CW00594692

CAMBRIDGE SERIES ON HUMAN–COMPUTER INTERACTION

The Social and Interactional Dimensions of Human–Computer Interfaces

Cambridge Series on Human–Computer Interaction

Titles in the Series
1. J. Long and A. Whitefield, eds., *Cognitive Ergonomics and Human–Computer Interaction*
2. M. Harrison and H. Thimbleby, eds., *Formal Methods in Human–Computer Interaction*
3. P. B. Anderson, *The Theory of Computer Semiotics*
4. J. M. Carroll, ed., *Designing Interactions: Psychology at the Human–Computer Interface*
5. J. Darragh and I. Witten, *The Reactive Keyboard*
6. S. Greenberg, *The Computer User as Toolsmith*
7. G. Marchionini, *Information Seeking in Electronic Environments*
8. K. Y. Lim and J. Long, *The MUSE Method for Usability Engineering*
9. P. Thomas, ed., *The Social and Interactional Dimensions of Human–Computer Interfaces*

The Social and Interactional Dimensions of Human–Computer Interfaces

Edited by
Peter J. Thomas
University of the West of England

Published by the Press Syndicate of the University of Cambridge
The Pitt Building, Trumpington Street, Cambridge CB2 1RP
40 West 20th Street, New York, NY 10011-4211, USA
10 Stamford Road, Oakleigh, Melbourne 3166, Australia

First published 1995

Printed in the United States of America

Library of Congress Cataloging-in-Publication Data
The social and interactional dimensions of human–computer interfaces /
edited by Peter J. Thomas.
p.   cm. – (Cambridge series on human–computer interaction ;
9)
Includes index.
ISBN 0-521-45302-X
1. Human–computer interaction. I. Thomas, Peter J. II. Series.
QA76.9.H85S63   1995
302.2 – dc20   94-36921
                                                                    CIP
CIP

A catalog record for this book is available from the British Library.

ISBN 0-521-45302-X hardback

Contents

List of contributors   *page* vi
Acknowledgments   ix

1   Introduction: The social and interactional dimensions of human–
    computer interfaces, *Peter J. Thomas*   1
2   Ethnography and human–computer interaction, *Geoff Cooper,*
    Christine Hine, Janet Rachel, and Steve Woolgar   11
3   Toward foundational analysis in human–computer interaction,
    James M. Nyce and Jonas Löwgren   37
4   Representing the user: Notes on the disciplinary rhetoric of
    human–computer interaction, *Geoff Cooper and John Bowers*   48
5   Conceptions of the user in computer systems design,
    Philip E. Agre   67
6   On simulacrums of conversation: Toward a clarification of the
    relevance of conversation analysis for human–computer
    interaction, *Graham Button and Wes Sharrock*   107
7   Wizards and social control, *Robin Wooffitt and*
    Catriona MacDermid   126
8   Sociology, CSCW, and working with customers, *Dave Randall*
    and John A. Hughes   142
9   Expert systems versus systems for experts: Computer-aided
    dispatch as a support system in real-world environments,
    Jack Whalen   161
10 Conversation analysis and human–computer interaction design,
    Sarah A. Douglas   184
11 Multimedia tools for social and interactional data collection and
    analysis, *Beverly L. Harrison*   204
12 Social interaction in the use and design of a workstation: Two
    contexts of interaction, *Deborah Lawrence, Michael E. Atwood,*
    Shelly Dews, and Thea Turner   240

Index   261

Contributors

Philip E. Agre Department of Communication, University of California, San Diego, La Jolla, California, USA.

Michael E. Atwood NYNEX Science & Technology, Westchester Avenue, White Plains, New York, USA.

John Bowers Department of Psychology, University of Manchester, Manchester, UK.

Graham Button Rank Xerox EuroPARC, Regent Street, Cambridge, UK.

Geoff Cooper Department of Sociology, University of Surrey, Guildford, Surrey, UK.

Shelly Dews NYNEX Science & Technology, Westchester Avenue, White Plains, New York, USA.

Sarah A. Douglas Computer and Information Science Department, University of Oregon, Eugene, Oregon, USA.

Beverly L. Harrison Department of Industrial Engineering, University of Toronto, Toronto, Ontario, Canada.

Christine Hine Centre for Research into Innovation, Culture and Technology, Brunel University, Uxbridge, Middlesex, UK.

John A. Hughes Department of Sociology, Lancaster University, Cartmel College, Lancaster, UK.

Deborah Lawrence NYNEX Science & Technology, Westchester Avenue, White Plains, New York, USA.

Jonas Löwgren Department of Computer Science, Linköping University, Linköping, Sweden.

Catriona MacDermid Social and Computer Sciences Research Group, University of Surrey, Guildford, UK.

James M. Nyce Center for Information and Communication Sciences, Ball State University, Muncie, Indiana, USA.

Janet Rachel Centre for Research into Innovation, Culture and Technology, Brunel University, Uxbridge, Middlesex, UK.

Dave Randall Department of Interdisciplinary Studies, Manchester Metropolitan University, Manchester, UK.

Wes Sharrock Department of Sociology, University of Manchester, Manchester, UK.

Peter J. Thomas Centre for Personal Information Management, University of the West of England, Bristol, UK.

Thea Turner NYNEX Science & Technology, Westchester Avenue, White Plains, New York, USA.

Jack Whalen Institute for Research on Learning, Palo Alto, California, USA.

Robin Wooffitt Social and Computer Sciences Research Group, University of Surrey, Guildford, UK.

Steve Woolgar Centre for Research into Innovation, Culture and Technology, Brunel University, Uxbridge, Middlesex, UK.

Acknowledgments

The task of shepherding a volume of chapters such as this from initial discussions to publication in the Cambridge Series on Human–Computer Interaction has been made simple, primarily through the help and cooperation of the authors, and with the help of John Long of University College, London, managing editor of the series, and Julia Hough, editor for psychology and cognitive science at Cambridge University Press in New York. I hope the resulting book reflects their contributions.

1

Introduction: The social and interactional dimensions of human–computer interfaces

Peter J. Thomas

The aim of this book is to reflect the range and diversity of research currently being carried out in what might be loosely called "the social and interactional dimensions of human–computer interfaces." Such a project, to those who are active in fields of research such as human–computer interaction (HCI) and the sociology of technology, might seem to be a considerable undertaking. And indeed, as the chapters in this volume demonstrate, the work currently being undertaken under this loose banner is diverse, drawing on a number of disciplines, theoretical orientations, methodological commitments, and with many and varied potential impacts on the design of human–computer interfaces. Perhaps then, in lieu of a definite and comprehensive summary of what might constitute the "social and interactional dimensions of human–computer interfaces," what is represented here is a snapshot of a program of work currently being carried out that in some way involves a distinctive sociological perspective on the design of technology.

The fact that we can speak of distinctive social and interactional dimensions of human–computer interfaces is attested by the volume of work that bears this distinctive orientation in the research forums concerned with the design of computer technology: from studies of design practice, detailed studies of the design of interface features, and studies of the discipline of HCI and its relationships to design practice, software engineering, and systems development. And, although there is no one program in evidence – with cogent research themes, findings and clear contributions to human–computer interaction – there are several assumptions and perspectives that are embedded deeply in the chapters that constitute this volume.

Work by the anthropologist Lucy Suchman at Xerox PARC is perhaps the most familiar point of contact with the social and interactional dimensions of human–computer interfaces for many readers of this book. Suchman clearly demonstrated that "social issues" enter alongside "technical" and "psychological" issues in the design of human–computer interfaces. Her critique of cognitivism suggested that users' interactions with systems are, in the most thoroughgoing way, informed by existing social practices, skills, norms, and by users' reliance on constructed moment-by-moment understandings rather than abstract characterizations or procedural "technical" knowledge. What this points to is that we must consider, when designing human–computer interfaces to technical artifacts, two dimensions: the interactional and the social.

We can take "interactional" here to mean the mechanics of users' behavior: the use of systems is not simply the interaction between software and psyche; rather it is the situated, particular, detailed, gritty, error-prone, and largely nondetermined reality of using an artifact. Several of the chapters in this volume draw particular attention to the importance of detailed observational studies of the use of computer systems as a way into understanding "the real world" of human–computer interaction.

We can take "social" here to mean the larger context that is implied in the use of computer systems: the use of systems is not only a matter of an individual user and an individual system; it is situated in a context that involves other users, organizational constraints, policies, and realities, and a culture of understandings that are created by, and determine, the uses of technology. Again, several of the chapters in this volume point to the importance of considering the ways in which wider cultural and social issues enter into the uses of technology, particularly when redefining terms such as "user," "user interface" and "task" in HCI.

Yet there is much more than this implicit in the contributions to this book. One theme recurring throughout the chapters is a concern with the adequacy, form, and nature of modes of study current within HCI. One manifestation is a concern that, in sociological terms, we must develop a sociology *for* rather than *of* human–computer interaction. The issue here is that sociology should not simply assess, value, or comment upon the design and use of technology; rather it must move toward a situation where sociological theory, methodology, and modes of analysis can provide direct and unambiguous input into the design of technology. Such a concern is manifested in several of the chapters in the collection.

Another theme, which is implicit in the closing chapters of the collection, is that such sociological, theory, methodology, and modes of analysis are applicable to a range of situations and systems: not only for the design of human–computer interfaces that one might assume involve "social" and not only "technical" concerns, such as CSCW (computer-supported cooperative work) systems, but to systems which mediate between organizations, users, and customers – such as those described in chapters by Randall and Hughes (Chapter 8), Whalen (Chapter 9), Douglas (Chapter 10), and Lawrence et al. (Chapter 12).

Further themes in this collection are suggested by the specific topics that the chapters address, and the volume falls naturally into three parts, with the chapters arranged sequentially to form the themes. The first theme, represented by the four chapters by Cooper et al. (Chapter 2), Nyce and Löwgren (Chapter 3), Bowers and Cooper (Chapter 4), and Agre (Chapter 5), is essentially concerned with what kinds of understanding we might seek of the "social and interactional dimensions of human–computer interfaces" and what modes of study and analysis are possible. A particular focus here – as it has been in many research studies – is on the nature and uses of ethnographic approaches to the study of the phenomena of human–computer interaction, and the understandings and categories that can be usefully captured and analyzed using such techniques.

Cooper et al. specifically examine the contribution of ethnography to the design of human–computer interfaces. Although ethnography is commonly regarded in primarily empirical terms – ethnography reveals the details of actions and interaction in ways not possible by "laboratory-based" methods – Cooper et al. suggest that ethnography is not only "a way of gathering data" but also a conceptual orientation that provides a distinctive contribution to the analysis and design of human–computer interfaces. The distinction that Cooper et al. seek to make is between ethnography as a "technique" and ethnography as an "orientation." Anthropologists' sensitivity to the "strange" or "exotic" in the everyday world is the kind of orientation that they seek to emphasize. Therefore, in terms of technology and in particular computer technology, and specifically the technology of human–computer interfaces, the aim is to untangle the contributions of the technical and social to the ways in which an artifact constrains and implies actions, behaviors and users' understanding of it. Their core concern is to understand how "the attributes of technical artifacts such as computer systems embody features of the antecedent circumstances in which they are produced and used." Part of this orientation has specific implications for human–computer interaction and for the phenomena involved in the design of human–computer interfaces. For example, the core concern of HCI with "the user" – in cognitive approaches toward design that aim to develop typographies of cognitive skills, abilities, and limitations – has a particular significance. Cooper et al.'s approach questions, makes strange, and renders exotic the very notion of "the user" and the users' role in interaction, design, and development of human–computer interfaces. More important, the very assumption they set out to challenge – that ethnography is primarily a method or technique for getting at "the real world" of user's interaction with computer systems – is that which is commonly taken for granted in discussions of ethnography and its value for HCI: that the setting is somehow separate from the analyst's and observer's understanding of it. The import of their chapter is that there is much leverage to be gained by questioning, or "rendering strange," what are taken-for-granted features of situations such as the ways in which entities such as users, designers, and computers are understood.

Nyce and Löwgren's chapter tackles the same concerns, suggesting why the relegation of ethnography to method or technique might have come about, and suggesting how ethnography might be revitalized in HCI. Their historical sketch of the roots of HCI shows the move – as evidenced in many of the chapters in this volume – toward forms of "contextual inquiry," characterized by approaches to design that are intended to reflect both the user's and developer's understanding of the contexts in which systems are used. As part of this move, the use of ethnography has come to miss what they term "foundational analysis." This they attribute to ethnography's attempt to find a niche within the traditional concerns of HCI – which they see as opposed to a view of user–system interaction as contingent, situated, informed by context and seldom rule-bound – and its resulting "rewriting" into a directly applicable method.

The attention paid to the analysis of the situated practices of design and use of computer systems, illustrated in several of the chapters in this volume, can also be directed toward HCI itself. The premise of this volume is that there are "social and interactional dimensions of human–computer interfaces" – with its assumption that the field is characterized by relationships between HCI, computing, and sociology. In their chapter, Cooper and Bowers suggest that we might usefully look to the "discourses" of the human sciences and see that the distinctive character of a disciplinary discourse is not the object of study itself (in this case, users or interfaces) but the framework that renders certain objects and certain statements about those objects as being legitimate. The characteristic of a domain of discourse, then, is the ways in which it succeeds in marking out certain territory as a professional activity. In particular, they note that the field of HCI is "fragmented, contested, and dynamic." As with other chapters in this volume, the issue turns upon conceptions, definitions, and understandings of the terms "user" and "user interface." What Cooper and Bowers suggest is that far from being abstract, concrete, unequivocal references for familiar referents in the world, such terms are heavily bound up with the social organization of the scientific endeavor of HCI. Yet these are not simply distinctions with no difference: the notion of "representing the user" is one that sits at the center of much work in HCI, from representations of "user cognition," through the definition of "user requirements" to the rhetoric of "user empowerment," which underpins the whole notion of "user-centered design." The rhetoric that portrays users as frustrated, anxious, and in need of the liberating influence of human–computer interaction and "design for usability" is, suggest Cooper and Bowers, a way of providing a legitimating force for the very existence of HCI. As do Nyce and Löwgren, Cooper and Bowers examine HCI research literature from this perspective. Card, Moran, and Newell's early work is seen as a way of legitimating the involvement of cognitive psychology in the enterprise of HCI, and what they identify as the "second wave" of HCI is a similar attempt to legitimate the development of the field toward a rejection of early directions represented by Card, Moran and Newell's work, toward a focus on the nature of design itself rather than the ostensible object or interest, the user interface. What comes with this is reformulation of the nature of the user from frustrated, anxious, and in need of rescue, toward users who have valuable expertise, which is embedded in, and illustrated through, the complexities of their work practices.

Agre's chapter explores the relationships between designers and users from a different and broader perspective, and focuses on two contrasting and problematic conceptions of the user – the "technical" and "managerial." Agre suggests that the term 'user' is often taken to mean a human extension of a machine, rather than something more appropriate – an understanding of the situated and contextual uses of systems by people in various professional roles. Cautioning against oversimplistic views of terms such as "technical," "managerial," and "computer system," Agre suggests that there is essentially an institutional – that is, entrenched professional and cultural, rather than personal – gap between designers and users. One of these conceptions of the user, the "technical," assumes that "the user lives in the same world as the programmer." Agre suggests the falsity of such an assumption by noting that, for example, the work environment of the user and the programmer are often radically different or more important, that users' work practices are not amenable to description in the mechanistic and procedural terms employed by conventional programming methodologies. However, Agre notes, attempts to influence the design process by opening them up to the details of users' practices may allow "weak formalization," which can uncover the stranglehold of formalization in the design process as an embedded institutional phenomenon. Similarly, the managerial conception of the user is centered around the idea that technical systems cannot be developed outside the social arrangements into which they are introduced; this in turn implies an attention to the nature of employee perceptions, and in particular the expectation that users will be "resistant" to new technologies. In the managerial conception this means that these perceptions need to be managed in particular ways such that technologies are not perceived as threatening. Here the design and deployment of technical artifacts is a process of systematically managing user perceptions through a variety of means, which Agre illustrates in his analysis of work in the development of "active badge" systems. Agre's chapter clearly illustrates a further facet of the social and interactional dimensions of human–computer interfaces: the ways in which deep-rooted conceptions of users have profound effects in shaping the design and deployment of technology.

The following three chapters, by Button and Sharrock (Chapter 6), Wooffitt and MacDermid (Chapter 7), and Randall and Hughes (Chapter 8) explore in detail, and through examples of specific technologies, how systems are profoundly "social artifacts." Button and Sharrock's chapter reprises an issue concerning sociology's precise contribution to the the social and interactional dimensions of human–computer interfaces: the "conversational" nature of human interaction with machines. This is more than a matter of mere terminology – an issue of the metaphorical use of the word "conversation" to describe the interaction between humans and computer systems. The deeper issue, claim Button and Sharrock, concerns the relevance of a particular kind of sociological inquiry (conversation analysis or CA) to the design of human–computer interfaces, the utility of sociological findings and methods more generally, and potentially the status of human agency vis-à-vis computational artifacts. What Button and Sharrock attack is the notion that, by applying conversation analytic findings to the design of conversational interfaces, we could create machines that "converse" with their users. They suggest that such attempts are merely "going up a blind alley" conceptually and practically: that to even make the claim that through the application of conversational analytic "rules for speaking" it is possible to create conversing machines betrays a deep confusion about the nature of human conduct. The central notion here concerns the notion of rule – does programming a machine to operate in terms of certain rules derived from an analysis of human conversation mean that the system is conversing in the same way? No, claim Button and Sharrock, since even though humans might appear to be acting according to rules, what they are actually doing is *embodying* such rules in their actions. People do not behave according to the rules, but "orient" themselves to certain normative features of interaction. With respect to simulations of conversational behavior on computers, such simulations could never be considered to be conversation, no matter how accurate, verisimilitudinous, sophisticated, or seemingly genuine. In one sense, Button and Sharrock's arguments have force at the level of detail: the critique and explanation of the notion of "rule" in accounts of human conversation and in accounts of how computers use rules strike at the core of the nature of actions of human and machine, as prefigured in the accounts by Weizenbaum and Turing. However, the arguments also open up the essential instability of the whole enterprise of employing sociological findings in the design of human–computer interfaces. They indicate that the ways in which such findings, specifically conversation analysis, can contribute to human–computer interfaces is still a live issue.

Wooffitt and MacDermid's chapter describes exactly the attempt that Button and Sharrock focus on – interfaces that employ speech recognition and synthesis technology. The development of speech systems can only be said to have produced unsophisticated interactional artifacts since the focus in creating such systems has traditionally been on techniques for processing of speech signals. This has led to systems that are simply incapable of producing appropriate behaviors of the kinds that humans employ in their routine interactions with each other. Wooffitt and MacDermid suggest that system designers are in fact committed not to producing interfaces that allow the expression of a full range of behaviors, but are actually implementing "social controls" on users. Speech recognition systems, in this case, must constrain the possible allowable range of behaviors so that the available technical mechanisms are able to deal with user actions and interactions in a way that optimizes those mechanisms. As Wooffitt and MacDermid suggest, "system-friendly" is the key concept here, in contrast to the concept of "user-friendly" from HCI. Yet it is not clear that such a "system-friendly" approach is likely to be unsuccessful in interacting with users since there are few data available in advance of the actual use of such systems that can allow designers to evaluate the ways in which putative users will interact with the system. The technique described by Wooffitt and MacDermid is the (strangely but accurately named) "bionic WOZ simulation" in which a human stands in for part of the system being evaluated in concert with other working parts of the system. Here the particular sociological assumptions employed are again those of conversational analysis. Conversation analysis, as discussed earlier, is an approach to the description of human interaction that focuses on the minute details of interactional patterns. The detailed accounts of particular forms of organization and, in particular, "communicative breakdowns" provide suggestions as to how such problems might be handled in a technical way:

the social control involved in designing such systems is one way of ensuring certain measures of success. However, and more important, such attempts provide the analyst with valuable data as to the operation of the interactional practices of humans who use such technological artifacts: the attempt at social control through technical innovation allows analysts to see how users react, and thus in turn to reshape the design of those systems appropriately.

The following chapter, by Randall and Hughes, takes up the theme of creating a sociology for social artifacts. Randall and Hughes's focus here is on a subdiscipline of HCI – computer-supported cooperative work (CSCW). CSCW is an interesting and pertinent object of attention since, as Randall and Hughes caustically note of HCI, it has meant the "discovery of sociality by computer science and by HCI." Issues concerned with the world of work, the organization in which work takes place, and the environment in which the user and the computer are embedded, are taking a place alongside those cognitive issues which previously defined "traditional" HCI. The challenge is to allow such concerns to enter into systems design, and sociology has a key place in this. What is required is more than the gross simplifications provided by sociological studies of work, and the development of detailed accounts of the everyday activities that contribute to the effectiveness or otherwise of human–computer systems. The aim of Randall and Hughes's chapter is thus to suggest and exemplify how studies of "doing work" with technology can be performed, and what an understanding of "work" can mean for the design of technology. Taking the concept of "division of labor" common in sociological theory, Randall and Hughes explore what it might mean to employ a "working division of labor": not "division of labor" as an abstract concept, but as something understood by those involved in it. Much of this has roots in ethnomethodology, a form of sociological inquiry that seeks to provide an account of how events, actions, and behavior – including in this case those surrounding technology and its use – are construed, understood, and used in practical situations, and how the "sense-making" activities of those involved in work actually operate. In the case of Randall and Hughes's study of working with customers in a building society, the results of such an inquiry are to point up important relationships between the work to be done, the procedures by which such work is specified by an organization, and the technologies used – including paper-based and computer technologies. One of these is the finding that technology is extremely sensitive to the apparent unpredictabilities of the environment – customer requests, the nature of teamwork, dealing with inadequacies in available data, and the relationships between the organizational procedures and the larger concerns of an organization.

The final four chapters of the book can be read as studies in the social and interactional dimensions of human–computer interfaces, although they are more than mere case studies, and address and extend a range of issues covered in other chapters. In Chapter 9, Whalen illustrates the shaping and molding of technology through the kinds of fine-grained analysis of situational context that are discussed in earlier chapters. Whalen concentrates on obtaining an understanding of the use of computer-aided dispatch technology. Such an understanding is important since, although the technical capacity exists to build ever more complex and powerful support systems, it is not clear how far such technology is sensitive to the work practices of those who use it routinely, and the demands of the environment in which such systems are situated. The danger of not pursuing such an understanding is that such systems may fail spectacularly, a phenomenon that has been of considerable interest to the user interface design and information systems development communities. Whalen looks specifically at the ways in which a system designed to support users' assessment and actions on the basis of complex information displays organizes that information, and how an "intelligent" support system might remedy some of the problems that users encounter. Whalen looks at the ways in which users of precomputational support technology use that technology to understand the nature of the situation they are dealing with – essentially the use of expert knowledge to complement and make sense of available information. Whalen also describes how a computerized version of the system aimed to make the exercise of that expertise more "efficient" by centralizing diverse information previously held in paper-based form. However, a further form of technology support was instigated in the form of an "intelligent decision support system," which aimed to automate as far as possible the decision making involved. Embedded in such a system, Whalen notes, is the assumption that providing intelligent support is equivalent to providing an answer: something that fails to acknowledge, draw upon, and complement the expertise possessed by the operators of the system. Yet the issue Whalen addresses is not the obvious one of whether the operation of the system reflects or embodies adequate or useful decision-making policies, but the question of how one might construct a system that creates a "shared frame of reference" between the user and the system itself. Here an ethnographic approach can demonstrate exactly what the notion of "expertise" consists of and how this can usefully feed into the design of "systems for experts."

A similarly detailed approach to the fine-grained details of interaction with systems is evident in the chapter by Douglas (Chapter 10). Here again, conversation analysis is contrasted with psychologically oriented studies characteristic of traditional HCI. Approaches such as conversation analysis, Douglas suggests, provide a way into the details of users' interaction and valuable accounts of how, for example, users "manage their troubles" with computer systems. Instead of an abstract characterization of human–computer interaction, the promise is of an account that emphasizes the situated, managed, and accomplished nature of activity with and around computer systems, again a theme that has been taken up by previous chapters. What might be useful is an approach that is amenable to influencing the process of software design and provides ways in which designs can drive new theoretical insights. Douglas's approach to this is to employ "constructive interaction," a method of generating the rich contextual information required.

Constructive interaction is essentially a way of unifying observational analysis with protocol analysis based on simulated joint problem-solving exercises. The output of constructive interaction studies is then systematically analyzed using the methodology of conversation analysis – recording the features and events of conversational interaction such as pauses, the overlaps of actions and utterances, and simultaneous actions and events. Douglas demonstrates, through an extended example of using this approach in the design of a cardiovascular construction kit, that such methods can be systematically used to benefit human–computer interface design.

Approaches such as Douglas's, which involve fine-grained ethnographic analysis of the details of users' interactions with systems, are coming to rely on the use of video recording for data capture. In Chapter 11, Harrison describes tools that can support this process. Techniques such as exploratory sequential data analysis (ESDA) require that data concerning situational and temporal context, users' performance, and system behavior are analyzed. In particular, Harrison focuses on the challenges of dealing with multimedia data and the integration of video and other data such as observer's annotations, impressions, and notes about events in progress, which this requires. The tools that will be most useful will allow analysts to explore and visualize patterns which are relevant in users' interactions with systems. One approach is to view video as a form of "document" that combines the characteristics of a structured data file and other documents. Such systems as VANNA, VideoNoter, or Timelines, all described by Harrison, provide the necessary functionality for such fine-grained analysis and allows analysts to create, for example, indexes to locations in the video document that are sensitive to temporal events and that also support annotation. Harrison's chapter reviews the challenges for developing such systems that can ease the processes of observation and interpretation of video data.

The final chapter in the volume, by Lawrence et al. (Chapter 12), looks at the contribution of sociological methods and findings to the design of a specific piece of technology – a workstation for telephone operators. In this kind of task, users are not interacting with a system, but using the system as part of their interaction with customers, in the same way that Randall and Hughes examined the use of system in customer inquiries in building societies. This has the effect that the operator of the system is in effect a "surrogate user" who acts as intermediary between technology and user. In analyses of the performance of workstation designs, even when a proposed design fulfilled criteria of "usability" as normally defined, it was found that a dominant feature of the interactions was in fact the interaction between the humans involved in the system, yet such interaction was not able to be dealt with by the traditional usability tests run in laboratory conditions, and was therefore effectively factored out as a critical component of the design. In their studies of dialogues between operators and customers, using dialogue and timeline analysis, Lawrence et al. suggest that operators use their expertise and knowledge of both technical and everyday contexts of interaction to accomplish the task of providing directory assistance. The implications of such a conclusion is that the technology designed to support interaction profoundly affects the interaction – for example, "technology-oriented dialogue" required on the parts of the customers, or the requirement that operators, by virtue of the design of the technology support, mediate between "technical" and "social" dialogues.

As Lawrence et al.'s chapter demonstrates, a consideration of the social and interactional dimensions of human–computer interfaces is central to any formulation of the concerns of HCI. Their chapter demonstrates their considerable relevance not only to the study but to the design of technology.

Their chapter, and the other chapters in the book, illustrate the breadth and depth of this relevance.

2
Ethnography and human–computer interaction

Geoff Cooper, Christine Hine, Janet Rachel, and
Steve Woolgar

2.1 Introduction

Recent years have seen the recognition of the potential of a range of sociological research for work in the design, implementation, and use of computer technologies. In general, this latter work has been undertaken under disciplinary auspices other than sociology, ones predominantly informed by psychology and component disciplines within cognitive science. One consequence is that there is as yet no very clear view of the different sociological approaches on offer – ethnography, ethnomethodology, conversation analysis, interaction analysis; nor is it clear exactly how such approaches can be of use in the variety of domains which have shown interest – for example, human–computer interaction (HCI), requirements analysis, and computer-supported cooperative work (CSCW). The specific aim of this chapter is to examine the potential contribution of ethnography to HCI.

Ethnography is commonly regarded as a "bottom-up" alternative perspective that – by contrast with, for example, laboratory based methods – can do justice to the richness of action and interaction in actual settings.[1] While subscribing to these empirical commitments and their value, we see the key import of ethnographic study in different terms. Accordingly, this chapter seeks to set out the actual and potential significance of a version of ethnography that has been developed from the tradition of laboratory studies (Knorr-Cetina, 1981; Latour and Woolgar, 1986; Lynch, 1985; Traweek, 1988) in the sociology of scientific knowledge (SSK). We argue that, both in methodological and substantive terms, this approach has much to offer HCI. We emphasize that the significance of this version of ethnography is primarily epistemological. This means that it is more than just a different way of gathering data, or a way of gathering different data. Instead it is a distinctive conceptual approach in which the relation between researcher and object of study is radically reformulated.

We begin by setting out some key features of this approach, and delineating it from some received views of ethnographic work within HCI. We then present four brief descriptions – tales from the field – taken from recent ethnographic studies of technological settings, in order to illustrate the approach. We aim to show how these studies, conceived within an ostensibly different set of interests to those of HCI as it is commonly defined, offer new dimensions to current thinking about human–computer interaction. Finally we discuss the significance of ethnography for HCI, and suggest that it promises a valuable reformulation of both the methodology and object of study of HCI.

2.2 Ethnography

Ethnography derives from efforts by anthropologists and others to record the culture of exotic and (usually) primitive foreign tribes. From the origins of this work, the term ethno-graphy has denoted a commitment to the empirical recording of these cultures, often taken to exemplify humankind in its pure form, before they vanish or become modernized. Ethnography has since been interpreted in many ways. The contemporary and more familiar variant is that ethnography entails extended participant observation at a chosen field site, as the observer attempts to become part of the tribe. The rationale is that a prolonged period of intense immersion in the culture best enables the ethnographer to experience the world of her subjects, and hence to grasp the significance of their language and actions for, in our case, the production and consumption of technical artifacts.

Despite historical variations in the form of ethnography, it has generally retained the two elements of commitment to empirical study and concern with the exotic and/or strange.[2] In social studies of science and technology it has been particularly important to emphasize the latter element. This is because a general thrust of SSK has been to challenge the taken-for-granted character of the technical capacities and characteristics of scientific knowledge and technology (see Woolgar 1991a for discussion). The argument is that instead of assuming that actions and behavior stem from the given, inherent technical qualities of an artifact, we should view technical characteristics as the upshot of various social and cultural practices.[3] This means in particular that the attributes of technical artifacts such as computers and computer systems embody features of the antecedent circumstances in which they are produced and used. Thus, for example, the relative merits of a particular screen display should be understood in terms of the cultural preconceptions and values that inform its design and use, rather than as a reflection of technical capacity.

It is strategically important to stress the second element of ethnography – the exotic – when attempting to understand the social dimensions of science and technology, because it is precisely in these realms that the phenomena under study are most taken for granted: since the physical, material, and technical qualities of technology seem so much less effable than more traditional social and psychological attributes, it is an important analytic advantage to be able to resist and challenge the apparently "obvious" characteristics of the technology under study. At the same time, it is part of the tradition of research in SSK that the most persuasive aspect of the claim for the socially and culturally constituted character of technologies is that the argument is worked through with reference to detailed example. The ethnographer's persuasive powers – the rhetorical value of "actually having been there" – is combined with the claim to "take the content of the technology seriously"[4] in detailed case studies of specific examples of technological development – hence the continuing commitment to demonstration through empirical study, and the methodological commitment to the usual paraphernalia of participant observation: the use of field notes and diaries, collection of documents, and audio and video recordings.

It follows that the version of ethnography we offer here necessarily emphasizes the virtues of critically examining both the technical attributes and the form of relations between humans and technical artifacts. The analytic moment of this approach requires us to make these features of the situation exotic, while offering an argument based on close empirical observation. Our approach thus represents a particular and distinctive set of analytic emphases, some of which, as we will discuss, are derived from or reinforced by features of the particular technological domains that we have studied. The four main themes that characterize our version of ethnography are the observer's role and the definition of the setting being described; analytic skepticism; particular challenges relating to new conceptions of the unit of analysis and to the new forms of social relation involved; and dialogue between ethnographer and the "subjects" of study.

2.2.1 The observer's role

The ethnographer is conceived as part of the setting, deliberately included within the epistemological space of the practice of research (cf. Bourdieu, 1990). As indicated, the ethnographer's primary task is that of observation, but "observation" is only a partial description of what is happening. Rather he or she is differentially embedded within the practices that constitute the setting, and this provides much of the frame for interpretation. This claim is epistemological rather than empirical. The ethnographer faces the usual problems of gaining access to the practices of the setting, and even of deciding (and defining) what constitutes the setting. However, these practical problems provide the basis for examining the ways in which the ethnographer (and other "natives"; cf. Sharrock and Anderson, 1982) is necessarily bound up in the definition of the observational "space." In other words, these "difficulties" are the motor for reflection on the place and sense of observation that is possible in a particular setting. This reflexive dimension to ethnography is often overlooked by approaches that prioritize the need to produce reliable or objective descriptions of removed objects of observation.[5]

2.2.2 Analytic skepticism

The ethnographer seeks to maintain a stance of analytic skepticism toward the phenomena under investigation. As mentioned, this is especially important in a technical setting, which is characterized by relatively rigid hierarchies of specialized technical knowledge. Thus the ethnographer has to work hard not simply to accept that, for example, a particular software application or development standard is the best available; and instead question how and why, for example, this standard has emerged, how and by whom it is being promoted, which audiences are being enrolled in the definition of its quality, and so on. In the same way, in systems development settings, the ethnographer does not merely accept the producer and consumer (or user) categories as given, but seeks to investigate the ways in which these distinctions are created and sustained.

In some ways the aspiration toward analytic skepticism is in tension with the ethnographer's attempts to become an accepted member of the setting, although the schizophrenic nature of his or her position can also be put to good use. Crucially, such skepticism would include not simply resisting the adoption of members' views but also being prepared to change the focus of the study, to reconceptualize what constitute the objects of study and, in general, continually to challenge the preconceptions with which one entered the field.

It must be stressed that (what we are calling) analytic skepticism is not proposed as a formulaic method for achieving epistemological distance from one's objects of study. Rather, it is intended to denote an ongoing and necessarily always inconcludable process of critical questioning. For example, in the way that we have briefly formulated it here, analytic skepticism can *itself* be interrogated in terms of its apparent ties to a particular phenomenological version of subjectivity, and the extent to which it elides possible distinctions between some form of cognitive effort in the field and the production of the ethnographic text. In other words, we are describing an orientation that suggests the need for a continual practical and textual struggle against the acceptance of the given, whether in the categories and classifications of those we are studying or in the connotations of our own ethnographic discourse.

2.2.3 The unit of analysis

The ethnographer recognizes that particular domains pose particular challenges for ethnography. Thus, for example, in studying domains in which much "communication" is electronic, in which "interaction" is geographically spread across different sites, the ethnographer must question what "being there" in the field might mean, and whether a particular (and increasingly peripheral?) form of social interaction – informal face-to-face – is being inadvertently privileged if the traditional norms of ethnographic presence are not themselves subjected to critical scrutiny. In addition, it may be profitable to consider technologies as themselves parties to interaction: that is, to resist the assumption that interaction takes place only around or through computers (Bench-Capon and McEnery, 1989). It further follows that the ethnographer needs to be circumspect about approaches that give cognition (situated or otherwise) a central explanatory role (cf. Woolgar, 1989). In all these respects, the consideration of the problems and challenges of doing ethnography in technological domains can connect to, and highlight, aspects that were always problematic and that have been raised as theoretical issues elsewhere. For example, our ethnography can criticize prevailing conceptions of context (cf. Cooper, 1991); or it can require us to reconsider the most appropriate unit of analysis through raising questions about the role of agency (Callon 1986; Latour, 1992; Law, 1991; Woolgar, 1989, 1991b).

2.2.4 Ethnography as dialogue

The ethnographer enters into a dialogue both with those in the setting and with nonethnographers beyond it. In contrast to attempts to control for the researcher's presence, the ethnographer makes a virtue of it, giving feedback to those who are interested, and treating the resulting interactions as further material for analysis.[6] This is particularly germane to the theoretical concerns of our version of ethnography, since this aspect of our work asks in what sense and to what extent the insights and observations of the ethnographer can be of value to the subjects of study, as well as to others. This is thus a rather more thoroughgoing form of reflexivity than advocated in many texts on ethnography (e.g., Hammersley and Atkinson, 1983): the definition and negotiation of social and organizational boundaries, and their relevance for settings in which the ethnography takes place are explored as both theoretical and practical issues.

Conceptualizing ethnography as dialogue brings into focus its textual nature: the aim is not merely to produce a rich description of an objective reality, but to construct artfully a representation that enables and embraces a dialogue with those under study. This links back to the focus on analytic skepticism, since the utility of ethnography in HCI is not simply to present a detailed description of the work at the study site, instantly recognizable to the participants, but to produce a representation less familiar to them that questions their fundamentally held distinctions and thus promotes fruitful exchange.

2.3 Ethnography and HCI

In comparing our work with that of HCI, two interrelated strands of divergence, substantive and epistemological, become apparent. By a substantive divergence, we mean simply that while our ethnographies address phenomena that, inter alia, can be described as aspects of human–computer interaction, these do not necessarily constitute the kind of phenomena that HCI, in its practice, understands by such a term. For example, in Section 2.4 below, we consider some of the ways in which "the user" is represented within the design and development process. In so doing, we not only implicitly assert the importance of studying empirically a wider range of phenomena than the user interface and the individual using it,[7] but also argue the need to go beyond the notion of the "user" as an empirical and prediscursive given.[8]

This reformulation of the phenomena of HCI derives from an underlying epistemological divergence with respect to the latter's prevailing conceptions of sociologically derived work. Thus far there has been relatively little work within HCI that has explicitly defined itself as "ethnographic."[9] However, a range of approaches including contextual inquiry (Whiteside, Bennett, and Holtzblatt, 1988), activity theory (Bannon and Bodker, 1991), Suchman's use of ethnomethodology (1987), and Winograd and Flores's theoretically heterogeneous critique of cognitive science (1986) is commonly understood as forming a particular and coherent approach to the study of interaction outside the laboratory. It is the understanding of the nature and value of this work that is our concern here.[10] The chief characteristic of discussions of the value of this work is the imputation of naturalism as the methodological foundation and warrant for sociologically derived approaches.[11]

For example, Kellogg sees Suchman's work as a contribution to the general task of analyzing "*real* people in *real* situations" (Kellogg, 1990: 193, emphasis in original), her use of laboratory experiments notwithstanding. Similarly, Carroll articulates the challenge of this kind of work in terms of its perceived implication that system design must somehow try to accommodate the infinite details that emerge from an artifact's use in situ, and that can have substantial effects on its usability (Carroll, 1990: 322). It is significant that the "real" situations of use are further defined as posing a problem of quantitative detail, rather than, for example, as an opportunity for investigating the significance of different actors' definitions of the situation.

A central difficulty with this interpretation of the relevance of sociological work is that it is perceived and implicitly defined in terms of its attention to the empirical.[12] We would not wish to deny the strategic importance of studying interaction in a variety of settings. However, we suggest that to take the main significance of sociological studies in terms of a "bottom-up" methodology is to miss its more radical potential.[13] Specifically, the emphasis on "bottom-up" empirical description ignores the very important questions of selection, interpretation and, in particular, the way in which the setting is formulated (Cooper, 1991). More crucially, such a neglect leaves the epistemological metaphor of observation unchanged: the prevailing view is that the observer remains separate from the phenomenon being studied, and his or her own role in its formulation is left, discretely, to one side.

By contrast, we suggest that the more significant aspect of the ethnographic approach lies, as we have indicated, in its epistemological commitment to challenging this metaphor of separation and observation; and that central to this challenge is the explication and interrogation of the role of the ethnographer within the setting and its textual representation.

2.4 Tales from the field

In order to illustrate some of the advantages of this version of ethnography, we now present four brief accounts of ongoing or recently completed studies in four settings.[14]

2.4.1 Presence, community, and observation in technological settings

In the course of an ethnographic study of computer scientists, I (GC) was confronted with some practical problems of access with respect to certain kinds of empirical materials. These "problems" are discussed in terms of the analytic purchase that they provide, not just for the setting in question, but for more general issues of ethnographic methodology.

This study was centrally concerned with the practice of research, and the ways in which this could be seen to have been affected by changes in its organization, funding, criteria of evaluation, and modes of accountability. To this end, I was given office space in a prominent computer science department in order that I might discern the significance of such changes. One issue immediately became apparent. Whereas the implicit model for the study was the ethnography of scientific practice (Knorr-Cetina, 1981; Latour and Woolgar, 1986; Lynch, 1985; Traweek, 1988), in which the laboratory provides a central locus in which work is done, much of the work of computer science is done in the individual's office. Consequently, those occasions in which researchers did gather collectively and talk, notably coffee breaks, became crucially important for the study, for it was on these occasions that I was able to get "news" of recent developments, which I could then follow up in various ways – talking to individual researchers, borrowing documents, attending meetings, or whatever. Thus to a large extent, "observation" was prearranged and managed, and settings in which informal face-to-face interaction took place were the primary site for deciding on and selecting what was to be observed.

This kind of situation provides material for ethnographic investigation since these constraints are themselves aspects of the social organization of the workplace.[15] But before discussing the significance of the spatial organization of the local setting for ethnographic study, I want to point to a further aspect of researchers' interaction: their use of electronic media, and in particular electronic mail (E-mail), to communicate with a wider distributed collection of researchers. This problematizes a whole series of assumptions about ethnographic presence within, and observation of, a given object of study (a scientific community).

In one sense, the use of E-mail could be said to present an observably pervasive aspect of work at this site, an unproblematic empirical phenomenon; but attempts to access some of the materials being sent and received prompted further reflection.

For example, two researchers suggested that I might like to look at two more or less complete electronic archives that they held relating to the setting up of major international research projects. However, there were problems of access: since I was not connected up to the network in my own office, and had to go elsewhere to read my E-mail, I suggested that this material be transferred to diskettes (as ASCII files), which I could then take away. Neither individual knew whether or how this was to be done, and the sheer volume of data (5 megabytes in one case) suggested that the task might, in any case, be impractical. Not wishing to burden them with unnecessary chores, I therefore suggested that they E-mail them to me at my "home base." This also proved difficult, since it would entail each researcher forwarding, one by one, an extensive list of messages that had accumulated over time. Consequently, this course was not pursued either.

Finally, it was agreed that I would use one researcher's office while he was away to look at these materials on his own computer, and in due course this was how I finally got to look at them. This was a highly informative experience: for as I scanned through this enormous archive, new messages continually arrived, and were announced with an orchestral chord: and the system had been set up so that I was flipped out of the message that I was examining to the electronic in-tray. The combined effect of this, and the ringing telephone, contributed to a sense of occupying the researcher's personal electronic space.[16]

These events can be read as stages of an attempt to overcome technological barriers in order to access particular data; but more significantly they provide interesting data in themselves. Two aspects are especially noteworthy. First, difficulties were related to the temporal order of work practice. As my use of the researcher's machine illustrated, although messages were kept for reference – partly, of course, for my reference – they were managed on a moment-to-moment basis: read, forwarded, and acted upon (to some degree) as and when they were received. To forward a large archive at a later date was anomalous, since it was not within the parameters of researchers' everyday practice, and thus problematic: messages are dealt with contemporaneously. Second, the question of community was raised. There are a number of aspects to this. It was clear that the problem of access could be described in terms of my not being connected to, and thus a part of, the relevant community in question: had I for instance been a named participant in the mailing list for the proposed project, materials could have been forwarded to me as and when they arrived – again, the temporal dimension is important. Moreover, I was forced to critically examine some different senses of community that I had unproblematically accepted: in particular, the extent to which I had privileged the (most easily) observable versions of community in the modality of face-to-face interaction. For, as these events help to show, researchers, in their everyday life, are members of communities defined by many different modalities.

Here we see an example of how different interpretations of ethnography can lead in different directions. For the tacit ascription of primacy to the most easily observable and, in the most traditional sense, the most "social" form of interaction will privilege a particular version of community. A more reflective, and less formulaic ethnography will problematize such assumptions and lead to the production of new questions. Thus, I was able to consider different senses of community and their interaction. For example, within a particular electronic community (another collaborative international research project) different E-mail lists had been set up so that electronic communication of a more critical kind – with respect to other collaborators – could take place at the site that I was studying.[17] But it is worth commenting that my knowledge of this project was at least partly derived from a paper archive in which E-mail designated as important had been printed out: thus, a further distinction is possible insofar as messages have a transformed significance if a decision is made to save them as part of an observable archive of hard copy.[18] Considerations such as these transform "community" from a sociological variable to an interpretively flexible resource: in which settings, on which occasions, and in which modalities do members claim and ascribe membership to which communities (cf. Moerman, 1974)?

It should be stressed that while these issues are vividly highlighted in technological settings, they are not confined to them: for example, it could legitimately be argued that laboratory studies have consistently privileged face-to-face interaction in their quest to find out what is going on behind the cleaned-up facade of the scientific method as enshrined in research papers.[19]

In the sense that we give to the word, ethnography must therefore include questioning even those very tenets that would appear to be central to its rationale: in this case, that ethnography entails being present within a given community in order to observe what goes on: for "presence," "community" and "observation" are all problematized.

2.4.2 Ethnography and "being there"

The initial remit of a second line of ethnographic research was to study the interactions of information technology with the research process in science, focusing on the intensive use of information technology in human genetics. The first part of this ethnography has involved joining a computer services department providing a system of on-line facilities for accessing and analyzing research data to the U.K. genome community. I (CH) began updating the user manual for the services on offer. In many ways this role was ideal for ethnographic purposes – in my situation the questioning of features of the system and its relations with users was routine. One drawback, however, was that this position limited my (analytic) mobility; I was situated at one particular pole of the user–producer dichotomy that I wished to bring into question. Rather than being limited to explaining the detailed doings of users to the computer services team, and vice versa, the aim was to question the existence of the categories of "producer" and "user" and to examine the various ways they were deployed, in both organizational and technological terms. This is to be achieved by viewing the system from various vantage points: having completed a phase of ethnography in the computer services department, I now intend to follow the system to the laboratory and observe its construction in use. We thus see that although the initial sites of observation are suggested by an analytic interest in the categories of producer and user (they preconfigure the ethnography), the ethnography remains free to dissociate itself from them as preexisting, real categories. This approach, however, could be taken to ground any analytic purchase of the ethnography in physical presence on site. A part of my argument in the following section is that the epistemological insights of ethnography are not intrinsically coupled with being there in the field: that it is more about the efforts one makes to enter the field, wherever and whatever the field may be.

The idea that ethnography requires the actual presence of the ethnographer at the field site, observing the intricate details of daily life, is brought vividly into question by the dominance of electronic communication in the computer services department. Much of the work of these individuals is done on the computer; their information gathering and communications appear largely to be carried out in the virtual world provided by the Internet. How can I enter this world and yet retain my ethnographer's skepticism toward the taken-for-granted features of this technology? One way is to examine which kinds of communication this virtual world is considered suitable to host, and which it cannot substitute. There are virtual adepts and virtual novices: in large part the members of the computer services department are adepts and the users, the biologists whom they serve, are novices. The majority of the cries for help from users arrive via the telephone lines, despite the provision of an option on the computer system menu designed for just this purpose. When members of computer services leave the office for meetings, it is to meet with these users. It is thus tacitly acknowledged that the virtual world gives insufficient indication of what users really want – the staff members "try to talk to users" when they visit the center. The virtual world seems only to provide some of the computer services staff's requirements for communication; and it is deemed inadequate in communication with virtual novices.

Within computer services much is made of the need to resort to paper and face-to-face communication for the specific training task of transforming virtual novices into virtual adepts. Yet this is by no means a paperless office. Although I have yet to see a memo passed around the office, postcards are regularly passed around, and the fortnightly progress report and schedule of work to be done for the coming fortnight is reproduced on paper for each individual and ceremonially filed.

The ceremonial function of paper seems paramount. The manual itself, while acting as a means of teaching users how to read the system and as a technology for reattributing agency from human beings to inanimate technical artifacts, also carries a ceremonial status. When I ask about a particular part of the system, a brief informal chat is followed by what seems like a formal handing over of the manual. I feel I have just been handed the keys to the City of London. The recipient of the manual is symbolically given access to inner workings and, hence, power over the system. This is not an accolade accorded to everyone; with its connotations of ability to control and intervene, access to inner workings carries status in this environment. The appropriateness of a form of communication varies according to the particular circumstances. For example, in one bizarre concatenation of media, one of the staff of the computer services department E-mails me to ask where I am, comes to that room when I reply in order to arrange in person a virtual meeting the next day over the network, then hands me a representation on paper (a map) of the virtual territory we are to traverse to allow me to locate myself within that territory.

So, one way of incorporating the technology in a technologically driven ethnography is to try to figure out the functions that the network serves by looking at the functions that it does not serve. However, it seems that by taking this route I am adopting some of the very assumptions with which I should be taking issue: I have made a distinction between the virtual world and face-to-face contact, and have taken the virtual world as less real than face-to-face interaction. I reflect on the impact that information technology has had on the definition and conduct of my own research – both in the communications media through which it is conducted and the substantive focus. At an early stage of the research, in trying to track down likely candidates for interviews, I telephoned a funding agency for details of its grants to researchers working on the human genome and was told they could only give me all genetics researchers or nothing: human genome was not a keyword in their database.

Once I step into the world of electronic communication the very boundaries of the ethnographic inquiry become blurred. While sitting in my university office I can participate in the virtual world of the ethnography site, and yet while on site I can return to the comforts of my own office, my own system, and the company of friends from the world beyond the ethnographic study. This begins to bring home one of the fundamental features of this style of ethnography. It is not so much about being at the field site as opposed to being at home; rather, it is about the passage between the two. Since the very idea of ethnography depends on the boundedness of ethnographer and of the field site, fundamental insights may be gained by reflection upon the transgression of this boundary.[20] Similarly, features of the division between computer services and users are illuminated by my own passages across the boundary: the circumstances under which I am accepted as "one of the boys" and those on which I am judged suitable to act as the "naive user" in judging the comprehensibility of the manual or the usability of a new piece of software.

The maintenance of a strict boundary between computer services and its users appears to act for the computer services staff as a way of constituting a valued and professional identity for staff members and a hierarchical relationship in which users are subservient due to their lesser display of knowledge of internal workings, machines, and communications media. The human genome project has been construed as a case of unprecedented collaboration between biologists and computer scientists (Erickson, 1992). It appears more, however, that the computer system itself is performing the collaboration, leaving biologists and computer professionals to retain discrete communities.

The applications of this form of ethnography do not lie in the suggestion of better and more effective styles of user interface for the system, nor are the stages of ethnographic research and dissemination of results as distinct as many models of the research process would imply. The participation of the ethnographer in the research setting entails an interaction with those in that setting during the research process. In the study in the computer services department, staff members are keen to hear my findings about the behavior and expectations of users, the effectiveness of training courses, and the ways in which these may be improved. However, the challenge for the ethnographer is to conduct this dialogue in a way that is true to the stance of questioning taken-for-granted assumptions. In particular, this means that the ethnographer has to avoid reproducing the strict producer–user dichotomy, which participants in the setting seem to hold as fundamental to their identity, and which is reflected in their questions to the ethnographer. One way of achieving this may be to look at situations in which the computer services department itself could be construed as users and the frustrations which they experience in these circumstances – in their dealings with commercial software and hardware producers, the providers of external databases, and the authors of programs. By exposing the mosaic of these interactions, it may be possible to bring into question the maintenance of that one boundary which seems so fundamental to the identity of computer services and which allows the information system to act as a kind of border customs post. In effect a study of the interface between users and the information system, traditionally construed as the subject of HCI, needs to take into account that this is also the interface between two communities, two cultures, and two organizational styles.

2.4.3 Configuring the user

Thus far, our tales from the field have particularly exemplified two aspects of the version of ethnography we are advocating. First, we have seen that questions about the observer role can generate a whole new sense of the community of relevance for study: in particular, we find that membership of relevant communities is a matter that participants themselves experience as flexible and negotiable. Second, we see that, especially in technical settings, the observer role can be transformed in virtue of the electronic spaces in which "the observer" engages with participants: the passage between field and "home" becomes the crucial focus of study. In both cases, questions about the observer role raise further questions about the appropriate unit of analysis for ethnographic inquiry.

A third line of study particularly stresses the analytic skepticism associated with this style of ethnography. In this case, the skepticism is brought to bear on taken-for-granted assumptions about two key entities: "the machine" and "its user(s)."

The study focused on the development of a new range of personal computer (PC) in a medium-sized company whose main business was the manufacture of computer hardware and systems, primarily for education. A main objective of the study was to track the evolution of the new PC product, looking in particular at the social, cultural and organizational influences upon design. After protracted negotiations, I (SW) joined the company as part of the recently expanded project management team; it was thought that my acting as assistant project manager would be particularly useful (for my observational purposes) because it would involve extensive liaison between sections.

It quickly became clear that different sections and groups in the company held often quite distinct views about the kinds of people who would be using the machine and about their attitudes and needs.[21] Members of different sections at different times offered varying accounts of "what the user is like." Knowledge and expertise about the user was distributed within the company in a loosely structured manner, with certain groups claiming more authority in specific matters such as the need for a "welcome screen," the style in which the manual was to be written, the nature and number of the bugs that had to be fixed before release, and so on. In each case, discussion and argument included consideration of what the user would expect, how the user would react, and, especially when the discussion took a more technology driven turn, whether the user mattered. It occurred to me that the whole history of the development of the machine could be construed as a struggle to configure (i.e., to define, enable, and constrain) the user. The architects of the new machine, its hardware engineers, product engineers, project managers, salespersons, technical support, purchasing, finance and control, legal personnel, and the rest were both contributing to, and sometimes fighting over, a definition of the user and of the appropriate parameters for her actions; and it was these that were becoming embodied in the emerging machine.

The "usability trials" provided an especially interesting focus of attention because they turned out to involve explicit articulation of whether prevailing ideas about the user were correct. The start of the trials was delayed on several occasions by the late availability of (what the users product section regarded as) a "finished" product.[22] Members of the user products section took the view that usability trials could only properly take place when a cased version of the machine was available. The machine would not count as a real machine unless it was in its case: an appropriately physically bounded entity. "Real" in this usage evidently denoted "the kind of machine a user would expect." This contrasted markedly with what counted as a real machine within the company: especially in the engineering sections, machines were routinely left open on desks, their innards on full display, precisely so that engineers had quick access to the inside of the machine.

It became evident that the machine's boundary – the case – symbolized that of the company, so that in many respects gaining access to the inner workings of the machine was tantamount to gaining access to the inner workings of the company. This was evident, for example, from the surprise of novices in joining the company when they found the pieces of technology they had been taught to revere in such a state of "undress"; from the experience of being taught for the first time how to assemble a computer during the company "induction program"; from my varying enthusiasm about actually buying one of the new machines (depending on whether I was situated in the company or at the university); and from confidential "insider" advice (from a senior member of the hardware team) that I should wait at least six months after launch before ordering a machine.

A central ostensible concern of the usability trials was to evaluate the draft documentation that was to accompany the machine on its shipment: "is the documentation sufficiently clear to users?" In the light of the symbolic importance of the machine/company's boundary, we can understand this question as asking how easy it was for users to gain access to the interior of the black box, to negotiate the machine/company boundary, in order to extract what they need. The documentation is adequate if it contains instructions that ensure that users gain access to the company in the prescribed fashion: by way of preferred (hardware) connections or through a predetermined sequence of (keyboard) operations. Other routes are barred; labels on the case itself bear warnings of the dire consequences of unauthorized boundary transgression: electrocution, invalidation of the warranty, and so on. Often, these same labels redirect users to sources – such as "user documentation" or the company technical support hot line – which can reestablish the preferred patterns of user action, in line with the approved configuration of the user's relationship with the company.

In planning the trials, particular attention was given to the selection of subjects. How could we find subjects who were most likely to act like users? A main aim was to try out the machine and its documentation on relatively novice users. However, a prevailing need for secrecy forced the selection of subjects from within the company. Although this finessed the secrecy problem, the problem of finding subjects who could act like novice users still remained. In the end, the users products group had to draw on personal contacts within the company, to find insiders who could act like outsiders.

In each trial, the subject was confronted with machine, peripherals, and documentation. The tester introduced the general purpose of the trial, pointed out the equipment available, set a task, and asked the subject to say how he or she might go about it and to estimate the length of time it would take. The bulk of the trial comprised the subject then trying to complete the task. Finally, there was a "post mortem" when the tester and other observers would discuss the trial with the subject.

Although (especially in the introduction to the trial) the testers cast themselves as objective observers – not wanting to intrude upon the "natural" process of a user interacting with the machine, and wanting an unbiased picture of how users "actually" went about the completion of the tasks – a whole series of contingencies arose that seemed to demand their frequent intervention. For example, where subjects were thought to be going hopelessly wrong, or where they were clearly about to get into trouble, it was felt necessary to retrieve the situation. Testers also intervened to explain the origin of a problem in terms of a machine fault, where this prevented (or made difficult) the completion of the task by the subject. In general, testers offered considerable commentary on the subjects' performance in what seemed to be attempts to encourage and reassure the subject. An examination of the video and audio records shows how these interventions and commentary depend upon formulations both of "what users are like" and of "what the machine is doing."

What makes these trials so interesting in respect of accounting for interaction between machine and user is that they depend on and involve assessments of the character of both machine and user. The interactions are part of the process of establishing the identity of the interacting entities. In other words, the interaction between machine and user involved assessment both of whether the machine was acting like a real machine *and* whether the user was acting like a real user. For example, the trials reveal participants' attention to the possibility that the machine was not (yet) working as required, that things might yet go wrong. In other words, the capacity of the machine, what it can do, what it is, whether it works "properly," and so on are all open for negotiation in and through the putative user's dealings with it. Similarly, the nature and identity of the user was essentially open. A large number of prompts and interventions pursued the issue of whether the subject was acting sufficiently like a real user. In each case, the tester explored with the subject the way they would have behaved, if in fact they had been acting like a real user.

In one particular trial, Ruth was asked to connect the machine to a printer. In order to see if the "machine" worked, the observers used as criterion the successful operation of a "peripheral." Ruth was initially confronted by the machine (switched on, with its keyboard and monitor); various instruction booklets and an as yet unconnected printer. After some considerable time and various faltering efforts to make sense of the instruction manual, Ruth announced she was stuck. The difficulty was eventually resolved by a sequence of questions from Nina and Nina's eventual declaration that the task is, after all, impossible. It turned out that Ruth had been asked to connect a printer to the new machine using a lead designed for use with a previous range of computers.

This and similar episodes show vividly that the testers' assessment of the adequacy of the (putative) user's actions heavily involves testers' knowledge of "what users are like." Throughout, the testers provide comments on the subjects' actions; they suggest which aspects of the machine and its documentation should be attended to in order to achieve a correct interpretation; and they offer advice on whether the subject is behaving "correctly" qua user. The subject is encouraged to interpret the testers' actions in relation to the machine, and feels she has to display her actions in accordance with their expectation of users.

In all this, the importance of the machine boundary is paramount. I noticed that testers spoke authoritatively about "their" machine; they spoke as insiders who could dispense advice about the machine to outsiders. The importance of insider–outsider contrasts was underscored when it came to attributing blame for (what turned out to be) the impossible task set for Ruth. Indeed, the machine boundary is crucial to the resolution of "Ruth's problem." First, the resolution retrospectively defined who or what has been on trial: in virtue of the resolution we see that the machine, not Ruth, had been the subject of the trial all along. Second, it turned out that the machine on trial is incompatible with the previous range of machines produced by the company. It transpired, in other words, that the entity at the center of all this attention was an imposter. In this form, the "machine" on trial was not, after all, a machine; it was a deviant, not (yet) one of us.

The user's character and capacity, her possible future actions are structured and defined over the course of a long social process of design and development. However, as is dramatically illustrated in the usability trials, interactions between machine and user entail considerable negotiation both about the nature and capacity of the machine, and about the identity and character of the user. Rather than conceptualizing interaction as exchange between two stable, given entities, it is better to think of the machine as its relationship to the user, and vice versa. In this, the machine is a metaphor for the company so that the boundaries of the machine are the boundaries of the company. The machine's case symbolizes the user's relationship to the company. Insiders know the machine, whereas users have a configured relationship to it, such that only certain forms of access or use are encouraged. Of course, this never guarantees that some users will not find unexpected and uninvited uses for the machine; but such behavior will be categorized as bizarre, foreign, perhaps typical of mere users (Woolgar, 1993).

2.4.4 The dialogue: Our interface between humans and machines

This fourth account of recent fieldwork is included for three particular reasons. First, it illustrates the nature of the "dialogue" entered into by the ethnographer and the ethnographed. Second, it demonstrates the way that this ethnography was itself shaped by the dialogue. And third, it displays the ways in which the material from the ethnography was used in the process of translating findings into forms that could more easily be taken up by the subjects of the study.

Toward the end of an ethnographic study of information system design I (JR) was told a story. I was told it twice, in the space of two weeks – each time by a senior manager at the end of a senior management meeting. You've probably heard it yourself. It goes like this:

Systems design used to be done by a bunch of techies, deep deep deep within some head office building somewhere. Here they would build their system. Test it, test it, test it, until they were sure it would work, and then they would throw it over this great high brick wall, and hope that the user would catch it, on the other side.

I might have thought no more of it, but I was faced with the prospect of presenting some "results" of the ethnography to the company. I seized upon the story, then, as it seemed to offer a practical interface between my sociological inquiry and their project management problems.

This fourth ethnographic study was conducted in, on, and with the Customer Project Team in the Management Systems Division of Freshwater (a recently privatized water company). The team was made up of experts from a variety of different communities. When I first joined, there were three or four individual contractors (experts in various database packages); half a dozen brand new Freshwater recruits with experience or potential in programming and systems analysis; ten or so programmers from a consulting company (some of whom worked part time); another six Freshwater employees seconded onto the project from different parts of the company to contribute their experience and knowledge of organizational practice; another seven or eight members of a large prestigious, international consulting company (which I shall call here DC); and always at least one, sometimes four or five, visiting students.

As the project progressed it grew in size, and the consultants and contractors changed names and appearances, but overall each community continued to be represented in the project. Even on this crude measurement, "the" project already contained a variety of interfaces between different organizational communities.

Overall, the project was managed jointly by DC and Freshwater. In practice this meant that DC bore responsibility for project planning and control. Its claim to be able to do this rested (to a large extent) on the reputation of its methodology – a complex set of manuals and computerized machinery, which (DC said) provided the basis for the whole process of systems development and design.

The primary feature of DC project management was to divide the overall Customer Project Team into two: the systems team (with about three-quarters of the total headcount) and the change management team. The methodology reflected this split in the amount of detail it went into for each team's work. Whereas the work of the systems team was highly prescribed, change management was a heading tacked on to the reporting system. The systems team had available a complex map laying out work packages and timing to plan out the design and development phase; the change management team was left to make up its own as it went along.

By the time I heard the mythical "brick wall" story I had already been with the Customer Project Team for a year. I had by then come to have my own idea of the way the team was working. However, when the story was told to me it was told as a story of the past, about the way systems used to be designed. Or perhaps it was a story about somewhere else, a competing company perhaps. The important point, I gathered, was that this story was *not* a description of the Customer Project. Indeed, the point of the story was to portray the Customer Project in favorable light. How had the Customer Project overcome the problem of the great high wall? It had Change Management.

This set me thinking how the story might sound if it were to describe the Customer Project, taking into account the Change Management role. I thought it might go something like this:

Systems Design is done by a bunch of techies deep deep deep within some head office building somewhere. Here, they build their system, test it, test it, test it, until they are sure it will work, and then, just before the day of the great toss, they send out the Change Management guys to explain to the users how to catch.

I told this (version of the) story myself during the last few weeks of my stay at Freshwater. First, I told it as part of my "farewell party" on my last day "in the field." Then I was invited back by the director, to give the talk at a large middle-management meeting. I realized that I was using the story as an interface device. It was making it possible for two communities to communicate effectively. Its use opened a channel through which I was then able to speak more specifically about the mechanisms that kept users out of the design process. And it was this that enabled me to have an effect on the process of design, and to change the way "the humans" interacted with "the machine."

The story tells of a group of people who are isolated from the others who will nevertheless be affected by them. As we have seen (Section 2.4.3) the boundary between designers and users can be symbolized and reinforced by the physical boundary of an encased machine. At Freshwater the boundary was instead symbolized and reinforced by the consultants' (that is DC's) methodology. Following the analogy one stage further, we would expect to find that the methodology is a metaphor for the DC.

Although the Customer Project had succeeded in removing the brick wall from around the system designers, it had erected a wall in other forms. But as far as the systems team was concerned, there was no (longer any) wall. My first problem, then, was to convince the project that there was indeed still a "wall" to be addressed. The second was to show how the practice of developing the information system behind this wall was constraining future use of the system. The third was to suggest some solutions. These three issues are not just practical problems to be overcome, they are also interesting ethnographically. In this process I, as ethnographer, was in the process of being defined. The ethnographer in this setting was being given the chance "to be useful." By using my experience in this process as further data, I was able to draw conclusions about the place of "usefulness" in this community. In particular "usefulness" involved organizing a description of a situation to produce "a problem," which could then be used as a space in which I (as "useful" person) could offer a solution. My solution, in this case, was "to see epistemologically" – that is, to offer the ethnographic way of seeing brick walls produced by social practices.

Retelling the "brick wall" story was enough to persuade the Customer Project that there was a problem to be addressed. The smiles and laughter around the room when I spoke signified wide recognition. The next step was not so straightforward, the real target of my campaign was the deeply entrenched view that systems design *should* be done a long way away from users. But this was so deeply entrenched that it was difficult to point to it. It was so much a part of the epistemological ground, so to speak, that it affected the growth of everything. And as we have seen from the telling of the (first version of the) story, the systems designers were unaware of this fact. Indeed, they thought of themselves as acting in opposition to the bad state of affairs which the story portrayed.

My solution to this in my presentations to Freshwater was twofold. The first tack was to describe some aspects of the work of change management and the systems designers to illustrate the operation and effects of the boundary:

A small subteam within the system team had been working on Release 2 of the main system. In December, one of the men, calling himself a design analyst, visited various parts of the business and interviewed a number of key managers about the current organizational practice. Throughout January and February he and two others used this interview material to devise data flow diagrams, and to work out "entities" and "data elements." Quiet discussions were held with the database manager and the technical architect at casual moments during the normal working day. A "prototype" was constructed (a string of screens) and a presentation was delivered to a few carefully selected senior managers. Commitments were made. Documents were written. Then, only THEN, was the Change Management Team brought in to begin its own process of interviews and designs. By this time the System Team was already firmly established along the path laid out in the prestructured methodology. It was entering a time phase it called Technical Design as the Change Management team was beginning to get a feel for the size of the problem. As far as the team were concerned (and as far as the methodology predicted) it had gotten what was needed (it was a matter of management expectation that the team wouldn't need to go out again) to design and make its computerized system. It was for the Change Management people now to go out and interview again, to find out what else must be done (what procedures should be written, what training given, what practices changed, what new forms to be designed, what new Radio System to be developed, how many new vodaphones to be bought, what new people to be employed, what new wires to be laid . . .) to allow the system to work. The Change Management Team had to create the new world into which the computer system would gracefully glide, dignity and integrity intact.

My second tack was to highlight the boundaries between the various professional groups that made up the Project Team as a whole:

I was shadowing one of the young DC consultants who had been brought over especially from the United States to contribute to the design of the system. Early in the
morning I sat by while he "inducted" another DC consultant, also just over from the
United States, in the protocol of writing pc20s. It was one of those casual office meetings, between peers, sharing jokes and information in the same breath. A little later the
same day, another young DC consultant approached John and quietly asked John to
help him understand some of the documentation. After a couple of minutes Frank began
to gain confidence and ask more complex questions about the potential problems of ap-
proaching the design in this way. I began to take more obvious interest in the conversation by writing in my notebook. I noticed Frank's eyes slide quickly in my direction
and back again to John. He closed his mouth and interlocked his fingers. Then, as he
stood to leave, he said "I'll catch you later." The next thing in John's diary was a
scheduled meeting with William, a Freshwater employee, and a member of the System
Team. When William sat down at the conference table John leaned back in his chair,
folded his hands behind his head, and asked, "What can we help you with?" William
floundered in his reply. He didn't know what John could help him with, that was the
main reason he had come down to see him! William had hoped that John would tell
him how he could help William. The meeting lasted fifteen minutes and was characterized by short questions and short responses. It was uncomfortable. And as William
testified later, unsatisfactory.

These three encounters illustrate that the nature of interaction is a function of the
nature of the relationship. The different relationships between these three people
governed the extent to which they could then effectively design the new system. In
a sense, their interaction with John represented an interaction between the humans
and the computer. John, as expert in the new system design, could govern the
quality of input to the design process from different members of the *system* team to
the design process.

2.5 Conclusion

In these four brief accounts we see the richness of a version of ethnography that can
offer important pointers to ways of reshaping the traditional concerns, problem-
atics, and objects of HCI. We have introduced a kind of ethnography which, while
committed to argument through empirical example, emphasizes the analytic value
of rendering strange and/or exotic some of the key taken-for-granted features of the
setting. This has four clear implications. First, the straightforward idea of observation as a disengaged relation between discrete entities must be replaced by much
greater sensitivity to the various ways in which participants, objects, and other
entities mutually constitute each other. Second, in technological settings in particular, our approach challenges preconceived ideas about the primacy of face-to-face
communication as the medium of social relationship. Third, we have suggested that
this kind of ethnography establishes the significance of contingency in presumptions about the capacity and character of both technical artifacts and humans; this

especially makes problematic those approaches which depend on fixed ideas of "what the machine can do" and "what the user can do." Above all, it is crucial to understand the ways in which the definition and negotiation of social and cultural boundaries are implicated both in characterizations of users, suppliers, designers, and their machines, and in attempts to explain interaction. Finally, we have noted how, in line with our views on the need to interrogate the social and cultural boundaries that underpin interaction between the different entities of our study, much is to be gained through dialogue with the subjects and objects of our investigation.

One aspect of the form of dialogue we favor finds resonance with increasing demands that academic research should demonstrate its relevance and utility for domains outside its particular areas of scholarly expertise (cf. Cooper and Woolgar, 1993a). Thus, for example, it has been noted that HCI constitutes a new challenge for cognitive psychology insofar as the latter discipline is asked to provide practical recommendations for design, implementation, and use (see, e.g., Landauer, 1987). Similarily, much of our work, although building on early laboratory studies in SSK, is increasingly asked to produce more than a disengaged critique by, for example, contributing to producers' and designers' understanding of their own practice. Our emphasis on the embeddedness of researcher in the setting, and on the virtue of a continual dialogue with those being studied, suggests one way of addressing this new challenge. Rather than looking to the social scientist for once-and-for-all solutions to design problems and issues, the notion of dialogue suggests that ideas are fed back, discussed and negotiated as part of the ongoing practice of research.

Of course, the mere willingness to engage in dialogue hardly *guarantees* that our coconversationalists will find what we have to say of value. Instead, we need also to pay careful attention to the form and nature of the dialogue. This again underscores the point we made at the start of this chapter, that ethnography has to be much more than a mere mind-set or attitude. It also entails reflexive attention to the ways in which we tell our stories, the way in which we fashion our descriptions, and the likely readers of our tales from the field. As writers like Anderson (1993) and Button and King (1992) note, the most significant feature of ethnography is that, far from being an "observational technique," it is a form of reportage. The appeal and insights of ethnography stem in large part from the tales from the field.[23]

To the extent that we are suggesting the inadequacy of conceptualizing human–machine interaction as a straightforwardly observable exchange between discrete predefined entities, our argument will find sympathy with those already committed to broadening the focus of HCI.[24] However, it is perhaps important to emphasize that we are not claiming merely to be pursuing a better kind of HCI. Instead, our aims are more ambitious. We have suggested some ways in which concepts in HCI such as, for example, "user" and "interface" can be revised. But it is clear from our preliminary forays down the ethnographic path that a far more radical response is needed: these concepts probably require exorcism rather than mere revision! For our experience of trying to write critically about such matters reaffirms how entrenched are the concepts and related categories of action and behavior in conventions of language and representation. It follows that in order to critique the key categories we take for granted in HCI, we need to pursue a form of ethnography that attempts to destabilize current conventions of reportage.

Acknowledgments

Grant acknowledgments: ESRC/PICT; ESRC; SERC/ESRC and SERC. Part of one of the ethnographic studies reported in this chapter was funded by the ESRC Programme on Information and Communication Technologies (PICT). Thanks for comments to Anna Tsatsaroni.

Notes

1. As noted by authors such as Anderson (1993: 2), the rise of interest in ethnography is partly accounted for by a widespread disenchantment with conventional forms of "requirements capture" for the design of end-user systems (cf. Luff, Heath, and Greatbatch, 1992).
2. In fact, the relative emphasis given to each of these elements accounts for some of the key differences in the way ethnography has been interpreted. Where empirical study is prioritized we find a style of ethnography which emphasizes its value in terms of the reliability and objectivity of its observations; where the emphasis is on the strange and/or exotic, the value of ethnography is its ability to challenge taken-for-granted assumptions. In broad terms, the conception of ethnography as a "technique" fits the former element; the idea of ethnography as theoretical orientation better fits the latter.
3. Of course, this general formulation leaves open which of the myriad senses of "social and cultural practice" is germane.
4. In social studies of science and technology, calls for "taking the content (of the science or the technology) seriously" or "taking the content of the technology into account" are common to many otherwise different approaches and perspectives (cf. e.g., Bloor, 1976: 1; Button, 1993; Pinch and Bijker, 1987: 22). Although these programmatic declarations are valuable in reminding us not to focus solely on the "social" (or "nontechnical") elements, they are less clear about the rationale for any particular attempt to take the content into account. They appear to adopt widely differing criteria of what is to count as (seriously) taking the content into account. They also appear insensitive to a consideration of the audiences for whom their descriptions might count as adequate.
5. In Geertz's (1973) terms, we are saying that ours is an ethnography *in* a setting, not just an ethnography *of* a setting.
6. This goes beyond the rather restricted sense of dialogue advocated within "contextual research": see, e.g., Whiteside et al. (1988).
7. This is in line with some of HCI's programmatic statements, if not with prevailing practice: on the need to study a broader range of phenomena than the "interface," see Diaper (1989); and on the movement toward a more broadly defined notion of "interface," see Grudin (1990).
8. See Cooper and Bowers (this volume) for further discussion of the significance of such a move.
9. Explicitly ethnographic work has been more apparent in studies of the design process, in the field

of requirements analysis, and latterly within CSCW: see, respectively, Jirotka, Goguen, and Bickerton (1994); Low and Woolgar (1993); and Turner and Kraut (1992) for examples.

10. Tetzlaff and Mack, in their review of "perspectives on methodology" in HCI, note that much of this work "seem(s) to have much in common with field and ethnographic techniques" (1991: 302).

11. There is a further question here of how far naturalism is central to the claims of the work itself: but given the heterogeneity of the different approaches in question, discussion of this is beyond the scope of this chapter. On the unappreciated significance of this heterogeneity, see Suchman's comments (1993).

12. This is perhaps inevitable given the central place that cognitive psychology occupies within HCI, for the predominance of the experimental paradigm within that discourse transforms the significance of the routine sociological practice of studying people in everyday settings: for instance, it may be designated "ecological" or "realist" research (see, e.g., Forrester and Reason, 1990: 292).

13. This point has been argued in relation to ethnographic studies in the sociology of scientific knowledge by Woolgar (1982).

14. Of course, these brief acounts offer no more than a taste of the four extensive pieces of research from which they are taken. For further details of each of the studies see, e.g., respectively: (Section 2.4.1:) Cooper, 1992; Cooper and Woolgar, 1993b. (2.4.2:) Hine and Woolgar, 1993. (2.4.3:) Woolgar, 1991b, 1993. (2.4.4:) Hall, Low, and Woolgar, 1992; Low and Woolgar, 1993. We present the studies in this order for the purposes of the flow of the argument, rather than as a reflection of their chronology.

15. It was only after a considerable period in the field that I realized that the comparative isolation of the particular office that I was sharing was of direct relevance to my topic: for its occupant could be seen as a representative of "old" university culture in some respects, and did not take an active part in research. Consequently there was comparatively little traffic of colleagues in and out of his office.

16. When I subsequently mentioned to this researcher this sense of intruding into his personalized electronic domain, he laughed: "Well, if you're in my office, and you're logged into 'Keaton' as WFCA, then you ARE me!"

17. Perhaps predictably, there were stories about the accidental circulation of the wrong versions of documents on the wrong E-mail networks, in which the wider community received critical comments that had been intended for a more restricted community.

18. As discussed in Section 2.4.2, the relative social status of different media is a rich source of ethnographic information. The production of a handwritten piece of paper with columns of figures during one coffee break caused considerable derision when its owner suggested that it contained very important data.

19. This probably owes much to the anthropological roots of ethnography, which constitute a specific form of "logocentrism" (see Derrida, 1976). It was always difficult to shake off the feeling that sitting in an office on my own reading the research papers of those I was studying was not proper ethnography.

20. The ethnographer here seems to be finding herself in the situation described by Ong (1982: 80). He suggests that critics of new technologies tend to find themselves unavoidably availing themselves of the technologies they set out to criticize.

21. The company did not engage in extensive market research, nor in any systematic efforts at requirements analysis; rather they saw their business as primarily "technologically driven," bringing to a more or less stable customer base the latest instantiations of their vision of the future in PC and systems "solutions." Consequently, design decisions made during the evolution of the new machine tended to involve (often implicit) views about outsiders, largely unmediated by direct efforts at soliciting the views of potential customers.

22. Indeed, one of the main reasons for delay in the project as a whole centered on problems in subcontracting the manufacture of the case.

23. However, Anderson seems not to share our analytic skepticism about the epistemological status of observation and representation since, for example, his recommendation is to ground analytic

terms in the "'just-what' of the actualities of the (programming) activities themselves" (Anderson, 1993: 7).

24. See Cooper and Bowers (this volume) for discussion of this "second wave" in HCI.

References

Anderson, Bob. (1993). Representations and requirements: the value of ethnography in system design. Unpublished paper, Cambridge EuroPARC, February.

Bannon, L., and Bodker, S. (1991). Beyond the interface: encountering artifacts in use. In J. M. Carroll (ed.), *Designing interaction: Psychology at the human–computer interface* (Cambridge: Cambridge University Press), 227–253.

Bench-Capon, T. J. M., and McEnery, A. M. (1989). People interact through computers not with them. *Interacting with Computers,* 1 (1), 31–38.

Bloor, D. (1976). *Knowledge and social imagery* (London: Routledge and Kegan Paul).

Bourdieu, P. (1990). *In other words: Essays towards a reflexive sociology* (Cambridge: Polity).

Button, G. (1993). The curious case of the vanishing technology. In G. Button (ed.), *Technology in working order: Studies of work, interaction and technology* (London: Routledge), 10–28.

Button, G., and King, V. (1992). Hanging around is not the point. Unpublished paper presented to workshop on Ethnography and Design, ACM *CSCW '92 Conference,* Toronto October 31–November 4.

Callon, M. (1986). Some elements of a sociology of translation: Domestication of the scallops and the fisherman of St. Brieuc Bay. In J. Law (ed.), *Power, action and belief: A new sociology of knowledge?* Sociological Review Monograph 32 (London: Routledge), 196–233.

Carroll, J. M. (1990). Infinite detail and emulation in an ontologically minimized HCI. In J.C. Chew and J. Whiteside (eds.), *Empowering People: CHI '90* (New York: ACM Press), 321–327.

Cooper, G. (1991). Context and its representation. *Interacting with Computers,* 3 (3), 243–252.

Cooper, G. (1992). Narrative requirements and dilemmas in the construction of a proposal. *CRICT Discussion Paper 24,* March.

Cooper, G., and Woolgar, S. W. (1993a). Software is society made malleable: The importance of conceptions of audience in software and research practice. *CRICT Discussion Paper 34,* May. Also forthcoming as a *PICT Policy Research Paper.*

Cooper, G., and Woolgar, S. W. (1993b). Software quality as community performance. *CRICT Discussion Paper 37,* August. Also forthcoming in R. Mansell (ed.), *Information, control and technical change* (London: Aslib).

Derrida, J. (1976). *Of grammatology* (Baltimore: Johns Hopkins University Press).

Diaper, D. (1989). The discipline of HCI. *Interacting with Computers,* 1 (1), 3–5.

Erickson, D. (1992). Hacking the genome. *Scientific American,* 266, 4, 98–105.

Forrester, M., and Reason, D. (1990). HCI "intraface model" for system design. *Interacting with Computers,* 2 (3), 279–296.

Geertz, C. (1973). *The interpretation of cultures* (New York: Basic Books).

Grudin, J. (1990). The computer reaches out: The historical continuity of interface design. In J. C. Chew and J. Whiteside (eds.), *Empowering People: CHI '90* (New York: ACM), 261–268.

Hall, P. A. V., Low, J., and Woolgar, S. (1992). Human factors in information systems development: A project report. *CRICT Discussion Paper 31,* December.

Hammersley, M., and Atkinson, P. (1983). *Ethnography: Principles in practice* (London: Tavistock).

Hine, C. M., and Woolgar, S. (1993). Technology is ethics by other means. Presented at Sociology of The Sciences Yearbook Conference, Brandeis University, July.

Jirotka, M., Goguen, J., and Bickerton, M. (1994). *Reconceptualising requirements* (London: Academic Press).

Kellogg, W. A. (1990). Qualitative artifact analysis. In D. Diaper, D. Gilmore, G. Cockton, and B. Shackel (eds.), *Human–Computer Interaction: Interact '90* (Amsterdam: Elsevier North-Holland), 193–198.

Knorr-Cetina, K. D. (1981). *The manufacture of knowledge: An essay on the constructivist and contextual nature of science* (Oxford: Pergammon Press).

Landauer, T. K. (1987). Relations between cognitive psychology and computer system design. In J. M. Carroll (ed.), *Interfacing thought: Cognitive aspects of human–computer interaction* (Cambridge, Mass.: MIT Press), 1–25.

Latour, B. (1992). Where are the missing masses? Sociology of a few mundane artifacts. In W. Bijker and J. Law (eds.), *Shaping technology/building society* (Cambridge, Mass.: MIT Press), 225–258.

Latour, B., and Woolgar, S. (1986). *Laboratory life: The construction of scientific facts,* 2nd ed. (Princeton: Princeton University Press).

Law, J. (1991). Introduction: Monsters, machines and sociotechnical relations. In J. Law (ed.), *A sociology of monsters: Essays on power, technology and domination* (London: Routledge), 1–25.

Low, J., and Woolgar S. (1993). Managing the socio-technical divide: Some aspects of the discursive structure of information systems development. *CRICT Discussion Paper 33,* May. Also in P.Quintas (ed.) (1993), *Social dimensions of systems engineering* (Chichester: Ellis Horwood), 34–59.

Luff, P., Heath, C., and Greatbatch, D. (1992). Tasks in interaction: Paper and screen based activity in collaborative work. In J. Turner and R. Kraut (eds.), *Proceedings of the Conference on Computer-Supported Cooperative Work (CSCW '92)* (New York: ACM Press), 163–170.

Lynch, M. (1985). *Art and artifact in laboratory science: A study of shop work and shop talk in a research laboratory* (London: Routledge and Kegan Paul).

Moerman, M. (1974). Accomplishing ethnicity. In R. Turner (ed.), *Ethnomethodology* (Harmondsworth: Penguin), 54–68.

Ong, W. (1982). *Orality and literacy: The technologising of the word* (London: Methuen).

Pinch, T., and Bijker, W. E. (1987). The social construction of facts and artifacts: Or how the sociology of science and the sociology of technology might benefit each other. In W. E. Bijker, T. P. Hughes, and T. Pinch (eds.), *The social construction of technological systems: New directions in the sociology and history of technology* (Cambridge, Mass.: MIT Press), 17–50.

Sharrock, W. W., and Anderson, R. J. (1982). On the demise of the native: Some observations on and a proposal for ethnography. *Human Studies,* 5, 119–135.

Suchman, L. (1987). *Plans and situated actions* (Cambridge: Cambridge University Press).

Suchman, L. (1993). Response to Vera and Simon's situated action: A symbolic interpretation. *Cognitive Science* 17 (1), 71–75.

Tetzlaff, L., and Mack, R. L. (1991). Discussion: Perspectives on methodology in HCI research and practice. In J. M. Carroll (ed.), *Designing interaction: Psychology at the human–computer interface* (Cambridge: Cambridge University Press), 286–314.

Traweek, S. (1988). *Beamtimes and lifetimes: The world of high energy physicists* (Cambridge, Mass.: Harvard University Press).

Turner, J., and Kraut, R. (eds.). (1992). *Proceedings of the Conference on Computer-Supported Cooperative Work (CSCW '92)* (New York: ACM).

Whiteside, J., Bennett, J., and Holtzblatt, K. (1988). Usability engineering: Our experience and evolution. In M. Helander (ed.), *Handbook of human–computer interaction* (Amsterdam: Elsevier North-Holland), 791–817.

Winograd, T., and Flores, F. (1986). *Understanding computers and cognition* (New Jersey: Ablex).

Woolgar, S. (1982). Laboratory studies: A comment on the state of the art. *Social Studies of Science,*
    12, 481–498.
Woolgar, S. (1989). Representation, cognition and self. In S. Fuller et al. (eds.), *The cognitive turn:
    Sociological and psychological perspectives on science* (Dordrecht: Kluwer), 201–224.
Woolgar, S. (1991a). The turn to technology in social studies of science. *Science, Technology and
    Human Values,* 16, 20–50.
Woolgar, S. (1991b). Configuring the user: The case of usability trials. In J. Law (ed.), *A sociology of
    monsters: Essays on power, technology and domination* (London: Routledge), 57–99.
Woolgar, S. (1993). The user talks back. *CRICT Discussion Paper 40,* September.

3
Toward foundational analysis in human–computer interaction

James M. Nyce and Jonas Löwgren

3.1 Background

In the 1970s and the early 1980s, human–computer interaction (HCI) evolved out of what was then called "software psychology." In 1980, Shneiderman defined software psychology as "a new science which applies the techniques of experimental psychology and the concepts of cognitive psychology to the problems of computer and information science" (Shneiderman, 1980: 3). The growing field of HCI inherited from software psychology and from the human factors community both a laboratory-based, experimental program and a strong belief that such a program could alone answer whatever questions – applied and basic – computer and human interaction might raise.

Gaines (1985) dates the beginnings of experimental psychology's interest in HCI to 1973, when an article on a psychological evaluation of two computer language constructs was published in the *International Journal of Man–Machine Studies.* According to Carroll (1993), psychology played two major roles in early HCI. The first was to produce general descriptions of human interactions with systems and software. Results from this application of psychology were packaged either as analytical models or as general design principles. The work of Card, Moran, and Newell illustrates the analytical HCI models that emerged – all of them based on analogies drawn from information processing: described as "a sort of psychological civil engineering" (1983: 10), the different models they introduced were to make it possible to predict the performance of any joint user–computer system.

The other role for psychology was to verify the usability of systems and software. Given the experimental heritage, it is not surprising that laboratory studies of usability tended to be unrepresentative or oversimplified in order to yield "scientifically valid" results. Carroll (1993) gives examples such as using undergraduates in the place of programmers or studying organized versus disorganized menus in order to obtain statistically significant results.

The next phase of development could be described as "Why HCI?" Instead of aiming for general truths about user–computer interaction, researchers started to turn to systems development issues. The new goal was to provide knowledge that could be applied to the process of developing usable and useful computer systems. This often took the HCI community off in the direction of importing or devising methods and techniques (this will be part of our story) and then attempting to validate them. In the mid-1980s, usability engineering and related approaches became popular and usability labs were set up in academia and industry. These efforts typically promoted iterative systems development, where each iteration was tested for usability by the future users. In order to manage the problem of knowing when to stop, it was assumed that usability requirements could be specified along with the other requirements that, according to a long-standing software engineering tradition, are specified before the system is built. Representative examples of this approach include Bennett (1984) and Carroll and Rosson (1985).

The tension between an engineering approach to usability, which presupposed design problems could be specified before they were solved, and the realities of designing for complex, changing patterns of work, need, and context has become more and more evident. By the last half of the 1980s, researchers in usability-oriented systems development had begun to discuss the dialectic between usability and engineering (Whiteside and Wixon, 1987). Whiteside and Wixon define usability as the extent to which software supports and enriches the ongoing experience of people who use the software. They concluded that usability

extends the horizon for interactive software design towards issues that are really of concern to people. However, this orientation provides no commitment to action. On the other hand, engineering is by definition commitment to action. However, it is not inherently grounded in issues that are really important to people. Thus each aspect of usability engineering provides a focus that the other aspect lacks. (Whiteside and Wixon, 1987: 20)

This tension between experience and engineering has led to more consideration of context in HCI. Contextual design (Whiteside, Bennett, and Holzblatt, 1988; Wixon, Holzblatt, and Knox, 1990) is one such development approach. Contextual design explicitly rejects laboratory methods in favor of obtaining an understanding of the context in which users work. The process of acquiring this understanding is called contextual inquiry:

We talk with users while they are working. We see which aspects of a system support or interfere with work and how that system interacts with the whole work context. . . . Different users of a system are selected so that each user adds another dimension to the emerging picture of work breakdowns and opportunities to support work within the system to be developed. Because we engage the users as partners in this inquiry, we gather users' interpretations, language and the structuring of their work activities. (Wixon et al., 1990: 331)

Contextual design also attempts to deliver realistic designs under time and resource constraints. The key feature here is that the designs are developed so that they reflect both the users' and the developer's current understandings of the context. This kind of understanding necessarily evolves over time and, as it does, this helps guide design and redesign. The process can continue until the resources are exhausted.

3.2 To ethnography

This move toward contextual issues has led HCI researchers to ethnography. However, the laboratory heritage of this research community has meant that in HCI, ethnography has been used only to describe action and behavior. What this kind of ethnography has not dealt with well as a result are those categories of meaning that give behavior and interaction their significance and meaning. In other words, the most important part of ethnography – foundational analysis – has in HCI dropped out.

The reason, we believe, is a demonstrable, fundamental gap between the knowledge the HCI community has tended to value and build from and that which a strong ethnography can yield. For example, what ethnography tells us about practice – that it is contingent, often problematic, informed by context, and is seldom rule bound – challenges most of HCI's strategies, programs, and research agendas. Rather than address this issue head on (and risk losing a place in HCI), ethnography has essentially been trivialized – reduced to a method that "counts" and describes.

In the HCI community then, ethnography has been seen as just another field technique. As such, it becomes at best a way to describe (fill in) some set of already predefined research categories. When ethnography is used this way, it is reduced to an inventory of (someone's description of) behavior and belief. What this kind of ethnography can not pick up are those cultural categories that give behavior and interaction their significance and meaning.

What ethnography presupposes is both the willingness and the theoretical training to do analysis of the most fundamental kind – one that starts with questions about categories, meaning, and intention. It is this kind of foundational analysis that seems to be missing in much of the ethnographic work done in the HCI community. By foundational analysis, we mean the critical questioning and analysis of basic categories and assumptions. We argue that ethnography requires the investigation of "common sense." This includes both the enactment and production of common sense categories and meanings and how they inform those events – that is, work and technology – which the HCI community takes as its primary research interests. In other words, ethnography is not concerned just with what is meaningful but with how meaning is made, revised, and acted upon. Once again, it is this kind of ethnography that has not been brought into HCI. Nor for the most part has it been part of any of the HCI research agendas that so far have made use of ethnography.

This could have some unfortunate consequences. Ethnography, we believe, will move into the mainstream of HCI only as quickly as it can be reduced to one of HCI's structured research methods. For example, Cooper et al. in their discussion of ethnography and HCI (this volume) go out of their way to separate ethnography (a method) from a "theoretical orientation" and they do this to ensure the method's "reliability" and "objectivity." This, of course, requires a substantial rewriting or "forgetting" of what, since the late nineteenth century, ethnography has been. Although diminishing ethnography's aim and scope will help preserve HCI's dominant epistemology, the HCI research community stands to lose as a result a powerful instrument not only to understand others but also itself.

In short, HCI researchers will continue to try to identify rules and procedures of behavior and to turn these rules more or less directly into hardware and software. Even when we do find discussions in HCI, say, of meaning or agency, they quickly turn to issues of notation, procedure, and rules (Shultz, 1991). In short, and there is no polite way to put this, the HCI community for the most part believes in a taken-for-granted world where everyone pretty much knows what they want (or this can be "discovered" with little or no effort) and everyone understands and talks about the "good" and "desirable" in relation to systems in about the same terms as we do. It is not surprising then that in the HCI community ethnography has been used (and argued for) on the one hand as a commonsense strategy for observation and on the other as an equally commonsense "model" to talk about "meaning."

One result is that important categories in the HCI community like "work" are either taken for granted or read directly out of culture as "common sense." In short, for the reasons given previously, foundational analysis that takes apart the categories like "work" is not often part of HCI's research agenda. This is the reason why in HCI the theoretical structures, models, and languages we have to talk about, say, work are not particularly robust. To put it another way, it seems that common sense (I know what work is) and ideology (e.g., work [and the workplace] should be more collaborative, more democratic, more equalitarian . . . whatever), in a word direct, uncritical transfers from cultural to academic discourse, are more responsible for the direction HCI research and development efforts have taken than any kind of sustained analysis. The point is that, as the HCI agenda develops or even changes direction, it is seldom because commonsense understandings have been challenged or looked at critically.

This is true, in one way or another, of all the ethnographic work that has been published in the HCI literature. For example, although the papers Hughes, Randall, and Shapiro have published on air traffic control (1992; see also Bentley et al., 1992) raise some interesting questions about the nature of design and "cooperation" in design efforts, they do not look very critically at the categories they themselves use. Further, they take the air controller's categories either for granted or as self-evident. There is at work here, we think, a serious misreading of what the ethnographic project is about. While strong forms of ethnography can and should encourage dialogue, no set of practitioners, no matter how expert, can articulate analytic frameworks or categories. Nor for that matter can they abstract out of context and their experience information HCI researchers and developers can immediately use (Graves and Nyce, 1992). All this requires considerable, second-order ethnographic work – what we call foundational analysis. In fact, it is because this kind of analysis has not been done that members of the HCI community find it difficult to get "straight answers" out of ethnographers (Sommerville et al., 1992).

In short, Hughes, Randall, and Shapiro (1992) make no sustained attempt to separate or take apart the categories and resources that support either their own research or the kinds of work they are studying. Harper's study (1992) of two EuroPARC laboratories raises many of the same issues. Here, as in many social studies of science, the categories, resources, and agendas that characterize laboratory work but are embedded in and informed by culture tend to be ignored, taken for granted, or are much too quickly reduced to individual acts or events that can be observed and described. The few anthropologists who publish in the HCI literature also seem to ignore foundational issues.

For example, although Suchman (1987) has contributed in important ways to our understanding of the qualitative distinctions that set traditional models of "machine intelligence" apart from human knowledge and experience, her research on work seldom moves back and forth between taken-for-granted meaning, cultural categories, behavior, and interaction. This neglect of culture and culture analysis stems in part from Suchman's reading (1990) of Garfinkel: Garfinkel tends to reduce culture to normative rule. To avoid this, Suchman's work and that of her colleagues at Xerox PARC tends to focus on behavior. Nor do they, for the same reason, move in their studies of work much beyond the microparticular and the microanalytic. Again this is not surprising given the influence Garfinkel has had on their research.[1]

What HCI researchers and developers seem to value about this kind of anthropological work is its detailed descriptions of behavior – an endpoint that has much in common with their own naturalistic attempts to describe, observe, and inventory. The problem is that descriptions of this kind represent just the first step toward understanding what is going on, for example, in the workplace. They are certainly no substitute for any kind of foundational analysis. Nor are they something, as some in HCI community seem to believe, that rules or principles can directly be derived from.

Nardi's et al. study of neurosurgery (1993) argues that video groupware might be more useful and acceptable if it supported not face-to-face work but work events and objects directly (cf. Nyce and Timpka, 1993). Although this raises some interesting questions about how computer-supported cooperative work (CSCW) applications might emerge from and be fed back into the workplace, there is in this study a curious dislocation between findings and argument. This is because Nardi's conclusions do not seem to emerge from any principled analysis of neurosurgical work. In other words, in this article few if any questions are raised about the fundamental nature of neurosurgery. What is particularly striking is that the categories and constructs (like "brain") that underlie and inform work and labor in neurosurgery and separate it even from other kinds of surgery are taken as more or less self-evident.

Although Nardi describes her spreadsheet studies (Nardi and Miller, 1990; 1991) as ethnographic research (Nardi and Zanmer, 1993: 11), it is not at all clear that this is the case. This research is not naturalistic (it is done offstage, away from work, and consists of a series of interviews). Nor is it particularly analytic. (Like her work on surgery, it takes the categories and elements that constitute this workplace at face value.) Further, Nardi equates ethnography with "studying a small number of people in some depth" (1993: 11). This reduces ethnography to essentially small-group work and neglects both analysis and interpretation – the foundational elements in ethnography. In short, Nardi assumes that the "rich semantics" (1993: 17) of the workplace that she wants to build into design specifications are either locatable at some commonsense level or that they can be discovered relatively easily and without much analytic effort. Nardi is not alone in this. This stance toward work, the social world, and analysis itself seems to be shared by all those who have brought ethnography into the HCI community.

3.3 Participatory design: An example

To illustrate the consequences of relying on commonsense ways of talking about meaning and action, we will turn to participatory design. Even though there has been some crossover from industrial codetermination experiments in the United States and United Kingdom, participatory design rests on a Nordic tradition of collaboration and cooperation between employers and employees regarding work issues that goes back some fifty years (Sandberg et al., 1992). Over the years, this collaboration has been read and written into law and contract (legal and social) that governs the workplace.

Because there has been such a strong push–pull relationship between the development of Scandinavian society, particularly in labor relations, and participatory design, this design tradition took hold here more than ten years ago. (The results from UTOPIA, one of the first of these projects, a collaborative development project for the newspaper industry, started to appear in the 1980s.) Since then, cooperative projects have been carried out between designers, developers, researchers, trade unions, and companies (this historical development is summarized in Ehn, 1989).

As a result, in Scandinavia, industrial design and development cycles have progressively been opened for debate. This has allowed other views than those of designers and managers to be brought in. In participatory design, practitioners become directly involved in system analysis and artifact design. Efforts are also made to ensure that users will be active, equal participants in design efforts. With participatory design, the intention is to create an environment in which all the parties involved can exchange information, make informed choices, and thereby come to some reasoned stands about design and technology cycles for the workplace.

Participatory design also attempts to manage, even direct, change. Here, developers act as catalysts. They initiate a change process where the goals cannot be fully specified a priori and there are no objective stopping criteria (Bødker, Greenbaum, and Kyng, 1991). Drawing on dialectic materialism, some accounts of participatory design discuss worker emancipation and emphasize the political nature of this change process (Ehn, 1989). Other researchers start from Wittgenstein's notion of language games (Ehn and Sjögren, 1991).

We will argue here that participatory design tends to be based more on culture, ideology, and belief than on any sustained analysis. In participatory design, fundamental categories like "practice" and "change" are either treated as givens or taken for granted. As a result, participatory design tends to cover over more than lead to an analytic understanding of issues, categories, and agendas associated with HCI. This is not a trivial issue for it calls into question what actually supports and informs participatory design. Almost always what is left out of discussions of participatory design is that this design strategy reflects a particular set of cultural and historical features. When this issue is taken up, it is assumed that in other settings differences of this kind can be dealt with through "accommodation" (Muller et al., 1991). Consequently the problem of transfer outside of Scandinavia is seen as a relatively trivial one. However to treat these issues this way ignores the fact that participatory design both rests on and reflects some fundamental Scandinavian categories and assumptions. For example, how categories like change are read in Scandinavia not only informs the arguments for participatory design but underlies the method itself.

In Scandinavia, change is widely believed to be a force whose effects may not only be unwanted but can be actually inimical to society and its members. Some Swedes, for example, tend to perceive change as dangerous, presumably because its consequences are unpredictable. However Swedes also believe that change can be rationally managed and, in this way, its unintended or unwanted consequences can be avoided. What participatory design provides is a "rational" set of methods and theories that focus attention, both scholarly and lay, on the concept of change. More specifically, it provides a form where design and implementation efforts, change and the workplace can be discussed. In this way, it opens up (subjects) change and innovation to public debate and, in Sweden, this presumes rational scrutiny and control.

At work here is a particular set of beliefs about language and action, one where language has much in common with action. Although speech acts can inform, challenge, and question, here speech acts directly accomplish. Further, in Sweden language is understood to be a "strong" form of action. As such, language acts, particularly those that strive for consensus, are seen as "real" acts and they can have, it is believed, real and permanent consequences. In Sweden, it is as though power can be derived from speech, at least from certain "proper" kinds of speech, alone. To be effective then, language does not need to have any other kind of social referent. For example, it need not be linked to class or status. This opens up the possibility, at least with respect to speech, that hierarchy and structure do not matter.

In Sweden then, no one more than anyone else "owns" language, unlike property, and everyone has "equal" control of and rights to it. Therefore through language, rationality, equality, and "understanding" can be both worked out and achieved. This is in part why political, social, and cultural debate and discussion, are taken more seriously than, say, in the United States.

In short, participatory design rests on and works from some fundamental Scandinavian assumptions. For example, participatory design assumes that group work and discussion are necessary, that consensus is important, that from such agreements and group processes, adequate understandings about, say, work will emerge. This knowledge, to go on, should be and can be both achieved and best used collaboratively. There is in Sweden anyway a strong tendency to deny "difference" and that difference plays any significant role in social life (Löfgren, 1987; Scase, 1976). This need to flatten hierarchy, it should be pointed out, acknowledges the critical role power and formal structure, particularly in relation to authority, have in Sweden. At the same time however, it denies that this is necessary or inevitable. Hierarchy, the argument continues, no longer has any "real" importance: in Sweden, it is an artifact from the past.

Participatory design assumes that the differences in power, commitment, and expertise found in any development cycle, once discussed around a table, will be acknowledged and can be dealt with. What interests us here is how this is done. In participatory design, there is a strong push toward explicit contract, not informal "understandings," shared, not private, beliefs and goals and structure. Participatory design assumes that if all the stakeholders in a development effort are not already rational (i.e., cooperative) and "equal," group and language work of this kind will make them so.

In other words, structuring these speech events (this is a central tenant of participatory design) so that they are subject to prior, agreed upon rules and norms makes these speech events by definition "rational" transactions. Further, these rules, by their very presence, create or at least lead to participation, theoretically equal participation, and consensus. To put it another way, with participatory design, collaboration, compromise, and conversation can level any playing field.

Although the workplace is contingent and often problematic, what participatory design assumes is that it is, if not rule-bound, rule-specifiable. Through method and structure, as Swedes here take speech and rule to be, rationality is sought and applied and all this "goes away." In this way too, the issues that change and technology raise for the workplace can also be understood and "managed." In Sweden, it has to be kept in mind that change is a force, a natural force, of such an order that it can only be handled through what Swedes perceive to be the strongest of their cultural resources – rationality, language, and consensus. In short, participatory design both stands on and has been read directly out of culture. Further, this has been either glossed over or ignored in the literature (for an exception, see Whitaker, Essler, and Östberg, 1991).

3.4 Conclusion

What ethnography can and should help us discover is something about the nature of categories upon which HCI agendas, like participatory design, rest. This is true whether we turn to ethnography to understand the categories that inform HCI research strategies and agendas, or whether ethnography is used to help make sense of the categories and meanings that give behavior and interaction in the workplace their significance. To argue that ethnography, like other contextual methods, is too expensive to use in HCI research and development cycles is for the most part a red herring. To argue that ethnography is occult and "hermeneutic" – that is, not easily understood, taught, or practiced – is too. However, to argue that a strong ethnography could be too analytical, that it would only tear things apart, gets to the heart of the matter. This is because it reveals the hegemony that the laboratory, with its pragmatic, empirical stance toward the world, still has in HCI. The problem is that the terms and agendas we both use and study in HCI are contested, negotiated social domains and HCI needs foundational methods, like a strong ethnography, to deal with them.

Acknowledgments

We wish to thank Diana Forsythe and Bill Graves for their comments on drafts of this chapter.

Note

1. As a result, Suchman uses "situated" and "situation." However, this assumes that both these terms represent events that are unproblematic, sui generis, and as such require no further analysis.

References

Bennett, J. (1984). Managing to meet usability requirements: Establishing and meeting software development goals. In J. Bennett, D. Case, J. Sandelin, and M. Smith (eds.), *Visual display terminals* (Englewood Cliffs, N.J.: Prentice-Hall), 161–184.

Bentley, R., Hughes, J., Randall, D., Rodden, T., Sawyer, P., Shapiro, D., and Sommerville, I. (1992). Ethnographically-informed systems design for air traffic control. In J. Turner and R. Kraut (eds.), *Proceedings of the Conference on Computer-Supported Cooperative Work (CSCW' 92)* (New York: ACM Press), 123–129.

Bødker, S., Greenbaum, J., and Kyng, M. (1991). Setting the stage for design as action. In J. Greenbaum and M. Kyng (eds.), *Design at work: Cooperative design of computer systems* (Hillsdale, N.J.: Lawrence Erlbaum), 139–154.

Card, S., Moran, T., and Newell, A. (1983). *The psychology of human–computer interaction* (Hillsdale, N.J.: Lawrence Erlbaum).

Carroll, J. (1993). Creating a design science of human–computer interaction. *Interacting with Computers,* 5 (1), 3–12.

Carroll, J., and Rosson, M. (1985). Usability specifications as a tool in iterative development. In H. Hartson (ed.), *Advances in human–computer interaction,* vol. 1 (Norwood, N.J.: Ablex), 1–28.

Ehn, P. (1989). *Work-oriented design of computer artifacts* (Hillsdale, N.J.: Lawrence Erlbaum).

Ehn, P., and Sjögren, D. (1991). From system descriptions to scripts for action. In J. Greenbaum and M. Kyng (eds.), *Design at work: Cooperative design of computer systems* (Hillsdale, N.J.: Lawrence Erlbaum), 241–268.

Gaines, B. (1985). From ergonomics to the fifth generation: 30 years of human–computer interaction studies. In B. Shackel (ed.), *Human–Computer Interaction: Interact '84* (Amsterdam: North-Holland), 3–7.

Graves, W., and Nyce, J. (1992). Normative models and situated practice in medicine: Towards more adequate system design and development. *Information and Decision Technologies,* 18, 143–149.

Harper, R. (1992). Looking at ourselves: An examination of the social organisation of two research laboratories. In J. Turner and R. Kraut (eds.), *Proceedings of the Conference on Computer-Supported Cooperative Work (CSCW' 92)* (New York: ACM Press), 330–337.

Hughes, J., Randall, D., and Shapiro, D. (1992). Faltering from ethnography to design. In J. Turner and R. Kraut (eds.), *Proceedings of the Conference on Computer-Supported Cooperative Work (CSCW' 92)* (New York: ACM Press), 115–122.

Löfgren, J. (1987). Deconstructing Swedishness: Culture and class in modern Sweden. In A. Jackson (ed.), *Anthropology at home,* ASA Monograph 25 (London: Tavistock Publications), 74–93.

Muller, J., Blomberg, J., Carter, K., Dykstra, E., Halskov, K., and Greenbaum, J. (1991). Participatory design in Britain and North America: Responses to the "Scandinavian challenge." In *Human Factors in Computing Systems: CHI '91 Proceedings* (New York: ACM Press), 389–392.

Nardi, B., and Miller, J. (1990) The spreadsheet interface: A basis for end user programming. In D. Diaper, D. Gilmore, G. Cockton, and B. Shackel (eds.), *Human–Computer Interaction: Interact '90* (Amsterdam: Elsevier North-Holland), 977–983.

Nardi, B., and Miller, J. (1991). Twinkling lights and nested loops: Distributed problem solving and spreadsheet development. *International Journal of Man–Machine Studies,* 34, 161–184.

Nardi, B., Schwarz, H., Kuchinsky, A., Leichner, R., Whittaker, S., and Sclabassi, R. (1993). Turning away from talking heads: The use of video-as-data in neurosurgery. In *Human Factors in Computing Systems: INTERCHI '93 Proceedings* (New York: ACM Press), 327–334.

Nardi, B., and Zarmer, C. (1993). Beyond models and metaphors: Visual formalism in user interface design. *Journal of Visual Languages and Computing,* 4, 5–33.

Nyce, J., and Timpka, T. (1993). Work, knowledge and argument in specialist consultations: Incorporating tacit knowledge in system design and development. *Medical and Biological Engineering and Computing,* 31, HTA16–HTA19.

Sandberg, Å., Broms, G., Grip, A., Sundström, L., Steen, J., and Ullmark, P. (1992). *Technological change and co-determination in Sweden* (Philadephia: Temple University Press).

Scase, R. (1976). Inequality in two industrial societies: Class, status and power in Britain and Sweden. In R. Scase (ed.), *Readings in the Swedish class structure* (Oxford: Pergamon Press), 287–314.

Shneiderman, B. (1980). *Software psychology: Human factors in computer and information systems* (Cambridge, Mass.: Winthrop Publishers).

Shultz, T. R. (1991). From agency to intention: A rule-based computational approach. In A. Whiten (ed.), *Natural theories of mind: Evolution, development and simulation of everyday mindreading* (Oxford: Basil Blackwell).

Sommerville, I., Rodden, T., Sawyer, P., and Bentley, R. (1992). Sociologists can be surprisingly useful in interactive systems design. In *People and Computers VII: Proceedings of the HCI '92 Conference* (Cambridge: Cambridge University Press), 341–353.

Suchman, L. (1987). *Plans and situated actions: The problem of human–machine communication* (Cambridge: Cambridge University Press).

Suchman, L. (1990). Representing practice in cognitive science. In M. Lynch and S. Woolgar (eds.), *Representation in scientific practice.* (Cambridge, Mass.: MIT Press) 301–321.

Whitaker, R., Essler, U., and Östberg, O. (1991). Participatory business modelling. Research Report TULEA 1991:31, Luleå University, Sweden.

Whiteside, J., Bennett, J., and Holzblatt, K. (1988). Usability engineering: Our experience and evolution. In M. Helander (ed.), *Handbook of human–computer interaction* (Amsterdam: Elsevier), 791–817.

Whiteside, J., and Wixon, D. (1987). The dialectic of usability engineering. In H.-J. Bullinger and B. Shackel (eds.), *Human–Computer Interaction: Interact '87* (Amsterdam: North-Holland), 17–20.

Wixon, D., Holzblatt, K., and Knox, S. (1990). Contextual design: An emergent view of system design. In *Human Factors in Computing Systems: CHI '90 Proceedings* (New York: ACM Press), 329–336.

4

Representing the user: Notes on the disciplinary rhetoric of human–computer interaction

Geoff Cooper and John Bowers

> To throw some light on discussions about the "people" and the "popular," one need only *bear in mind that the "people" or the "popular" . . . is first of all one of the things at stake in the struggle between intellectuals*
>
> (Bourdieu, 1990: 150, original emphasis).

4.1 Introduction

The focus in this chapter is somewhat different from that of most of our cocontributors; for rather than pointing to some of the many ways in which action and interaction at the user interface can be construed, described, and analyzed as "social," we propose and explore the value of looking at the matrix of disciplinary relations that not only provide the background to but, we claim, constitute the *very possibility* of the entities "user interface" and, for that matter, "user." In other words, we argue for the importance of analyzing the discourse of human–computer interaction (HCI), with particular reference to its interaction and management of relations with other disciplines. Such a shift of topic has radical consequences: for those phenomena that occupy central positions within the domain of HCI emerge as discursive constructs that are crucial for the discipline's self-assertion and legitimacy. Thus, the question of "social dimensions" of interaction is completely reformulated.

A consideration of many of the early texts in HCI from the late 1970s and early 1980s reveals a number of important features of HCI discourse. Indeed, our argument will be that recent developments in HCI – far from contradicting the discipline's foundations laid in this early period – depend and build upon them. In the space available here, we cannot evidence all our claims fully. Although we take the features of HCI discourse that we identify to be constitutive of the field, we will make our points in relation to a comparatively small number of key texts, which, though, we will analyze in some depth.

The chapter is structured as follows. We begin by briefly indicating the theoretical and methodological underpinnings of our analysis of disciplinary discourse, and noting some of the specific issues that must be addressed in relation to HCI. We then identify and analyze, in turn, a number of themes we see as being of central significance to the discipline: the representation of the user, the user interface as the site of HCI knowledge; the rhetoric of progress, the artful management of disciplinary relations, and the emergence of crisis rhetoric as the early optimism of

HCI has begun to falter in recent years. Finally, we consider some of the implications of, and future directions for, our analysis.

4.2 Analyzing discourse

Our analysis draws implicitly on the perspective on disciplines elaborated by Michel Foucault (e.g., 1970; 1977), and on the work of Michel Callon (e.g., 1986), which, although it does not take the discipline as its unit of analysis, identifies a similar dynamic in the formation and organization of knowledge. We will briefly set out the main parameters of this approach.

Foucault focused on those institutionalized forms of discourse which he characterizes as the human sciences, whose legitimacy rests on their claim to speak some form of truth about, and on behalf of, the human subject. Of fundamental importance is his assertion that the distinctive character of a given discourse, that is the relative unity of the statements that it comprises, does not derive from the objects of study: such objects are the product of discourse, not its foundation. Rather, a discourse actively maps out a terrain of possible and valid statements, sets the boundaries of that terrain and constitutes the legitimate objects of study within it. Just as objects are produced in and through discourse, this process will also involve the definition of those who have rights of access to the discourse. In this way, experts, their professional self-interests and domains of exclusive expertise emerge. In other words, this is a constructivist and supply-driven view of disciplinary formation.[1] The legitimacy of the emerging discipline is tied to the extent to which it succeeds in formulating and asserting a distinctive domain and thereby, in Callon's terms, in constituting itself as the "obligatory passage point" for access to that domain's phenomena. Once this has been achieved, a discipline can speak *its* truth.

In the case of the human sciences, the constitution of a distinctive domain is reflexively tied to claims that the discipline in question, to differing degrees, acts as the representative of a particular constituency. In this respect, a discipline's rhetoric is of great significance: for no matter how well intentioned it may be, compassionate rhetoric – whether it be nineteenth-century criminology's claims to understand the criminal or HCI's advocacy of "user-centred design" – can be seen to serve an important legitimating function.

However, we do not wish to claim that Foucault provides a method that can be unproblematically "applied" to HCI. There are a number of methodological and historical obstacles to such a formulaic aspiration that we can do no more than note in passing. The identification of HCI as a unitary discipline is clearly problematic, for even preliminary analysis reveals a more complex configuration in which, for example, cognitive psychology constitutes both a defining core of an avowedly multidisciplinary field, and a skeptical competitor.[2] The field is fragmented, contested, and dynamic, and this is itself, we shall argue, germane to understanding the discourse of HCI. HCI has to work and be convincing within a field of competing and highly skeptical interests. For us then, "discipline" is retained not as a definitive label for HCI but as a provisional designation for an unstable process in which the constitution, ordering, and regulation of a domain exists in a mutually supportive relation with the attempt to found a legitimate discourse in which that domain is described.

HCI has to insinuate itself into an existing array of disciplines, notably but not exclusively, computer science and cognitive psychology. This creates a whole series of disciplinary dilemmas for HCI workers: to attain autonomy without losing one's audience, to attain novelty without losing one's legitimacy, and so forth.[3] This active and persistent management of interdisciplinary dilemmas emerges as a central feature of HCI discourse in our analysis.

We claim that the viability of HCI depends on its production and management of new categories in terms of which problems, issues, methods, theories, recommendations, and so forth get formulated. We identify two crucial categories that HCI has constructed: the user and the interface. It is not that users and interfaces lay undiscovered until HCI found them. Rather, HCI discourse actively produces users and interfaces where before there were none, and does this in ways that draw upon and reinforce disciplinary realignments. And users have an added significance in that they form the constituency that HCI claims to represent.

4.3 Representing the user

A pervasive, fundamental and highly visible feature of HCI discourse has been its representation of the user and his or her needs. Such representation constitutes, from our perspective, a valuable topic for analysis; and we argue that the rhetoric of representation is of fundamental importance for the attempt to assert the legitimacy of HCI as a discipline.

The representation of the user can be analytically broken down into three constituent and mutually dependent moments. In the first, the user is created as a new discursive object that is to be HCI's concern; this can be distinguished from, for example, "the operator" as found in ergonomics texts. In the second, HCI tends to construct cognitive representations of the user: that is, the discourse of cognitive psychology is typically conferred privileged access to and understanding of those aspects of "users" which are seen as being of particular relevance to the study of human–computer interaction. In the third, HCI represents the user in the political sense of "representation": as Landauer puts it, people within HCI should be the "advocates of the interests of users" (Landauer, 1987: 2) within the wider enterprise of system design. The last two senses are interrelated in that the legitimacy of political representation rests in part on the extent to which expertise in cognitive representation is accepted.

A notable aspect of the political representation of the user is its liberal, humanist, and antitechnicist rhetoric. The relatively ubiquitous notion of "empowerment" – see for example the subtitle of the CHI '90 conference *Empowering People* – provides a conspicuous example.[4] An even more telling one is provided by "user-centered design," which urges that design not simply take the user into account, but should "start with the needs of the user"; it emphasizes "that the purpose of the system is to serve the user, not to use a specific technology, not to be an elegant piece of programming" (Norman, 1986: 61). It is not insignificant, we suggest, that the implicitly moral assertions about the needs of users are here tied to the chronological place that such considerations should take in the design process. If design *starts* with the needs of users, then HCI will claim a more central place in system design.

The political and disciplinary connotations of representation become especially clear when we consider Shneiderman's (1987) text. The preface is called "Fighting for the user" and a political–war discourse is used throughout the first few pages. After a list all those who are concerned with problems of computer use, we read:

> However, our awareness of the problems and a desire to do well are not sufficient.
> Designers, managers, and programmers must be willing to step forward and fight for
> the user. . . . Victory will come to people who take a disciplined, iterative, and empiri-
> cal approach to the study of human performance in the use of interactive systems. . . .
> In this way, each designer has the responsibility of making the world a little bit warmer,
> wiser, safer, and more compassionate. (1987: v–vi)

In various places, Shneiderman's text characterizes users as frustrated, anxious, struggling, and suffering computer shock, terminal terror, and network neurosis. These characterizations of the woes of users are commonplace in creating simultaneously both the user as a fragile beast under threat from technology and a duty for HCI researchers to help rescue them. Booth (1989) adds in the first three pages of his opening chapter that users are not understood, angry, frustrated, insecure, frightened, stressed, not motivated to work well, unsatisfied with their jobs, and prone to absenteeism.

That users are not like designers (or computer scientists or system managers or programmers, etc.) is repeatedly emphasised in HCI texts. Consider Shackel (1985: 265): "the designers are no longer typical or equivalent to users; but the designers may not realise just how unique and therefore how unrepresentative they are."

It is important to recognize the rhetorical functionality of these characterizations of the user for HCI. It is not so much that users *are* angry, frightened, and different from designers, it is more that, for this way of legitimating HCI, they *have to be*. One would have no case for HCI, if – having focused on users – we found them to be happy, content, familiar, and already as warm as Shneiderman wants them to be! As long as HCI takes the (political) representation of the user as part of its justification and remit, the frustrated and slightly exotic user will have to be repeatedly rediscovered; while the essential difference of (ordinary) users from designers that Shackel identifies underwrites the need for specialized, mediating representations and representatives.

The sense that "user" serves HCI as rhetorical cipher is further reinforced by its relatively abstract and unexplicated quality: for example, there is comparatively little attention given to distinctions between the individual using the computer and the organizational constraints within which such use takes place. But our claim here is not that "real" users are being ignored (see the discussion of Bannon's work): rather that, in whatever form, users are a necessary construct for HCI's legitimacy, in that they form a constituency awaiting adequate representation. In Callon's terms, the construction of users is an essential part of the process by which HCI attempts to become an "obligatory passage point" (Callon, 1986).

4.4 The user interface: The site of HCI knowledge

The user interface[5] is the site of HCI knowledge and practice; for if HCI's legitimacy derives from its claimed knowledge of the cognitive user, the user interface is the object that it aspires to change. As such, it is itself fundamental to HCI's disciplinary aspirations.

The definition of the interface as a locus of interaction between user and machine is, however, subject to a number of flexibilities. We wish to note two of them. First, HCI disputes the presumed (computer science) view of the user interface as marginal to the functionality of the system. As Norman claims in his advocacy of user-centered design, "from the point of view of the user, the interface *is* the system" (Norman, 1986: 61, emphasis in original), and therefore central to design. Second, the interpretive flexibility of the interface can be put to use in validating the evolution and extension of HCI's domain of expertise. For example, Grudin (1990) points out that the widespread conception of the user interface as the screen (and its design) simply reflects the current state of computer technology in an evolution from punch cards to the distributed and embedded technologies of the future.

In both cases, the interface and its definition are put to use to assert the importance of HCI as a discipline. Grudin's argument is also of interest in that it graphically highlights, through its partial acknowledgment of the converse, the notion of the interface as predating its recognition. For, despite his acknowledgment that it was in a particular period that the term acquired widespread currency, and that the predominant disciplines involved were cognitive psychology and human factors, he explicitly conceptualizes the user interface as existing prior to its formulation in discourse: "Of course, systems have always had user interfaces: how have they evolved, prior to and since attracting attention?" (Grudin, 1990: 262).

The rhetorical effect of such an assertion is that HCI, whose field is interface development, represents a necessary response to a given but hitherto unrecognized set of design problems, and that their solution has become a matter of some urgency.

The further notable feature of Grudin's argument is a reliance on a notion of technological and theoretical evolution or progress. We now turn to examine this figure of HCI discourse in more detail.

4.5 The legitimating function of rhetorics of progress

HCI crucially depends on some notion of technical, social, or epistemological progress.[6] Pointing out or arguing for the existence of some form of progress is often important either to legitimating the stance taken in a text or for indicating responsibilities or "challenges" that we have which are profoundly "new" (or both). We take as our focus one of HCI's foundational texts: Card, Moran, and Newell's *The Psychology of Human–Computer Interaction* (hereafter *PHCI*), published in 1983, to see some progress rhetoric in action. On the first page, progress ("advances") in cognitive psychology is pointed to: "Recent advances in cognitive psychology and related sciences lead us to the conclusion that knowledge of human cognitive behaviour is sufficiently advanced to enable its application in computer science and other practical domains."

For *PHCI,* these advances are due to theorizing humans as information processors and a whole array of sources are cited to demonstrate the utility of this conception. Having founded the worth of the information processing approach, *PHCI* argues that it is already being applied in areas of practical importance. Eyewitness testimony and the design of intelligence tests are specifically cited. That two areas seemingly far removed from computer science and from each other are the first to be cited is presented as underlining cognitive psychology's claim – not merely to applicability but to generality.

PHCI then goes on to specify the particular relevance of this approach for future work by claiming that "there are already the beginnings of a subfield, for which various names (associating the topic in different ways) have been suggested: user sciences, artificial psycholinguistics, cognitive ergonomics, software psychology, user psychology, and cognitive engineering" (p. 2).

In this way, *PHCI* trades off its novelty with its legitimation in terms of past contributions. *PHCI* will be new and original without being groundless. And it will be justified by precedent without being derivative or merely rehashing its ancestors. Achieving this balance is quite an artful matter rhetorically. It is important to note the use of a notion of progress-not-yet-exhausted in bringing it off. "Our own goal is to help create this wave of application: to help create an applied information-processing psychology" (p. 3).

Here, a personalized ("our") goal is aligned with a "wave." The metaphor of wave is interesting here: it simultaneously situates "us" within a large-scale endeavor while giving an image of force. Again, *PHCI*'s enterprise is presented as being part of a composite. It is not marginal or idiosyncratic in such a way that a skeptic could readily dismiss it; but its force cannot yet be taken for granted. There is work for *PHCI* to do.

The management of a narrative of progress in relation to cognitive psychology then is crucial to the legitimation of *PHCI*. Narratives of progress also appear in direct discussions of technology and its status within society: "Society is in the midst of transforming itself to use the power of computers throughout its entire fabric – wherever information is used – and that transformation depends critically on the quality of human–computer interaction" (p. 3).

This statement employs a factual report on social change to justify consideration of human–computer interaction. "Society is in the midst of transforming itself." There is no guarding of this claim with "it is often supposed" or "we believe" or some such device. The change in society is presented as just there. It is also further emphasized by employing what Bowers and Iwi (1993) call a "total and uniform" construction of society. Society is not broken down to consider the relation between computers and different social groups, such a conception being entirely consonant with the unexplicated notion of individual "users" that was noted in the previous section. The whole of society is transforming. The emphasis on "its entire fabric" further underlines this.

This excerpt also employs a device similar to some others we have seen in earlier excerpts. We are "in the midst" of change. Earlier we saw "already the beginnings" of new disciplines. These devices present a version of historical change that combines a form of determinism but with a reinforced obligation for those aware of history to do the work of specifying the details. This account of history does rhetorical work in offering a narrative in which we are invited to see ourselves and our responsibilities. And it does so in ways consistent with how the "advances" in cognitive psychology are depicted and utilized. Processes which already exist "out there" justify "us" (they are not mere fictions!) but a (partially) open future gives us both latitude and responsibility.

Now consider the following excerpt, the first of a list of four "current interface deficiencies" told in the form of "mini-horror stories."

In one text-editing system, typing the word *edit* while in command mode would cause the system to select everything, delete everything, and then insert the letter t (this last making it impossible to use the system Undo command to recover the deleted text because only the last command could be undone). (pp. 5–6)

We have found the telling of such "horror stories" to be a prevalent feature of many early texts in HCI, and they exemplify the identification of a set of problems awaiting attention that we suggested was crucial to the assertion of the need for a new discipline. However, their use rhetorically is not unproblematic. The stories must be seen to have a general upshot (the world needs HCI) and not a particular one (the designers of this particular system were poor). In addition, they must be told in such a way as to not contradict any progress story that might be used elsewhere. It would be strange if the text used technical progress to justify the importance of HCI and then gave enough examples for us no longer to believe in technical progress! They must be told in such a way as to lead to the desired conclusion (a new discipline is needed) rather than to be taken in any other way (better software development methods would have avoided this). Finally, they must be told in a way that manages and mitigates potential accusations of blame. They must not be taken so as to offend and hence repel those whose support the teller wants to count on, for example, computer scientists. As such, just like pictures without a caption, the stories *do not* speak for themselves – indeed, anything but!

These are severe discursive dilemmas. *PHCI* manages them through again utilizing the hybrid picture – which we have seen emerge already – of progress-plus-responsibility with the interface as the site for study: "Yet, when one looks at the teletype interfaces of yesterday, it is clear that substantial progress has been made. . . . But despite considerable advancements, the systems we have are often ragged and in places are sufficiently poor to cripple whole ranges of use" (pp. 6–7).

In this excerpt the notion of progress appears again. This time we suggest that it is involved with managing and mitigating a reading of *PHCI* which the skeptical reader might happen upon. The reader is assured of progress so the "mini-horror stories" should not be taken as denying it. Furthermore, a general point is made about a general category – "the systems we have." They are often ragged and crippling. With this generalization, we are instructed to read the stories as indexing a general conclusion and not a specific accusation of blame to the designers of the systems in question.

We want to emphasize how a certain nuanced notion of progress does rhetorical work in *PHCI*. Specifically, we suggest that progress legitimates the novelty of *PHCI* (and hence HCI itself) without marginalizing it, while setting up a network of roles and responsibilities for readers and researchers which they are invited to fill.[7] All this is done in a way that attempts to manage the likely responses from skeptical readers who might happen upon *PHCI*. This includes dealing with some delicate dilemmas that arise whenever a text is inserting itself between other disciplines. The deftness with which *PHCI* manages the disciplines of cognitive psychology and computer science is the subject of the next section.

4.6 Disciplinary relations

Much of the foregoing excerpts from *PHCI* – on analysis – have been shown to legitimate cognitive psychology or information–processing psychology through narratives of progress. Cognitive psychology is central to *PHCI*'s HCI and emphasizing its progress is one way to manage those skeptical of cognitive psychology's worth. However, this is not the end of affairs. For one thing, there may be those within cognitive psychology who are skeptical of this application. Consider the following.

As with all applied science, this can only be done by working within some specific domain of application. For us, this domain is the human–computer interface. The application is no offhand choice for us, nor is it dictated solely by its extrinsic importance. There is nothing that drives fundamental theory better than a good applied problem, and the cognitive engineering of the human–computer interface has all the makings of such a problem, both substantively and methodologically. (p. 3)

Again, *PHCI* is at pains to point out how its approach is at one with the common practice of "all applied science." As before, *PHCI* gains its strength through precedent. This involves constructing an object of study: "the human–computer interface." However, it is important to note how *PHCI* emphasizes the nonarbitrary nature of the interface (i.e., a real, practical problem is being addressed), while saying that it is not just its practical importance that motivates the choice. If *PHCI* was only motivated by practical matters, this would be enough to marginalize it within psychology and cognitive science. Studying the interface can, as it is sometimes put in HCI texts, "drive fundamental theory." In this way, *PHCI* constitutes its endeavors as both and equally of theoretical and practical weight. Thus, skeptical psychologists are offered the opportunity to participate in a field where their theoretical vanguardism will be undiminished while contributing to any aspect of a practical problem that affects the whole of society.

Of course, there may still be skeptics from computer science, skeptics who are still prepared to read *PHCI*'s litany of horror stories as a veiled accusation. First, the authors of *PHCI* offer the statement that in addition to the arguments about the potential ubiquity of computing in society, "we have personal disciplinary commitments to computer science as well as to psychology" (p. 3) to attend directly to this skepticism of their orientation. In addition, *PHCI* gives an *explanation* of why there might be "all [those] little ways" through which poor designs let us down. This explanation does further work in managing possible readings of the text as being implicitly accusatory.

Interaction with computers is just emerging as a human activity. Prior styles of interaction between people and machines . . . are all extremely lean: there is a limited range of tasks to be accomplished and a narrow range of means (wheels, levers, and knobs) for accomplishing them. The notion of an operator of a machine arose out of this context. But the user is not an operator. He does not operate the computer, he communicates with it to accomplish a task. Thus we are creating a new arena of human action: communication with machines rather than operation of machines. What the nature of this area is like we hardly yet know. We must expect the first systems that explore the arena to be fragmentary and uneven. (p. 7)

This emphasis on the novelty of interaction with computers is at one with the management of progressivist rhetorics that we already have noted. HCI is a new area that we have a responsibility to study and, as it's new, our work cannot be reduced to what has gone before. However, here we also see a new relation between humans and machines being used to explain (or is it excuse?) early "fragmentary and uneven" systems prone to failures of the sort told in the horror stories. This gives *PHCI* a latitude in managing the apportionment of blame: designers are not to blame in any direct way as we are dealing with "a new arena of human action," which "we hardly yet know." Along the way, this argument constructs a further object for study in HCI – the user: "the user is not an operator." In contrast with the operator, the user performs a task by interacting with the machine in a much more intimate and cognitively sophisticated sense than the operator of, say, a motor car or factory machinery could be said to do. In this way, HCI can mark itself as distinct from traditional ergonomics. The extent of its success can be read in the decline of the use of the term "operator" and the correlative rise of "the user" in the literature; and in the extent to which claims for the importance of ergonomics have to acknowledge, and move within, the "discursive high ground" that has been marked out by cognitive psychology (see, e.g., Booth, 1989).

Having managed a possible reading of *PHCI* as blaming computer science, the text turns to indicating the advantages to that discipline of participating in HCI. We read:

It is our strong belief that the psychological phenomena surrounding computer systems should be part of computer science. Thus, we see this book not just as a book in applied psychology, but as a book in computer science as well. When university curriculum committees draw up a list of what "every computer scientist should know to call himself a computer scientist," we think models of the human user have a place alongside models of compilers and language interpreters. (p. 16)

Not only is *PHCI* proposing an addition to computer science, it is suggesting a refashioning of the very identity of computer scientists! New kinds of computer scientist should come into existence, knowledgeable in the ways of HCI. Furthermore, the disciplinary asymmetry of the claim that computer scientists should learn cognitive psychology is striking. *PHCI* does not contain the converse claim that cognitive psychologists should learn computer science.

In summary, our argument is that in early HCI discourse, texts have recourse to cognitive psychology as the source of representations of the user. We have seen how Card et al. (1983) bring off the importance, indeed priority, of cognitive psychology to HCI and how this required the artful management of some possible skeptical responses both from within cognitive psychology and without.

4.7 Crisis rhetoric and the second wave

In the very late 1980s and through to the time of writing, we detect a number of developments in HCI discourse. While the themes we identified in Card et al.'s

(1983) book are still very much in evidence, there is also a loss of confidence manifest in a number of sources. For example, a panel discussion at the CHI '91 Conference was called "HCI Theory on Trial."

To study this faltering optimism further, let us examine Diaper and Addison's (1992) report on a panel session called "HCI: The Search for Solutions." The report notes a series of problems that HCI has confronted: concerning its basic nature, its application to system development, and concerning the marketing of HCI and educating others in it. All these are presented as being in crisis. The authors suggest that:

> What is required is a general and integrated approach to HCI's problems that: agree what HCI should be; what HCI can do; how HCI can do it; and how HCI can be allowed to do it. Proposals that fail to address all four of these are likely to continue to doom HCI to being ineffective and for systems that include computers to continue to be inflicted on individuals, organisations and society that do little to enhance the quality of life, if not actually making the world a less attractive place for us all. (p. 493)

In several respects, we can characterize this as crisis rhetoric. The progress that HCI once promised has been thwarted. We are now already in a situation where we are "doomed," as individual users or as HCI researchers. It is worth noting how this crisis rhetoric depends on earlier promises of progress – one would not be convinced of the pertinence of these current troubles for HCI, if one had not been earlier convinced of its promise – and also on several of the elements of "first wave" HCI discourse: the hapless user inflicted with technology for instance.

In part, the solutions offered in the panel that Diaper and Addison report on involve reconstructing HCI itself but the reorientations are modest: some consist in a re-invigoration of the ergonomic tradition within HCI, some a heightened emphasis on "interaction" over "interface" as the "I" of HCI, some the necessity of an agreed vocabulary. Whereas crisis rhetoric has the effect of commending urgent reflection on us all, the foundations and disciplinary legitimacy of HCI are not questioned.

An alternative response is to focus on the constitution of HCI itself. This is evident in a number of different forms, which we cannot detail here;[8] but a common theme is the adoption of a critical stance toward first-wave HCI that is often reminiscent of the first wave's orientation to design! In the first wave, design was problematized for not taking account of the user. Now, HCI is problematized for not taking account of design.

We find many of these themes well developed in a chapter by Bannon (1991) called "From human factors to human actors: The role of psychology and human–computer interaction studies in system design" (henceforth FHF). Just as *PHCI* compressed many of HCI's foundational moves in a single text, so does FHF with respect to what we shall tentatively call "second-wave HCI."

FHF seeks legitimacy through very similar tropes as did *PHCI*. It invokes notions of progress or advancement. It points out that past achievements, though real, are partial. In short, FHF performs similar interdisciplinary footwork to *PHCI*. The difference is, however, that it is now HCI and applied psychology themselves that are accorded this treatment. Consider:

Although psychology, particularly as represented by the field of human factors . . . or ergonomics, has had a long tradition of contributing to computer systems design and implementation, it has often neglected vitally important issues such as the underlying values of people involved and their motivation in the work setting. (p. 25)

Psychology and psychologically informed approaches to human factors and ergonomics are characterized as "contributing" yet incomplete in "vitally important" ways. Similarly, HCI itself has grown and progressed but has failed to be relevant to design:

Over the last decade the area of human–computer interaction has grown enormously, both within academic research environments and corporate research laboratories. . . . Despite the legitimate advances that have been made . . . , there has been serious criticism of the field for its lack of relevance to practitioners in system design. (p. 33)

These remarks are worth comparing with our discussion of progress rhetorics in *PHCI* where the "legitimate advances" had been made by designers and technologists who had progressed from "the teletype interfaces of yesteryear" and so forth, yet they were unable to systematize the results of their trial-and-error explorations, their common sense, and their intuitions into a well-founded applied science.

This rhetoric is continued in the excerpt below where FHF situates itself in relation to human factors research and begins to reformulate the nature of persons as actors: for although traditional human factors work "has produced many improvements to existing technological systems," its view of the person has been a limited and reductive one (pp. 27–28). Bannon goes on to discuss and question the term "user":

Another term ubiquitous in articles about the HCI field that deserves scrutiny is that of users. . . . The focus of the system design or HCI research group is biased towards the technology; the view of people is often simply as "users" of this piece of technology and "naive users" at that. This can lead to problems. People may not know the technology, but they are not naive as to their work; rather it is the system designers who are "work naive." . . . [There] is a danger in thinking of people as nothing but users. In fact, it is often the case that computer users need to make some modifications to the system in various ways, tailoring the system before it is truly usable. . . . So in a very real sense users are designers as well. Focusing on people simply as users can also blind us to the fact that the user's view of the technology we are developing may be very different from that of the designer's view. . . . It is the ability to understand the user perspective, to be able to see a problem from other than the system viewpoint, to be able to empathize and work with the users of the intended system that marks the good design team. (pp. 28–29)

This excerpt involves a number of subtle reformulations of the notion of user. First, the notion of naive users is objected to as this can obscure the knowledge that users have of their work practices. Second, a reductive conception of user is objected to as this hides suppler user–designer relations that can exist. However, a disparity of user from designer and user from system is still employed here and the necessity of understanding users for good design is asserted again here much as in first wave HCI discourse. Thus, this passage from FHF can be seen to work with a modified conception of user. It does, however, still employ this category and puts it to use in similar ways to the HCI, which the text is critical of. In this way, FHF situates itself still within HCI yet in a (self-)critical orientation to it. This enables FHF to be read as a sympathetic criticism concerned to improve – and not overthrow – HCI. FHF, then, manages the sensibilities of a possible skeptical HCI reader much as *PHCI* had to manage the sensibilities of a possible skeptical computer science reader. In our terms, it deploys the moral and political priority of "representing of the user" in order to problematize and reorder representation in disciplinary terms; and to achieve this, it evokes an ontologically given user prior to representation.[9]

FHF goes on to argue that the differences between designer and user views are to be solved no longer through representing the user through cognitive psychology but by involving *users themselves.* Cognitive psychology is here dethroned and a number of other disciplines are invited to contribute to studies of the entire design and work context. Thus, FHF reconstitutes HCI by reformulating users and reordering the disciplines and HCI's relation to them. In so doing, it nevertheless avails itself of many of the tropes of first-wave HCI discourse (e.g., a notion of "attenuated" progress) as well as many of its constituents (e.g., a notion of "user"). FHF, in many respects, gains its legitimacy through an interdisciplinary critique much like *PHCI* did, only this time it is "first-wave" texts like *PHCI* that form the object of the critique. In a sense, then, FHF has an ironic dependence on texts like *PHCI.* Much as first-wave HCI discourse has to reinvent the hapless user whose cognitions are not understood by designers, so second-wave HCI discourse has a dependence on the hapless user whose working practice, motivations, values, or whatever are not understood by first-wave HCI.

Of course, FHF's is only one way to attempt to establish a legitimized yet critical orientation to first-wave HCI while still operating within HCI. But a recurrent theme within new-wave HCI is a shift of orientation with respect to design. HCI's disciplinary relations with(in) this enterprise are becoming an explicit focus of concern. Of particular interest here are question about the place of HCI within design, and the communication of HCI knowledge to designers. In a sense the very constitution of HCI discourse creates the possibility for this shift in discourse, for the first wave founded HCI as simultaneously *both* a discrete discipline, *and* as one that could contribute to the building of computer systems that already fall within the discourses of other disciplines.

Let us briefly note an interesting discursive manifestation of this shift: that is, the suggestive extension and transformation of some of HCI's key terms. "Usability" has been increasingly employed to describe the adequacy of information that is passed from HCI practitioners to designers. For example, Forrester and Reason (1990: 283) compare (ironically) the complexity of the material given to designers by HCI with the principles that it is supposed to be promoting. Young describes one of the criteria for assessing his simulation models as "usability: are the models practical for the designers who are the intended users?" (Young, 1990: 1056). The designation of designer as user here is further echoed by Carroll, who describes the goal of artifact analysis as attempting to "make it more feasible to take the important objects of HCI practice seriously and thereby to empower designers" (Carroll, 1990: 1057). We can note here that while the objects of "empowerment" are now designers, the term continues to serve an explicit disciplinary function within this displaced context:[10] HCI still has a duty to empower and, hence, a reason to be.

It is also worth asking what empowerment across disciplinary boundaries could mean, especially when we consider the rationalistic stance that much of HCI takes toward the design process: that is, it insists that explicating the principles underlying design will improve design. This takes many forms, from Carroll's own attempts to assess an artifact in terms of the reasonableness of its implicit "claims," to the suggestion that if a rationale cannot be given, then the software cannot be said to have been designed at all (Edmonds, 1989: 52). The stated aim of the design rationale framework is instructive here; it attempts to "help designers reason about design and produce an output which can help others to understand why design is the way it is" (MacLean, Bellotti, and Young, 1990: 207). Helping designers is inflected with disciplinary connotations. A normative and regulative sense is apparent: good design *is* design with rationale.

Let us stress that the "second wave" is highly varied and fragmented in comparison with early HCI. But what unites the divergence is a certain rhetorical dependence on first-wave HCI; for texts can gain legitimacy by analyzing its failings and contrasting themselves with it; and most situate their contributions still within HCI or are taken as such.

The multiplicity of second-wave formulations of HCI should not surprise us. We have argued that HCI was born in attempts to resolve the tension between a range of disciplines. We have suggested that this involves the management of a multiplicity of discursive dilemmas as the claims of different disciplines are invoked, managed, and played off against one another. Skepticism of the foundations of HCI could come, then, from any of a multiplicity of sources. Our analysis of first-wave

HCI – we hope – displays just how provisional and tenuous such discursive strategies can be. On this view, the current multiplicity of approaches is only to be expected. In a sense, it is foreshadowed in the very constitution of HCI.

4.8 Conclusion

We have argued that HCI discourse – and the phenomena, objects, problems, and issues that are formulated within it – can be fruitfully read against the matrix of dynamic and contested disciplinary relations within which it is situated. By analyzing a number of central and recurrent themes within this discourse, we have attempted to show how the domain of HCI is discursively constructed, and how this construction is rhetorically and functionally crucial both for disciplinary legitimacy and identity; that conceptions of technical and theoretical progress, and correlatively of crisis, form an indispensable part of the rhetorical structure of HCI; and that disciplinary relations have to be continually and artfully managed. In short we argue that, in an important sense, this discourse is constitutive of the discipline of HCI. This, it seems to us, provides for an enhanced understanding of both the content of HCI and of its development. Our suggestion is not only that this constitutive rhetoric has been vital for HCI's formation and emergence, but also that the increasingly heterogeneous nature of the field in the "second wave" can be seen in part as a response to the disciplinary tensions that have been integral to the foundations of HCI discourse and hence are immanent within HCI. This view suggests that the debate, disillusion, and dispersal of much HCI today will continue as long as HCI respects the disciplines and institutional settings into which it inserts itself. To go beyond this condition may require a reappraisal of not only the various academic disciplines but the very necessity of constituting disciplines in the first place.[11]

A point of some interest concerns the response of cognitive psychology and computer science to HCI's attempts to found a discipline and demarcate a distinctive domain; for as we have noted, HCI texts have to address themselves to, and attempt to manage a skeptical readership. Our conjecture is that, to the extent that the user interface appears to have a more prominent place within software engineering texts than hitherto – for example, the most recent edition of Sommerville (1992) devotes an entire chapter to it – that the moral rhetoric associated with the user has been successful. However, the very fact that such issues can be accommodated within competing discourses puts into question the extent to which HCI has managed to establish itself as an "obligatory passage point" in relation to knowledge of the phenomena that it has attempted to define as its own.

Finally let us consider the rhetorical and disciplinary status of our own arguments. For although our gaze has been securely fixed upon HCI, it has been implicit in our argument that the processes described have, at least, some degree of general applicability for understanding the formation and interaction of disciplines.[12] It might be assumed that an admission of generality amounted to an undermining of our own argument: for clearly our own text could be analyzed in terms of *its* use of tropes, *its* management of discursive dilemmas, and the matrix of disciplinary relations within which *it* moves. In our view, such a recognition – that is, the recognition of reflexivity – serves rather as an affirmation of the processes that we have attempted to articulate. For the suggestion that reflexivity leads to the negation of our argument relies on a mistaken assumption that this text is separate from what it describes.

By contrast, we assert the value of considering this text as an instance of the very phenomenon being described. In the first place, our shift of focus onto the discourse of HCI is itself an overtly disciplinary one, whose claim to novelty rests on an implicit comparison with work within HCI and an assertion of the relevance of work in different fields, such as the sociology of scientific knowledge. Moreover, the volume of which this chapter forms a part is itself a phenomenon consistent with our formulation of the "second wave," in which the dynamic and shifting field of disciplinary relations accommodates a wider plurality of more ostensibly critical approaches, which are nonetheless tied to foundational aspects of first-wave HCI. As such, our chapter should not be construed as species of metalevel criticism, but as part of this same matrix of disciplinary relations, and as displaying the same rhetorical dependence on features of HCI discourse that we have identified in recent work of others. However, while we assert that criticism is not our intention, we recognize that, as Latour has argued, since the deconstruction of others' work is a standard strategy for discrediting positions within science, it is not surprising that analyses such as ours are read in that light (Latour, 1987). Accordingly, and bearing in mind the book this chapter appears in, perhaps there is no escape from our text being read as itself a piece of second-wave HCI no matter what we mere authors would wish.

Acknowledgments

We wish to thank James Pycock and Phil Agre for many useful suggestions for this chapter and for comments on an earlier draft. John Bowers acknowledges support from the European Communities' ESPRIT Project, COMIC.

Notes

1. "Constructivist" is used in a general sense here, and not as a label for a particular methodology or theory within the social sciences. Neither Callon nor Foucault can be easily designated as constructivist in the latter sense.
2. "Problems" such as these can, of course, be profitably turned into topics and sources of substantive insight in themselves. E.g., the disjunction between programmatic claims for multidisciplinarity and the practical agendas set by cognitive psychology is itself a characteristic

feature of HCI, and one with considerable significance for putative contributions from other disciplines (see Cooper, 1991).

3. Cf. Ashmore, Mulkay, and Pinch's (1989) discussion of the founding of "medical economics."

4. Sometimes this liberal rhetoric coexists, somewhat uneasily, with an emphasis on productivity: e.g., Dertouzos's keynote address to the CHI '90 conference asked "let us then ask what we should do in tomorrow's user interfaces to increase productivity and empower people, as the theme of this conference charges" (Dertouzos, 1990: 1).

5. In another paper (Bowers and Rodden, 1993), one of us has proposed that the notion of interface (as designating some site where two separated objects are to be interrelated) can be made an empirical topic for study rather than taken as a theoretical resource for HCI. That is, just what is separated from what and just how the interrelations are made are issues to be studied in a relevant field setting, not taken as matters requiring an a priori, conceptual decision. Bowers and Rodden report a study from this perspective. The current chapter's discourse analytical approach is a complimentary alternative. Both strategies take "the interface" not as some entity with a fixed location and definition but as something whose sense and place are produced through practical activities of various sorts (the discursive practices of HCI in the current case, the practices by which a computer network is managed and used in the case of Bowers and Rodden's field study).

6. Cf. Woolgar (1985) on the rhetoric of progress within AI.

7. On the textual construction of responsible subject positions, see McHoul (1986); and on the role that this plays in "performing community," see Cooper and Woolgar (1994).

8. See, e.g., Carroll (1989), Suchman (1987), Whiteside and Wixon (1987).

9. Cf. Woolgar and Pawluch (1983) on "ontological gerrymandering."

10. It might further be argued that "designer" has come to occupy a familiar discursive position within recent HCI, i.e., crucial to disciplinary claims, yet relatively unexplicated as a category: e.g., it does not map easily onto job descriptions within IT or computer science.

11. The authors are divided over the practical feasibility or desirability of such an overcoming of the disciplines. One of us is eager to see the end of cognitive psychology, computer science, and the rest and the beginnings of "postdisciplinary research." The other is not so sure.

12. Bauman (1992) suggests that self-justificatory rhetoric is more important to those disciplines, such as the social sciences, which have to work continually at the definition and preservation of their boundary with respect to lay discourse: a problem, e.g., more for sociology than for physics. Our argument implies that *boundaries* with other disciplines are equally important. Beyond this, our response to Bauman would be that, in the first place, the differential specificity of disciplines is a matter for empirical investigation; and, second, that construing disciplines such as physics as not engaged in self-justification may rely on an unduly restricted conception of the nature of scientific work.

References

Ashmore, M., Mulkay, M., and Pinch, T. (1989). *Health and efficiency: A sociology of health economics* (Milton Keynes: Open University Press).

Bannon, L. (1991). From human factors to human actors: The role of psychology and human–computer interaction studies in system design. In J. Greenbaum and M. Kyng (eds.), *Design at work: Cooperative design of computer systems* (Hillsdale, N.J.: Lawrence Erlbaum), 25–44.

Bauman, Z. (1992). *Intimations of modernity* (London: Routledge).

Booth P. A. (1989). *An introduction to human–computer interaction* (Hove and London: LEA).

Bourdieu P. (1990). *In other words: Essays towards a reflexive sociology* (Cambridge: Polity).

Bowers, J., and Iwi, K. (1993). The discursive construction of society. *Discourse and Society,* 4 (3), 357–393.

Bowers, J., and Rodden, T. (1993). Exploding the interface: Experiences of a CSCW network. In *Human Factors in Computing Systems: INTERCHI '93 Proceedings* (New York: ACM Press), 255–262.

Callon, M. (1986). Some elements of a sociology of translation: Domestication of the scallops and the fisherman of St. Brieuc Bay. In J. Law (ed.), *Power, action and belief* (London: Routledge), 196–233.

Card, S. K., Moran, T. P., and Newell, A. (1983). *The psychology of human–computer interaction* (Hillsdale, N.J.: Lawrence Erlbaum).

Carroll, J. M. (1989). Evaluation, description and invention: Paradigms for human–computer interaction. In M. C. Yovits (ed.), *Advances in computers* 29 (London: Academic Press), 47–77.

Carroll, J. M. (1990). Towards an emulation-based design theory. In D. Diaper, D. Gilmore, G. Cockton, and B. Shackel (eds.), *Human–Computer Interaction: Interact '90.* (Amsterdam: Elsevier North-Holland), 1057–1058.

Cooper, G. (1991). Representing the user: A sociological study of the discourse of human computer interaction. Unpublished Ph.D thesis, Open University.

Cooper, G., and Woolgar, S. (1994). Software quality as community performance. In R. Mansell (ed.), *Information, control and technical change* (London: Aslib).

Dertouzos, M. L. (1990). Redefining tomorrow's user interface. In J. C. Chew and J. Whiteside (eds.), *Empowering People: CHI '90* (New York: ACM Press), 1.

Diaper, D., and Addison, M. (1992). HCI: The search for solutions. In A. Monk, D. Diaper, and M. Harrison (eds.), *People and Computers VII: HCI '92 Proceedings.* (Cambridge: British Computer Society, Cambridge University Press).

Edmonds, E. (1989). Judging software design. In A. Sutcliffe and L. Macaulay (eds.), *People and Computers V: Proceedings of the HCI '89 Conference* (Cambridge: Cambridge University Press), 49–56.

Forrester, M., and Reason, D. (1990). HCI "intraface model" for system design. *Interacting with Computers,* 2 (3), 279–296.

Foucault, M. (1970). *The order of things* (London: Tavistock).

Foucault, M. (1977). *Discipline and punish* (London: Allen Lane).

Grudin, J. (1990). The computer reaches out: the historical continuity of interface design. In J. C. Chew and J. Whiteside (eds.), *Empowering People: CHI '90.* (New York: ACM Press), 261–268.

Landauer, T. K. (1987). Relations between cognitive psychology and computer system design. In J. M. Carroll (ed.), *Interfacing thought* (Cambridge, Mass: Bradford/MIT Press), 1–25.

Latour, B. (1987). *Science in action* (Milton Keynes: Open University Press).

MacLean, A., Bellotti, V., and Young, R. (1990). What rationale is there in design? In D. Diaper, D. Gilmore, G. Cockton, and B. Shackel (eds.), *Human–Computer Interaction: Interact '90* (Amsterdam: Elsevier North-Holland), 207–212.

McHoul, A. W. (1986). The getting of sexuality: Foucault, Garfinkel and the analysis of sexual discourse. *Theory, Culture and Society,* 3 (2), 65–79.

Norman, D. (1986). Cognitive engineering. In D. A. Norman and S. W. Draper (eds.), *User centered system design* (Hillsdale, N.J.: Lawrence Erlbaum), 31–61.

Shackel B. (1985). Ergonomics in information technology in Europe – a review. *Behaviour and Information Technology,* 4 (4), 263–287.

Shneiderman, B. (1987). *Designing the user interface* (New York: Addison Wesley).

Sommerville, I. (1992). *Software engineering,* 4th ed. (New York: Addison Wesley).

Suchman, L. (1987). *Plans and situated actions* (Cambridge: Cambridge University Press).

Whiteside, J., and Wixon, D. (1987). Improving human–computer interaction: A quest for cognitive science. In J. Carroll (ed.), *Interfacing thought* (Cambridge, Mass.: Bradford/MIT Press), 353–365.

Woolgar, S. W. (1985). Why not a sociology of machines? The case of sociology and artificial intelligence. *Sociology,* 19 (4), 557–572.

Woolgar, S. W., and Pawluch, D. (1985). Ontological gerrymandering: The anatomy of social problems explanations. *Social Problems,* 32 (3), 214–237.

Young, R. M. (1990). Evaluating cognitive simulation models in HCI. In D. Diaper, D. Gilmore, G. Cockton, and B. Shackel (eds.), *Human–Computer Interaction: Interact '90* (Amsterdam, Elsevier North-Holland), 1056–1058.

5
Conceptions of the user in computer systems design
Philip E. Agre

5.1 Introduction

Some computer people build systems for people they know. Most often, though, relationships between the builders and users of computer systems are mediated by social arrangements that are shaped by forces far beyond these people's lives. Computerization, as Kling (1989) has pointed out, is a long-term process, and as computers have become ever more intimately involved in people's lives, the process of computerization has become increasingly inseparable from the social dynamics of the organizations and communities within which it is embedded. When a computer is simply meant to crunch numbers in an air-conditioned room, its designers may need only a rough understanding of the larger social arrangements in which it participates. But when a computer is meant to be used from minute to minute as part of somebody's job, its designer had better understand the larger organization of that job and its consequences for good design.

Unfortunately, the very social arrangements that made large-scale computer systems possible have often created enormous institutional and imaginative gaps between the people who build these systems and the people who use them. When the system's design is guided by an incomplete, distorted, or false understanding of the total setting of its use, the results can be unfortunate. Attempts to improve things may alleviate some symptoms but they may also obscure the systemic disorder underneath. This confusing situation rarely contributes to the humanization of work; indeed, users' resistance to misguided computer systems frequently leads to defensive appeals to technological rationality. It will be said, for example, that "users don't know what they want," that "there's no use bothering with the social angle because you can't predict the effects of these new technologies anyway," or that users exhibit "fear of change"; each of these claims contributes to the dehumanization so frequently ascribed to technological society.

It is thus worth investigating designers' conceptions of users, and particularly their conceptions of users' resistance to new technologies. Such an investigation might take place on many levels, but I propose the relatively modest task of marking out two fundamental conceptions of users, or perhaps two organizing schemes for such conceptions, which I shall call the *technical* and the *managerial*. Roughly speaking, the technical conception of the user has two facets: the worldviews of designer and user are assumed to coincide, and the user is understood to be a component in a larger system. Thus the user's resistance to this arrangement is understood as something external to the system and therefore as irrational. The managerial conception, again roughly speaking, understands that the real object of design is not just the technical artifact but the whole institutional system around it; the user is understood as a human agent whose perceptions of the proposed institutional arrangements become an object of inquiry and intervention in their own right.

Subsequent sections will explain these ideas at greater length, but for the moment I would simply like to issue a set of cautions about the phrase "technical and managerial conceptions of the user." Grudin (1993) has described several drawbacks to the phrase "the user." To start with, most systems are used by several people of varying backgrounds and varying (and potentially conflicting) relationships to one another; one rarely encounters an entirely isolated "the user." More importantly, the user is probably not wholly defined in terms of his or her use of a computer system; systems should be designed not for "users" but for clerks, lawyers, salespeople, engineers, waiters, drivers, and so on. The term "user" should not, in other words, reduce individuals to one-dimensional extensions of machines. Furthermore, several authors have developed useful distinctions among the users of a given system. Bjorn-Andersen, Eason, and Robey (1986: 170–172), for example, found in their comparative study that computer systems' designers paid more attention to users upon whom the system depends heavily for its operation than to the users who depend heavily on the system to do their work. Friedman (1989: 184–185) classified a system's users depending on which phase of the systems development process they are involved in. Blomberg (1987) has described the special role of advanced users, who sometimes channel information between other users and the technical support staff. Similarly, Nardi and Miller (1991) have described the sharing of code among spreadsheet users, with experienced users teaching others and joint use of the system providing occasions for domain learning and distributed debugging. Such taxonomies have the virtue of expanding the notion of "user" beyond the stereotype of the isolated "end user."

The term "conception" is not wholly satisfactory either. As Hedberg and Mumford (1975), Dagwell and Weber (1983), and Walton (1989: 131–132) have pointed out, designers' professed opinions about users may vary drastically from whatever is implicit in their actual design practice. A "conception" here is not an argument or a position or a set of beliefs. Instead, by the term "conception" I mean the view of users, their organizational environments, and their activities that is implicit in a given professional community's practices, regardless of any conscious opinions that this community's members might have. I wish to emphasize this distinction between conceptions and conscious opinions because many programmers *are* informed about the social aspects of computing and *do* consciously intend to engage in socially responsible system design. But I also wish to emphasize the tenacity of the underlying conceptions of users that are embedded in languages, tools, methods, and organizational arrangements. Although it is altogether unclear how to undo these conceptions or what might replace them, I hope to make a start by at least sketching them and indicating some of their properties.

Moreover, in speaking of "technical" and "managerial" conceptions of the user, I do not mean to imply that all technical people hold technical conceptions or that *only* technical people hold technical conceptions, and likewise for managers and managerial conceptions. When I do speak of technical people and managers, I will oversimplify by neglecting overlap between these categories and differences within them (e.g., analysts versus coders, technical managers versus marketing managers, line versus staff). A given individual may hold different conceptions for different purposes, since a conception is a property of a *practice* and not of an individual person as such. Finally, I do not mean to imply that all technological design practices must necessarily employ the technical conception of the user, nor that all forms of organizational coordination must necessarily employ the managerial conception. I do, however, believe that present-day technical and managerial practices do in fact overwhelmingly carry in them the conceptions of the user that I will describe. Of the two, the technical conception is the older and more entrenched, whereas the managerial conception is still evolving and taking hold, often displacing the technical conception for certain purposes.

The terms "computer" and "system" also require care. The classical computer was a mainframe with which users interacted through punched cards or through terminals consisting of alphanumeric screens and keyboards resembling those on typewriters. A computer system consisted of such hardware plus a software package that performed a definite, bounded set of functions for purposes such as bookkeeping, simulation, scheduling and dispatching, industrial process control, and statistical calculations. These days, however, the category of "computer" is multiplying and dissolving. Nearly anyone who uses a telephone is, strictly speaking, a computer user, particularly when the telephone is part of an integrated telemarketing system. And the notion of a singular, delineable system is breaking down as computer networks and wireless communications erase the boundaries among individual machines. Despite these complexities, the vocabulary of "computer systems" is in practice only slightly anachronistic, and I will stick with it here.

Let me also emphasize the narrow scope of my inquiry. My central topic pertains to conceptions of the user in system design, not the actual processes of design and management, the process of fielding implemented systems, the actual use of or resistance to a system by users, or the rest of the day-to-day politics of the "shop floor." Furthermore, I am not attempting (unlike, say, Noble 1986) a social history of these conceptions of the user, just a provisional sketch of them and some fragments toward a genealogy of their origins. Further research along any of these lines would no doubt force revision of my story.

Having established these caveats, let us return to the institutional gap between designers and users. Norman (1988), focusing on consumer products such as remote-control devices and architectural elements such as doors, has drawn attention to the many aspects of bad design that derive from designers' incomplete understandings of the actual ways in which their artifacts are used. Designers are not wholly indifferent to users, of course. Sharrock and Anderson (1994) watched a team of engineers designing a complex paper feeder and cataloged some of the references to users that pervaded the designers' discussions. In particular, they noted that "designers did not focus on users and their actions *for their own sake.* Rather, the issue of what users would or would not do arose in the context of some other topic" and that, in particular, "it is as a course of action type that 'the user' most often appears" (1994: 9). When faced with a technical decision, the designers would reason about users within a certain repertoire of themes. Users, for example, are presumed not to understand the internal workings of the machine, to understand new machines through reactions developed through using old machines, to attempt to minimize their effort, and always to have a particular task in mind and not an abstract interest in the machine itself. Knowledge about the users would arrive through a variety of indirect routes, but in no sense were the designers familiar with the users' worlds. Designers of complex technological artifacts do have certain kinds of indirect access to their users, then, but it is still unusual for them to have much personal acquaintance or systematic understanding of users' activities, organizational settings, interests, and subjective understandings of all these things.

In this chapter I wish to focus on a particular type of artifact use, namely people using computers – and particularly large, custom-built systems as opposed to mass-marketed packages or systems built for niche markets by small entrepreneurial firms – to do their jobs. Inasmuch as computers used in workplaces are a type of industrial machinery, it is worth reviewing some of the sociological literature on the introduction of new manufacturing technology. Perhaps the most relevant existing research is found in the labor process literature, which starts from the observation that people rarely own the machines they work with; nor is it at all common for them to have had a hand in designing those machines. In a book reflecting on his work as an operations researcher designing manufacturing processes for a large British chemical company, Hales (1980) reports finding it difficult to conceptualize the workers whose work processes he was designing, much less actually meet them. Those workers encountered machinery and plant arrangements that tended to channel their work activities in particular ways, with little information about the social processes that led to them.

The labor process literature was originally motivated by Braverman's (1974) theory of the appropriation by industrial management of workers' craft knowledge through the process he called "deskilling." Subsequent empirical research, though, shows things to be much more complicated. Automation sometimes brings lower-skilled jobs and sometimes higher-skilled jobs and sometimes a combination of both (Giordano, 1992; Thompson, 1989). Visible throughout these case studies, though curiously invisible in Braverman, is conflict of various types over control and definition of the work. Wilkinson (1983), for example, recounts an episode of shop-floor politics in which numerically controlled machine-tool operators learned to program their machines using a device originally intended for making small changes to programs written by professional programmers in another room of the factory; since the programmers had a hard time keeping up with the necessary stream of bug fixes and changes, many of the programming duties were effectively taken over by the machinists themselves.

The labor process literature, in short, has discovered that no single factor determines how a given form of technology will be used in practice. It has also focused attention on the possible roles of technology in management's simultaneous pursuit of the imperatives of efficiency and control. Edwards (1979), for example, distinguishes three types of control: simple, technical, and bureaucratic. Simple control consists in old-fashioned supervision, for example, by foremen watching over people as they work. Technical control is built into the workings of the machinery, for example, the establishment of separate stations on an assembly line that moves at a fixed pace determined elsewhere. And bureaucratic control is built into procedures of evaluation, pay schedules, and other forms of motivation, for example, in the incremental promotions and pay increases that attend continued good work in many firms. Recent developments, including the steady growth in computer-mediated work activities, make it possible to discern a fourth type of control, which I have referred to elsewhere (Agre, forthcoming) as "the empowerment and measurement regime." In this scheme, sophisticated forms of organizational communication encourage notions of "empowerment" while work outcomes are continuously and rigorously measured in market-relevant terms. Every model of control contains an implicit model of resistance and consent, and both the models and the realities of these things vary considerably across decades, cultures, industries, and degrees and types of professionalization.

Yet little has been written about resistance to computer-based technologies. Although Iacono and Kling (1987) have cautioned against any deterministic assumptions about the effects of computers on working life, Rule and Attewell (1989), among others, have remarked on the utility of computers in controlling work activities through automated surveillance and increased rationalization of policies and practices. The broader literature on resistance to computer technology is roughly divided between union-oriented literature, particularly in Europe, on shop-floor politics and collective bargaining strategy (Keul, 1983; Levie and Williams, 1983), and literature on organizations that makes little reference to larger economic conditions (e.g., Markus, 1984). For all their differences, these literatures share a refreshing awareness that resistance to new technologies stems directly from perceptions of the implications that new organizational arrangements hold for the distribution of power. Within the organizational literature, for example, Keen (1981) presents an elegant taxonomy, drawn on Bardach's (1977) analysis of the detours that legislation suffers on its way to implementation, of the political maneuvers that managers use at various stages in the design and implementation of computer systems to ensure their eventual failure. He refers to these tactics collectively as "counterimplementation" (CI) and recommends the systematic co-optation of likely CI practitioners as part of a project's early stages. Several other studies have also described the use of CI tactics by threatened managers (Ackoff, 1960; Argyris, 1976; Schreuder, 1987; Walton, 1989: 142–149).

The union-oriented literature, for its part, portrays industrial automation as a means of management control and recounts a centuries-old tradition of resentment toward automation and resistance against it through a variety of means, from simple carelessness to organized slowdowns to bureaucratic maneuvering to physical sabotage to attempts to discredit the system to collective bargaining on work practices to electoral politics (Garson, 1989; Howard, 1985; Rybczynski, 1983; Shaiken, 1985). Throughout this history, the technical artifacts of automation have stood as symbols, more or less consciously understood as such, of larger social arrangements whose logic is not specifically technological but political and economic. The contemporary literature, indeed, defines its concern not specifically in terms of technology but in relation to social arrangements such as teams, quality circles, and just-in-time production that threaten to wear down union bargaining power in the name of flexibility and productivity (Parker, 1985; Wells, 1987).

The two sections that follow treat the technical and managerial conceptions of the user, respectively, as independent phenomena. Inasmuch as the literature on the technical conception is relatively mature, Section 5.2 is organized in large part as a survey and synthesis of existing literature. Section 5.3 on the managerial conception, by contrast, develops a limited number of themes in relation to a report generated as part of one particular project. Section 5.4 introduces the much larger and harder question of the relationship between the two conceptions of the user by placing this relationship in some larger contexts of intellectual and social history. Section 5.5 concludes.

5.2 The technical conception of the user

The technical conception of the user is usually not a worked-out theory. It is, instead, a diffuse assumption, presupposed in various ways by deeply institutionalized professional practices, that the user lives in the same world as the programmer. Sometimes, of course, this is actually true. But more often it is radically false. To make this notion concrete, let us look at various aspects of the programmer's world and the ways in which they encourage a technical view of the user. The phrase "the programmer," of course, is almost as misleading as "the user"; programmers have a range of backgrounds, usually work in groups, have a variety of conscious opinions about users, and change somewhat as a profession over time. Despite all this, the picture I will paint is only slightly less true of the majority of programmers and their worlds today than it was fifteen years ago.

To start with, it helps to picture the programmer's physical work environment. Programmers work sitting at computer terminals. Periodically they gather in groups to go over specs and interfaces and schedules, but the actual programming is usually done in relative solitude sitting in a chair and looking at a screen. Coffee and recorded music are often involved. The work demands attention, and technical and management frameworks go to great lengths to impose structure on it. At any given moment a given programmer is probably contemplating a fairly small bit of code whose purpose can perhaps only be expressed in terms far removed from the average user's concerns. It might be, for example, the second subcase of the termination condition of a subsystem that performs various housekeeping functions so that all the other subsystems will have access to particular resources when they need them. Perhaps it is not working quite right, or perhaps it is unclear how to taxonomize all the logically possible situations that might arise at that point. The very fact that the programmer understands this bit of code is in itself an enormous imaginative gulf between programmer and user. Such detailed logical issues are at the center of the programmer's world; they are the stuff of day-to-day work. A programming project of any size generates thousands of small puzzles of this type, each of which must be solved consistently with all the others. And the puzzles matter, since the whole program has to work right for anybody to get any work done later. Simply coordinating the efforts of the numerous programmers who collaborate on large programming projects is a tremendous task; Krasner, Curtis, and Iscoe (1987) have categorized a wide variety of communications breakdowns among the various groups involved in such projects. Having spent a few years in such an environment, it becomes difficult to imagine the perspective of somebody who does not view a computer system as a logical anatomy, an ontology made into datastructures, a set of formal relationships and constraints, and a network of paths for data to move along. Since the programmer is imaginatively *inside* the system, the very concept of a user interface can be difficult to grasp or take seriously (Kling, 1977). It is little wonder that, at least perhaps until the recent emergence of a mass personal computer market, large numbers of novice computer users have experienced the machines as artifacts of a shockingly alien culture (Sproull, Kiesler, and Zubrow, 1984).

The culture of programming has historically had an element of monastic withdrawal. Corporate MIS departments are particularly notorious in this regard, often to the point of an us-and-them hostility to the distant and demanding users. Danziger and Kraemer (1986: 119) found that "problems with computing occur more frequently among those end users who find that computer specialists are more intrigued with the technology than with serving users' needs and are unwilling/unable to communicate in the users' language." Mumford (1972) documented these attitudes in her interviews with the members of one such department, who had developed a powerful value system based on constant technical change and innovation.

People who had been bank clerks for many years, once transferred to EDP, rapidly became technocrats, impatient with the resistance to change of their old colleagues. Similarly, in the present research, it was not unusual for members of line departments to be placed temporarily in the EDP group to act as link men for new systems that were being introduced. We found that many of these became so imbued with technical values during their stay that they were incapable for performing this linking role and became totally identified with the values of the computer personnel. . . . The reason for this rapid acceptance of EDP values appears to be the power of the technical ethic. This is able to capture people's enthusiasm and to make them feel, perhaps for the first time, that they are associated with work that is exciting and worthwhile. It can be argued that these technical values are being seriously challenged at present but this is not occurring, as a rule, in the organizations which use computers. (Mumford, 1972: 199–200)

Although not unusual, the attitudes that Mumford encountered are certainly extreme. But regardless of any overt attitudes, the underlying conceptions are embedded in institutions and practices. In particular, institutional factors tending to distance programmers and users have become especially clear as progressive computer people, particularly those motivated by the Scandinavian tradition of participatory design, have tried to bring users into the design process (Clement and Van den Besselaar 1993; Schuler and Namioka, 1993). Grudin (1991) has specifically cataloged several barriers between programmers and users, pointing out that they vary somewhat across the various development environments: competitively bid contracts, product development, and in-house custom development. Contracting, for example, typically requires a fixed, predefined specification, so that contact with users is viewed as a corruption of the bidding process. Marketing people are often afraid that programmers' contacts with users will blur the company's image. The users of a system are often unknown in advance or physically distant, many of them are unwilling or unable to participate in design activities, and it can be difficult to determine which users are "typical." Managers are sometimes afraid that users will slow the programmers down with endless requests for individualized help. And so on. And when "user involvement" does take place, significant changes in the design process do not necessarily follow, since technical people may confuse users with technical jargon or convert them to a technical conception of their own activities. These forms of institutionalized distance are, in themselves, of course not unique to computing but can be found throughout engineering (Noble, 1986: 44–45).

Together, these institutional and cultural forces create a formidable wall between programmers and users. Nonetheless, they are not the most fundamental determinant of the technical conception of the user. Indeed, many mainstream business publications now recommend the involvement of workers in system design (Quinn, 1992) and customers in product development (Peters, 1990), even though few serious instances of worker involvement in the redesign of computer-mediated work have yet been reported (Kling and Dunlop, 1993). It remains to be seen how genuine this involvement becomes (cf. Banks and Metzgar, 1989; Parker, 1985; Wells, 1987), but the current fashion for "downsizing" of companies certainly makes plausible the rhetoric of removing bureaucratic barriers to competitively remunerative cooperation.

Whatever the outcome of these changes, they do not in themselves significantly affect the most fundamental determinant of the technical conception, which is the ideology and practice that Kling (1980) refers to as "systems rationalism." Systems rationalists believe – or, more important, conduct their design work as if they believed – that it is possible and desirable to draw a firm line around the "technical" aspects of work practices and technology choices, treating the "political" aspects as someone else's problem – or even as irrational details to be stamped out altogether. The force of this point is often difficult for technical people to appreciate. Whereas the interpretive social scientist regards rationality as a social construction and a misguided repression of the political dimension of human life, the culture of technologists treats rationality as a positive value whose opposite is simply "irrationality."

Central to the systems rationalism is *formalization,* the recasting of human affairs in mathematical terms for purposes of implementation on computers. Design work begins with a process known as "systems analysis" or (a slightly different notion) "requirements definition," within which existing work practices are systematically represented in one or another formal language (Friedman, 1989: 257–265). These languages vary in their precise presuppositions, ontologies, and blindnesses, but each one incorporates a definite system of assumptions, loosely speaking an ideology, about workers, work tasks, work routines, information, efficiency, and so on. These languages are mathematical in the sense that they can be given a mathematically precise operational semantics that completely predicts, through the methods of mathematical derivation (i.e., proof), the input–output behavior of any computer that might be programmed to follow a given "text" in the language. Yet despite their close modern-day identification with computing, these languages trace their intellectual lineages to precomputer times, to the notation schemes originally developed for time and motion study in factory work, particularly by Gilbreth and his followers (Gilbreth, 1921; Shaw, 1952) – the main difference being that Gilbreth's schemes track the movements of human bodies and work materials, whereas the systems analysis schemes track the movements of information. The literature of this period exhibits an almost surreal neglect of the social and political dimensions of work; indeed, in surveys such as that of Couger (1973), it is hard to detect the presence of human beings at all except in the inclusion of "personnel" among the components of the information-processing regimes under study. (For a critical analysis, see Friedman [1989: 265], and for the beginnings of an alternative see Boland and Hirschheim [1987].)

Formal representation of human work activities for purposes of computer-based mechanization is, of course, only one instance of the much more extensive and deeply rooted practice of formalization. Formalization is first and foremost a discursive practice. Though its principal product is a mass of abstract symbolism seemingly far removed from ordinary language, this highly prized outcome should not distract attention from formalization as a *process*. People who engage in technical practices see formalization as a kind of trajectory in which some object (be it physical, social, or whatever) is worked over linguistically, described and re-described in successively more formal terms, so as to produce a mathematical representation that is demonstrably linked to the original object through a chain of incremental paraphrases (cf. Suchman and Trigg, 1993). Although a rhetorician or sociologist might see this as a process of "construction of a technical object," technical people normally see themselves as making clear something that was formerly obscure. They might sometimes regard particular formalizations as poorly done, as approximations, as incomplete, as needing revision, as inelegant, and so forth, but they rarely make any systematic attempt to enumerate the (possibly inadvertent) assumptions that are built into them, much less any systematic attempt to check these assumptions against reality. The more complex the formalization, indeed, the less thoroughly it is liable to be checked. The rhetoric of "clarity," "precision," "rigor," and so forth all too often permits divergences between formalism and reality – especially the more plainly "social" aspects of reality – to be blamed on reality.

It is perhaps easy to see the unfortunate synergy that can arise between the practice of formalization and the previously discussed institutional forces serving to separate computer people, both functionally and imaginatively, from the worksites for which their systems are destined. Predictably, the relationships between programmers and users that evolve in these conditions are frequently strained. The point, of course, is not that anybody is consciously malicious, but that institutional structures and disciplinary forms of language and interaction have tended to shape human relationships in certain ways.

Suchman and Jordan (1989) have described this relationship from the point of view of workers, and particularly women workers, whose highly developed but unsystematized work-expertise is often invisible to the representational practices of the systems analysts. This invisibility is usefully analyzed under five headings: (1) the scant acquaintance of the analysts with the actual complexities of the worksite; (2) the systems rationalist's neglect of the political dimension of the work; (3) the unarticulated ("tacit") nature of much of the overlooked expertise; (4) the misguided assumption that work that goes smoothly is necessarily simple and thus easily formalized; and (5) the inherent resistance of human activities to mathematical formalization. The final point is the most difficult; Suchman and Jordan, following Garfinkel (1984 [1967]), argue that the rules that govern, say, the procedures of a billing office, do not in themselves provide an adequate descriptive account of the actual day's course of work in that office – nor, they argue, *should* they. To the contrary, the rules provide a resource to the workers in their irremediably improvised efforts to make the files *turn out* a certain way in the face of the endless series of ambiguities, accidents, interpretations, exceptions, and so on that make up the ordinary contingencies of a day's work.

Programmers' misconceptions about the actual nature of work lead them to design computer systems that provide their users with characteristic patterns of frustrations. These patterns are, as one would expect, poorly documented. One of them, lamented by Bravo (1993), is the irritating tendency of software packages not to save your work until you ask them to. This scheme, thoughtlessly institutionalized for the benefit of the file-system designer rather than that of the user, leaves untold thousands of people, a large portion of whom experience ceaseless production pressures from their managers, permanently concerned that one false move will cause them to lose their work. Another pattern is the assumption, often false, that users have the time available to enter all the necessary data about their activities into the system (Hughes and Randall, this volume; Walton, 1989: 20). When these kinds of problems occur in isolation, of course, they are sometimes susceptible to isolated technical repairs. The real trouble begins when a pattern of problems points to fundamental misconceptions about the process of systems design and implementation in complex social settings. Benson (1993) has described the particularly telling case of a police dispatch system that reduced the dispatch process to a formally specified scheduling problem, thereby neglecting and disrupting the fragile system of social ties that had formerly been negotiated through the dispatchers' choice of which officers to send on which calls.

When insight into the social organization of computer use is lacking, programmers often blame users for the difficulties that arise with newly deployed systems. The roots of this tendency should be clear enough from the preceding discussion: (1) the programmer's imaginative perspective from within the system makes it difficult to identify with a perspective outside the system; (2) institutional forces nearly guarantee that programmers will develop an incomplete and superficial understanding of their users' worlds; and (3) the practice of formalization buries numerous assumptions – some of them contingently false and others perhaps necessarily false due to the very nature of formalization – beyond the normal scope of their own critical practices. Computer people *do* have their critical practices and many of them *do* feel an abstract sympathy for the user's situation; the point, once again, is that their distorted conception of the user is not simple sloppiness or malice but in fact deeply and multiply determined by the material and discursive organization of contemporary technical practices.

Forsythe (1992) has documented some of the manifestations of programmers' conceptions of users in the domain of medical informatics, a branch of artificial intelligence that develops knowledge-based systems to support medical decision making. Journals in that area exhibit a concern with the "user acceptance problem," but the practice of double-blind clinical trials largely prevents practitioners from gaining much insight into users' subjective reactions to experimental computer systems. Investigating this phenomenon, Forsythe identifies five problematic assumptions underlying standard practice in this area: (1) evaluation of systems primarily in technical terms, principally speed and accuracy; (2) neglect of the social contexts of use in favor of problem formulations that fit within simple numerical schemata; (3) a model of controlled clinical trials based on laboratory science that neglects whatever cannot be (or has not been) quantified; (4) the presupposition that experts' conscious models of work practices actually correspond to the reality of those practices; and (5) reliance on a single model despite the multiplicity of models employed by the diverse professionals in a typical work group. Unreflective use of all five of these counterfactual assumptions is guaranteed to produce trouble – and, in particular, to produce trouble whose nature nobody understands: a series of problematic situations, hitches, work-arounds, misunderstandings, impossible demands, and so forth, none of which is readily interpreted as a symptom of anything deeper, or indeed as forming any intelligible pattern at all.

Programmers, of course, are often intelligent and humane people, able to make at least piecemeal sense of such difficulties. Occasions of trouble can be, and routinely are, turned into streams of bug reports, feature requests, incremental improvements in the user interface, and so forth, and these things often do help. But the underlying problem is systemic. The practice of formalization can be taught with greater or lesser degrees of flexibility, humility, and critical insight. And some schools do better than others. Unfortunately, as Hacker (1981) points out, most technical people are trained at institutions with relatively rigid approaches that are liable to reproduce the destructive potentials of formalization in its normal institutional setting.

The technical conception of the user, then, is a phenomenon comprising several parts and requiring analysis at a number of levels. The analysis I have presented, of course, is wholly conceptual; it draws on others' empirical research in disparate places and times and in disparate application domains. The true picture can only be found in sustained investigation and theorization of particular sites of practice, whereupon additional factors would certainly demand to be taken into account. We can, however, at least make some provisional sense of the characterization of the technical conception that I offered at the outset, which is that it treats users as inhabiting the programmers' world and not their own. Much of this effect derives from simple lack of knowledge; in the absence of sufficiently obtrusive evidence or adequately penetrating critical paradigms, the natural tendency is to speak of "them" in the same terms that we normally speak of "us" – the nonprogrammatic ethnocentrism that derives from nothing more complicated than the tendency of disciplinary languages to encode worldviews. But, I have argued, the more fundamental determinant of the imaginative blurring between programmers and users (as between all technical people and everyone else) is the practice of formalization – and specifically the tendency of technical people to treat their formalizations as veridical representations of reality and also as cleaned-up but essentially equivalent versions of anyone else's clearly understood conceptualizations of that reality. The problem arises when the users do not, in fact, view their reality through the mediation of formal representations; not only do the users run afoul of the false assumption built into the system via its motivating formalization, but the programmers and users will have great difficulty communicating about the problem because one is thinking and speaking in formalized terms and the other is not. Of course, some users, such as scientists, technical people, and accountants, *do* see their domains in formal terms, and these users generally have an easier time of things – subject, of course, to all the other sources of discoordination between themselves and the programmers who build the systems they use. Likewise, computers are often introduced to help automate tasks that were already heavily formalized and routinized (e.g., through detailed paperwork and filing systems), and these applications often proceed less painfully than others (cf. Danziger and Kraemer, 1986). The plight of nontechnical users is made even worse by the invidious comparison to these relatively satisfied customers and by the widespread misunderstanding, among programmers and users alike, of the true nature and real pitfalls of formalization as it is usually practiced as an element of computer system design.

Given this understanding of the dynamics contributing to the technical conception of the user, it becomes possible to predict and explain many forms of user resistance to computer systems, as well as the technical conception of this resistance. First of all, the systems analysis process, whatever its detailed use in practice, is deeply geared to replacing people rather than assisting them. If people are simply conduits and processors of information, no economic reason remains to keep them on. Resistance to such a notion is understandable, and the technical conception views such resistance as the purest and most arbitrary backwardness.

A second form of resistance manifests itself as an endless series of complaints, requests, accusations, and so forth, one for each individual symptom of the systemic divergence between the programmer's worldview and the actual nature of the work. Lacking any evident unifying coherence, these complaints seem shortsighted, arbitrary and picayune.

A third form of resistance involves name-calling: the system is "too complicated," "incomprehensible," "more trouble than it's worth," "hard to use," and so forth. These complaints seem strange to the programmer who is thoroughly familiar with the internal logic that confers order on the manifold features of the system's behavior.

Finally, the user community develops a complicated set of work-arounds, based on a folk theory of the system's behavior: "when you do this it does that," "to get it to do this, first you have to do that," "to avoid losing such-and-such, create a dummy record," "when it says X it really means Y," and so forth (Gasser, 1986). These bits of lore are usually symptoms of the formalization's failure to capture the full situational flexibility of the user community's indigenous language and work practices. The point is not that users' work-arounds and improvisations are necessarily pathological; quite the contrary, the difficulty lies in the failure of technical forms of representation to comprehend fully the inherently improvisational nature of human work. But since the users understand work situations in their own terms and not those of the programmers, they can only explain the system's behavior as a piecemeal and superficial set of generalizations and tricky procedures. To the programmers, of course, these practices may appear to run across the grain of the clear logic of the system.

This list is, of course, incomplete, and its elements should be regarded as ideal types rather than ironclad generalizations. The dynamics around the technical conception of users will not explain all types of resistance or all aspects of programmers' understandings of this resistance. But perhaps the analysis I have presented will provide a vocabulary for better formulating and legitimizing the wide range of justified complaints that issue from the technical conception of users and its larger institutional embedding.

The picture, fortunately, is not entirely bleak. Research in the area of computer-supported cooperative work, particularly in Europe, has begun to formulate a novel and more attractive conception of formalization, its relation to users, and its place in the design process. Perhaps the most explicit statement of this conception is found in Robinson's research on participatory design within worker-owned cooperative businesses. In a review of successes and failures in a series of such projects, Robinson (1991a; 1991b) found that the most significant factor affecting a system's acceptance by its users was the presence of "double-level languages." A system and system design process employ double-level languages when they rigorously distinguish between (1) the formalization in virtue of which the system operates and (2) the language(s) that the community members use in discussing the matters that the system's operation bears upon. This should be contrasted with the normal practice of formalization, in which programmers routinely draw on the vocabulary of the indigenous language in preparing their formalization of the application domain. Using the same term for the employees' concept and the program(mer)'s concept has the virtue of simplicity, but it also legislates a particular mapping between the two vocabularies that might obstruct proper comprehension and use of the system.

A system employing double-level languages, by contrast, allows its users wide latitude in interpreting the system's datastructures and processes. This is particularly important when the program is used as part of a complex, difficult, and politically subtle interaction such as salary negotiation in a cooperative enterprise (Robinson 1991a; 1991b). In such a setting, it is vital for different professional groups to be able to discuss, examine, and interrelate their different conceptions of money, work standards, fairness, job duties, and so forth without these things being covertly pinned down to a particular model by the program's formal claims on particular words and concepts.

In the notion of double-level languages it is possible to discern an emerging distinction between (at least) two uses of formalization, which I will call "strong" and "weak." Strong formalization is the conventional style; it is characterized by the claims it makes on the language of a system's user communities. In its strongest form, this actually results in users' activities being regimented in terms of what I have called a "grammar of action" (Agre, in press), drawn on indigenous categories of work practices but systematized into a definite formal space of possible action sequences that the system captures in real time.

Weak formalization, by contrast, makes few if any claims on users' language. The process of creating weak formalizations will presumably draw its inspiration from existing practices, and the process will still result in a set of interlocking mathematical definitions that can be made into the basis for a computer program, but it does not make any strong claims about the *semantics* of these formal structures; in particular, it leaves a certain amount of room for users to negotiate how they will be interpreted in a given situation. The design process leading to the system will take care to distinguish between the categories of social analysis and the categories of systems implementation, rather than automatically supposing (along the lines of systems analysis) that a system "supports" a given fact about its environment by formally representing it. Perin (1991), for example, points to the case of the "social fields" of informal communication in an organization, which are useful to know about without it making sense to include them in a technical specification.

In current practice, the most common type of weak formalization calls for users to represent their activities to a computer system not within a formal grammar of possibilities but with bits of text in natural language. The program presumably stores these bits of text and allows them to be retrieved in some useful way, so that they can be interpreted by (possibly different) users according to the demands of their particular (possibly different) situation. The users who enter these bits of text will, if Garfinkel's (1984 [1967]) research on professionals filling out medical forms in hospitals is any precedent, design their entries according to their notions of who will be reading them, and in what circumstances, and for what purposes.

For example, one line of research on design rationale capture (MacLean, Young, and Moran, 1989) does not attempt to impose on users the (probably impractical) burden of expressing their own reasoning within some wholly formal language as they go along. Instead, the program offers a structure within which particular bits of reasoning can be entered and stored in whatever form seems most useful.

One line of criticism of such schemes is that they sacrifice the precision and clarity of meaning that are the whole point of formalization; if the representations must be interpreted afresh by every user then it seems unlikely that anybody will ever be able to agree about what any given machine-state means. It is crucial to see the fallacy in this argument. Formal representations are only formal and precise in an internal sense; they license certain inferences and exclude others on purely mathematical grounds. But they do not, in themselves, say anything about the semantic relationship between the formal structures and the actual states of affairs in the world to which they are supposed to refer. This semantic relationship is underwritten entirely by the system's physical interactions with its environment (if any) and by the users' situated interpretations (Collins, 1990). These interpretations are never "precise" or "clear" in a mathematical sense (unless, of course, their referents are themselves mathematical structures). But they *are,* nonetheless, constrained by all manner of conventions and other social arrangements. Strong formalization is precisely one type of conventional social arrangement, implemented through a pointwise suturing of particular tokens of the formal language to particular lexical items of the natural language. This scheme does not eliminate the need for interpretation, and it introduces many opportunities for frustration and confusion. Sometimes it is good enough. But other times different kinds of social arrangements are required. Among these is just about any situation in which members of different professional communities must negotiate interpretations among themselves; if a computer system's operation is going to be the object of a great deal of ongoing semantic negotiation then its development process should probably employ some type of weak formalization (Hutchins, 1990; Robinson and Bannon, 1991).

It is still hard to say what conception of the user attends the use of weak formalization. No doubt it varies with the institutional setting. A setting such as Robinson's cooperatives is instructive because its members have the power to refuse computers that do not help them. The physicians in Forsythe's study of medical informatics have a similar power, and this may account for the otherwise disproportionate attention paid to "user acceptance" in that area. Likewise, the tradition of strong unions and technology bargaining in Europe, and particularly in Scandinavia, presumably contributes to the growth of participatory design research in those countries. The relations of power in these settings are contributing to an evolution of the very practice of formalization; in the United States, where the complexities of military procurement and sharp competition in computer-intensive industries are the principal drivers of reform in system design, the evolution of formalism-qua-practice may take a different path. But a growing understanding of the nature of formalism and its institutional embedding can only contribute to a more democratic conception of computer systems development. This understanding is useless without the equity in power relations that true democracy requires, but perhaps it can play a role in envisioning what this equality would consist of and making sense of the otherwise confusing circumstances that call for it.

5.3 The managerial conception of the user

Programmers and managers – by which I principally mean users' direct managers, as opposed to top-level executives – stand in radically different relationships to the users of computer systems. The differences are worth enumerating for the light they cast on their respective conceptions of the users:

- Programmers are usually distant from their users; managers are routinely in close proximity to the people they manage.
- Programmers imagine users in generalization and the future tense (at least very often in the initial design of a system); managers deal with particular employees from day to day.
- Programmers are responsible for building tools; managers are responsible for ensuring that work gets done with those tools.
- Programmers interact mostly with machinery and identify themselves with technical progress; managers interact mostly with people and identify themselves with corporate goals.
- Programmers hear about resistance to their systems second- or thirdhand through bureaucratic channels; managers encounter resistance immediately and are charged with overcoming it.
- Programmers, as line workers with relatively clear technical goals, generally do not experience themselves as particularly political creatures; managers live and die by bureaucratic politics.

Management as a distinct and generic activity in the United States emerged after World War I, during the consolidation of the large business organizations that had arisen in the decades before the war; the manifesto of this emergence was Chester Barnard's *The Functions of the Executive* (1962 [1938]). Management as an object of institutionalized professional training emerged after World War II, during the first serious proliferation of systematic guides to management; the manifesto of this professionalization process was Peter Drucker's textbook *Management* (1945). The verb "to manage" carries a definite complex of connotations that closely reflects the manager's situation. Managers' fundamental dilemma is that they are responsible for the outcome of processes they cannot wholly control. To manage something is to perform a range of operations on it over time: monitoring it, continually assessing it within a rational framework of concepts, and regularly intervening in it in accordance with strategies and goals established at higher staff levels. "To manage" is a transitive verb, of course, and business discourse allows this verb's object to include absolutely any aspect of a business' operations, from inventory levels to corporate image to job stress to information resources. Above all, managers manage people. This process is understood to entail, as a normative matter if not in practice, that managers set clear objectives, provide regular evaluations, secure the necessary resources, and exert their authority to deal with problems as they arise. Managers' conceptions of their world are shaped by these concepts, by their objective situation, and by their personal interests.

The managerial conception of workers qua users of computer systems differs considerably from the technical conception. It begins with the understanding that technical systems cannot be designed or fielded independently of the social arrangements that surround them. Managers, after all, have a variety of objectives in pursuing technical changes, and these are rarely focused on the technology as an end in itself (Buchanan, 1986). The introduction of new workplace technology is normally an occasion for organizational rearrangement, and the technology only succeeds if the social structures around it succeed too. This lesson has taken many years to become fully established as a principle of computer systems design. The history of this evolution begins with managers' attempts to field systems designed wholly within the technical conception of the user; encountering unexpected and poorly understood resistance, they resorted to a motley combination of sales tactics, control regimes, training courses, and so forth (Friedman, 1989: 207–208; Mumford, 1972: 142–147, 200; Walton, 1989: 93; cf. Desanctis and Courtney, 1983), and they often developed user support systems at the last minute, as a reaction to unanticipated user needs (Bjorn-Andersen et al., 1986: 87).

Responding to the manifest limitations of this approach, a distinctive managerial conception of computer users developed. Simplifying only moderately, this process had two stages, which it is the purpose of this section to analyze. The first stage is the idea of sociotechnical systems (STS), according to which the social and technical aspects of work processes are viewed as interlinked systems that should ideally be designed together. The second stage has integrated STS ideas with the broader managerial practice of organizational communication, which is a kind of public relations aimed at employees. After briefly describing the tenets of STS and organizational communication, together with their respective conceptions of employees and their resistance to technological change, I will sketch a case study drawn from an industrial project that raises some strongly debated ethical concerns.

The practice of sociotechnical system design began after World War II at the Tavistock Institute, which comprised a group of psychologists and organizational theorists based in London who applied their skills to Britain's difficult labor–management relations (Trist, 1981). Their research began, as I have mentioned, with the notion that the social and technical aspects of an organization are mutually constraining subsystems of a larger system. This notion plays on the ambiguity or vagueness of the word "system." The technical sense of "system," of course, derived from the ideology of systems analysis; and although the STS notion of a social system is not developed enough to discern a definite intellectual provenance, the phrase is used equally by a broad range of social theorists. As an empirical project, STS research has investigated the interactions between the social and technical subsystems (Markus, 1984). As a prescriptive project, STS provides a conceptual framework for designing social and technical systems that are, in some sense, well fitted to one another (Taylor, 1987), with a particular emphasis on enabling employee groups to organize their activities in a "democratic" fashion with a minimum of external management. As can well be imagined, the practice of STS has been an improvement in humanitarian terms over conventional British management practice. Yet, as critics in unions and elsewhere have pointed out, sociotechnical systems design does not envision a broadly participative design process and tends to accept existing technology as a given rather than applying humanistic values to the development of new technology. To the contrary, the continued use of the systems-analytic notion of "design" speaks of a unilateral process initiated and conducted by management, though perhaps with some broader consultation – more in some countries, such as Norway, than others, such as the United States.

Markus (1984) has clearly described the application of STS methods to computer system design. Her analysis proceeds by taxonomizing types of organizations and types of computer systems and then generalizing about the kinds of untoward interactions that can arise as a given type of system is installed in a given type of organization. Markus views resistance as resulting from concerns about loss of organizational power, and specifically as resulting from a design process that did not adequately address issues of power. She remarks that programmers tend "to apply the term *resistance* quite freely to any unintended (by them) use of systems" (1984: 74). And since she views resistance as a symptom of bad design, she (like Mumford and other STS practitioners) is suspicious of attempts to paper it over through training, coercion, or disciplinary procedures.

Resistance and negative impacts [of a new computer system] cannot be effectively attacked by focusing independently on the problems that arise in each phase of the system's life cycle. Rather, an implementer of systems must create designs that take into account, in some way, the intentions, desires and motivations of all parties affected by the system; when the design differs from current organizational functioning, it must be reinforced by corresponding changes in other dimensions such as culture, structure or people. Furthermore, to assure that this design is accurately embodied in procedures and/or information technology, the implementor must also design a system-building process and an implementation process that is capable of producing and introducing the intended system. (Markus, 1984: 97)

Sociotechnical systems design, then, introduces the idea that the designed artifact consists of both the technical artifacts and the social arrangements that surround them, including the actual processes of implementation and use. Resistance becomes a kind of system failure, comparable with a blown fuse or a software bug, and designers must work to anticipate such failures and adjust their designs accordingly. What the STS method lacks is a way of designing the actual human interactions that implement the social aspects of the sociotechnical designs. That function is being served by organizational communication, a rapidly evolving practice whose most ambitious version is concerned with the management of "corporate culture." My exposition will concentrate mainly on these ideas as they are applied to the implementation of computer systems in organizations.

Perhaps the easiest way to understand organizational communication is as a variety of public relations. The central concepts of public relations are "publics" and their "perceptions" (see Grunig and Hunt, 1984). A public is any group of people who stand in a shared functional relationship to some organization. A typical company's publics include its customers (who may themselves be divided into several distinct segments), its employees, its distributors and retailers, its stockholders, the officers of its unions, the relevant government regulators, the relevant consumer activists, reporters for the local press, people who live near the company's operations, and so forth. An organization of any size will have a written-down communication plan for most or all of these publics. Central to this plan will be an assessment of those publics' perceptions of the company. Perceptions are typically glossed as simple and somewhat vague statements such as "high-quality products," "technologically backward," "polluters," "well-managed," and so forth. These catalogs of inferred perceptions motivate a communication strategy aimed at dissolving negative perceptions or creating positive ones; the perceptions are formulated in a simple and vague way in order to provide maximum flexibility in the means employed to change them.

A given communication plan will begin with a "message" carefully designed to adjust given perceptions in a given public without interfering with other organizational goals. Supporting materials for the message will include stories, statistics, slogans, expert opinions, legal arguments, and so on. The dissemination of this message will typically involve a range of media: advertisements in the newspaper, inserts in customers' bills, stories that publicists might suggest to journalists, and so forth. Other opportunities might arise unexpectedly, for example when a new public controversy provides a rhetorical tie-in to an element of the organization's message. Some communication tactics openly present the organization's point of view on a controversy, but most are more indirect, and many (such as a speaking tour by a friendly scientist) have no obvious connection to the organization at all.

When applied to the marketing of a new product, public relations planning will be integrated with the design of the product. Marketers believe that people do not buy artifacts; rather they buy much larger packages of social interaction that include advertising information, promises and guarantees, repair services, the availability of add-on products, customer service, symbolic values such as prestige, and so forth. Having assembled such a package, the marketers will try to present it in a coherent way, starting with an assessment of the customer's perceived needs and likely perceptions of the offering as a whole. What is designed, then, is not simply the product itself, nor simply the larger package of social arrangements, but this whole package plus the manner in which it is presented to prospective customers. The design will include the product's precise set of features, its physical

design (Forty, 1986), brochures and manuals, sales pitches, customer service interactions, and so forth. It will also include a communication plan addressing what
Goldman (1984) calls the company's "vulnerability relations" – for example, perceptions of poor quality, financial troubles, or excessive cost. The themes, images,
and strategies of this communication plan, in other words, are part of the overall
product design. If this communication plan fails then the product is likely to fail as
well.

The design and implementation of a new computer system are analogous to the
design and marketing of a new consumer product; the principal difference is that
the salient publics consist principally of the company's own employees. (The
picture is, of course, more complex for a system that is to be sold to another
company; in this case, responsibility for the communicative function will be
divided in some way between the vendor and customer.) As with the design of a
consumer product, the managers responsible for a new computer system will assess
employee perceptions of the company, its managers, its existing work practices and
technologies, and so forth. They will then try to anticipate perceptions of various
possible systems, work practices, and ways of introducing these things. In particular, they will try to anticipate perceptions that might form the basis for resistance to
the new system, for example "too complicated," "trying to monitor and control us,"
"taking all the interest out of the job," "breaking the union," or "speedup pressure"
(Wynn, 1983). In particular, they are aware that the same technical system can be
perceived in opposite ways, for example "intrusive and controlling" versus "opening up the organization" (Walton, 1989: 42). As with STS design generally, resistance is understood as a failure mode of the design, and the object of design is
not just the computer itself but the whole package of social arrangements around it
(Kling, 1980: 79–80), together with the manner in which all of this is communi-
cated to the users. The design will ideally take into account the way in which the
communication strategy itself is perceived; common troublesome perceptions include "empty promises," "hype," "treating us like children," "heartless bu-
reaucrats," or "just the latest management fad." Managers generally are highly
attuned to the symbolic dimensions of their behavior, and they will design a mode
of comportment for themselves which aims to dissolve existing negative perceptions, avoid new ones, and encourage enough positive perceptions to keep the work
moving smoothly (Jackall, 1988). More generally, the technology, by bringing new
symbols and new patterns of activity, will provide the occasion for broader cultural
change-making in the organization, a process that Schein (1986) calls "technological seduction."

The research on organizational communication contains numerous theories
about the formation and evolution of employee perceptions. It is common to speak
of a "corporate culture" that shapes those perceptions in roughly the same manner
as the cultures that anthropologists study (Czarniawsk and Joerges, 1990; Kilmann,
Saxton, and Serpa 1986; Kunda, 1992). I will concentrate on one element of

corporate culture: the metaphors that organize meanings into coherent wholes. Corporate cultures are often said to have root metaphors in the sense that anthropologists have adapted from Pepper (1961 [1942]). Smith and Eisenberg (1987), for example, trace employee disgruntlement at Disneyland to a shift from the "drama" metaphor (putting on a show) to the "family" metaphor (taking care of one another), which gave rise to perceptions of an inadequately nurturing maternal company.

Computer systems provide a rich medium for metaphor design. A good metaphor not only lends conceptual coherence; it also, if only inadvertently, carries a larger social meaning. The metaphor of electronic mail, for example, tends to promote the idea that electronic messages are private in the same way as paper mail, with the result that the widespread management monitoring of these messages (Piller, 1993; Rothfeder, 1992) is frequently perceived as an invasion of privacy. The desktop metaphor for computer screens suggests a similar notion of inviolate personal space, though less strongly. On the managerial view that I am describing, a well-designed computer system will employ a set of metaphors whose broader social meanings, when applied to the actual social organization of work on the system, will not lead to perceptions that bring unmanageable levels of resistance. By analogy with concepts such as "design for testing" and "design for manufacture," we might call this "design for perception."

Although I speak of design for perception as a manifestation of the "managerial conception" of users, I should reemphasize that it is not the sole province of managers, just as the technical conception is not the sole province of technical people. The complicated professional and organizational dynamics through which the two conceptions interact to produce a synthesis in any given design process are beyond the scope of this chapter. Instead, I will simply assume such a synthesis and speak of "the designer" who practices it, even though relatively few such fully integrated individuals exist right now. This designer has a broad range of concerns, from the narrowly defined technical specifications of the system to the organizational exigencies of implementation. In particular, this designer has a broader and more sophisticated approach to the potential for users' resistance to the systems being designed.

As a practical matter, the designer will integrate the technical and managerial aspects of the design process through an incremental, back-and-forth movement among issues on various levels. The designer who anticipates that a given user community will resist a given system has several options: choose new metaphors, perform a focus group or a trial run to assess how serious the problem is, plan to co-opt potential leaders of resistance through "participation" or concessions tailored to their specific concerns (Dickson, 1981), create some additional communication tactics (stories to be spread, assurances to be given, and so on) as a part of the design, investigate further the precise cognitive structures that give rise to the negative perceptions, change the artifact so that additional or different affordances became available for compensatory metaphor making, and so forth. These are design decisions every bit as much as the choice of algorithms, materials, architectures, and so on. All of these decisions, furthermore, can interact strongly with the design of the physical artifact. A change of metaphors, for example, will probably require a change of interface and possibly a change of architecture as well.

To make these issues concrete, let us briefly consider an example of this type of design reasoning. It derives from a project of the Xerox Corporation to design a software architecture for the Olivetti "active badge" (Want et al., 1992). The active badge is a credit card–sized black plastic rectangle that employees of a company might wear on their clothing. On the face of the badge is an infrared LED, which flashes in a characteristic pattern that serves to identify the particular badge; the flashing light (invisible to the eye) can be detected by devices mounted on the walls of rooms and hallways throughout a workplace. These devices are connected to a local area network and periodically transmit whatever signals they receive to a continuously running computer program that keeps track of where all the badges are. The metaphor of "badge," of course, suggests that every individual carries a badge as an electronic form of identification. A typical application of active badges would be to automatically forward individuals' phone calls to whatever room they are in.

As might be expected, active badges are controversial. They regularly call up associations to Orwell's *1984,* Bentham's *Panopticon,* and other images of technological dystopia. That they do so, of course, is a cultural fact shaped by a particular set of metaphors and a particular set of historical experiences, literary symbols, and other elements of public discourse. Xerox's laboratory in Cambridge, England, is engaged in research on the interactions between the technical and social aspects of active badge systems (cf. Harper, 1992; 1993; Harper, Lamming, and Newman, 1993). The researchers are using themselves and their fellow scientists as the first experimental subjects for the technology, and they are conducting ongoing ethnographic research on the social and technical dynamics that ensue. Since much of this research has been published in the open literature, it makes an unusually accessible case study in design for perception. To be fair, at least some active badge researchers within Xerox have discussed the necessity of legislation to regulate the uses to which active badge data are put (Weiser, 1993: 82). Nonetheless, the principal innovation that aims at alleviating such fears is a software architecture whose features are under the control of the individuals wearing the badges. As Bellotti and Sellen (1993) point out in their thorough and principled catalog of privacy concerns around the badges, getting this right is easier said than done.

To listen in on some of the reasoning in the active badge design process, I will quote in full a paragraph from a paper about some experiments with active badge software architectures (Graube and O'Shea, 1991). Space does not permit a detailed account of all of the research on active badges, and I do not wish to make this single passage stand in for other projects at Xerox or elsewhere. Nonetheless, the forms of reasoning it exhibits repay careful consideration:

Obvious uses of badges which come to mind are those related to tracking and locating people. Other applications relate to the spread of distributed computing services, inter-connecting badges with computers, transforming the active badge into a generalized remote-control operator. A common denominator in these applications is the importance of dealing with privacy issues. Our experience has shown that tracking is generally not the fundamental problem associated with badges, but more what becomes of the collected information. Concern soon starts to be raised about this transformation of apparently transient data into permanent data. It seems that what makes the active badge such [a] sensitive device is that it initiates the capture of information (somehow private and public) which in turn, because of the inter-connectivity, can be disseminated. Thus this is not really the Active Badge which is at stake but the captured information's future. However as the only visible part of this complex process is the active badge device, it is understandable that it becomes the focus of users' fears. Moreover because active badges have been introduced with no particular purpose other than their obvious locating property, the focus of user concerns on this aspect of badges is not surprising. This contrasts with the case of cellular phones, which are nonetheless tracking devices, where these issues never have been so clearly raised, essentially because cellular phones offer a more visible purpose related to the conventional use of the telephone. In fact the active badges have very much less in common with ordinary badges [than] cellular phones have with non portable phones. Perhaps if badges had been introduced as primitive portable lightweight computers or "cordless mice" the pattern of user reaction would have been quite different. One of the goal[s] of the Activated Active Badge project is to focus on applications of active badge technology which emancipate the individual user from some particular chores and which should not be regarded as ways of providing third parties with real-time or historical access to records of user movements, meetings or technology use. (Graube and O'Shea, 1991: 2)

Note several things about this paragraph:

First, its question is not "what is the philosophically or sociologically soundest way to think about active badge privacy issues?" but rather "how do users think about these issues?" The "fundamental problem" they describe is not a danger forecast by the designers but a perception of danger by the users; "dealing with privacy issues" means "dealing with the users' privacy concerns." Problems not perceived by users are not a topic. Indeed problems as such are not a topic at all; the topic is users' perceptions. In making this observation, I do not mean to endorse any simple distinction between real and imaginary problems; the point, rather, is that the paragraph – and the larger discourse with which it is continuous – locates its problematic within users' cognition and not, for example, within the social organization of the users' activities.

Second, the users are interpreted as ascribing this "problem" to a particular piece of the technical system, the badge rather than the software, and not (for example) to the social embedding of the system (for which the badge might stand as a more or less conscious synecdoche). Although the idea of ascribing problems to the badges is introduced by the authors themselves ("tracking is generally not the fundamental problem associated with badges"), this tendency is soon discovered to be irrational, if understandable. The practical suggestion is to reframe the technology in a less open-ended way and to draw attention away from the badge itself and toward the immediate practical purpose that the badge system serves. What would change on this proposal is not the possibility of disseminating the data but rather the users' perception of this possibility.

Third, the authors then explore a series of metaphors for the active badge system, each of which carries social implications about privacy. They speculate, for example, that active badges would be perceived as less threatening if likened to cellular phones, portable computers, or mice. The reader is presumed to be capable of drawing out the implications of each metaphor. The badge-as-mouse metaphor, for example, casts the badge as a sort of pointing device used to indicate physical locations through body motions instead of screen locations through hand motions. The mouse is a particularly benign technology, and the authors imply that the badge-as-mouse metaphor would carry this connotation of benevolence to the badge as well. They leave it as an empirical matter whether users would actually make this association. And, indeed, the point is that the authors are concerned with this empirical question about users' response to the metaphor and not with whether the metaphor supports an intellectually adequate argument for the benevolence of the technology. Furthermore, the various alternative metaphors for active badges have the rhetorical effect of presenting users' perceptions as contingent, and thus in some sense arbitrary, having been structured by unreflected, or at least undermotivated, metaphors.

Fourth, the authors' argument about cellular phones is particularly subtle. It simultaneously promotes the legitimacy of one metaphor (to cellular phones) that generates few threatening perceptions and pours cold water on an existing metaphor (to ordinary badges). The authors suggest that such a substitution ought to alleviate concern about active badges, but this argument is questionable in that it is unclear whether negative perceptions of active badges are generated by the badge metaphor and not, say, the panopticon metaphor. It is also questionable in that cellular telephones and workplace tracking devices have different institutional embeddings; users of cellular telephones may feel that tracking data are secure through the analogy to ordinary telephone records, which belong to the phone company and (or so the users believe anyway) can only be released by subpoena, whereas the operative precedent for users of workplace tracking devices might be the uses and abuses of personal information by a different organization, such as their employers. But the authors' concern, again, is not with valid forms of reasoning but with the actual forms of reasoning exhibited by prospective users of active badges as a function of various modes of packaging and presentation. If the substitution of one analogy for another alleviates users' fears, then it is an adequate sociotechnical proposal. Furthermore, any resistance might be met with the argument that it is inconsistent to be worried about one of these technologies and not the other. Once again, the point is not whether such an argument would be reasonable but whether it would placate worried users.

Fifth, the final sentence formulates the overall goal of the research in terms of perceptions. On the positive side, the term "emancipates" emphasizes the theme of freedom – the users are to be emancipated from certain chores. This is a striking formulation, given that the active badge system is perfectly capable of going beyond the elimination of existing chores to the provision of useful new functionalities. The term may serve to counterbalance the metaphors of oppression called up by conventional cultural associations to automated tracking devices. On the negative side, the newly repackaged technology "should not be regarded" in terms of its negative potentials. The phrase is peculiar. To say "could not be regarded" would plainly be false; to say "would not be regarded" seems unduly optimistic given the strong feelings that active badges routinely provoke. The suggestion, more likely, is that such perceptions would be possible but that managers would have the rhetorical resources available to rebut them. The system, in other words, would be adequately defensible as a practical matter.

Sixth, a running theme in these observations is the passage's neglect of the institutional context of active badge use. To be sure, the authors are describing an experiment organized by scientists within a peripheral laboratory in a large company, not a system being implemented for day-to-day production purposes. Nonetheless, they are treating their subjects as adequately representative to support generalizations about users' responses. And closer examination reveals several devices through which the passage suppresses the larger context of the experiment by avoiding mention of the social actors in the drama of workplace privacy. The users, for example, are not mentioned explicitly when they are taking actions ("Concern soon starts to be raised") but only when they are reacting to something ("fears," "concerns," "reaction"), or when they are objects of others' actions ("applications . . . which emancipate the individual user," "access to records of user movements"). The passage employs the passive voice to avoid explicit mention of the users' employer ("information . . . which . . . can be disseminated," "active badges have been introduced"), and although the authors speak of themselves as a group of experimenters ("Our experience," "the Activated Active Badge project"), they do not mention the employment relationship at all. The passage also treats technological changes as givens ("the spread of distributed computing services") and not as human choices, and treats the uses of technology likewise (as "uses" and as "applications").

The passage I have quoted, then, illustrates some general properties of design for perception. Above all, design for perception depends on a kind of cognitive map of the users. In the present case this map is derived through a combination of field trials and introspection by authors who share some cultural background with the relevant user community. More advanced cognitive mapping employs a combination of practical experience, survey research, arguments and objections that users and others have raised in conversation, and so forth. The managerial conception of the user begins with this cognitive map and fashions technical systems and strategies of personal interaction that engage with the contents of this map in structured ways. Although managers rarely think of this process in "technical" terms, they understand it as continuous with the design and deployment of technological artifacts. The technical and social aspects of the process are articulated through the symbolic dimensions of the behavior of both the machines and the managers.

A cognitive map includes representations of a user community's metaphors, experiential precedents, and idea systems. And of course these things all depend on the users' cultural and personal backgrounds. A given user community's response to an active badge system might be influenced, for example, by an extensive understanding of computer networking; or through lack of exposure to wireless communications, or a belief in spirits and sympathetic magic; or through personal experience with electronic monitoring of the users' work, the tracking devices sometimes attached to the ankles of prisoners, or the secret police apparatus of totalitarian societies. Likewise, a given user community might have a worldview derived from Scandinavian notions of democracy, Mediterranean notions of honor, or Confucian notions of wise governance. Interpretations of new technologies, moreover, are regularly shaped and contested in complex ways even after implementation is complete. And new technologies frequently undergo intensive processes of gendering, for example, as the various jobs associated with them become positioned symbolically as "men's work" or "women's work" (Cockburn, 1988). As a result of these many cognitive and cultural factors, a sociotechnical design that "works" with one user community might not work with another. The key to the managerial conception of the user is precisely an awareness of this fact, together with a design methodology that can adapt to different cultural conditions. As a result of these context-sensitive design methods, user communities with different backgrounds might encounter identical artifacts presented with different metaphors, or they might encounter identical artifacts embedded in different organizational arrangements, or they might very well encounter different artifacts altogether. (An example of the last case would be the control regimes found specifically in factories employing women from developing countries.) In each case it will be a critical managerial goal to shape the users' perceptions of their newly changed work lives.

In the case of active badges, users' perceptions will be shaped in large part by cultural understandings of privacy. Most discussions of privacy in the English-speaking world (outside of legal theory) rapidly turn to the vocabulary of George Orwell's dystopian novel *1984*. This understanding of privacy is structured by a specific system of ideas that I have called the "surveillance model" (Agre, 1994):

1. visual metaphors, as in Orwell's "Big Brother is watching you";
2. the assumption that this "watching" is nondisruptive and surreptitious (except perhaps when going astray or issuing a threat);
3. territorial metaphors, as in the "invasion" of a "private" personal space, marked out by "rights" and the opposition between "coercion" and "consent";
4. centralized orchestration by means of a bureaucracy with a unified set of "files"; and
5. identification with the state, and in particular with consciously planned-out malevolent aims of a specifically political nature.

These ideas help to structure public debate on a wide variety of issues, from sexual freedom to credit reporting laws to management access to employees' electronic mail. Their influence can be seen in some of the views attributed to users in the passage I have quoted, for example, in the fear of unbounded circulation and centralized gathering of information derived from the badges. These notions are laced with images of secrecy, omniscience, and malevolence that derive from the experience of bureaucratically organized state terror that Orwell extrapolated in his novel.

Unfortunately, as I argued in the same place, these ideas are ill-suited to understanding issues of workplace privacy. One of their many unfortunate consequences is that critics of problematic technologies such as electronic work monitoring and active badges are routinely made out as proposing implausible "sinister conspiracies." Another unfortunate consequence is the assimilation of organizational communication schemes to the Cold War notion of "brainwashing," both by critics and by proponents who are paraphrasing the arguments of critics. But more to the present point, it is precisely the inadequacy of the surveillance model that provides the points of entry for the cognitive interventions of design for perception. The authors of the passage quoted note that their users are concerned that firm boundaries be drawn around their personal information, and accordingly they explore various metaphors that suggest such boundaries – for example, the relatively firm organizational and legal boundaries around information on private telephone usage. The designers need not have spelled out the whole conceptual background of the surveillance model, any more than they need to spell out the totality of the other operating conditions of the systems they design; it suffices that they map the users' cultural and cognitive processes well enough to arrive at a sociotechnically workable system.

Before concluding my exposition of the managerial conception of the user, I should emphasize once again that conceptions, as I am using the term, reside not in individuals' conscious commitments but in the logics of practices. The designers of active badge systems may or may not employ the precise vocabulary of publics, perceptions, and messages, although analogous vocabularies are readily available. To instantiate the managerial conception of their users, it suffices that the designers' actual practices include the constitutive procedures of this conception: cognitive mapping, the exploration of metaphors, the simultaneous design of physical and social technologies, and so forth. In the paragraph I have quoted, this hypothesis accounts for features of the authors' rhetoric that would otherwise be mysterious; further research will be required to spell out the precise workings of the managerial conception in particular projects.

I have been arguing that the managerial conception of the user, even more than the technical conception, is profoundly shaped by anticipated user resistance to new technologies and their associated organizational arrangements. Given this, the question arises of how users' resistance ought to proceed on the occasions when it is actually called for. Resistance, of course, is a collective enterprise, and nothing can substitute for the basics of workplace and community organization. But an analysis of the managerial conception suggests some detailed tactics. One of them, perhaps surprisingly, is to avoid arguing with managers about issues like workplace privacy. Managements engaged in cognitive mapping routinely encourage argumentation (sometimes called "venting") about the relevant issues as part of the mapping process. It is certainly important to conduct arguments about the nature of proposed workplace changes, and these arguments should lead to public statements, policy proposals, and so forth. But little is gained and much is lost by revealing these arguments prematurely (cf. Scott, 1992).

Another tactic, already widely applied in organizing campaigns, is the creation of alternative metaphors that might in turn shape alternative perceptions. These alternatives work best when they provide clear, powerful ways of understanding technologies and organizational arrangements in a broad social context. In the domain of privacy, for example, I have argued that it might be useful to supplement the surveillance model with the *capture model,* which focuses its attention on the rearrangement of work activities so that they can be captured in real time by computers, as well as on the broader organizational dynamics and political economy of this kind of sociotechnical strategy (Agre, 1994). Future work might explore the consequences of this view for an oppositional consciousness and a policy analysis of workplace privacy issues.

5.4 Some bigger pictures

Previous sections have sketched some of the institutional forces that have shaped the technical and managerial conceptions of the user. These separate sketches are inevitably misleading, though, unless the two conceptions and the relationships between them are placed in larger social and intellectual contexts. For present purposes it will suffice to outline in the most schematic way three of these contexts: (1) the tension between rhetoric and technical reason in the history of Western ideas; (2) the tension between the bureaucratic and corporatist strains in American management practice; and (3) the respective constructions of self (i.e., the programmer and manager) implied by the technical and managerial conceptions of the user and its larger institutional embedding.

Considered purely as systems of ideas, the technical and managerial conceptions clearly trace their lineage back through the dual Western traditions, respectively, of technical reason and rhetoric. Ever since classical Greece these two strands of thought have been in tension with one another. Their practical aims have always been readily distinguishable: technical reason assists in the manipulation of things through an analysis of their causal place in the natural order; rhetoric assists in the manipulation of people through an analysis of their cognitive place in the social order. Even the accusations that partisans of each side made against the other in antiquity are still thoroughly familiar today: technical reason, it is said, either excludes human beings from the natural order of things or else abuses them by reducing them to this order; rhetoric, it is said, flouts the principles of disinterested inquiry by abandoning truth for ornament, emotion, and style. Descartes complained against the empty rhetoric of the decadent scholastic tradition, viewing mathematics as the language of nature; Vico (1990 [1743]) complained against the subsequent impoverishment of the humanities in European universities by Cartesian reason, viewing rhetoric as the language of wisdom.

Historical defenses of rhetoric and technical reason have always presupposed a set of institutional contexts for their practice. Aristotle's *Rhetoric,* for example, distinguishes three types of rhetoric according to their listeners: political oratory in the legislative assembly, forensic oratory in the courtroom, and epideictic oratory in ceremonies of praise or censure in the marketplace. The *Rhetoric,* like many of Aristotle's other texts, synthesized the most effective practices of the day into textbooks for elite young men training to participate in these institutions. Vico, likewise, viewed rhetorical training as accustoming elite young men to adjusting their language to suit their interlocutors, thereby of knitting them into the social worlds around them. Yet these institutional contexts of rhetoric are treated as given and not as contested and changing sites of practice. Defenses of technical reason, for their part, have almost uniformly omitted any mention of the social arrangements that provide the leisure for technical design work and the physical materials and social force for technical implementation. Yet these too certainly exist and change and have material consequences for what "works" and does not "work" in practice.

The managerial conception of the user clearly descends, if distantly, from the classical theory of rhetoric. The rhetorical strategies surrounding computer systems extend classical rhetoric in some significant ways, for example, through the vocabulary of perceptions, the notion of managing a culture through metaphors and stories and the like, and the integration of rhetoric with the design of physical artifacts. And the managerial practices presuppose a different institutional setting, the corporate bureaucracy in which managerial rhetors, working together, present a coordinated message to an audience of line employees using rhetorical devices chosen through an analysis of the audience's perceptions and cognitive structures. The persuasive force of this message depends in part on its rhetorical structure (e.g., its metaphors), in part on management's possession of privileged information and claim to a broader perspective on questions of business rationality, and in part on the formal relationship of employment.

The technical conception of the user, and the broader practice of which it is part, are likewise clearly recognizable as a chapter in the tradition of technical reason. The technical conception actually establishes a dual conceptual relationship between the programmer and the user: it understands the user as a component in a system understood in mathematical terms and it presupposes that the user shares the programmer's epistemological relationship to this system. So far as technical reason is concerned, the system is finite and bounded, and can be completely represented through its "spec." The systems analyst looks down upon the system the way that God looks down upon the whole of Creation; and indeed no other perspective is imaginable within the technical conception (Haraway, 1991). The enormous institutional and imaginative distance between programmer and user permits this disembodied understanding of the material work to flourish with little impediment. The actual implementation of the system must proceed without God's intercession, of course, but the technical staff is able to presuppose that adequate power is available elsewhere for this purpose.

The vocabulary of the computer industry can make it difficult to appreciate this point. The term "user" frequently blurs the distinction between the actual user, the line employee whose everyday work is conducted through the system, and the customer – the managerial coalition that establishes strategy, defines the social arrangements of work, specifies the system's behavior, manages its implementation, and oversees the subsequent work processes (Friedman, 1989: 184). (The term "programmer," likewise, often blurs the distinction between the people who write the software and the managers who direct them.) A further source of confusion is the term "personal computer," which might be suitable for computer hobbyists or independent professionals but is greatly misleading in the dense system of social and technical interactions of the average work setting (Pfaffenberger, 1988).

Consideration of the practical settings of computer system implementation requires practitioners to somehow reconcile the technical and managerial conceptions of the user. For managers, as I have explained, this is partially a matter of integrating technical design with the design of organizational communication strategies. But the problem has many other dimensions as well, and together these issues identify the central tension in the development of American management. Waring (1991) makes this tension concrete through his historical reconstruction of two traditions of management thought, which he refers to as "bureaucratic" and "corporatist." (He argues that both traditions originate in Taylor's theories of work rationalization, but I will put this question of origins aside.) The bureaucratic tradition, as originally identified by Weber, seeks rational (scientific, impersonal, apolitical) principles of organizational structure and decision making. The corporatist tradition, which originates in nineteenth-century European political thought, likens the corporation to a polity that functions through individuals' identification with assigned roles. The bureaucratic tradition reached its apogee in the reign of financially trained manager-technicians at Ford in the 1950s and 1960s; it has invested enormous effort into quantitative techniques for modeling business operations and determining technically optimal forms of work organization. The corporatist tradition is best exemplified by the ongoing "quality of work life" (QWL) movement with its rhetoric of "participation" and "empowerment" (Parker, 1985; Wells, 1987); it emphasizes human agency, creativity, and motivation, as well as the inevitability of ambiguity and change in business operations.

It is enormously difficult to trace the intellectual history of these two traditions, much less their practical history, because of the peculiar social dynamics of ideas in American business. Managers seeking promotions and consultants seeking to differentiate their services have an interest in exaggerating the novelty of newly instituted methods, with the result that business people routinely introduce new terms to name incrementally novel ideas, thereby obfuscating their genealogy. As a result, commentaries on the history of business ideas often go to extremes, either announcing radical breaks at the drop of a hat (as with the promoters of new methods) or claiming that nothing is new under the sun (as with the skeptics of these methods – and, I am afraid, Waring himself).

The truth, of course, is more complex. Perhaps the central tendency in the development of business thought and practice is the progressive integration of bureaucratic and corporatist ideas and methods. A recurring theme in this integration was already noticed by Weber: organizations generally benefit from decentralized decision making, and decision making can be decentralized to the extent that operations are controlled through a detailed accounting system and formalized through the imposition of a uniform method or language on work activities. I have written elsewhere (Agre, forthcoming) about a particularly compelling example of this theme, the simultaneous use in emerging management practice of a rhetoric of "empowerment" and computerized real-time capture of work activities. Yet because attempts to implement this kind of formalized control invariably bring other problems, and because of the fads that sweep ceaselessly through American business practice, bureaucratic and corporatist ideas tend to surge and retreat like tides of different oceans on the same shore. Nonetheless, it is crucial to understand that each tide leaves a great deal behind it when it recedes, and that the relationship between the two traditions is ultimately dialectical in nature.

This understanding casts some light on the relationship between the technical and managerial conceptions of the user. The technical conception is not exclusively the property of computer programmers but resides in a larger bureaucratic tradition. The managerial conception, likewise, does not exhaust managerial ideas about technology, people, and organizations, but participates in a larger corporatist tradition. It is impossible to give any simple, ahistorical account of the way in which managerial practice integrates the two conceptions of the user because there is no simple, ahistorical account of the larger traditions that encompass them. What is possible, however, is the disciplined tracing of the dialectical relation between the traditions and the ways in which they articulate with both the shop-floor politics of computer systems implementation and with the political economy of the firm and its place in the unfolding structures of markets (e.g., Porter, 1980).

To conclude, though, I wish to return to the theme of "conceptions." Although I have sketched some of the institutional forces that shape the managerial and technical conceptions, there still remains the existential question of what kind of human relationship each of these conceptions brings with it. In the case of the technical conception of the user, I see no reason to amend the widespread idea that technology is, in a particular sense, dehumanizing: while technologies may contribute to the elimination of certain degrading forms of work, nonetheless the programmer, insofar as he or she participates in the technical practices I have described, spends the day making plans for other people's lives without knowing those people or even recognizing their humanity beyond their place in a formally specified system. Heidegger (1977 [1954]) characterized the technologist's way of seeing the world as "enframing": a relentless effort to reconstruct various situations of human life within a finite vocabulary of technical schemata. The institutional forces that structure the distant relationship between programmer and user abet – and help reproduce – this kind of foreshortened social vision. The situation should not be seen as a simple human failing, of a sort that might be repaired through reading matter or moral exhortation. Visions of an alternative relationship between programmers and users *are* available in the ongoing participatory design movement, to which I alluded toward the end of Section 5.2. And the plain inefficiencies of bad design may induce market pressure toward reform. But these tendencies have only begun to reckon with the social relations of work that structure technical practice, and it is not entirely clear how to proceed.

That much is largely familiar; what is newer is the emerging critique of the emerging managerial conception of the user. Like the corporatist tradition in American management thought of which it forms a part, the managerial conception largely escapes the conventional vision of the rational, dehumanizing, technology-driven bureaucracy. The managerial conception does not ignore human beings, neglect their agency or resistance, or reduce them to quasi machinery. Quite the contrary, the managerial practices I have described take these aspects of human culture and cognition as their starting point, seeking to circumvent the causes of resistance through symbolic action rather than through force. As such, they can appear even to skeptical observers (e.g., Kellner and Heuberger, 1992) to reconcile the split between "system" and "lifeworld" that Habermas (1987) regarded as a central feature of technological society.

Nonetheless, the fact is that managerial practices, precisely in the way in which they engage with human beings as social actors, bring their own form of dehumanization. The symbolic strategies that I described in the context of active badge research are manipulative. They begin with the goal of fielding a certain category of technology, and they seek the communicative means to achieve this goal. As such, they exemplify the phenomenon that Jackall (1988), in his extraordinary phenomenological ethnography of managerial practices, referred to as "alertness to expediency." The paragraph I analyzed is, when viewed from this perspective, not far different from the managerial practice that Jackall (1988: 188–189) calls "rehearsal," whereby managers collectively work out the most convincing rationalization for actions already decided on – and, more specifically, that rationalization whose casuistry the participants "feel comfortable" animating in public performance against the anticipated arguments of target publics. This process, it is important to understand, is just as much an objectification of the manager himself or herself as it is an objectification of the computers and people that compose the sociotechnical system being designed:

In effect, one makes oneself alert to expediency by projecting outward the objectifying habit of mind learned in the course of self-rationalization. That is, the manager alert to expediency learns to appraise all situations and all other people as he comes to see himself – as an object, a commodity, something to be scrutinized, rearranged, tinkered with, packaged, advertised, promoted, and sold. The mastery of public faces described earlier is only the outward reflection of an internal mastery, a relentless subjection of the self to objective criteria to achieve success. Such self-abnegation, such stripping away of natural impulses, involves a self-objectification that in fact frames and paces the objectification of the world. To the extent that self-objectification is incomplete – and, of course, even the most thorough secular ascetic has uncharted areas of the self – to that extent do managers experience moral dilemmas with [in?] their grapplings with the world. In my view, this is the nub of the moral ethos of bureaucracy. Managers see this issue as a "trade-off" between principle and expediency. They usually pose the trade-off as a question: Where do you draw the line? (Jackall, 1988: 119)

Such attitudes are already deeply embedded in the practice of organizational communication, as an examination of the literature on corporate culture makes plain (see, e.g., Sathe, 1986). Their elaboration into components of the technical design process is perhaps most significant in that technical artifacts heavily condition the bodily practices of the people that use them. This systematized extension of the symbolic engineering of consent into the very habitus of ordinary work activities should be an occasion for critical reflection and concern.

5.5 Conclusion

I have been painting a generally dark picture of the social organization of computer system development. In particular, I have been sketching a transition from the generally familiar picture of the technical reification of human affairs to an emerging picture of the managerial reconstruction of human symbolic life in the service of organizational expediency. Each picture brings its own version of the objectification of human beings – "users" – in the service of a fundamentally unilateral understanding of systems design as social practice. And in particular, each picture brings its own conception of resistance to unilateral design practices. The emergence and interaction between these two pictures stands on its own as a chapter of the social history of productive work.

Nonetheless, inasmuch as I have focused on *conceptions* of users and their resistance, rather than on the actual human beings in the fullness of their lives, my own analysis threatens to recapitulate in a more insidious form the unilateral character of conventional system design. Resistance, after all, is a category predicated upon, and limited to, a reaction or response to an agenda already determined somewhere else. It is only in this restricted perspective, for example, that workers who are dying to change their world can be portrayed as exhibiting "fear of change" (e.g., Fine, 1986).

In order to turn things right side up, it will be necessary to understand the ways in which the social practice of "users" makes its own sense while simultaneously being conditioned by technical and managerial practices. It is perhaps unsurprising that the empirical basis for this kind of research, particularly with regard to the users of computer-based technologies whose design has been informed by the managerial conception, is largely lacking. The analysis presented here, though, suggests elements of an agenda for such research. Managerial communication practices, unlike the conventional practices of technical design, presuppose a two-way symbolic exchange that can be viewed as symmetrical in some limited and formal way (Grunig and Hunt, 1984). Managerial work, on this view, is cultural intervention, and as such is indissociable from the encounter between popular culture and the processes of commodification in the larger culture. The surveillance model of privacy, for example, is a cultural phenomenon par excellence, and as such it helps structure individuals' and communities' engagements with numerous forms of domination.

Just as managerial design is learning to adapt to existing structures of popular resistance, then, a challenge for democratic social practice is the development of equally adaptive systems of meaning. Put another way, the acceleration of technical and organizational change must be met with an accelerating reaffirmation of human values. The resources for such a project derive not from the rejection of technical and managerial practices but from their transformation: from a unilateral to a participatory technical practice and, more important, from managerial simulacra of participation to the authentic item.

Acknowledgments

This chapter has benefited from comments by Paul Dourish, Diana Forsythe, Jonathan Grudin, Richard Harper, Mike Robinson, Lucy Suchman, and Randy Trigg, who nonetheless do not necessarily endorse its conclusions.

References

Ackoff, R. L. (1960). Unsuccessful case studies and why. *Operations Research,* 8 (2), 259–263.

Agre, P. E. (forthcoming). From high tech to human tech: On the sudden market for social studies of technology. In G. Bowker, L. Star, L. Gasser, and B. Turner, (eds.), *Social science research, technical systems and cooperative work.*

Agre, P. E. (1994). Surveillance and capture: Two models of privacy. *Information Society,* 10 (2), 101–127.

Argyris, C. (1976). Resistance to rational management systems. In G. B. Davis and G. C. Everest (eds.), *Readings in management information systems* (New York: McGraw-Hill).

Banks, A., and Metzgar, J. (1989). Participating in management: Union organizing on a new terrain. *Labor Research Review,* 14, 1–55.

Bardach, E. (1977). *The implementation game: What happens after a bill becomes a law* (Cambridge, Mass: MIT Press).

Barnard, C. I. (1962). *The functions of the executive* (Cambridge, Mass.: Harvard University Press). Originally published in 1938.

Bellotti, V. M. E., and Sellen, A. (1993). Design for privacy in ubiquitous computing environments. In G. de Michelis, C. Simone, and K. Schmidt (eds.), *Proceedings of the Third European Conference on Computer-Supported Cooperative Work* (Dordrecht: Kluwer), 77–92.

Benson, D. (1993). The police and information technology. In G. Button (ed.), *Technology in working order: Studies of work, interaction, and technology* (London: Routledge).

Bjorn-Andersen, N., Eason, K. and Robey, D. (1986). *Managing computer impacts: An international study of management and organization* (Norwood, N.J.: Ablex).

Blake, L. (1992). Reduce employees' resistance to change. *Personnel Journal,* 71 (9), 72–76.

Blomberg, J. L. (1987). Social interaction and office communication: Effects on user's evaluation of new technologies. In R. E. Kraut (ed.), *Technology and the transformation of white-collar work* (Hillsdale, N.J.: Lawrence Erlbaum).

Boland, R. J., Jr., and Hirschheim, R. A. (eds.). (1987). *Critical issues in information systems research* (Chichester: Wiley).

Braverman, H. (1974). *Labor and monopoly capital: The degradation of work in the twentieth century* (New York: Monthly Review Press).

Bravo, E. (1993). The hazards of leaving out the users. In D. Schuler and A. Namioka (eds.), *Participatory design: Principles and practices* (Hillsdale, N.J.: Lawrence Erlbaum), 3–11.

Buchanan, D. A. (1986). Management objectives in technical change. In D. Knights and H. Wilmott (eds.), *Managing the labour process* (Aldershot: Gower).

Chaiklin, S., and Lave, J. (eds.). (1993). *Understanding practice: Perspectives on activity and context* (Cambridge: Cambridge University Press).

Clement, A., and Van den Besselaar, P. (1993). A retrospective look at PD projects. *Communications of the ACM,* 36 (4), 29–37.

Cockburn, C. (1988). *Machinery of dominance: Women, men, and technical know-how* (Evanston, Ill.: Northwestern University Press).

Collins, H. M. (1990). *Artificial experts: Social knowledge and intelligent machines* (Cambridge, Mass.: MIT Press).

Couger, J. D. (1973). Evolution of business system development techniques. *Computing Surveys, 5* (3), 167–198.

Czarniawsk, B., and Joerges, B. (1990). Linguistic artifacts at service of organizational control. In P. Gagliardi (ed.), *Symbols and artifacts: Views of the corporate landscape* (Berlin: Walter de Gruyter).

Dagwell, R., and Weber, R. (1983). System designers' user models: A comparative study and methodological critique. *Communications of the ACM, 26* (11), 987–997.

Danziger, J. N., and Kraemer, K. L. (1986). *People and computers: The impacts of computing on end users in organizations* (New York: Columbia University Press).

Desanctis, G., and Courtney, J. F. (1983). Toward friendly user MIS implementation. *Communications of the ACM, 26* (3), 732–738.

Dickson, J. W. (1981). Participation as a means of organizational control. *Journal of Management Studies, 18* (4), 159–176.

Drucker, P. (1945). *Management: Tasks, responsibilities, practices* (New York: Harper and Row).

Edwards, R. (1979). *Contested terrain: The transformation of the workplace in the twentieth century* (New York: Basic Books).

Fine, S. F. (1986). Technological innovation, diffusion and resistance: An historical perspective. *Journal of Library Administration, 7* (1), 83–108.

Forsythe, D. E. (1992). Blaming the user in medical informatics: The cultural nature of scientific practice. In L. Layne and D. Hess (eds.), *Knowledge and society* 9 (Greenwich, Conn.: JAI Press), 95–111.

Forty, A. (1986). *Objects of desire* (New York: Pantheon).

Friedman, A. L. (1989). *Computer systems development: History, organization and implementation* (Chichester: Wiley).

Garfinkel, H. (1984). "Good" organizational reasons for "bad" clinic records. In H. Garfinkel (ed.), *Studies in ethnomethodology* (Cambridge: Polity) 186–207. Originally published in 1967.

Garson, B. (1989). *The electronic sweatshop: How computers are transforming the office of the future into the factory of the past* (New York: Penguin).

Gasser, L. (1986). The integration of computing and routine work. *ACM Transactions on Office Information Systems, 4* (3), 205–225.

Gilbreth, F. B. (1921). *Motion study: A method for increasing the efficiency of the workman* (New York: D. Van Nostrand).

Giordano, L. (1992). *Beyond Taylorism: Computerization and the new industrial relations* (New York: St. Martin's Press).

Goldman, J. (1984). *Public relations in the marketing mix: Introducing vulnerability relations* (Chicago: Crain).

Graube, N., and O'Shea, T. (1991). An architecture for user control of active badge systems. Technical Report EPC-91–123, Rank Xerox, Cambridge EuroPARC.

Grudin, J. (1991). Interactive systems: Bridging the gaps between developers and users. *IEEE Computer, 24* (4), 59–69.

Grudin, J. (1993). Interface: An evolving concept. *Communications of the ACM, 35* (4) 110–119.

Grunig, J. E., and Hunt, T. (1984). *Managing public relations* (New York: Holt, Rinehart and Winston).

Habermas, J. (1987). *The theory of communicative action*, vol. 2: *Lifeworld and system: A critique of functionalist reason* (Boston: Beacon Press).

Hacker, S. L. (1981). The culture of engineering: Woman, workplace, and machine. *Women's Studies International Quarterly,* 4 (3), 341–353.

Hales, M. (1980). *Living thinkwork: Where do labour processes come from* (London: CSE Press).

Haraway, D. J. (1991). Situated knowledges: The science question in feminism and the privilege of partial perspective. In *Simians, cyborgs, and women: The reinvention of nature* (New York: Routledge), 183–201.

Harper, R. (1992). Looking at ourselves: An examination of the social organisation of two research laboratories. Technical Report EPC-92–108, Rank Xerox, Cambridge EuroPARC.

Harper, R. (1993). Why do people wear active badges? Technical Report EPC-93–120, Rank Xerox, Cambridge EuroPARC.

Harper, R. H. R., Lamming, M. G., and Newman, W. M. (1993). Locating systems at work: Implications for the development of active badge applications. *Interacting with Computers,* 4 (3), 343–363.

Hedberg, B., and Mumford, E. (1975). The design of computer systems: Man's vision of man as an integral part of the system design process. In E. Mumford and H. Sackman (eds.), *Human Choice and Computers: Proceedings of the IFIP Conference on Human Choice and Computers,* Vienna, April 1–5 1974 (Amsterdam: North-Holland).

Heidegger, M. (1977). The question concerning technology. In *The question concerning technology and other essays,* translated from the German by William Lovitt (New York: Harper and Row). Originally published in 1954.

Howard, R. (1985). *Brave new workplace* (New York: Penguin).

Hutchins, E. (1990). The technology of team navigation. In J. Galegher, R. E. Kraut, and C. Egido (eds.), *Intellectual teamwork: Social and technological foundations of cooperative work* (Hillsdale, N.J.: Lawrence Erlbaum), 191–220.

Iacono, R., and Kling, R. (1987). Changing office technologies and transformations of clerical jobs: A historical perspective. In R. E. Kraut (ed.), *Technology and the transformation of white-collar work* (Hillsdale, N.J.: Lawrence Erlbaum).

Jackall, R. (1988). *Moral mazes: The world of corporate managers* (New York: Oxford University Press).

Keen, P. G. W. (1981). Information systems and organizational change, *Communications of the ACM,* 24 (1), 24–33.

Kellner, H., and Heuberger, F. W. (1992). Modernizing work: New frontiers in business consulting. In H. Kellner and F. W. Heuberger (eds.), *Hidden technocrats: The new class and the new capitalism* (New Brunswick, N.J.: Transaction).

Keul, V. (1983). Trade union planning and control of new technology: Experiences from research projects with Norwegian trade unions. In U. Briefs, C. Ciborra, and L. Schneider (eds.), *System design for, with, and by the users* (Amsterdam: North-Holland), 207–218.

Kilmann, R. H., Saxton, M. J., and Serpa, R. (eds.). (1986). *Gaining control of the corporate culture* (San Francisco: Jossey-Bass).

Kling, R. (1977). The organizational context of user-centered software design. Technical Report 108, Department of Information and Computer Sciences, University of California, Irvine.

Kling, R. (1980). Social analyses of computing: Theoretical perspectives in recent empirical research. *Computing Surveys,* 12 (1), 61–110.

Kling, R. (1989). Theoretical perspectives in social analysis of computerization. In Z. W. Pylyshyn and L. J. Bannon (eds.), *Perspectives on the computer revolution,* 2nd ed. (Norwood, N.J.: Ablex), 459–518.

Kling, R., and Dunlop, C. (1993). Controversies about computerization and the character of white collar worklife. *Information Society,* 9 (1), 1–29.

Krasner, H., Curtis, B., and Iscoe, N. (1987). Communication breakdowns and boundary spanning activities on large programming projects. In G. M. Olson, S. Sheppard, and E. Soloway (eds.), *Empirical studies of programmers: Second workshop* (Norwood, N.J.: Ablex), 47–64.

Kunda, G. (1992). *Engineering culture: Control and commitment in a high-tech corporation* (Philadelphia: Temple University Press).

Levie, L., and Williams, R. (1983). User involvement and industrial democracy: Problems and strategies in Britain. In U. Briefs, C. Ciborra, and L. Schneider (eds.), *System design for, with, and by the users* (Amsterdam: North-Holland), 265–286.

MacLean, A., Young, R. M., and Moran, T. P. (1989). Design rationale: The argument behind the artifact. In K. Bice and C. Lewis (eds.), *Proceedings of the Conference on Human Factors in Computing Systems: CHI '89* (New York: ACM Press), 247–252.

Markus, M. L. (1984). *Systems in organizations: Bugs and features* (Boston: Pitman).

Mumford, E. (1972). *Job satisfaction: A study of computer specialists* (London: Longman).

Nardi, B. A., and Miller, J. R. (1991). Twinkling lights and nested loops: Distributed problem solving and spreadsheet development. In S. Greenberg (ed.), *Computer-supported cooperative work and groupware* (London: Academic Press), 29–52.

Noble, D. F. (1986). *Forces of production: A social history of industrial automation* (Oxford: Oxford University Press).

Norman, D. A. (1988). *The psychology of everyday things* (New York : Basic Books).

Parker, M. (1985). *Inside the circle: A union guide to QWL* (Boston: South End Press).

Pepper, S. C. (1961). *World hypotheses: A study in evidence* (Berkeley: University of California Press). Originally published in 1942.

Perin, C. (1991). Electronic social fields in bureaucracies. *Communications of the ACM,* 34 (12), 75–82.

Peters, T. (1990). Get innovative or get dead (part one). *California Management Review,* 33 (1), 9–26.

Pfaffenberger, B. (1988). The social meaning of the personal computer: or, Why the personal computer revolution was no revolution. *Anthropological Quarterly,* 61 (1), 39–47.

Piller, C. (1993). Bosses with x-ray eyes. *MacWorld,* 10 (7), 118–123.

Porter, M. E. (1980). *Competitive strategy: Techniques for analyzing industries and competitors* (New York: Free Press).

Quinn, J. B. (1992). *Intelligent enterprise: A knowledge and service based paradigm for industry* (New York: Free Press).

Robinson, M. (1991a). Double-level languages and co-operative working. *AI and Society,* 5 (1), 34–60.

Robinson, M. (1991b). Pay bargaining in a shared information space. In J. M. Bowers and S. D. Benford (eds.), *Studies in computer-supported cooperative work: Theory, practice and design* (Amsterdam: North-Holland), 235–248.

Robinson, M., and Bannon, L. (1991). Questioning representations. In L. Bannon, M. Robinson, and K. Schmidt (eds.), *Proceedings of the Second European Conference on Computer-Supported Cooperative Work* (Amsterdam: Kluwer).

Rothfeder, J. (1992). E-mail snooping. *Corporate Computing,* 1 (3), 168–174.

Rule J., and Attewell, P. (1989). What do computers do? *Social Problems,* 36 (3), 225–241.

Rybczynski, W. (1983). *Taming the tiger: The struggle to control technology* (New York: Viking Press).

Sathe, V. (1986). How to decipher and change corporate culture. In R. H. Kilmann, M. J. Saxton, and R. Serpa (eds.), *Gaining control of the corporate culture* (San Francisco: Jossey-Bass).

Schein, E. H. (1986). How culture forms, develops, and changes. In R. H. Kilmann, M. J. Saxton, and R. Serpa (eds.), *Gaining control of the corporate culture* (San Francisco: Jossey-Bass).

Schreuder, H. (1987). Organization, information, and people: A participant observation of a MIS-carriage. In W. J. Bruns, Jr., and R. S. Kaplan (eds.), *Accounting and management: Field study perspectives* (Boston: Harvard Business School Press), 146–165.

Schuler, D., and Namioka, A. (eds.). (1993). *Participatory design: Principles and practices* (Hillsdale, N.J.: Lawrence Erlbaum).

Scott, J. C. (1992). Domination, acting, and fantasy. In C. Nordstrom and J. Martin (eds.), *The paths to domination, resistance, and terror* (Berkeley: University of California Press), 55–84.

Shaiken, H. (1985). *Work transformed: Automation and labor in the computer age* (New York: Holt, Rinehart, and Winston).

Sharrock, W., and Anderson, B. (1994). The user as a scenic feature of the design space. *Design Studies,* 15 (1), 5–18.

Shaw, A. G. (1952). *The purpose and practice of motion study* (Manchester: Harlequin).

Smith, R. C., and Eisenberg, E. M. (1987). Conflict at Disneyland: A root-metaphor analysis. *Communication Monographs,* 54 (4), 367–380.

Sproull, L. S., Kiesler, S., and Zubrow, D. (1984). Encountering an alien culture. *Journal of Social Issues,* 40 (3), 31–48.

Suchman, L. (1988). Designing with the user: Review of *Computers and democracy,* edited by Gro Bjerknes, Pelle Ehn, and Morten Kyng. *ACM Transactions on Office Information Systems,* 6 (2), 173–183.

Suchman, L., and Jordan, B. (1989). Computerization and women's knowledge. In K. Tijdens, M. Jennings, I. Wagner, and M. Weggelaar (eds.), *Women, work and computerization: Forming new alliances* (Amsterdam: North-Holland), 153–160.

Suchman, L. A., and Trigg, R. H. (1993). Artificial intelligence as craftwork. In S. Chaiklin and J. Lave (eds.), *Understanding practice: Perspectives on activity and context* (Cambridge: Cambridge University Press), 144–178.

Taylor, J. C. (1987). Job design and quality of working life. In R. E. Kraut (ed.), *Technology and the transformation of white-collar work* (Hillsdale, N.J.: Lawrence Erlbaum).

Thompson, P. (1989). *The nature of work: An introduction to debates on the labour process.* 2nd ed. (London: Macmillan).

Trist, E. (1981). *The evolution of socio-technical systems: A conceptual framework and an action research program* (Toronto: Ontario Quality of Working Life Centre).

Vico, G. (1990). *On the study methods of our time,* translated by Elio Gianturco (Ithaca: Cornell University Press). Originally published in 1743.

Walton, R. E. (1989). *Up and running: Integrating information technology and the organization* (Boston: Harvard Business School Press).

Want, R., Hopper, A., Falcao, V., and Gibbons, J. (1992). The active badge location system. *ACM Transactions on Information Systems,* 10 (1), 91–102.

Waring, S. P. (1991). *Taylorism transformed: Scientific management theory since 1945* (Chapel Hill: University of North Carolina Press).

Weiser, M. (1993). Some computer science issues in ubiquitous computing. *Communications of the ACM,* 36 (7), 74–84.

Wells, D. M. (1987). *Empty promises: Quality of working life programs and the labor movement* (New York: Monthly Review Press).

Wilkinson, B. (1983). *The shopfloor politics of new technology* (London: Heinemann).

Wynn, E. H. (1983). The user as a representation issue in the US. In U. Briefs, C. Ciborra, and L. Schneider (eds.), *System design for, with, and by the users* (Amsterdam: North-Holland), 349–358.

6

On simulacrums of conversation: Toward a clarification of the relevance of conversation analysis for human–computer interaction

Graham Button and Wes Sharrock

6.1 Introduction

Within the sciences of design, there has been an increasing inclination to seek an understanding of "the social" in order to improve the quality of designs.[1] This turn toward the social may be conceived as having implications of varying significances, ranging from those which would simply enable incremental improvements in design to those which involve the fundamental rethinking of the nature of the activity of design. In the field of human–computer interaction (HCI) the turn to the social has been a strong one, presumably because the "interface" provides the crucial point of contact between the interstices of the machine and the activities of the individuals operating them.[2] Also, as the concern to design systems – as manifest in the growth of distributed computing – that will support complex and collectively conducted patterns of activity increases, designers have become much more sensitive to the need to relate the behavior of individual users to the setting of group and organizational life within which that is located (Bowers and Rodden, 1993; Grudin, 1990). A consequence of turning to the social has been the invocation of social science approaches to assist designers, and among social science approaches ethnomethodology and conversation analysis have drawn attention (Goguen, 1992; Goguen, forthcoming). In this chapter we discuss issues surrounding the way conversation analysis in particular is applied in HCI.[3]

Facilitating the transactions between machine and user(s) has been a central and long-standing objective of interface design. Both cognitive and social scientists have attempted to make the operations of the computer as "natural" as possible, for example, by seeking to reproduce, through the computer, operations already familiar to users. In the notorious case of "the desktop," users are invited to treat their on-screen work after the fashion of their office proceedings – creating documents, keeping documents in files, keeping files on the desktop, and putting documents in a wastebasket.

The increasing sophistication of computer and information systems has meant that they can be used in increasingly complex transactions. This is occasioning the attempt to develop means to allow the user to make elaborate "interrogations" of the machine and has encouraged the idea that one of the most natural forms of interaction to people is the verbal exchange, as instantiated by conversation. Further, the growing complexity of user–system exchanges will necessitate much greater flexibility in the range of responses available from the system; because conversational exchanges are open-ended and highly adaptable, it seems logical to suppose that building into the system the resources available to conversationalists would permit the design of systems with readily adjustable responses. Thus, it would be reasonable to think that if one is designing a system involving a complex interaction between users and the computer, an effective way to do this might be to treat the operations as dialogical ones, modeling them after conversational exchanges.

The fact that some sociologists have already undertaken the analysis of the organization of "naturally occurring conversation" and have, furthermore, constructed a model of the system for turn taking in such conversation (Sacks, Schegloff, and Jefferson, 1974) has caught the attention of those to whom the possibility of natural language, dialogical interfaces has occurred.[4] That these sociologists have gone some way toward assembling a formal analysis of aspects of the organization of conversation, focused upon an explicit model of "conversational turn taking,"[5] might also promise to facilitate the adoption of the conversation metaphor for computer systems by making it seemingly amenable to programming.

In an essay entitled "Going up a Blind Alley," (Button, 1990), one of us has already entered into the discussion of the possible utility and significance of "conversation analysis" in the service of the conversation metaphor in computer and system design. It was certainly not his intention – nor is it now ours – to cast doubt upon the worth of the conversation metaphor as a device for designing comfortable and effective computer systems. We say this because this intervention in the debate has been wrongly construed as an attempt to interdict efforts to (1) simulate conversational sequences on computers and (2) develop the conversational metaphor in computer system design.[6] This certainly was not the purpose of that piece, and we have difficulty in understanding how such motivation could be assigned to it by some of its detractors.

The argument, as clearly expressed, was not against the pragmatic pursuit of exercises in computation or of design objectives, for there is no way of being sure how any strategy might eventually pay off, but was, rather, against *the claims* made about what success in such pursuits would prove. The central objection in "Going Up a Blind Alley" was to the idea that the construction of a system that could reproduce features of dialogic organization in a detailed and intricate way would mean the creation of a computer that could "talk like you and me" (Reichman, 1985). The case was put via two main points:

1. that programmatic argument on behalf of the conversation metaphor was overlooking the fact that it was a metaphor (a confusion that has not, we think, afflicted the "desktop" case);
2. that these arguments were misguided by superficial resemblance in the notion of "rule" between conversation analysis and computing.

Because both of these arguments have been misunderstood, we will seek to clarify them here as a way of addressing the possible relevance that conversation analysis could have to HCI design.[7] We will take up two issues. First, distinction between rules of human conduct and programming rules is crucial for any consideration of the relationship between conversation analysis and HCI design. Second, those seeking to simulate conversation will need to confront certain problems if they are to be successful in such *practical* endeavors. Thus, our concern is not to deny the relevance of conversation analysis in the design of HCI systems but to point out the way in which conversation analysis has been misappropriated.

Why do we consider these matters consequential? Why shouldn't we just let the matter drop, as Wooffitt and MacDermid (this volume) seem to imply that they are doing by handing the matter over to system designers "to decide the success (or otherwise) of speaking machines"? There are two reasons. First, despite avowals to the contrary, programmatic claims are being made with respect to these ventures that are intendedly consequential but in fact misleading, and their advocates persistently misrepresent the nature of the opposition to them. Second, we are concerned that the overambitious claims made about ethnomethodology and conversation analysis will result in disappointment with them and eventually an underestimation of their potential in HCI.

The programmatic claims rerun the debates that have been going on for decades over the prospect of intelligent machines. They are, for example, another attempt to persuade us that we need to revise some of the fundamental distinctions – such as that between human and machine – that we make in our lives generally (Fraser and Wooffitt, 1990) and thus to downgrade our assessment of the difference between the human species and machines or other species of animals (McIlvenny, 1990). We object to such efforts on the grounds that they do not seem to make the necessary distinction between arguing about whether one could in fact build a system that could simulate conversations in close and fine-grained details, and arguing about what it would mean to have built such a system. It is exactly the same order of mistake that has bedeviled much of the debate about the possibility of "intelligent machines."

The second reason for taking up these issues is, in some ways, a more parochial one, for we are concerned, as partisans of ethnomethodology and conversation analysis, with the way in which exaggerated expectations of their potential utility may lead to disillusionment with the actual results of their application, and that the failure of such ventures to deliver may then be attributed to ethnomethodology and conversation analysis, when, in fact, the "failure" is merely one relative to unduly inflated claims. This is not to question whether ethnomethodology and conversation analysis might be useful to designers and researchers, for we are ourselves, though tentatively, satisfied that they could be useful, as we will explain in a later section. However, the likelihood that they will be effectively exploited depends, in important part, on their actual character being correctly appreciated, and it is our contention that the portrayal of these approaches to designers and researchers is sometimes misleading – slanted in a way that minimizes the difficulties that those attempting to simulate conversation will practically confront. We use the term "simulate" here because the source of their confusion is an inability seemingly to comprehend that this is *all* that is possible.

6.2 The Turing Test error

Frohlich and Luff (1990) and Fraser and Wooffitt (1990) tell us that the objections that were formulated in "Going up a Blind Alley" to the conflation of conversation analysis and computer modeling are without substance because they have actually succeeded in doing what they insist Button had denied could be done, namely, to equip computers to follow rules and to engage in conversation. Further, Chapman, (1992) describes his intention to build with his colleague, Susan Stucky, a natural language system of which he says:

We do not expect to claim that the implemented system *does* engage in conversation, act as a social agent, perform conversation repair, and so on. We view it rather as a mechanized philosophical Gedankenexperiment. Here, we will say, is a system that does things that *look* like conversation, social action, repair, and so forth; and that it meets criteria that have been set forth for those activities. (Chapman, 1992; italics in original)

The way in which Chapman phrases the argument is important because it does not just reduce the matter to a hypothesis to be tested as Frohlich and Luff and Wooffitt and Fraser seem to do (to paraphrase: Button says we cannot build a system that converses, we say we can; the test is to build one or fail, and we believe that we have succeeded). The important question, however, is: *even* if a system was built (which Chapman seems to be confident about) that produced in some way something that looked like conversation, could we intelligibly say that the machine is conversing? Chapman's argument is that Button's previous argument does not preclude us from saying yes.

We would, however, have hoped that people would have learned from the mistakes of AI. Hubert Dreyfus's (1993) persistence in mapping the discrepancy between the overweening claims made for work on computer design and the realities of those achievements, together with his insistence on pointing out the intrinsic implausibility of those claims might have brought about greater caution in the interpretation of the achievements effected by computer simulations. The ready and optimistic assumption that machines can do what human beings do nonetheless seems to persist and be uncritically held.

The fact that human beings carry on conversations in accord with rules (of turn taking, inter alia) and the fact that computers run according to programs (which can be formulated as expressions of rules) lead some to think that there is therefore no difference between a person following a rule and a computer being programmed in terms of a set of rules, and that, therefore, the programming of a computer in terms of the model of conversational rule following would establish that the computer is now "conversing" in the same sense as a human conversationalist. The idea that modest "empirical" exercises in computational simulation of activities, including those of conversation, should invite fundamental revaluation of our place within the scheme of things seems to be seriously disproportionate: the modest empirical exercises that are offered[8] are merely a distraction in relation to what is in fact a *conceptual* controversy.

There is a difference between conceptual and empirical issues, and the resolution of the latter does nothing to contribute to the former. The construction of more elaborate and, in terms of simulation, successful systems does not support the argument that a dialogic machine can really converse in the sense in which human beings do. It merely reproduces the same issues as are presented by the simplest of devices. Thus, when Wooffitt and MacDermid (this volume) assert that "the debate seems to have been conducted around 'in principle' issues" and has involved "an argument that the nature of conversational interaction is such that it is in principle pointless trying to model it in computer systems," they follow the persistent pattern of treating the "in principle" argument as though it was meant to restrict practical exercises (which, since the conceptual and empirical issues are independent, it could not do).

The claim that, by modeling, on computers, language, conversation, or any other human activity, one cannot thereby endow the system with the capacities involved in the human use of language, engagement in conversation, and so forth is most decidedly not to suggest that one cannot model language or conversation on a computer, let alone that it is "pointless" to do so. The argument is *necessarily* an "in principle" one, because it is not – at least in its central features – about whether one in fact could build systems capable of passing the Turing Test. The argument is over the interpretation that is to be set on the passing of such a test. Searle's "Chinese room" argument, for example, is specifically designed to grant that it would be possible, in principle, to design a system – even out of beer cans – that would pass the test, but Searle then goes on to deny that the passing of the test establishes that the system understands the language that it so convincingly simulates. It has, in his terms, no syntax. In the same way, our argument allows that it may be both interesting and productive to simulate conversations on computers, without thereby granting that the line between person and computer system must be redrawn.

As we have said, the issue as to whether computers can converse or follow rules are not new ones; they are merely renewed applications of the reasoning that underlies the Turing Test. The mistake is with respect to understanding what is demonstrated by simulations. The Turing Test is based upon the idea that if people cannot discriminate one thing from another, there is no essential difference between them. Thus, if one can generate computer output – by voice synthesis, say – that cannot be distinguished from the contribution of a human participant in a conversation, then one has shown that a computer can do what a human being can, and that if the performance of the corresponding role by a human being would involve intelligence, then so too must the performance of the machine.

However, by the canons of the Turing Test, a whole range of intelligible human action is ruled out of court. For example, there would be no such thing as forgery. The fact one could produce a note or coin or signature that is indistinguishable from the officially issued currency or from the authentic signature does not mean that the note, coin, or signature is therefore an instance of a bone fide currency or of a legitimate signing. A forgery may be indistinguishable on immediate inspection – or indeed after intense examination – from a genuine item, but it remains a forgery nonetheless: its status as a forgery may be revealed by its serial number or the like. The fact is that formal similarities do not ensure identity, and the fact that one may be able to reproduce, on the computer, many sequences of conversation that *formally* resemble the sequences of conversation, which may indeed be formally indistinguishable from them, does not demonstrate that one has thereby enabled a computer to converse in the way that human beings do. However successful simulations of conversational sequences may be with respect to their indistinguishability, this does nothing to meet the objection that there is a difference between a genuine performance and its simulation. No matter how sophisticated (certainly they would have to be more sophisticated than the efforts of those who have claimed to have "done it" to pass) a computer simulation of a conversational sequence might be, it could not be described as "conversing" in the way in which humans can be so described.

Actually, the production of simulations that can pass a Turing-type test for conversational sequences does not in fact seem all that difficult. Weizenbaum's (1976) case of the Eliza program was one such, but its contrivance was a matter of great simplicity. Similarly, Harold Garfinkel (1967), using a graduate student and a table of random numbers, was able to simulate the verbal exchanges of a counseling transaction to the extent that it could deceive some people, but this does not mean that any *counseling* was taking place. That one could contrive much more sophisticated ways of simulating conversational sequences, much more closely modeled on the ways in which conversationalists organize their talk, would not make a qualitative difference to the question of whether the machine's products are simulations of conversational sequences.

The claims that conversation analysis has been or could be used to inform the development of conversing computers is, on these arguments, fallacious. If the argument cannot be appropriately clarified then the specification of appropriate role for conversation analysis in HCI is wrong-footed. In order to continue to try to restore the balance we will now turn to the vexed and troublesome issue of the relationship between following rules and programming computers.

6.3 Following rules and programming computers

The argument of "Going up a Blind Alley" was directed centrally at the question of whether computers, however sophisticated the model of conversation used to program them, could follow rules. This argument had two parts: (1) that the way in which conversationalists are described (in ethnomethodology and conversational analysis) as following rules is not in fact the way they are imagined to by those who want to argue that computers can follow rules as conversationalists do; (2) that computers do not themselves follow rules of conversation when they are programmed on the basis of a model of conversation, which may itself be formulated in terms of rules. Both parts of the argument addressed the question of what it is to follow a rule. Critics have argued that it is possible for computers to follow rules in the way that human beings do. Thus Hirst writes:

> Button seems to be saying nothing more than that CA rules must be represented declaratively, not procedurally, so that they can be deliberately and explicitly invoked with a view to their effect. But far from precluding their use by a computer, this argument suggests that they fit very nicely into present-day AI reasoning systems! (Hirst, 1991)[9]

The initial claim was that rules of conversation do not determine the conversationalist's sequence of actions but are "oriented to" by conversationalists in the organization of their talk and that in order to program a computer these rules would have to be deterministically conceived. Critics have sought to assert that computers *do* orient to rules and *are not* themselves determined by those rules. However, it seems to us that the crucial point about conversation has nothing to do with the character of computer programming and modeling, and everything to do with the understanding of the nature of what is being modeled, namely, conversation.

The failure to understand the role of "rules" in conversation that the previous critics have shown is, for the practical purposes of this chapter, to fail to understand the role of the "simplest systematics" model in the work of conversation analysis.[10] The actual issues have to do with the understanding of how language, conversation, and social action are related. In order to lay the ground for understanding what the appropriate relationship between conversation analysis and HCI is, we will turn to these issues in three steps: first, we will argue that the simplest systematics is about utterance design, and that those who dissociate the formal model from the body of the paper are likely to misinterpret the status of that model; second, that utterance design is essentially unformalizable; and, third, that the simplest systematics is about the organization of action and interaction, not about linguistic structures.

6.3.1 Utterance design

The appeal of the simplest systematics to those engaged in computer design may relatively easily be understood: the model expressed in the paper would seem to emulate a computer program, and it comprises a formal, recursive representation of the ways in which turns at talk are distributed in succession.

However, the simplest systematics was not intended to be a thoroughgoing formalization of the procedures whereby conversation is conducted or through which the business of turn transition management was arranged. On the contrary, one of conversational analysis's basic objectives was to oppose the view that ordinary talk could be extensively formalized in the ways envisaged by those who would see speaking as the application of a calculus. The simplest systematics was an abstraction out of a rich and detailed description of the practices whereby conversationalists ascertain who should speak next and determine what business the turns so allocated should do. It is only for purposes of simplified exposition that the question of turn transition management can be separated from the business of utterance design, a point which Sacks, Schegloff, and Jefferson not only state clearly in the following passage, but which they also persistently demonstrate in their analytic practice:

By contrast with . . . other speech-exchange systems, the turn-taking organisation for conversation makes no provision for the content of any turn, nor does it constrain what is (to be) done in any turn. That is not to say that there are no constraints on what may be done in any turn, for that is clearly not the case. "First turns" in a structurally characterizable set of circumstances properly take "greetings," and "next turns" can in a variety of closely describable ways be constrained by "prior turns." We note only that in conversation such constraints are organised by systems external to the turn-taking system. (Sacks et al., 1974)

The simplest systematics, and the analysis of other aspects of the turn-taking arrangements, operates at the level of alternating *utterance types*. The example of "adjacency pairs" (Sacks, 1993a; Schegloff and Sacks, 1973) is often used to exhibit these relations. Thus, it is the case that there is a normative requirement that, given a question is asked in the current utterance, the appropriate and immediate next utterance should be the provision of an answer. The grasp on the normative requirements of the adjacency pair thus solves this problem for the conversationalist: given an utterance of the first type, a question, has occurred, what kind of next utterance is appropriate? It is, of course, an answer. Note, however, the relationship in any actual conversation is not between "a question" and "an answer" but between *"the* question" and "an *answer to that* question." It is not, therefore, the case that conversationalists produce "utterance types"; they produce utterances which instantiate those types, and to be aware of the requirement to produce an answer in the next position is not to be in possession of any indication as to *what* answer to locate in that slot. Furthermore, the fact that the adjacency pair requirements specify that an answer should follow the question must not only be considered from the point of view of the alternation of the utterance types, but also from the way in which the structure of the utterance achieves the perpetuation of the turn transitional arrangements.[11]

The fact that the model specifies that one utterance type should succeed another says nothing about how the occupants of the type's slot should be designed to fulfill their sequential function or how they should be designed to articulate the further organization of the turn-taking sequence, to manifest their appropriate place within that sequence, to effect their tying with the prior utterance, or to achieve a further orderly transition of speaker turns. This will become particularly important when we consider the conversationalist's "problem" of locating "turn transitional relevance place" by projecting the completion of a turn.

6.3.2 The unformalizable character of conversation

A great deal of conversation analysis has been concerned with what we are here calling "utterance design" and the "turn articulation" aspects of such design – that is, with the way in which the utterances making up the turn are assembled in relation to their sequential placement among other utterances. It is not, for example, that the "answer" position is to be filled with something that provides an answer to the question, but that it be constructed such that it is recognizably, from its outset, going to provide the answer to that question. Thus, there has been a considerable amount of work on, inter alia, the ways in which turns at talk exhibit, in their construction, sensitivity to the identities of the conversationalists (Sacks, and Schegloff, 1979), their placement within a protracted sequence of utterances (Button and Casey, 1985a; 1985b; Sacks, 1975), the sound patterns that have antedated them (Schegloff, 1986), the purposes of interlocutors, the availability of shared knowledge (Sacks, 1986), the specifics of the relationship being carried out by the talk (Sacks, 1975), the business being done (Drew and Heritage, 1992), and the delicacy of the matters to be handled (Schegloff, 1980). There is an extensive literature on such matters.

Similarly, there have been extensive examinations of the ways in which pauses (Schegloff and Sacks, 1973), overlaps (Sacks et al., 1974; Schegloff, 1987), self-corrections (Schegloff, Jefferson, and Sacks, 1977), other-corrections (Schegloff et al., 1977), anticipation of errors (Jefferson, 1974), laughter (Jefferson, 1984), and multifarious other features of talk play their part in relating utterances in sequences. The relevant point about the extensive collection of such studies is, here, however, that they are *unformalized*. This is not, however, necessarily an accidental fact, but a representation of the fact that the phenomena are themselves intractable to formalization. Defense of this latter claim cannot be extensively made again here, and we will only say that the thrust of Sacks's work, and the work of conversation analysis in general, was to highlight the localized and particularized nature of the "determinants" of utterance design and turn articulation and to exhibit the ways in which these are evasive of efforts at representation in formal abstractions. The *isolation* of the simplest systematics from the analyses of the ad hoc situated work of the organization of "a single conversation" will inevitably result in a misreading of the nature of the former.

6.3.3 The organization of human action and interaction

There seems to be a strong temptation to overlook the extent to which conversation analysis is concerned with the organization of social actions, not with structures of language. The fact that many of those taking an interest in conversation analysis have backgrounds in linguistics and related disciplines may lead them to think that the study of conversation is primarily about "utterances" as linguistic forms but this is not so; it is very predominantly concerned with the "actions that utterances do."

The analysis of the turn-taking mechanism was itself subordinate to the fact that the utterances that conversationalists generate are produced to construct "the unit of a single conversation," with that unit being understood to be a self-organizing entity. Thus, the turns at talk do not merely "occupy" slots that are preallocated for them but in fact constitute the organization of the conversation of which they are a part, projecting and managing its unfolding and developing course. It is often the function of one utterance to generate another, and that same utterance thereby projects the character and course of the conversational sequence to which it might constitute, for example, the beginning.

For the very simplest example, consider the question: "Are you busy?" It calls for an answer, perhaps of a yes/no kind. However, the question "Are you busy?" often projects a course of conversation, and perhaps a kind of conversation. To ask "Are you busy?" may be to preface the asking of yet another question, which might be the question "Do you want to come round to our house for dinner?" (Schegloff, 1980). It might, alternatively, be that the question "Are you busy?" might project the possibility of a long conversation – it asks whether one is free to talk extensively now.[12] Thus, the production of utterances is not the mere allocation of talk to slots, but the construction of the very sequence that the utterances will compose. The design of turns at talk is, then, a matter of managing social interaction, and the ways in which such design accomplishes that management is also unformalized.

Furthermore, conversations are not only exchanges of talk, they are vehicles through which the conduct of social life is done, and particular turns at talk must be designed to perform the social actions relevant to the occasion or setting within which they are situated and of which they are constituent. As Sacks (1993a) aptly demonstrated in the very first lecture in his collected lectures,[13] the talk he was examining is organized by a person staffing the phone line at a suicide prevention center to elicit the caller's name for the organizational business of creating a client record. The recipient of the call, the suicide prevention volunteer, is not merely seeking a name as part of an exchange of identifications, but because the collection of a name is a bureaucratically required operation, and the fact that such a quest for identification is undertaken is not a requirement of "conversation" but of the record-keeping procedures of the bureaucracy.

The relationship between an utterance's linguistic form and the social action that it performs is not one that is formally specifiable. That something is "an answer," let alone that it is "*the* answer," is not something that is determinable from its formal features: that an utterance is a "candidate answer" might be determinable from the fact that it occurs in adjacency to a prior question. And, of course, whether it is *the* answer depends upon (1) what the question asks about and (2) what would answer the question. Thus "Are you busy?" may ask "Are you free to talk to me?" in which case "I'll be free in five minutes" might be the answer. If the question "Are you busy?" asks a taxi driver whether he has been working hard overnight, then the reply "I haven't had a fare for two hours" could then constitute the answer. "I'll be free in five minutes" gains its status as an answer not from its intrinsic features but from its placement as a response to the question, for the same utterance could, of course, provide an opening utterance or the preparation for an invitation.

6.4 Simulations of conversation

The force of the preceding remarks relates to two distinct issues. The first is the extent to which, in drawing upon the model of turn taking in conversation one can hope to construct simulations of conversations, and whether, in so doing, one would have simulated the procedures and practices of conversationalists. The second is whether, indeed, one has done more than *simulate* the procedures and practices of conversationalists, whether one has equipped the computer with the same conversational capacities as human beings. We will address these issues in turn.

6.4.1 Simulations of conversation and human practice

In the light of the arguments we have put forward in the preceding section we can now argue that the programming of computers to simulate conversational exchanges with users would require being able to program in vastly more than the rules of conversational sequences and the categorical titles of utterance types – for example, question, answer – that compose such sequences. One would have to equip the computers with the capacities of "utterance design" for (1) turn articulation, (2) the management of the conversation's course and organization, and (3) the capacity to conduct the social actions constituent of particular activities. Plainly, the fact that these topics are very far from systematically worked out, let alone specified in any formal way, means that the use of the turn-taking model to deliver simulations of conversational sequences must be a long way from setting them up to do anything directly comparable with what conversationalists do. It is not, after all, a matter of programming a ready-made model onto a computer, but of having to construct a model de novo and in instances in which the phenomena may resist formalization (as the phenomena of natural language use have persistently done).

6.4.2 Let's pretend conversation can be formalized

For the sake of argument, let us pretend, however, that one could achieve such formalizations. Suppose that one could specify the way in which conversationalists organize their activity so that this could be exhaustively implemented in a program. Would this not then ensure that computers *can* do what conversationalists do?

In this regard consider the fact that Wes Sharrock, after much practise, can now write out a perfect replication of Graham Button's signature. However, he cannot thereby be said to sign Graham Button's checks. Wes Sharrock can write Graham Button's signature so impeccably that a check on which he had inscribed it would pass all tests as to its payability, but this does not mean that Wes Sharrock, because he signs himself Graham Button is Graham Button, or that, in so signing himself he does what Graham Button does when he signs that name: Wes may sign himself Graham, but in so doing he does not (as Graham does when he uses that signature) sign with his own name. He signs with someone else's name, and the action of signing with someone else's name is a very different action from signing with one's own name. Further, of course, the action that is accomplished by signing with the other's name is very different from that accomplished by signing with one's own. Graham withdraws money from his bank account by signing his name, Wes steals money from Graham's bank account by signing with Graham's name. That Wes can only simulate Graham's signature, that he can only simulate drawing checks on Graham's account and cannot *validly* sign checks drawing on Graham's account has got nothing to do with his capacity to simulate Graham's signing behavior and everything to do with his being Wes and not Graham. It is his being *who* he is that determines the validity of his action of signing a name, of how he stands to the signature that he writes, *and so it is with computers and the utterances that they generate.* It is because it is *Wes* signing Graham's name that Wes is *only simulating* Graham's signature and it is because it is *a computer* printing out, or even sounding out something that looks or sounds like contributions to a conversational sequence that the computer can *only simulate* what a human conversationalist is doing.

There is the matter, if we may borrow his terminology, of what J. L. Austin labeled felicity conditions (Austin, 1962). The capacity of an utterance to perform an act or to have a certain force depends upon certain *conditions of its production* being appropriately arranged. Among those conditions are, of course, the endowment of the utterer with appropriate characteristics and capacities, and to endow a computer with the capacity to utter declarations of marriage, invitations to dinner, expressions of affection or contempt (and not just simulate these) would require one to endow it with *capacities,* not to equip it with programs.

We are arguing then, that the claims accompanying the suggestion that it is possible to build a conversing computer make the same order of mistake as that made by AI. In "Going up A Blind Alley" the point was made that the practical consequence of this is to deflect attention away from what is practicable and, with respect to conversation analysis, what the practical utility of its work might be for computer designers. We have here, been trying to lay the specter of the conversing computer in the same grave as the intelligent computer. We do not fool ourselves that we will have let these inflated claims down, but we have at least been trying to clear the field of unnecessary obstacles so that those in HCI can better see what is available and have a better appreciation of what is possible.

6.5 So, what use is conversational analysis to HCI?

We have insisted that conceptual and empirical arguments be kept separate, and we have been giving a conceptual argument against the conflation of human actions and computer simulations, a problem that is by no means unique to controversy about the development of natural language interfaces.[14] We now turn to a more detailed consideration of the problems in advancing the development of natural language interfaces. The fact that we have rejected suggestions that the development of complex natural language interfaces will eliminate the difference between human beings and machines says nothing about our views as to whether complex natural language interfaces can be built. The attribution to us of a 'conservatism' about the possibility or value of attempts to build such interfaces would be entirely misplaced, for the objective seems a reasonable one, though we must add, without the large significance attributed to it. Our skepticism about some current developments in HCI and about the role of "conversation analysis" is not, we hasten to add, a general skepticism about the utility of conversation analysis in the development of natural language interfaces. On the contrary, we certainly see it as a reasonable expectation that conversation analysis could be used in this context.

Our reservations pertain to *the way* in which conversation analysis is being brought into this. In respect of our first argument, we have objected to the way in which some (very simple) simulations attempting to use conversation analysis are associated with the unjustified claims about the capacity of computers "to behave like human beings." In respect of our second theme, our reservations are about the way in which conversation analysis is being (mis)understood. The ways in which current advocates of conversation analysis approach the problem of implementing the rules, for example, is conceived as a matter of mapping the potential distribution of utterance forms in sequence – thus Gilbert, Wooffitt, and Fraser (1990) enumerate a range of possible combinations in which adjacency pairs might succeed one another, but characterize those sequences entirely in formal terms of utterance types. When it comes to the issue of what is to occupy these turns, however, we are offered only characterizations of sentences in terms of their formal grammatical features. Since conversation analysis has persistently argued that the interactional function of utterances does not relate in any one-to-one way to their form, it is difficult to see how one could program a machine not merely to permute the sequence of possible slots but to generate occupants for them. These efforts appear to be stepping boldly – but perhaps unwittingly – into the gulf between conversation analysis and formal linguistics.

Since there is not available any *systematic* way of mapping sentences onto utterance type sequences, the basis for generating sequences of "turns" rather than mere enumeration of formal possibilities must be something other than the systematic resources of either conversation analysis or formal linguistics. It is, of course, the commonsense understandings that the would-be programmers have of the organization of talk in the domain for which they are building their simulation, a domain with an appropriately restricted set of possibilities, such that they can specify certain utterances in advance. In other words, the computer's contribution is specifically programmed in, and the user is provided with a set of prescribed possibilities, as is manifest in the example of an *Advice System* provided by Frohlich and Luff (1990: 191). Frohlich and Luff have had to use their commonsense understandings of the range of possibilities within the limited domain the system is relevant for and have had to program in those possibilities. Thus if the system was placed within another domain, it could not possibly work, or would only work, in ways different to what they might suppose.[15] We do not want necessarily to derogate such attempts to develop workable interfaces or to contest any suggestion that this one might be useful. Our only point is that such systems *do not* in anything other than the most limited possible ways realize "conversational procedures."

There is a considerable distance, then, between the understanding of conversation as a mechanical permutation of sequencing possibilities (something that can readily be programmed) and of understanding actual, naturally occurring conversation as an essentially *improvised* activity, something that is not prescribed in advance with respect to its constituent utterances and activities. Clearly, then, the development of natural language interfaces that aim to enable the possibility of elaborate exchanges that are not predominantly formated in advance will need to be much more sensitive to the ways in which conversational sequences are actually put together. It is with respect to sensitizing researchers to the ways in which improvised sequences of talk are *methodically* developed in relation to the specifics of the occasion and the activities involved in it that conversation analysis may have a significant role to play.[16]

We do not mean here that one can gut conversation of its findings and offer those up as possible programming rules. That is what we have argued against and that has been the way in which those against whom we rail have proceeded. We mean, instead, that conversation analysis may provide a way of elucidating the design specifications for particular applications by showing what *functional equivalents* of conversational mechanisms would have to be built. Thus, rather than conceiving of conversation analysis as a treasure chest to be pawed through for valuable rules of conversation to be then turned into programming rules, we want to argue that conversation analysis may provide designers with an understanding of the specifications of a system and that designers will then have to develop functional equivalents to the conversational mechanisms. We can illustrate this with one simple example which is that in order to build a simulacrum of conversation it is necessary to develop the *functional equivalent* of *the projection of turn transition relevance places.*

The system for turn taking prescribes that upon the completion of a speaker's turn, a next speaker should commence speaking. The immediate completion of the first speaker's turn is the occasion for the commencement of the next speaker's turn. The "massive fact" of human conversation is that there is minimal gap and overlap between turns at talk, that immediately upon the termination of one speaker's turn another begins to talk (Sacks et al., 1974). There is an issue of timing and coordination between speakers here. The putative next speaker must be able to determine the point at which the current speaker has finished a turn and also what to say in response to that turn. The putative next speaker must be able to determine, then, what a completed turn at talk would be, and must, indeed, be able to anticipate how a turn at talk that is currently in its course will have turned out. If matters were otherwise, then the putative next speaker would have to wait until an utterance was already completed to determine its character and closing. One could determine that a speaker had finished a turn by the fact that silence had fallen but this would require a gap before the commencement of a next turn. In any case, there are "within turn" silences, such that silence itself is not a sure indicator of a completed turn.[17]

Sacks et al. (1974) describe how it is that this timing and coordination is organized around what they call "possible turn transition relevance places." It is a foundational feature of their model that the occurrence of such places can be *projected* by conversationalists in the course of a given turn at talk. It is possible for natural language users to anticipate, from the beginnings and early stage of its production, what the resulting character of a completed utterance is going to be, and therefore what kind of construction would compose a complete utterance of that type. Thus, in the simplest case, the commencement of an utterance with a "wh" may project that it is going to turn out to be a question, and hearers can determine what a complete question might be; though, in the course of talk, the anticipation about the shape of the turn may be revised.

That conversationalists *can* undertake such projections of turn completion is something on which the simplest systematics is entirely dependent. *How* they do this is, however, something that, from the point of view of conversation analysis, is unknown. Furthermore for a sytematic analysis of this capacity we should not look to a linguistics built upon a top-down conception of language structure, for the projection of a turn's shape is assuredly a "left-to-right" feature. One can determine from the-turn-so-far what the character of the-turn-as-a-whole might be. This obviously has, in part, to do with the functional character of the utterance, with the kind of utterance type that is projected, but only in part.

In the immediate present, the prospect of constructing a simulation of ordinary conversation is going to be lacking in procedures for achieving this essential feature of *projecting* turn completion, and thus the management of turn transition will *not* be arranged in the way that it is in conversation. However, the necessity for turn transition relevance is something that conversation analysis would suggest, and a requirement for the development of dialogue systems will therefore be, among a host of other requirements, the *functional equivalent* of a turn transition relevance place, though not perhaps one that is directed toward meeting the no gap–no overlap requirement.

It is in this respect that we do not believe that the role that conversation analysis may play in the development of natural language interfaces is to provide rules of conversation, such as the rules involved in Sacks et al.'s turn-taking model, to be then turned into programming rules, for the model does not, nor was meant to, account for the capabilities of the projection of utterance completion. However, if designers are building a natural language system, then conversation analysis clearly provides specifications for the system, for the system will need to have some functional equivalent of the projection of utterance completion. We are arguing that conversation analysis has an important part to play in the development of requirements for a natural language system in terms of its use in the development of functional equivalents to the organizational activities it has described as being engaged in by speakers and hearers.

6.6 Conclusion

We have been attempting to clarify some of the issues that surround the attempt to develop natural language interfaces and the role of conversation analysis in this process. We have been pursing two major themes in this respect. The first is to disentangle conceptual issues from empirical issues, and the second is, in the light of this, to argue what we understand to be the appropriate and practical use of conversation analysis in the design process for language interfaces.

We have pursued the first theme not only because we think that it is as important to understand that the idea of a conversing machine is as wrong as the idea that machines can be intelligent but also because we believe that the conflation of conceptual and empirical issues has resulted in some confused thinking with regard to attempts to address the second theme. It is in part because we understand conversation analysis to have a role in the design of natural language interfaces through its unique position within the human sciences to provide specifications of utterance design that we want to argue our point forcefully, and have attempted the present clarification, for it seems to us that the role of conversation analysis in natural language interface design has been promulgated not only with a poor understanding of what computers as machines are, but also without a proper understanding of what conversation analysts have attempted with respect to their descriptions of talk-in-interaction. Conversation analysis has a role in the development of specifications of simulacrums of conversation, not as the provider of programming rules for conversing machines.

Notes

1. The range of concerns with the social has become quite wide. See Grudin (1988) for an early and interesting development, and Robertson (1993) and Seely Brown and Duguid (forthcoming) for recent suggestions as to the further development of the social within design.
2. To a very large extent the development of CSCW has been occasioned by the attempts of some previously associated with the cognitive foundations of HCI turning to the social. See Schmidt and Bannon (1992).
3. We are not surveying the range of possible uses that conversation analysis might have in HCI, but only debating certain claims about its use and significance in the development of natural language interfaces. We do not consider, e.g., the use of conversation analysis as a methodological device for HCI, encouraging the closer and more systematic examination of data-recording transactions between users and systems as pioneered by Suchman (1987) and as recommended by Wooffitt and MacDermid and by Douglas in this volume.
4. See the contributions to Luff, Gilbert, and Frohlich (1990).
5. We are careful to state that it is turn taking that has been (relatively) formally modeled, for though turn taking is a fundamental feature of conversation we must add that the organization of "naturally occurring conversation" does not by any means consist only in its turn-taking arrangements.
6. Within the collection in which it appeared, it was so rebuffed by Frohlich and Luff (1990) and by Gilbert, Wooffitt, and Fraser (1990). In addition, other aspects of the argument have been challenged by Fraser and Wooffitt (1990), Hirst (1991), and, in part, Chapman (1992).
7. We are also mindful that, while some may have been convinced by some parts of the previous argument, they have been less convinced by other parts, offering what they see as exceptions to the exclusion of conversing machines, and requesting that these exceptions be addressed through rethinking and sharpening what they construe as criteria for exclusion (Chapman, 1992). This seems, to us, a perfectly reasonable request and this an opportunity to oblige.
8. E.g., see Fraser and Wooffitt (1990).
9. We find Chapman's (1992) response to Hirst an interesting one. Chapman writes: "This valiant attempt fails to answer Button's criticisms. First, the rules are still representations. Hirst's analysis is exactly wrong: the point is not that rules should be represented declaratively, but that they should be represented *at all*. Second, though individual rules are not causally efficacious, the system as a whole is; the logic of the combined rule set cannot be violated. Third, there is no account of the sense in which the rules have the force of social norms" (italics in original).
10. We are aware that some in HCI have found in conversation analysis more resources to aid them in their work than just the model of the turn-taking system. However, we cannot discuss the whole range of such resources here and so have taken the interest shown in the turn-taking model as our focus.
11. Sacks's extended examination of adjacency pairs in a series of five lectures given in 1972 forcefully illustrates the interrelationship of utterance design and the management of the turn-taking system, for Sacks describes how adjacency pairs are a major device for the selection of next speakers, and how they are a systematic means for achieving two of the massive facts about conversation, which is that turn taking takes place with the minimization of gap and overlap (Sacks, 1993b: 521–569, lectures 1–5).

12. These examples display the reason why it is that conversation analysis places much store in the use of empirical material, for it is only in the context of actual courses of action and interaction that people can make these determinations.
13. Sacks (1993a: 3–11, lecture 1): "Rules of Conversational Sequence."
14. We would like to remind readers that we are only limiting ourselves to a consideration of the role of conversation analysis in the design of natural language interfaces and that we see it having further and other roles to play in the design of computer systems.
15. Garfinkel's (1967) study that we cited is relevant here, for he found that randomly given counseling advice to student questions was made intelligible by the students.
16. The intelligibility of the machine output to a user will, after all, be an increasingly delicate problem as the transactions being programmed for become more complicated.
17. Schegloff and Sacks (1973) consider these issues in their discussion of the closing section of conversation.

References

Austin, J. L. (1962). *How to do things with words* (Oxford: Oxford University Press).

Bowers, J., and Rodden, T. (1993). Exploding the interface: Experiences of a CSCW network. In *Human Factors in Computing Systems: INTERCHI '93 Proceedings* (New York: ACM Press), 255–262.

Button, G. (1990). Going up a Blind Alley: Conflating conversation analysis and computational modelling. In P. Luff, N. Gilbert, and D. Frohlich (eds.), *Computers and conversation* (San Diego: Academic Press), 67–90.

Button, G., and Casey, N. (1985a). Generating topic: The use of topic initial elicitors. In J. Atkinson and J. Heritage (eds.), *Structures of social action* (Cambridge: Cambridge University Press).

Button, G., and Casey, N. (1985b). Topic nomination and topic pursuit. *Human Studies,* 8.

Chapman, D. (1992). Computer rules, conversational rules. *Computational Linguistics,* 18 (4).

Drew, P., and Heritage, J. (eds) (1992). *Talk at work: Interaction in institutional settings* (Cambridge: Cambridge University Press).

Dreyfus, H. L. (1993). *What computers still can't do: A critique of artificial reason* (Cambridge, Mass.: MIT Press).

Fraser, N. M., and. Wooffitt, R. C. (1990). Orienting to rules. In N. Gilbert (ed.), *Workshop on ethnomethodology and conversation analysis* (Boston: American Association For Artificial Intelligence), 69–80.

Frohlich, D., and. Luff, P. (1990). Applying the technology of conversation to the technology for conversation. In P. Luff, N. Gilbert, and D. Frohlich (eds.), *Computers and conversation* (San Diego: Academic Press), 187–220.

Garfinkel, H. (1967). *Studies in ethnomethodology* (Englewood Cliffs, N.J.: Prentice-Hall).

Gilbert, N., Wooffitt, R., and Fraser, N. (1990). Organising computer talk. In P. Luff, N. Gilbert, and D. Frohlich (eds.), *Computers and conversation* (San Diego: Academic Press), 235–257.

Goguen, J. A. (1992). The dry and the wet. In E. Falkenberg, C. Rolland, and El-Sayed Nasr-El-Dein (eds.), *Information system concepts* (Amsterdam: Elsevier North-Holland).

Goguen, J. A. (forthcoming). Requirements engineering as the reconciliation of technical and social issues. In M. Jirotka and J. A. Goguen (eds.), *Reconceptualising requirements* (San Diego: Academic Press).

Grudin, J. (1988). Why CSCW applications fail: Problems in the design and evaluation of organisational interfaces. In *Proceedings of the Conference on Computer-Supported Cooperative Work (CSCW '88),* Oregon. (New York: ACM Press), 85–93.

Grudin, J. (1990). The computer reaches out: The historical continuity of interface design. In *Human Factors in Computing Systems: CHI '90, Proceedings* (New York: ACM Press), 261–268.

Hirst, G. (1991). Does conversation analysis have a role in computational linguistics? *Computational Linguistics,* 17 (2), 211–227.

Jefferson, G. (1974). Error correction as an interactional resource. *Language in Society,* 3 (2).

Jefferson, G. (1984). On the organization of laughter in talk about troubles. In J. Atkinson and J. Heritage (eds.), *Structures of social action: Studies in conversation analysis* (Cambridge: Cambridge University Press).

Luff, P., Gilbert, N., and D. Frohlich (eds.). (1990). *Computers and conversation* (San Diego: Academic Press).

McIlvenny, P. (1990). Communicative action and computers: Re-embodying conversation analysis? In P. Luff, N. Gilbert, and D. Frohlich (eds.), *Computers and conversation* (San Diego: Academic Press), 91–132.

Reichman, R. (1985). *Getting computers to talk like you and me* (Cambridge, Mass.: MIT Press).

Robertson, R. I. (1993). What to do with the human factor: A manifesto of sorts. *American Centre for design,* 7 (1), 63–73.

Sacks, H. (1975). Everyone has to lie. In B. Blount and M. Sanches (eds.), *Sociocultural dimensions of language use* (New York: Academic Press).

Sacks, H. (1986). Some considerations of a story told in ordinary conversations. *Poetics,* 15.

Sacks, H. (1993a). *Lectures on conversation,* vol. I (Oxford: Blackwell).

Sacks, H. (1993b). *Lectures on conversation,* vol. II. (Oxford: Blackwell).

Sacks, H., and Schegloff, E. A. (1979). Two preferences in the organization of reference to persons in conversation and their interaction. In G. Psalthas (ed.), *Everyday language: Studies in ethnomethodology* (New York: Irvington).

Sacks, H., Schegloff, E. A., and Jefferson, G. (1974). A simplest systematics for the organization of turn-taking for conversation. *Language,* 50, 696–735.

Schegloff, E. A. (1980). Preliminaries to preliminaries: "Can I Ask You a Question ?" *Sociological Enquiry,* 50.

Schegloff, E. A. (1986). The routine as achievement. *Human Studies,* 9 (2–3), 111–151.

Schegloff, E. A. (1987). Recycled turn beginnings: A precise repair mechanism in conversation's turn-taking organisation. In G. Button and J. R. E. Lee (eds.), *Talk and social organisation* (Clevedon: Multilingual Matters), 70–85.

Schegloff, E. A., Jefferson, G., and Sacks, H. (1977). The preference for self-correction in the organization of repair in conversation. *Language,* 53, 361–382.

Schegloff, E. A., and Sacks, H. (1973). Opening up closings. *Semiotica,* 7.

Schmidt, K., and Bannon, L. (1992). Taking CSCW seriously: Supporting articulation work. *Computer Supported Cooperative Work,* 1 (1–2), 7–40.

Seely Brown, J., and Duguid, P. (forthcoming). Borderline issues: Social and material aspects of design.

Suchman, L. (1987). *Plans and situated actions: The problem of human–machine communication* (Cambridge: Cambridge University Press).

Weizenbaum, J. (1976). *Computer power and human reason* (London: Freeman).

7
Wizards and social control
Robin Wooffitt and Catriona MacDermid

7.1 Introduction

Compared with the development of other forms of sophisticated computer-based technological artifacts, the production of interactive speech systems is at a relatively early stage in its history. The systems currently in production or already existing are unsophisticated machines. One feature of this unsophistication is their inflexibility in their dealings with actual human users. The primary problem is that systems simply cannot cope with the full range of spontaneous and natural verbal behavior that humans produce and deal with routinely in the course of everyday interaction. System designers are reacting to this problem by developing speech-based interactive computer systems in such a way that they can constrain the range of behaviors produced by a human user, thereby ensuring that the system has a better chance of engaging in successful and useful dialogue with real people.

We can apply a sociological gloss to this development (albeit loosely). We can characterize contemporary system designers as being in the business of trying to devise methods of social control. This is because interactive systems are being designed in such a way to ensure that normal spontaneous human behavior is being curtailed, and other, more restricted patterns of behavior are being implemented and encouraged. System designers are forced, by the sheer complexity of the task they face, to design the speech recognition facilities of their systems so that they can constrain and control the actions of human users. Of course, these methods of social control are in no way as insidious as methods of social control normally considered in sociological and political studies: for example, the use of armed forces or media propaganda in totalitarian states. But they are forms of social control nonetheless.

This is, of course, a paradoxical state of affairs: for so long the overriding ethos within the community of system designers has been to try to ensure that the system is *user-friendly*. This has certainly dominated the work of those engineers who design non-speech-based system interfaces. Considerable effort has been expended to ensure that systems not only facilitate work practices that seem natural, but also avoid the imposition of working conditions that perplex and impede the user.

In the development of speech-based interfaces, however, this ethos seems to have received little support.[1] It certainly seems to be of little concern to those who devise menu-led systems. And although interactive systems are being designed to sound as much like humans as is possible, and to respond in ways that humans might recognize and with which they may feel comfortable, a primary underlying motivation is to constrain human behavior to assist the system's overall performance. Speech systems are being designed so that the system's output will facilitate those forms of human verbal behavior which, given the current speech recognition limitations, the technology can cope with. The system is deigned to ensure the user's speech is *system-friendly*. This is a neat but ironic reversal of what has come to be conventionally accepted design practice.

Examples of such social control designed to circumscribe human users' natural verbal behavior are easy to find. Telephone home-banking services often rely on inflexible menu-led systems; here the complex problems of word recognition are avoided by ensuring that a menu of turn options guides the user through a series of prerecorded or "canned" questions that require no more than elementary answers. The system then has to recognisze no more than a few simple words, and is therefore unlikely to be overburdened either by lengthy and complex utterances, or the use of words that the system cannot recognize.

Systems that seek to be interactive and more responsive to user initiatives are clearly a more advanced technological accomplishment than menu-led voice recognition systems. Yet even in the case of such (relatively) sophisticated technology, there is a premium on ensuring that various features of ordinary human verbal behavior are discouraged or modified, while other discursive practices are encouraged.

In producing systems that constrain humans to be system-friendly, designers face a chicken-and-egg type of problem: how can system designers know how people will react to the behavior of speaking computers prior to the development of an experimental system, and how can an experimental system be developed prior to an understanding of users' behavior and requirements? That is, in advance of the actual system being built and operational, there is little knowledge about the way people will interact with it to inform the design of the system so that it facilitates easy use by a human.

Wizard of Oz (WOZ) simulations are becoming increasingly popular as designers attempt to anticipate the behavior of human users in their dealings with interactive systems (Fraser and Gilbert, 1991). The name of the simulation technique is derived from Baum's (1974 [1900]) novel *The Wizard of Oz,* in which the "great and terrible" wizard is revealed to be no more than a device operated by an ordinary man hiding behind a screen. Similarly, WOZ simulations require an accomplice (the wizard) to play the role of a projected technological artifact while experimental subjects are led to believe that they are interacting with a piece of existing technology. WOZ experiments can be designed so as to incorporate components of the actual system. In these cases, because the wizard pretends to be only part of the system, these experiments have come to be known as *bionic* WOZ studies. The name of this simulation technique is derived from the mid-1970's television program, *The Bionic Man.*

In this chapter we will examine data generated from a bionic WOZ study that was set up to assess the effectiveness of a feature of system performance that was designed to constrain human behavior.

The bionic WOZ study we report on was undertaken as part of the ESPRIT II project, SUNDIAL: Speech UNDerstanding in DIALogue. This is a collaborative project with partners in four European countries to design a speech-based computerized information service that can interact as naturally as possible with human users over an ordinary telephone system. The researchers from each of the four participating countries elected to model the system on a specific information service. The SUNDIAL partners in the United Kingdom elected to model the British Airways flight information service.

Early in the SUNDIAL project it was thought that, due to technological problems, the system would be unable to register (or "hear") anything said by the human user for half a second after it had finished its turn. This presented a problem. Any detailed transcript of conversational interaction will reveal that, in everyday talk, participants are particularly adept at starting turns with such precision that there is rarely a gap between successive turns. If users of the SUNDIAL system were to employ such precise "end-pointing techniques" in their interactions with the SUNDIAL system, it would be likely that a substantial portion of their requests (or whatever utterance they were producing) would go unheard. It was important, then, to ensure that users would only speak after the system's "deafness window" had passed, when the speech recognition components were again fully functional.

One proposed solution was the use of a tone or beep at the end of each system utterance which would signal to the human the point at which he or she could start speaking. It was decided to use the bionic WOZ simulation technique to test the adequacy of this solution. So unlike, for example, menu-led telephone banking systems, this particular bionic WOZ experiment was not attempting to constrain the range of different words a human user might employ in an exchange; nor were we attempting to circumscribe speech production variables: volume, emphasis, sound stretching, and the like. Rather, we were interested in constraining a temporal feature of speech production – specifically, precise synchronization with the verbal behavior of others. Such precision placement of talk is in a sense quite natural; it is a feature of discursive practices, which are routinely accomplished in unconstrained, naturally occurring verbal interaction. The attempt to use a tone to constrain this natural verbal behavior is therefore an attempt at social control; and the use of the tone is the strategy used to try to implement that aim.

In this chapter we are concerned with those occasions in which this attempt at social control failed; in particular, we look at some instances in which the subjects in the bionic WOZ experiment began to talk after the end of the system utterance but before the production of the tone; and those occasions in which they began to speak before the tone, but end up talking in overlap with the onset of the tone.

In the analysis of these instances, we have adopted a largely conversation analytic approach. So instead of merely counting the number of instances of failure and the relative frequencies of such instances distributed amongst users and classes of users, we are concerned to describe the sequential organizational properties which underpin the users' disinclination to withhold their talk until after the tone. There have been other attempts to adopt a conversation analytic approach to inform the development or analysis of interactive systems, most notably the papers in the collection *Computers and Conversation* (Luff, Gilbert, and Frohlich, 1990). Consequently, we feel there is no further need to justify the use of a conversation analytic approach for the analysis of these data. Indeed, a conversation analytic perspective lends itself to these data in a distinctive way. Conversation analysts have emphasized that the study of talk-in-interaction is also the study of perhaps the primordial form of social organization. In the bionic WOZ study we are reporting here, attempts were made to impose conditions upon a limited range of discursive procedures through which that social order is routinely produced. Consequently, it seemed appropriate to adopt a conversation analytic perspective in the study of attempts to impose forms of verbal behavior on a social order, the properties of which have already been mapped in detail.

As this work is still in progress, we will not in this chapter attempt a comprehensive analysis. Rather we will try merely to identify some consistent organizational features of our data, and thereby attempt to specify the structural locations in which this particular form of social control was vulnerable and likely to fail.

7.2 Methodological protocol and experimental design

7.2.1 System details

This Bionic WOZ simulation incorporated an Infovox Text to Speech Synthesizer (TTS), driven by an X11 R4 interface written in Prolog (v.3.1.1) in the UNIX operating system. The interface, run on a Sun "Sparc" workstation, allowed the wizard to simulate recognition errors and manipulate other variables such as the synthesizer's (nominal) gender and particular confirmation strategy. Subjects were provided with a list of ten flight-inquiry scenarios. These scenarios were based on calls to the British Airways flight information service. For each scenario, subjects telephoned the "system" and tried to obtain the relevant flight information. The wizard's simulation tool used prepared utterances with slots that were filled with values appropriate for each of the scenarios given to the subjects.

The simulation tool was run in synchrony with a front-end processing tool, which digitized the subjects' speech data for later analysis and training purposes. Feedback from this tool about the level at which the subject had spoken was relayed to the wizard's screen, and a "repeat" or "please speak louder" message could be generated by the wizard as and when necessary.

The system utterances were logged as they were produced and the whole dialogue was also recorded on audiotape using an analogue recorder as a backup for transcription purposes, providing details of timing and overlap in the dialogue.

The information about the importance of the tone was presented to the subject in the system's first turn in the exchange. Extract (1) provides an illustration.

(1) Subject 11 ("Sys." is the wizard,[2] "Sub." is the subject. Throughout this chapter we will be using conversation analytic transcription symbols.)

```
 1   Sys.   hel↑lo
 2          (.6)
 3          this is british airways flight
 4          inquiries service
 5          (.6)
 6   Sys.   I can only give you information on
 7          british airways flight arrivals
 8          and departures
 9          (.6)
10   Sys.   please speak after the tone
11          (.5)
12          -----                                        ((tone .4 seconds))
13          (.4)
14   Sub.   hello I understand there's
15          a flight from heathrow to sydney
            ((subject continues to request information))
```

7.2.2 The sample

Subjects were members of a local subject panel for social science experiments; none had participated in previous WOZ studies. They were paid five pounds for participating. Ten men and ten women participated; ages ranged from 22 to 65 years. The mean age was 48.2 and 49 for women and men respectively.

7.2.3 Procedure

Ten relatively straightforward scenarios were used in this simulation, of which four were flight arrival time queries, two were departure time queries and the remainder were miscellaneous queries. These proportions were based on the number of these types of inquiries found in a corpus of recorded calls between members of the public and the agents of a telephone-based flight information service.

To generate output, the wizard simply selected a prepared utterance from a list of keywords on the screen, using a mouse. The task parameters for the scenario were inserted automatically by the simulation software, and the utterance was then synthesized using the TTS synthesizer. Thus, subjects would only hear synthetic speech formulated in standardized structures, which in turn would facilitate the impression of a "talking machine." Utterances were also in some sense constructed in real time when, for example, confirming a series of parameters. The wizard would select one or a series of flight parameters to be confirmed, and then the appropriate confirmation phrase was constructed by the tool. The wizard could also compose utterances directly from the keyboard.

To facilitate further the subjects' belief that they were talking to an actual version of the entire system they were asked to fill in a questionnaire requesting information about their familiarity with various types of computer and speech technology. One question asked if they believed it was possible to have a conversation with a speaking computer. During interviews and questionnaires completed after the experiment, it was clear that all subjects believed they were actually talking to the entire system and not just a simulation of parts of it operated by a human.

In addition to the use of the tone to constrain subjects' behavior, various other contingencies were simulated. For example the wizard ensured that certain user requests were misheard, thereby generating specific kinds of user repair techniques. For example, in one scenario the system understood Stuttgart for Stockholm; and in other scenarios, the system understood Birmingham and Melbourne for Montreal. In some calls the system failed to understand the user's specification of dates relevant to the flight being queried.

There was evidence of a learning curve over the ten dialogues, with most problems occurring during the subjects' first dialogue. Since the subjects were only completely naive during the first dialogue, this is the one most worthy of attention for the purposes of developing a system for use by the general (untrained) public. Consequently our analytic remarks will be restricted to features of the subjects' first trials.

7.3 Analysis

In this section we will sketch some of the sequential properties of two types of instance in which the subject fails to wait for the appearance of the tone before starting to speak.

7.3.1 Confirmation insertion sequences

In the following two extracts the system seeks clarification of one of the parameters of the flight request. In both cases the subjects reply before the tone.

(2) Subject 8

```
14   Sub.   can you tell me when flight bee ay (.)
15          four eight one from (dusseldorf) is
16          expected to arrive
```

```
17        (7.2)
18   Sys.  you want to know the arrival time?
19        (.4)
20   Sub.  ye s:
21           [ -----                                              ((tone))
22        (7)
23   Sys.  please speak after the tone
```

(3) Subject 9

```
29   Sub.  I'd like to book a flight to florence
30        (.3)
31        this afternoon if possible (have you)
32        any seats available
33        (1.4)
34   Sys.  to florence?
35        (.3)
36   Sub.  please
37        -----                                                  ((tone))
38        (6)
39   Sys.  please speak after the tone
```

There are some consistent features of these sequences. In both cases, the subjects confirm the parameter the system is seeking to clarify with minimal, one-word utterances. These are produced with little delay after the end of the system's utterances. After the respective tones, neither subject attempts to repeat a prior turn. After some seconds have elapsed, the system indicates that there is a problem in the dialogue by reminding the subjects that they should speak after the tone.

The subjects seem to have ignored the tone and its significance in the dialogue. There are two "intuitive" explanations for these data which we need to address. Could it have been the case that the subjects did not hear the tone? This is unlikely; there seems to be little that could have interfered with ability to hear what was being produced at the other end of the line. There were no technical difficulties at that point in the experiment. Furthermore, in extract (2), although the tone does occur slightly in overlap with the last sounds of the subject's turn, it then continues clearly beyond the end of that turn; and in extract (3) it occurs adjacent to, but clearly after, the subject's confirmation. There are grounds, therefore, to suggest that the subjects should have heard the tone, or at least part of it.

We reported earlier that the request that the subjects speak only after the tone was made in the first system utterance in the dialogue. Could it be the case that the subjects were under the impression that the tone was relevant only to that specific moment in the dialogue after the system's first turn and before the subject's first turn? This would imply that subjects were treating the tone as having the same functional properties as the tone produced on an answering machine to announce the end of the prerecorded message. This is plausible. However, even if the subjects did believe that the relevance of the tone was restricted to the opening exchanges in the dialogue, they would have realized that this assumption was incorrect when they heard it again. At that point they would have been able to infer that the request to speak after the tone was going to be recursive throughout the dialogue, and not limited in its application.

Why, then, is the tone treated at that moment as having no interactional import? We can offer a speculative account via a consideration of some of the properties of adjacency pair sequences.

The subjects' first utterances in the dialogue are requests for information, and thereby constitute the first part of a *request–offer of help* adjacency pair. The provision of the first pair part generates a conversational "slot" in which the normatively expected second pair part should be produced. In this case, the second pair part is an offer of information, or an account as to why the information can not be provided. This means that the system's request for clarification is the first part of an insertion sequence (Shegloff, 1972) in the overarching request–information pair. This insertion sequence consists of a confirmation-seeking confirmation–disconfirmation pair.

In ordinary conversational interaction, insertion sequences are sites in which participants can address business which is preliminary to, or a prerequisite of, the production of the normatively expected second pair part.

This feature of insertion sequences is particularly evident in calls to public service agencies. For example extract (4) comes from a call to the police.

(4) (From Whalen and Zimmerman, 1987: 174.)

1	A	Mid city Emergency
2	B	Um yeah (.) somebody jus' vandalized my car,
3	A	What's your address.
4	B	Thirty three twenty two: Elm
5	A	Is this uh house or an apartment.
6	B	Ih tst uh house
7	A	Uh- your las' name.
8	B	Minsky,
9	A	How do you spell it.
10	B	M.I.N.S.K.Y.
11	A	Wull sen' somebody out to see you.

The call to the police constitutes a request for help, the appropriate second pair part to which is an offer of assistance. And, eventually, in line 11, the operator provides that offer of help by saying that someone will be dispatched to investigate the complaint. But in between the request for help and the offer, there are four separate question-answer sequences in which a range of business gets sorted out: where the caller lives, his name, the kind of accommodations he has, and so on. All these items of information are elicited through the agent's initiation of question–answer insertion sequences.

During these insertion sequences, however, the normative expectation that the request should receive an offer of help is not diminished. Evidence for this comes from the fact that the caller at no time seeks to treat the intervening questions as somehow irrelevant to his primary concerns. His compliance with the agent's requests for information exhibits his understanding that these insertion sequences are leading up to the offer of help.

So, in calls to service agencies, the request for information constitutes the first part of an adjacency pairing; and the expectation that that first pair part will receive the appropriate second pair part is enforced by normative conventions. But there is a sense in which the power of normative expectations binding the production of first and second pair parts may be enhanced in such calls. That is, it is commonly known that the only (genuine) reason to call such a service is to elicit a particular kind of help; and that the primary business of such agencies is to provide it. So the strong link between first and second pair parts may be enhanced by considerations that are specific to such agencies.

These observations may cast light on the subjects' behavior in extracts (2) and (3).

The system's attempt to confirm a flight parameter is recognizable as the first part of an insertion sequence. This feature of the system's utterance is recognizable not only to us as analysts, but will have been recognized by the subject (albeit tacitly). The subject will have drawn on ordinary conversational conventions to infer that the system's utterance is not the appropriate second pair part of the overarching *request–information* pair, but is addressing business that is preliminary to the production of the appropriate second. So, the work of the overarching adjacency pair – the framework of the call – is momentarily deferred. (But not, of course, abandoned: the expectation that the system will provide information, or an account for its failure to do so, would still hold.)

Recall that the subject's first introduction to the tone and the system's declarations of its significance to the dialogue came after the system's first turn. So the initial appearance of the tone is produced prior to the subject's production of the first part of the overarching adjacency pair sequence. However, as we have seen, the subjects are treating the subsequent clarification request from the system as a legitimate (i.e., nonaccountable) insertion sequence during which time the central business of the call is deferred. Could it be, then, that for these sequences the interactional "guidelines" established earlier are also deferred, so that insertion sequences are treated as constituting interactional enclaves in which guidelines associated with the overarching *structural organization* of the call are deemed to have no relevance?

This is admittedly a speculative account. But if it is true, it suggests that some current practices in system design may be dangerously misguided. For example, because speech-based interactive systems are so prone to error, it is deemed sensible to design a system so that it is constantly checking and confirming the flight parameters, the type of request, and so on. This means that dialogues with human users will be liberally peppered with small confirmation insertion sequences of the type we see in extracts (2) and (3). But, as we have seen from these extracts, it is during precisely these kinds of insertion sequences that attempts to constrain human behavior may be ineffective. Of course, we are not claiming that the system's initiation of a *clarification–confirmation* pair will inevitably result in the subject ignoring the tone. Rather, we are merely pointing to organizational contingencies in which the subjects' sensitivity to previously imposed behavioral constraints may be diminished. And there is an additional irony. Insertion sequences are one of the routine everyday conversational practices that have been modeled in speech systems precisely *to ensure* the smooth progression of the dialogue. Yet the ineffectiveness of the tone at these points may be in part a consequence of the unanticipated properties of such interactional sequences.

7.3.2 Execution of corrections or repair

(5) Subject 12

```
34   S   I would like to know (.3) WHAt time (.) it
35       arrives (.4) a::nd which (.) terminal
36       (5)
37   W   please tell me where the flight leaves from?
38       (.5)
39       -----                                            ((tone))
40       (.7)
41   S   ibi:za,
42       (2.2)
43   W   from cairo?
44       (.2)
45   S   I:⌈: (.) b⌈i:za
46      ⌊ ---- ⌋                                          ((tone))
47       (.5)
48   S   ⟩ibiza⟨
49       (3.3)
50   W   I am having trouble with the name of
51       the departure city (.3) can you
52       please spell it for me?
```

(6) Subject 3

```
14   S   ehm: the question I wanted to
15       ask is: *urh ·h when the
16       flight from athens is scheduled
17       to arrive (.3) the flight number
18       is bee ay (.) four (.) six (.)
19       fi:ve.
```

```
20        (7.5)
21   W    you want to know the arrival time?
22        (.5)
23        -----                                                    ((tone))
24   S    Yes:
25        (8.8)
26   W    flight bee ay four six five from
27        amsterdam to london?
28   S    )fr'm⟨ from athe⌐ns
29                       └ -----=                                  ((tone))
30   S    =from athens
31        (.7)
32        to london
33        (4.2)
34   W    from athens?
```

In extracts (5) and (6) we see sequences in which the system has made a recognition error: respectively, Cairo for Ibiza and Amsterdam for Athens. It is after the system's production of these errors that the subjects begin to speak before the onset of the tone.[3] In their "offending" turns, the subjects correct the system. For these extracts, the issue of conversational *repair* appears to be implicated in the subject's failure to observe the significance of the tone.

Several studies have investigated the structural properties of the organization of repair in conversation (e.g., Schegloff, 1987; Schegloff, Jefferson, and Sacks, 1977). These studies have revealed, for example, that the first two positions in which repair can be executed fall within the same turn as the trouble source; and that three out of the four places in which repair tends to occur are in turns of the person who produces the initial trouble. Therefore, there is evidence of a structural preference for *self*-repair over *other* repair.

However, consider the following extract, which comes from a corpus of calls to the British Airways flight information service. The caller requests information about a flight carried by an airline about which the British Airways agents have no information. In her first turn after the request, the agent identifies the trouble source and offers the correct information number as a repair.

(7) [BA 16] T1:SB:F:F ("A" is the agent, "C" the caller.)

```
1   A:   flight information
2        may I help you⌐:
3   C:            └good morning um I was
4        wondering if you can tell me what time um:
5        (.) iberia flight six one four (.3) from
6        valencia scheduled to arrive tomorrow
7        please
```

8   (.5)
9   A: ah you'll have to check with iberia I'll
10   give you their number

It is notable that, in the British Airways corpus, agents show a marked tendency to initiate and execute repair in the same turn, invariably the turn after the turn that contains the trouble source. There are relatively few instances of other-initiated self-repair: that is, cases in which agents initiate caller's self-repair. This is unusual, as the organization of repair in everyday conversational interaction facilitates self-repair. In the light of this observation, it is useful to consider the way that the institutional context of calls to a flight information service may impinge upon and influence the shape of repair.

There is an asymmetry in the relative status of the participants with respect to calls to public service information agencies. Agents are flight information "experts" and, in most cases, the callers have little or no knowledge of the services about which they are inquiring. Thus, on those occasions in which an agent recognizes that the caller has, for example, formulated a request involving an incorrect flight detail, it is probably the case that the caller simply does not know the correct flight parameter, rather than that the caller has made a "slip of the tongue." There is, then, little likelihood that next-turn *repair initiation* by the agent will lead to successful *self-repair* by the caller.

There are occasions, however, in which this relative asymmetry may be inverted. It is likely that there will be occasions in which the agent has made a mistake, for example, mishearing the name of a departure city. With respect to that item of information only, it is the caller who is in the position of "expert," and it is she who must identify and repair the error. This is the case in extracts (5) and (6): the subjects know that the system has made a mistake, and that it is incumbent upon them to repair the problem.

To ensure that errors in conversation do not confuse subsequent interaction, it is necessary to be able to identify and repair problem sources as soon as possible. Consequently, repair organization is ordered so that the execution of repair can be located as close as possible to the repairable item. The first place in which repair occurs is within the same turn construction unit as the trouble source. The second structural position for repair occurs immediately at the next transition relevance place (Sacks, Schegloff, and Jefferson, 1974) after the trouble source. These same turn repair positions facilitate speedy self-repair. But to assure that *other* repair is closely positioned to the trouble source, it is necessary to begin the turn in which the repair occurs as near as possible to the end of the turn that contains the repairable item.

This feature of repair organization informs the subjects' behavior in extracts (5) and (6). In (5) there is a .2 second gap before the subject's execution of repair, but in extract (6) the subject initiates the repair without any delay after the system's prior turn. So, the significance of the tone is disregarded in the attempt by the subjects to lodge their first opportunity to execute repair as close as possible to the system's error. The behavior of the subjects displays their orientation to the conventions and organization of conversational repair activity: they both attend to the repair quickly after the turn in which the error has been exposed.

Although this accounts for the subjects' interjections before the onset of the tone, it does not explain why the subjects then repeat the turns that were produced prior to, or in overlap with, the tone. In extracts (2) and (3) the subjects did not repeat their confirmations after the tone. So why does it happen here?

There are two considerations. One difference between the extracts (2) and (3), and (5) and (6) is that in the first two cases, the offending turn was the second part of an adjacency pair; but in cases (5) and (6), the subjects are doing repair. As such they initiate a two turn sequence of conversational action: repair–acceptance or rejection. In the following extract, for example, one speaker is corrected by another, and then in the next turn the first speaker acknowledges the correction and incorporates it into a modification of the "final comment" of her previous utterance.

(8) (From Jefferson, 1987: 87.)

Milly: . . . and then they said something about Kruschev has
         leukemia so I thought oh it's all a big put on.
Jean: Breshnev.
Milly: Breshnev has leukemia. So I didn't know what to
         think.

So the production of a next-turn repair generates a slot in which that repair can be accepted or rejected. The projection of a slot in which the repair can be accepted or challenged is important in that it allows the producer of the trouble source to demonstrate that the repair has been successful (or at least that it has been recognized). Without such a display there is no way that the producer of the repair can know that the producer of the trouble source has recognized that they have been corrected, or that the error has been addressed.

The subjects' pretone turns in extracts (5) and (6) therefore initiate an important course of action. As the dialogue cannot proceed satisfactorily without confirmation from the system that it has registered that it had made a mistake, it is necessary to ensure that it is aware of the error: that the system "realized" that the subjects were engaging in repair activity. In extracts (5) and (6), the subjects' production of the correct departure city overlaps with the tone. The subjects therefore have grounds to infer that their utterances may not have been heard. It is therefore necessary to repeat the repair in "open space," the first appearance of which is after the tone.

There is one immediate upshot of this account. Although the subjects do repeat their utterances after the tone, it may not be due to a recognition of its significance as a guide as to when to speak. The repeat of the corrections may be motivated more by sequential considerations relevant to the execution of next-speaker repair in everyday conversation.

7.4 Conclusion

It is important to stress that the analytic approach we have adopted here does not lead us to make claims about the relative frequencies or distribution of occasions in which subjects speak prior to the tone. Attempts to count these instances provide little useful information about why such failures occur. Instead, we have tried to examine the organization of the subjects' offending turns; and particularly we have focused on the ways that the properties of conversational action sequences have become relevant at specific moments in the subjects' dialogues with the system. Consequently, we have provided a speculative account of instances of failure by drawing on some properties of insertion sequences within calls to public service agencies; and we have been able to account for the details of other instances of failure in terms of the general procedures for repair, and some features of the organization of next-turn repair in particular. In the exploration of the ways that communicative resources are so deployed and modified to meet the practical contingencies of actual dealings with artifacts, we can start to sketch the weak points in the fabric of social control that system designers may try to impose upon prospective or actual human users of speech-based computer systems.

In this chapter, we have used the notion of 'social control' as a heuristic to illuminate some of the dilemmas faced by designers of speech-based, interactive computer systems, and to characterize some features of their subsequent responses. Conventionally, within social and political sciences, programs of social control are viewed negatively: they are treated as constraining human behavior and impinging on cherished individual freedoms. We do not, however, regard the attempts of system designers to constrain human users' verbal behavior so negatively; indeed, we welcome them, for the following reason.

Is it reasonable to try to build truly conversational computers (Button, 1990; Gilbert et al., 1990; see also Button and Sharrock, this volume)? This is just one strand of a wider debate about the claims of the proponents of the strong AI position (see, e.g., Dreyfus, 1979; McCorduck, 1979; Searle, 1984; and Winograd and Flores, 1986). The debate seems to have been conducted around "in principle" issues: for example, there is an argument that the nature of conversational interaction is such that it is in principle pointless trying to model it in computer systems.

Of course, while "in principle" debates continue, system designers continue to develop new technologies and refine existing systems. What we should be doing, then, is studying the ways in which humans interact with these systems. But we do not wish to become embroiled in a debate about the appropriate criteria by which we can decide the success (or otherwise) of speaking machines. That is a job for system designers. As social scientists, we consider that it is more important to investigate *how* humans use everyday communicative competencies to make sense of *their* dealings with interactive systems. It is through the use of culturally available interactional and inferential resources that human users will fashion the utility of speech based interfaces.[4]

WOZ and bionic WOZ studies are undertaken by the community of speech system designers to facilitate the development of interactive systems; but in doing so they generate data that permit the examination of the interactional work done by human participants, which ensures the smooth progression of the dialogue. And in those occasions when the system is technically incapable of interacting successfully, such that the behavior of the human subject has to be constrained, we are in a particularly privileged position, because it is in the human response to those forms of social control that the analyst is given access to the operation of seen but unnoticed communicative practices. The attempts of system designers to impose a form of verbal social control thus inadvertently highlight those conversational resources, rooted in the domain of everyday talk-in-interaction, which are marshaled in exchanges with computerized artifacts and simulated versions of those artifacts, and through the use of which human–computer interaction may be realized.

Notes

1. An exception is the ESPRIT II project, SUNDIAL, in which, at the outset, there was a commitment to producing a speech-based system that could interact as naturalistically as possible with human users.
2. As our analytic observations concern the behavior of the subjects, and as they seemed to believe that they were talking to an actual speaking computer rather than a simulated version, we will refer to the utterances of the bionic wizard as *system* utterances.
3. In this respect it is interesting to note that in both cases, the subjects have, in previous turns, displayed their orientation to the relevance of the tone. In (5) in line 37, the system asks for specific flight information, and the subject waits until the tone has finished before answering; and in (6), the subject produces the second pair part of a clarification confirmation pair after the tone.
4. In this, we share assumptions that inform the social constructivist accounts of science, which emphasize that the success of scientific work rests upon the operations of a largely unseen and unnoticed network of cultural skills and practices (Collins, 1985; Collins and Pinch, 1982; 1993). To detect the operations and significance of such practices, sociologists of science have had to enculturate themselves into specific scientific communities. Only at such close range can the sociologist tease out the extent to which social factors impinge on the production of scientific knowledge, particularly in the case of controversial scientific disputes.

References

Baum, F. (1974). *The Wizard of Oz* (London: Collins). Originally published in 1900.

Button, G. (1990). Going up a blind alley: Conflating conversation analysis and computational modelling. In P. Luff, G. N. Gilbert, and D. Frohlich (eds.), *Computers and conversation* (London: Academic Press), 67–90.

Collins, H. M. (1985). *Changing order: Replication and induction in scientific practice* (London: Sage).

Collins, H. M., and Pinch, T. J. (1982). *Frames of meaning: The social construction of extraordinary science* (London: Routledge and Kegan Paul).

Collins, H. M., and Pinch, T. J. (1993). *The golem: What everyone should know about science* (Cambridge: Cambridge University Press).

Dreyfus, H. (1979). *What computers can't do* (New York: Harper and Row).

Fraser, N. M., and Gilbert, G. N. (1991). Simulating speech systems. *Computer Speech and Language,* 5, 81–99.

Gilbert, G. N., Wooffitt, R., and Fraser, N. M. (1990). Organising computer talk. In P. Luff, G. N. Gilbert, and D. Frohlich (eds.), *Computers and conversation* (London: Academic Press), 245–257.

Jefferson, G. (1987). On exposed and embedded correction in conversation. In G. Button and J. R. E. Lee (eds.), *Talk and social organisation* (Clevedon: Multilingual Matters), 86–100.

Luff, P., Gilbert G. N., and Frohlich, D. (eds.). (1990). *Computers and conversation* (London: Academic Press).

McCorduck, P. (1979). *Machines who think* (San Francisco: W. H. Freeman).

Sacks, H., Schegloff, E. A., and Jefferson, G. (1974). A simplest systematics for the organisation of turn-taking for conversation. *Language* 50, 696–735.

Schegloff, E. A. (1972). Notes on a conversational practice: Formulating place. In D. Sudnow (ed.), *Studies in social interaction* (New York: Free Press), 75–119.

Schegloff, E. A. (1987). Recycled turn beginnings: A precise repair mechanism in conversation's turn-taking organisation. In G. Button and J. R. E. Lee (eds.), *Talk and social organisation* (Clevedon: Multilingual Matters), 70–85.

Schegloff, E. A. (1991). Conversation analysis and socially shared cognition: repair after next turn and the defense of intersubjectivity. In L. B. Resnick, J. M. Levine, and S. D. Teasley (eds.), *Perspective on socially shared cognition* (Washington, D.C.: American Psychological Association), 150–171.

Schegloff, E. A., Jefferson, G., and Sacks, H. (1977). The preference for self-correction in the organisation of repair in conversation. *Language,* 53, 361–382.

Searle, J. (1984). *Minds, brains and science* (Harmondsworth: Penguin).

Whalen, M. R., and Zimmerman, D. H. (1987). Sequential and institutional contexts in calls for help. *Social Psychology Quarterly* 50, 172–185.

Winograd, T., and Flores, F. (1986). *Understanding computers and cognition: A new foundation for design* (Norwood, N.J.: Ablex).

8

Sociology, CSCW, and working with customers

Dave Randall and John A. Hughes

8.1 Introduction

Sociology has, almost since its origins in the nineteenth century, had a preoccupation with technology. As a reaction to Enlightenment individualism, sociology's argument that reason has only a limited application in the explanation of human conduct, and that the social environment in which human beings lived had at least as big a role to play, not surprisingly drew for its examples the effects of industrialization, perhaps the most thoroughgoing application of technology in human history. In brief, the main target of this critique of reason was the way in which the application of technology had degraded the sense of community and belonging that had allegedly typified the era before the advent of industrialism. But the effort to found a science of society carried with it the hope that such a discipline could play its part in the redesign of society itself to achieve a more desirable state of affairs. Of course, such a vision depended a great deal upon whether the visionary detested or embraced the potential of technology. Marx, for example, saw the way in which the ownership of the means of technological production had created two antagonistic classes and, in the process, dehumanized both. His objective was nothing less than the redesign of society through political means so that human beings might, for the first time in their long history, realize their nature as free creatures unfettered by the needs of a society incapable of doing other than subjugating the mass of its people. Later in the century, Durkheim saw sociologists more as physicians whose task was to diagnose and cure the pathologies of the social order, many of which were, in modern society, brought about by technological change and rampant individualism. And, to complete the trilogy of the classic writers, much of Weber's pessimism concerning the modern age was prompted by the way in which instrumental rationality, that attitude of mind which had played such a large part in creating Western science and technology, had permeated much of modern life.[1]

Since these heady days, however, the idea that sociology might be an applied discipline, on even a modest scale, has fallen into abeyance or, in some instances, into disguise.[2] Though the reasons for this change are too various to go into here, the more recent tradition in sociology – unlike, for example, that in economics or psychology – has tended to see the discipline as one with little or no direct application to social affairs. It has, of course, retained its interest in technology, in industrialization, in work, but apart from highly generalized theoretical and perspectively driven complaints, or critiques, about the "state of the world" hardly sees itself as a discipline that can be applied to the design of technology or of work.

For this reason the recent involvement of sociology in human–computer interaction (HCI), through its offshoot, computer-supported cooperative work (CSCW), is something of an embarrassment, not least because despite well over a century of endeavor in studying the effects of technology on work and society, there is a dearth of ideas and concepts that can be "fed into" the system design process in ways that do not simply critique design efforts but contribute in some positive way to more effective system design. Much of sociology has been, we suggest, a sociology *of* technology and work rather than a sociology *for* the design of work and technology (Hughes and King, 1992).

One or two aspects of this, and about the potential relationship of what sociology might offer to CSCW, are worth a brief note. The first of these has to do with what we understand a sociology *for* design to be. We are not claiming, for example, that sociology, the whole of sociology, should suddenly redirect its attention to issues of system design. Sociology, and it is not alone in this as a discipline, exhibits a variety of perspectives and methods of inquiry that constitute the core arguments and issues of the discipline. These arguments and issues, what in another context T. Hughes (1987) describes as the "heartland," are not likely to go away. What we have is a discipline whose unity lies in its fundamental disagreements about the nature of the discipline itself as a fact of sociological life. However, even if we examine the corpus of sociology to find any approach or collection of findings that could be applied to system design, the choice is extremely limited. We shall return to this point in a moment after we have dealt with another brief comment, this time from CSCW itself.

One of the main stimuli for extending to sociology the invitation to join the interdisciplinary table of HCI through CSCW is the discovery of sociality by computer science and by HCI. There are a number of threads to this. First, the criticisms voiced in HCI about the inadequacies of the overly cognitive approach to human–computer interaction issues (Bannon, 1991); second, the failure of a number of implementations that had not acknowledged the sociality of work (Grudin, 1989); and, finally, the movement of the interface, to use Grudin's (1990) formulation, away from the computer, away from the individual user, into the world of work and the organization. These are obviously summary statements of what are often detailed, and contentious, points of view. Nevertheless, they add up to the conclusion that systems find their voice within domains that, whatever else they may consist in, are social, and system design needs to take this into account.

This is captured, though not unequivocally, in the very notion of CSCW and the idea of "cooperation."[3] However, as is to be expected in a new field, much of what is involved in the idea of sociality for the purpose of system design is "contested terrain" (Proctor and Williams, 1991; Wilson, 1991). And sociology is not likely to resolve this issue in short order; in fact, it is more likely to bring its own problems into the field of system design to sow even more confusion.[4]

Of course, acknowledging the need for effective studies of the sociality of work is one thing; achieving this is quite another. It is difficult for sociology itself regardless of the connection with CSCW systems design. Developing a suitable apparatus that is capable of informing the requirements specification for systems design adds to the problems and is but still a promissory note (Hughes and King, 1992). As has already been hinted at, one of the major stumbling blocks is the lack of an agreed conception within sociology of a suitable analytic framework for the analysis of the sociality of work activities. Even empirical sociology has demonstrated an extraordinary unwillingness to address the details of work and its activities with anything like the attention that is needed for system design. Typically, the conventional sociology of work takes for granted the details of the work itself in favor of rather gross typifications, which, it is argued, display the social character of work. Such typifications tend to be constituted out of allegedly significant properties of work settings and activities, which are then presumed to be highly generalizable across work environments, industries, organizations, and so on. Thus, and for example, the well-known categories of manual and non-manual work are intended to provide 'theoretically illumined' descriptions which are held to be highly generalizable across a range of extra-work characteristics, such as educational opportunities, life chances, remuneration, status, power, and more. What these do not do is tell you about what the work consists of except as decontextualized "examples." The work itself is seen as exemplifying abstract sociological theoretical categories rather than as a set of activities done and reproduced by those who perform the work. The upshot of these strategies is to leave us with little detailed knowledge of the work with which to inform system design, for it is often the very small, the undramatic, the prosaic, the everyday, which has the greatest bearing on the effectiveness, or otherwise, of human–computer systems.

Within CSCW there are two broad, and not necessarily incompatible, strategies to repair this deficiency. The first is to develop conceptual schemes that attempt to bridge the gap between the analysis of the domains of work and the needs of system designers for systematic descriptions of the relevant properties of the work (Schmidt, 1991). The other, and in its origins an inadvertent rather than a deliberate choice, is to make use of the relatively submerged sociological tradition of ethnography. Though pioneered as a research method, if so it needs to be called, in anthropology, through the Chicago School it became associated with symbolic interactionism as the preferred method of social research. Even though the remit of ethnography extends beyond symbolic interactionism, the properties of the method that so appealed to this sociological point of view was its commitment to naturalistic inquiry; that is, its methodological injunction that the researcher "be there" in the settings and the circumstances into which the inquiry was directed. In this respect, it is a naturalistic method rather than a method of social research of the kind pioneered by Lazarsfeld and his associates, which included the questionnaire, multiple-variance methods and other statistical methods, the survey, and so on.[5]

Such methods, it was claimed, not only distance the researcher from the persons and their settings but also impose "theoretical" categories that owe little or nothing to the sense of the settings for those who have their lives within them.

This naturalistic stance and its attention to the actualities of work rather than any particular sociological theoretical position has proved attractive to some within CSCW.[6] Suchman's (1987) pioneering work has been followed by studies of air traffic controllers (Harper and Hughes, 1992; Harper, Hughes, and Shapiro, 1991), underground control rooms (Heath and Luff, 1992), among others. What typifies such studies is their detailed observation of how, in the natural setting of the work, persons go about the business of "doing the work" of "making a photocopier work using the manual," "keeping air traffic flowing," "dealing with problems of the movement of trains in the London Underground," and so on – all of these glosses for the manifold prosaic activities involved in "doing a job of work." All of them, though some more directly than others, have been concerned to describe the details of work activities as they occur within work settings and relate these to system design.

In the remainder of this chapter our objectives are relatively modest; that is, to present some "analytic vignettes" from an ethnographic investigation of work in a branch office of a building society. The invitation to do the study arose out of a request by a financial services systems developer for a "sanity check" on a highly structured model of the transactions and information flows within the organization that was to serve as the possible basis for system development. Our brief was to look at the daily work of the office and to see to what extent the presumptions made in the model about the nature of the work were consistent with the work as actually done on a day-to-day basis. Although we were unable to do an "in-depth," prolonged investigation, the ethnographer was able to provide sufficient material to suggest that in crucial respects the model poorly expressed some of the facets of financial processing particularly in respect of the work of the cashier, the "interface" between the customer and the organization.[7]

There are a number of points we want to illustrate using these vignettes. The first is a general one about the importance of studying work in its natural setting as it "actually happens" and not just for sociological reasons but in order to inform the design of CSCW systems. Rather than rely upon idealizations, as instantiated, for example, in highly structured models of transactions of information flows, job descriptions, procedural rules, and the like, it is important that design have a good grasp of the thorough ways in which work is socially organized. The second point, and perhaps an obvious one but one that recurs and recurs, is how, within the course of work, the technology can support as well as hinder the performance of the work, but that this can be a situated matter rather than an endemic one. The final point is to suggest some of the very difficult problems faced by CSCW. System design is a difficult business at best; designing for the sociality of work makes it even more difficult.

8.2 The interdependencies of work

The division of labor is one of the central and enduring concepts in sociology. Arising out of the work of Adam Smith (1970) and the political economists, from them incorporated, though with different implications, by Marx in his analysis of the production process, and enshrined by Weber in the notion of bureaucracy as the most thoroughgoing application of instrumental rationality to the organization of human affairs, it has become a virtually standard term within the sociological glossary. It refers to the ways in which functions, personnel, and their activities are organized and distributed within some unit, be this a business firm, a government organization, or even a family. It also draws attention to the ways in which activities are interdependent, and often explicitly designed to be so, in that no one person performs all organizational functions but only contributes to them.[8] It draws attention, too, to the ways in which the organization of the division of labor, the interdependence of activities if you will, is normative, institutionalized as not only a distribution of functions and activities, but also as a distribution of rights and obligations within the unit concerned. In this respect it is a term that draws attention to the ways in which the organization of the division of labor, the interdependence of activities if you will, is normative and institutionalized as not only a distribution of functions and activities, but also as a distribution of rights and obligations within the unit concerned.

The concept had, as already indicated, played a large part in sociological analyses of work and other domains. However, the notion is more than an analytic construct in sociological theories. It is also a notion to which members themselves orient in various ways. Members of organizations see themselves as part of a division of labor in which they are involved and not just bystanders. It is a notion used by them to explicate and make sense of the ways in which "what goes on" in the daily round of organizational life consists of a more or less intelligible, sensible organization of activities done by persons in their everyday world of work (Anderson, Hughes, and Sharrock, 1989; Bittner, 1974). It is exhibited in a myriad of small and large details of working life in, for example, job titles and descriptions, power and responsibility, the ecology of work settings, as well as in the actual work activities in which persons engage.

A predominant model of the division of labor in conventional sociology is to represent it as a structure, a container if you will, within which persons perform their actions. Thus, and for example, persons supposedly orient to the normative framework of the division of labor in ways that, allegedly, "carry out" the diktats of what the division of labor requires. Except that, as many studies of bureaucracies discovered quite early on, they often do not. Thus, the discovery of the 'informal' contrasted with the 'formal' aspects of the organization of interdependence and its instantiation in structural forms such as those of the bureaucratic organization. The clear implication of this kind of thinking was that the formal description of the organization of the division of labor did not capture all that went on within organizations. "Beneath" this formal structure lay an "informal" one which could betray the formal goals, support them, expedite them more effectively, or whatever, but which, nevertheless, was as much a part of organizational life as the formal structures.

However, one of the many methodological troubles that beset this kind of analysis was highlighted by Bittner (1974) who convincingly argued that, in empirical studies of organizations, one of the main problems is determining whether any instance of behavior is an instance of the formal or the informal organization? In effect, the solution of this problem involved invoking a rule, by theoretical fiat, which could assign these characterizations independently of how the members themselves construed their activities. In effect, the "formal" rules of the organization were treated as "external" causative factors but ones that bore an unexplicated relationship to actual behavior characterized as "informal." The result was, paradoxically, to allow a members' category, that of "organization," to do theoretical and analytical work, without paying proper attention to the ways in which the category entered into and made sense of the activities for the members themselves. The implication of this kind of argument is that the theoretical distinction between "formal" and "informal" organization is irretrievably dependent on distinctions formulated and used by organizational members in the course of their activities.

A major implication of this is that studies of the division of labor, or of organization, need to begin, not conclude, with the organization of activities as understood, made sense of, and performed by parties to those activities – seeing, that is, the division of labor as a "working division of labor" within its natural setting. What this notion draws attention to is the need to look at the actual division of labor, not its idealization as this might appear on some organization chart or some job description. This is not, we hasten to add, an argument that such idealizations have no part to play in the organization of activities, an argument that they are simply myths or chimeras that belong to a fictional world of organizational functioning. On the contrary, they are in intrinsic part of what we are characterizing as the "working division of labour."

However, what is necessary is to analyze job descriptions, organizational plans and charts, mission statements, and the like as features of the working setting – features that are oriented to and used by persons in the course of their everyday working activities. Suchman (1987) speaks of plans as resources that persons use in the course of making sense of their other activities, rather than as determinants of actions. Plans, and the like, cannot determine actions in any strong causal sense of the term. Just as no rule can dictate its own application, plans, job descriptions, and such, are "filled in" by persons who use or are subject to them since such formulations cannot, could not, explicate with the necessary exhaustiveness all the multiplicities of behaviors the rule, the plan, the job description entails *within their settings of use.* Plans, job descriptions, and the like vary in their specificity and the details that they contain but, in any event, do not seek to prescribe and describe every detail of what a person must do to satisfy them. They are not "external determinants" of actions. Rather what actions satisfy the plans or the job description or the rule are matters that are "internal" to them – matters to be decided and judged by those who use the plans, the rules, and so on within their work settings.

Thus, the important methodological implication for understanding the division of labor as a "working division of labor" is to understand it from the point of view of those who use its formulations as features of their practical actions within particular organizational settings. Acting-in-conformity-to-the-plan-or-the-job-requirements is to exercise competence in knowing the "just whats" that will satisfy these. It is knowing, too, that from the point of view of any participant, the work being done is only part of the total flow of work activities. An individual has his or her task to perform and its completion is merely a step in a larger scheme of processing of tasks done by others (Anderson et al., 1989).

In the building society concerned, as it is for many organizations, an important part of the ways in which tasks are integrated is through computer technology, which sends information and transactions to be processed in various ways. This is not, of course, the only way the integration of tasks is achieved because, and again as is typical, much of this takes place in the locally situated activities of the setting.

An important part in dealing with the tasks to be performed is dealing with what Garfinkel (1967) refers to as the "normal, natural troubles" that the work produces – that is, the kind of difficulties that arise in the course of activities and which have to be dealt with in and through the work activities in the course of a "typical" working day. In the cases we shall look at here, the technology is one of the precipitants of "normal, natural troubles" for cashiers in the building society.

8.3 Working with customers

The cashier's task is to process customer inquiries and perform transactions in response to customer requests, which can be either at the counter or over the telephone. Typically the cashier works from behind a counter that fronts a larger office space containing desks, telephones, cupboards containing files and ledgers, customer details, and other familiar artifacts of office work. To hand the cashier has a menu-driven computer screen, which can be used to provide information about accounts, recent transactions, and so on. Under the counter are relevant and routinely used forms, such as paying-in slips, cash drawers, and stationery. Round the desk space is other relevant information including memos from the head office as well as "post it" notes for more local reference.

In terms of the division of labor it is the cashier who directly services the customer and passes on other information and materials for others elsewhere in the organization to deal with. The cashier is the "interface" of the organization with its customers. The flow of work and information with which the organization deals begins with the cashier. To hand is most of the equipment and information that will be needed in the matter-of-course treatment of customers and their requests.

Thus, a customer request or a transaction is entered into the system by the cashier and starts its journey through the organization. It is coded and standardized as information and fed into the bureaucratically organized channels. Though no doubt complex, the process lends itself to computerization. In many ways, it can be modeled as the classic office in which activities are defined by procedural rules that determine what should follow from what. In this way, the system achieves a high level of predictability and efficiency of functioning in much the way proposed by the rationale for the office information systems effort of some years ago.

As DeZisman (1977) defined it, an office procedure is composed of a number of steps or activities which are "event-driven" and characterized by a "local focus of attention." Office Procedure Specification Language (OPSL) was intended as a facility for describing office procedures as a flow of written documents. Although a methodology intended for use in nonprocedural domains, it does presume that much of office work is well structured, for example, in having procedures for sending a letter only when very exact conditions are fulfilled.

In a large portion of office procedures, the clerical staff is trained to *react* to input from the environment, as opposed to *responding* to these inputs. The difference is subtle but important. By "react" we mean that the action to be taken for a given stimulus is to a high degree predetermined by the organization's management. Once a clerk is told about a situation, s/he can consult a predefined procedure (formally or informally) to determine what action should be taken by the organization. The organization does not rely on the clerk to *decide* what to do; instead the organization provides a procedure which instructs the clerk how to react to a situation. (DeZisman, 1977:16–17)

Thus, the presumption is that the clerk, or in our case, the cashier, simply *reacts* to an event by consulting an already predefined procedure. No decision or judgment is required. However, the point is that information flows are not descriptions of the work activities that produce the information in the first place. Nor can they necessarily be recovered from the information itself or the procedures for producing it. Information, of whatever kind, is the outcome of work and producing that information is likely to be someone's work. But it is not an adequate description of the way in which the work produced it, or how the work of making the information flow was achieved as part of a working division of labor, itself produced and reproduced by parties to it making judgments and determinations as to what and how the information provided is to be rendered into "information-required-by-the-system." As a number of field studies of office work note, clerical personnel often make judgments, interpretations, and decisions based on these in their work, and describing these as stimulus–response patterns is not only too simplified but the office *work* disappears from the descriptions. Suchman and Wynn (1984) comment:

The operational significance of a given procedure or policy on actual occasions is not self-evident, but is determined by workers with respect to the particulars of the situation at hand. Their determinations are made through inquiries for which both the social and material make-up of the office setting serve as central resources. (1984: 152)

If we turn to the cashier, as the "interface" between the customer and the organization, the flow of work begins with the customer; it is customer-driven in that what *this* customer wants *here and now* determines what kind of work the cashier will have to do *here and now*. Although there is plenty of routine work to do, such as bringing ledgers up to date, filing, and all the typical activities of an office, although there are variably "busy" periods by hours of day and days of week, it is the customer who takes priority, a priority reinforced by the building society's explicit "customer care" policy. Customers structure their requirements in a variety of ways, including making a series of requests at the beginning of the encounter or, alternatively, waiting for the completion of an initial request before making a second. Thus, the cashier not only does not know the nature of the request until the encounter has begun, but also cannot predict the way in which the request will flow. It may be a single request to withdraw a sum of money or may be multiple requests.

Transactions can, thus, become more or less problematic according to the various ways in which cashiers and customers jointly orient to them. These "normal, natural troubles" of cashier–customer relations make the "flow of work" notion rather less than straightforward.

Such "normal, natural troubles" can include problems generated by a customer's oversight, such as passbooks not signed, other identification not provided, failure to understand account rules, and more. Even the simplest of transactions can become complicated, as the following extract from the field notes illustrates:

Customer wishes to withdraw two cheques:

Cashier: Uh, I'm sorry, but there's only Mr. Smith's signature on the passbook . . . it hasn't got yours . . . have you got a signature with you?

Customer: No.

Cashier: I'll have to find a signature. . . . [Searches through card index file of customer details, application forms, etc.] I'm just trying to find your signature card . . . we should have a card for you and I can't find it . . . I'll just get you to sign your passbook for the next time . . .

[Gives customer passbook with waxed paper strip attached.]

Put simply, for the cashier the effective processing of transactions is problematized by the element of unpredictability that any customer represents.[9] Although it is perfectly possible to provide aggregate descriptions of a typical day, such as how and when such and such transactions are likely to be more or less frequent, what cannot be known in advance is what *any* particular customer transaction will be.

From the customer's point of view, and one of the main concerns of the building society's customer care policy, satisfaction is an amalgam of a number of factors, not least the cashier's ability to keep a queue moving so as to minimize waiting time while at the same time meeting the expectation that requests and inquiries will be adequately expedited at the appropriate time.[10] Branch officers speak of the need to maintain "customer confidence" and a significant part of this is avoiding unnecessary waiting as well as dealing with customer requests. The important point is that maintaining customer confidence is not a single, discrete activity such that the cashier completes the transaction and then performs the actions of maintaining customer confidence; rather it is one that permeates throughout every activity that involves dealing with customers, from the interaction over the counter, to handling requests and inquiries promptly, not allowing queues to build up, and so on. It is developed in and through the activities of the cashier.

From the point of view of the cashiers, along with other workers within the building society but mainly the cashiers, to effect these goals means dealing with the "normal, natural troubles" customers can bring and which can interfere with the orderly flow of work. This requires the cashier to engage in a significant amount of demeanor work in order to maintain customer confidence and trust in the system that customers are confronting, though, more often than not, without overmuch regard for the fact that *their* requests might well interfere with the smooth and relatively seamless production of the flow of work by the cashier.

Part of this demeanor work consists in explaining to the customers the steps as they go along, what inquiries they are making of the screen, to whom they are telephoning, and so on. The cashiers' competence becomes evident in the way in which the flow of interaction is maintained, without palpable gaps, in the routines of the interactions with the customer. In the case of those transactions which take time, especially when the customer introduces another complication, this involves making decisions as to whether this is something with which the cashier can deal, whether it can be dealt with here and now, or whether it is best dealt with "in part" so as to minimize the waiting time of others in the queue.

By far the most common source of complication, and the most difficult to deal with, is the customer inquiry. These may be in person or by telephone and may be about a range of matters including the status of an account, standing orders and direct debit payments, advice about insurance claims, advice about new accounts, or what to do about a lost passbook. Inquiries are frequently made in the course of other transactions and are nearly always time-consuming, not least because they interfere with the smooth execution of the transaction itself. From the cashier's point of view they are also unpredictable. Whatever the transaction, customers can, at any time, make what is for them a relevant inquiry regardless of how irrelevant it may be for the cashier's work in hand. The customers may not know who it is they need to speak to; the cashier is simply the first point of contact for inquiries that may, in the end, have to be redirected to sales, financial advisors, or others in the organization. Inquiries do, of course, have to be handled. The cashier must make a decision immediately about how to deal with them bearing in mind the dual need to maintain customer confidence and keep the queue moving. The cashier must determine as a matter of immediate priority whether he or she can provide an adequate answer now, whether information needs to be obtained from others, which may be by telephone, or whether the inquiry can be deferred and dealt with by making an appointment for the customer.

As we have suggested, trying to keep the customer satisfied and, as a part of this, maintaining customer confidence entail a complex and potentially conflicting set of demands: broadly those to do with expediting the requests of *this particular customer* to his or her satisfaction and maintaining the flow of customers through the process. However, another ingredient in this balancing act is the technology to hand. For example, inputting information to the static displays is probably the most single time-consuming aspect of the whole process of opening a new account. Within reason, cashiers will sometimes leave this work until the customer has left rather than get them, and others who may be waiting in the queue, to wait for a relatively long period. This is, however, technically a breach of procedure. As one cashier explained:

We're supposed to get the customer to sign and check the headers . . . and they get impatient 'cos they're having to wait while you put it all in . . . and the number of times you get communication failure and have to do it all over again . . . that woman who wanted to open four accounts . . . I just had time to get them open . . . there was a queue right out the door . . . there was no way I was going to get the Statics done.

Thus far we have argued that even the simplest of transactions can become complicated and part of this dealing with customers inevitably means the cashier must also deal with the technology to hand. In the act of processing transactions the cashier must routinely weave use of the technology into the flow of the current interaction with customers. The technology to hand is based on a range of likely customer requests and is designed to process these. Once the customer has requested a particular service, then the screen display is interrogated to expedite that service. Such systems are becoming a routine feature of many customer–client interactions. Ideally, of course, such technology should be "invisible" in the way that biros and forms are routine, invisible features of most customer–cashier interactions rather than intrusive within the encounter.

However, consideration of the kinds of "troubles" that can arise when dealing with customers illustrates just how the currently available technology can problematize these encounters. The following is a lengthy extract from an interview that arose from a customer's discovery that he was in arrears on his mortgage payments and his subsequent inquiry as to how this arose. It portrays quite dramatically how both the operator's and the customer's confidence eroded due to "inadequacies" in the screens.

Customer: I came in and got told I was £700 in arrears and then, no, it was only £220 and I want to know why . . . we left our payments running at a higher level thinking we were paying the interest off, which we obviously weren't . . . and I came to in to find I was £220 in arrears and I said "No, it couldn't be . . ."

Interviewer: Are you on Annual Review? [No] You've not been on arrears since the beginning. What we've got to try to do is find out where it's gone wrong . . . let's have a look . . .

[INTERROGATES SCREEN]

What it is, your insurance has just gone in, which is not on your mortgage . . .

Customer: I thought it was

Interviewer: No, only if you're on Annual Review

Customer: It doesn't account for the £700 I got told I was in arrears by first of all . . . that figure there [POINTS TO SCREEN]

Interviewer: No, but this column doesn't mean much, only the last figure. If you're not on Annual Review we'll have to work it out annually. . . . It's the 29th September every year, it should be on your statement . . .[FIVE MINUTE DISCUSSION OF ANNUAL STATEMENTS].

Customer: At one point I was told I was £900 in arrears . . . where did they get that from?

Interviewer: I can only apologise . . . you shouldn't have been told that . . . your arrears balance has been reducing as you've been paying over the odds

Customer: But shouldn't there be another eight months of £30 [overpayment]?

Interviewer: Have you ever been on Annual Review?

Customer: I'm not trying to be awkward like . . . I just want to know . . .

Interviewer: Well, your arrears must have been getting worse and worse 'cos you've never paid your insurance. . . . there's four lots altogether since 1988 . . . this column here is what we charge and this column is what you actually pay . . . [CALCULATES INSURANCE ARREARS] Now that comes to 31200 . . . what we've got to do now is find out what you've overpaid . . . [POINTS] . . . that was the first overpayment you made . . . your £159.80 . . . now what's this £274.46? [SPENDS SOME TIME TRYING TO FIGURE IT OUT] . . . ah . . . I know what it is, you've paid your first insurance payment and your mortgage together . . . there should be another £144. . . . It might be on the next screen [ENTERS CODES] . . . there it is . . . we've charged it to you'cos you haven't paid it . . . the £144 is the additional premium for your contents 'cos you took out Buildings and Contents . . . can you see that? Do you agree with that?

Customer: Yes, yes . . . I can see that . . . where did that £510 come from?

[INTERVIEWER USES SCREEN AND CALCULATOR TO TOTAL SUMS]

Interviewer: Can you see what I'm doing? [CARRIES ON USING SCREEN]

So it comes down in the end to [EVIDENTLY REALIZES THAT THE APPARENT ARREARS ARE STILL TOO HIGH] you must have paid one or two of those insurances . . . so I'll have a look [SCROLLS THROUGH SCREENS AGAIN]..nowhere near it.

[EVIDENTLY HAVING CONSIDERABLE DIFFICULTY]

Interviewer: You've never been on Annual Review?

[PHONES MORTGAGE ACCOUNTS]

Interviewer: Can you give me a hand on this one? Annual Review, he doesn't think he's ever been on it but I'm wondering whether in fact he has. . . . I've taken all that into account . . . Screen 09, is it? . . . Start of year. . . . I've added all the insurance premiums together. . . . they're coming to over a thousand . . . it's got to be at least two on the insurances, but usually it tells you the day they've come off, doesn't it, on an 07? [POINTS]. . . . that was for your bikes . . . [ON PHONE AGAIN] . . . so where's the rest of the payments coming from? . . . 'cos I'm still in arrears

Interviewer to Customer: She'll do a breakdown and send it out to you 'cos it's going to take some time.

Customer: I just can't understand it . . . they keep sending us letters if we want to reduce and at the same time they're letting the arrears build up [INTERVIEWER TRIES TO REASSURE CUSTOMER] Am I looking at £700 arrears or £200? It doesn't fill me with a great deal of confidence.

Interviewer: I imagine the computer will be right, but no, I understand . . .

Customer: Do you need any more information from me?

Interviewer: You can't recall making any payments over the counter? Cash sums? [No] . . . I'll have a word with my boss, 'cos she's very good at this sort of thing.

Customer: And when will I hear?

Interviewer: Oh . . . first thing next week?

Customer: Shouldn't I have been told . . . don't you think I should have been told?

This particular problem is not one where the queuing problem is relevant. The interview lasts for well over thirty minutes. It is a good example of the difficulties that can arise in weaving in the technology into interaction with customers despite the fact that the computer included proprietary software designed specifically to manage financial information. The initial problem arose because a cashier who originally dealt with the inquiry was unable to establish the exact reason for arrears on a mortgage account and, indeed, gave the customer three different estimates of the amount concerned.[11] There were pressing reasons for providing a satisfactory and plausible explanation for the confusion. But this is not what occurred despite the fact that the officer approached the problem with the confidence associated with an experienced practitioner. At a very early stage, a likely cause for the confusion is identified and attempts are made to demonstrate the source of the error, namely, the "failure" to pay an insurance premium. The problem gets worse as candidate explanations fail. The realization that the problem is not at all clear from the information available on the screens prompts an appeal to further expertise via the telephone and, eventually, an apologetic admission that it will take further investigation to locate the source of the problem.

What was also clear, though not from the edited extract, was that interaction with the screens in the course of the interview caused a number of difficulties. Interrogating the screens is time-consuming and officers report that they have considerable difficulty in conducting smoothly flowing conversations with their clients. In the words of one of them:

It's the seconds in between . . . you have to make conversation and keep it going even when you make a mistake otherwise your customer loses confidence in you. But the screens strike you dumb . . . you've developed your interview technique . . . the things you've always said and in order and so on . . . and all of a sudden you've got this THING in front of you.

As we have suggested, demeanor and the display of competence is an important aspect of maintaining customer confidence and satisfaction. Difficulties in inter-rogating the database can be a major factor in the erosion of that confidence.

Closely related to this is that one of the major problems with the screens is that the information they display is structured according to a flow of transactions, not to the flow of enquiries. The display of an account, for instance, will record every transaction, the amount and the overall balance. It will, however, give no clear indication of what payments are for, and for whom they are made. The orientation brought to a given inquiry by a customer, however, will be driven by particular relevances that are the concern of *that* customer. The problems of taking these into account in an elegant way often disrupts the flow of competent work and generates a substantial amount of further inquiry, often to other departments.

In the context of these problems with the available technology, it is hardly surprising that in many instances cashiers are reluctant to use the screens and prefer, instead, to rely on paper-based information:

The thing is . . . we get an awful lot of queries at the cash desks, but most of us don't know what all the information on the screens means . . . sometimes its just easier to go to the leaflets . . . when you can.

As another officer put it,

All this could be on the screen. You could have your frauds, like your dodgy solicitors and accountants, telephone lists and other useful info, but we want it all organised so you'll use it.[12]

As the preceding quotation indicates, there is an expressed wish for appropriate computer technology to aid the work of these branch officers. What they have at the moment is a system that though a fairly standardized one for such offices, is cumbersome, inelegant, and a source of troubles and irritations given the "unpre-dictability" of customer requests. The latter is, of course, made worse when the branch is busy and there are queues building up. And yet, the available technology has to serve all situations and, it is true, is reasonably serviceable in most routine transactions.

This is not the only work that cashiers do in the branch. As already indicated, there is work "behind the counter," such as filing, completing ledgers, bringing manual records up to date, answering correspondence, and the myriad of other activities that constitute office work in a building society. Even this work, however, is frequently interrupted by the customer to be "finished later." It has to be "put down" as customers appear. The ecology of the workspace reflects the fact that, at any given moment, there will be tasks awaiting completion. Significantly, this staccato completion of work is often accomplished by more than one person.

Not surprisingly perhaps, much of the work, not only mortgage processing, is paperwork using ledgers, customer files, and other documents, records, forms, and, just as in the cashiers' workspaces, a number of locally relevant information resources pasted up around the office. The way in which branch officers orient to each others' skills and local knowledge exhibits a division of labor at work in getting the practicalities of the task done. Personal "bibles" are mutually used as resources for solving problems and making decisions on a regular basis. The pooling of expertise, both in decision making and checking information, is illustrated in the following:

Officer 1: If the advance is dead on 90%, would you times it by three or by 2.75?
Officer 2: Does she need to have a multiple of three?
Officer 1: Yeah, its dead on now . . .
Officer 2: Well, why not put it in as 89% then and times it by three [CALCULATES] no, you're alright . . . just . . . doing it by 2.75 . . . do it by 2.75.

and also in the following:

Officer 1: This isn't a tax reference . . . its a personal tax number. If we send that to the Inland Revenue they'll just send it straight back again . . . we'll have to ring him.
Officer 2: Oh, you're right. Ok, I'll do that . . . I'll get in touch with him.

Officers draw on each other's records and do each other's work. The constant amending of the progress sheets is vital to these cooperative activities in that it would be extremely difficult for any individual to process another's mortgage application without a clear and reliable record of what has been done so far and what needs to be dealt with.

The variety of such documentation and the way in which it is deployed in and through the working division of labor, creates a series of constraints and allowances. On the one hand, the robustness of paper and its public availability is a resource for cooperative work, for teamwork. In addition, there are occasions when the materiality of paper constitutes a valuable resource for mutual checking of information. On the other hand, paper no doubt contributes to the time taken to process applications and to errors of various kinds. A considerable amount of time is spent "file chasing," seeking the whereabouts of a relevant document; a problem compounded when the customer is present either at the branch or on the telephone. Files can go to other departments but customer queries tend to come into the branch office. Further, it can be surmised that much delay and error is caused by an unnecessarily large variety of documents, some legally required of course, and the need for their flow to be regulated in some way, which, in turn, generates time-consuming procedures.

8.4 Conclusion

This situation must be familiar to most offices within many different kinds of organizations in different kinds of business, excepting perhaps the few advanced system research laboratories, in which there are not only computer systems, of varying sophistication, but also a considerable amount of paper organized by conventional manual procedures. Such systems have, of course, stood some test of time in that, as a mixture of formal and informal procedures, they serve the kinds of demands that branch officials routinely, and locally, face. They are not perfect, of course, and are subject to their own "normal, natural troubles," such as "missing" files, incomplete records, and more. What is also clear is that such systems rely very much on teamwork and the ability to share expertise, knowledge, and work within the branch.

Although the "paperless office" vaunted some years ago turned out to be a chimera, there remains at least a prima facie case for developing and introducing systems that would, at least, support much of the routine work that is involved in producing, maintaining, and organizing documents. However, most office systems seem to have been designed for a world without the customer, with all the "unpredictabilities" this can routinely bring to those, as in this branch, who are in direct contact with the customers. Although there is a strong sense in which the information required by building societies is relatively restricted (and for most transactions, such as withdrawing money from one's account, exceedingly restricted) and relatively easy to formalize and standardize, there are issues here to do with how that format is presented in a sufficiently flexible way to allow for smoother interactions with customers.

An important part of the problem is determining an effective mix of human–machine elements given that there are many options here, not all of which are technological but also have to do with the redesign of work. The current menu-driven screens seem to have been designed for a minimum of training with an interface that requires laborious scrolling through screens to find the one required. This type of system is, no doubt, more than ready to be superseded by more effective ones, which assume more competence on the part of the operator. On the horizon are note pads, touch screens, and so on, which have possibilities in this connection, and a little way over the horizon are systems likely to involve a radical rethinking of the possibilities here.

Meanwhile, businesses and other organizations have to face the realities of a current situation in which hard choices have to be made whether to commit large investments to current technology that has a reasonable expectation of working or to highly innovative technology that is likely to have all the familiar problems of new technologies. And, of course, all the mixes in between. However, from the point of view of CSCW it is not straightforwardly obvious in what ways the work could be more effectively supported since much of it exhibits the "intangibles" of human interaction that defy formal elucidation and modeling. Teamwork, the "unpredictability" of customer requests and what consequences this may have for keeping the flow of customers within "acceptable bounds" (a notion that defies precision), dealing with "inadequacies" in the data, demeanor work – all of these, and more, are the "front end" of information systems, which, while intended to support work and, through this, feed information into the larger system, do not do this as well as they might.[13] Of course, as in most cases, those who use the technology manage to "make it do," which is a major disincentive for investing in appropriate training and system design.

What is also surprising, though we suspect fairly common, is how relatively little training is given to enable users to make more effective use of the system. As Bannon et al. (1993) note, systems are rarely evaluated properly though doing so might well suggest significant ways in which better training might help make better use of even a poorly designed system. It might even be informative about the design of subsequent generations of that system.

Acknowledgments

The authors thank Geoffrey and Moksha Darnton, John Williams, Val King, Tom Rodden, Dan Shapiro, Catherine Fletcher, and Wes Sharrock.

Notes

1. One might also mention here, especially since it is much less voiced in the histories of social thought, the social reform tradition in the United States, which had an important, if indirect, impact on the early Chicago School. See Turner and Turner (1990).
2. We are thinking here of the moral and political stances exhibited in a number of social theories, Marxism and feminism being, perhaps, the most salient examples. Though not applied in the sense in which one might speak of "applied science," nevertheless, like all political and moral viewpoints there is a logical commitment to the idea that society, or the views and behavior of its members, should be changed through appropriate action.
3. The equivocation is about the notion of "cooperation." A significant portion of CSCW still tends to think of this as a specific kind of interaction involving the synchronous "working together" of a set of individuals, either distributed over distance or locally sited. This is, for example, much of the thrust of shareware, coauthoring, electronic meeting rooms, and so on (Grief, 1988). For sociology, however, "cooperation" tends to signify "interdependence" and, as such, is a generic feature of socially organized activities. This is an issue to which we shall return. See Bowers (1991) for an illuminating discussion of some of the issues attaching to the notion of cooperation.
4. Some of these issues are addressed in COMIC Deliverable, Strand 2, Informing CSCW System Requirements (1993). In brief, the point is that some critiques of software engineering methodologies, including many of those which have been used within CSCW, tend toward the metaphysical, amounting to critiques of work in modern society, and critiques of formalism and representation particularly. This has merely produced more confusion for what is a very practical and difficult business of system design and development.

5. Lazarsfeld allowed that his quantitative approach could also handle qualitative data. In the early days, unlike today, there was no necessary conflict between the quantitative approach of Lazarsfeld and that of participant observation, as ethnography was commonly referred to.
6. See, e.g., Bentley et al. (1992); Hughes, Randall, and Shapiro, (1993); Hughes and King (1992).
7. The model did, of course, deal with far more of the activities of the financial organization than with front office work.
8. The notion of specialization is important in this connection and goes back to the original Smithian idea that by specializng on a single activity and organizing relevant specialisms, gains in efficiency result.
9. The authors are indebted to Kjeld Schmidt for his comments on "introduced unpredictability."
10. See Zimmerman (1970) for a study of rule following with respect to queuing and allocation to office personnel.
11. Cashiers in the building society concerned do not receive substantial training in the complexities of mortgage transactions, which was why this inquiry was referred to an officer with over a year's experience of mortgage processing. The officer in our extended example was relatively practiced in the use of the system. However, the requirement for an effective knowledge of information resources, such as the inquiry screens at the same time as trying to maintain the confidence and trust of the customer, is a daunting one especially in an organization that, historically, has not placed a high priority on training. Explicit reference to the inadequacy of training was common and a typical example is as follows: "It's the training really . . . course people in the branches are keen to do this kind of thing, to learn about it, 'cos it makes their life easier. But they don't have the information in front of them . . . they have to look for it . . . even the basic information screens.
12. This officer was clearly unaware of some of the implications of the Data Protection Act.
13. This remark should not be taken too critically since, at the time, the current system was, no doubt, "state of the art."

References

Anderson, R. J., Hughes, J. A., and Sharrock, W. W. (1989). *Working for profit: The social organisation of calculation in an entrepreneurial firm* (Aldershot: Gower).

Bannon, L. (1991). From human factors to human actors: The role of psychology and human–computer interaction studies in systems design. In J. Greenbaum and M. Kyng (eds.), *Design at work: Cooperative design of computer systems* (Hillsdale, N.J.: Lawrence Erlbaum) 25–44.

Bannon, L. (1993). Use, Design, and evaluation: Steps towards an integration. Working Paper, COMIC-RISØ-2-3.

Benson, D., and Hughes, J. A. (1992). Evidence and inference. In G. Button (ed.), *Ethnomethodology and the human sciences* (Cambridge: Cambridge University Press).

Bentley, R., Hughes, J., Randall, D., Rodden, T., Sawyer, P., Shapiro, D., and Sommerville, I. (1992). Ethnographically informed systems design for air traffic control. In J. Turner and R. Kraut (eds.), *Proceedings of the Conference on Computer-Supported Cooperative Work (CSCW '92)* (New York: ACM Press), 123–129.

Bittner, E. (1974). The concept of organisation. In R. Turner (ed.), *Ethnomethodology* (Harmondsworth: Penguin), 69–81.

Bowers, J. (1991). The janus faces of design: Some critical questions for CSCW. In J. Bowers and S. Benford (eds.), *Studies in computer-supported cooperative work: Theory, practice and design* (Amsterdam: North-Holland).

Button, G. (ed.). (1993). *Technology in working order: Studies of Work, Interaction and Technology* (London: Routledge).

COMIC Deliverable 2.1. Informing CSCW System Requirements. Department of Computing, Lancaster University.

DeZisman, M. D. (1977). Representation, specification and automation of office procedures. Department of Decision Science, The Wharton School, University of Pennsylvania.

Garfinkel, H. (1967). *Studies in ethnomethodology* (Englewood Cliffs, N.J.: Prentice-Hall).

Grief, I. (ed.). (1988) *Computer-supported cooperative work: A book of readings* (San Mateo, Calif.: Morgan Kaufmann).

Grudin, J. (1989). Why groupware applications fail: Problems in design and evaluation. *Office Technology and People,* 4 (3), 245–264.

Grudin, J. (1990). The computer reaches out: The historical continuity of interface design. In *Human Factors in Computing Systems: CHI '90 Proceedings* (New York: ACM Press), 261–268.

Harper, R., and Hughes, J. A. (1992). "What a F-ing System! Send 'em all to the same place and then expect us to stop 'em hitting": Making technology work in air traffic control. In G. Button (ed.), *Technology and working order: Studies of work, interaction and technology* (London: Routledge), 127–144.

Harper, R., Hughes, J. A., and Shapiro, D. (1991). Harmonious working and CSCW: Computer technology and air traffic control. In J. Bowers and S. Benford (eds.), *Studies in computer-supported cooperative work: Theory, practice and design* (Amsterdam: North-Holland).

Heath, C., and Luff, P. (1992). Collaboration and control: Crisis management and multimedia technology in London Underground line control rooms. *Computer Supported Cooperative Work,* 1 (1–2), 69–94.

Hughes, J. A., and King, V. (1992). Sociology for large-scale system design. *CRICT Conference on Software and Systems Practice: Social Science Perspectives,* December 1, Reading.

Hughes, J. A., Randall, D., and Shapiro, D. (1993). From ethnographic record to system design. *Computer Supported Cooperative Work,* 1 (3).

Hughes, T. P. (1987). The evolution of large technical systems. In W. Bjiker, T. P. Hughes, and T. Pinch (eds.), *The social construction of technological systems* (Cambridge, Mass.: MIT Press).

Procter, R. N., and Williams, R. A. (1992). HCI: Whose problem is IT anyway? *CRICT Conference on Software and Systems Practice: Social science perspectives,* December 1, Reading.

Schmidt, K. (1991). Cooperative work: A conceptual framework. In J. Rasmussen, B. Brehmer, and J. Leplat (eds.), *Distributed decision making: Cognitive models for cooperative work* (Chichester: Wiley), 75–109.

Smith, A. (1970). *The wealth of nations* (Harmondsworth: Penguin). Originally published in 1776.

Suchman, L. (1987). *Plans and situated actions: The problem of human–machine communication* (Cambridge: Cambridge University Press).

Suchman, L., and Wynn, E. (1984). Procedures and problems in the office. *Office Technology and People,* 2, 133–154.

Turner, S. P., and Turner, J. H. (1990). *The Impossible science: An institutional analysis of American sociology* (Newbury Park: Sage).

Wilson, P. (1991). *Computer-supported cooperative work: An introduction* (Oxford: Intellect Books).

Zimmerman, D. (1970). The practicalities of rule use. In J. Douglas (ed.), *Understanding everyday life* (Chicago: Aldine), 221–38.

9

Expert systems versus systems for experts: Computer-aided dispatch as a support system in real-world environments

Jack Whalen

9.1 Introduction

The delivery of police, fire, or emergency medical service depends on a complex communications system. The hub of this system is the dispatch center, which is responsible for receiving and processing citizen telephone calls for service, and for mobilizing and coordinating the organizational response. Prior to the 1970s, dispatch facilities in the United States relied almost exclusively on manual methods – paper and pencil-based techniques and devices, essentially – for accomplishing these exacting tasks. For rural areas and small towns, where the population base being served was usually under 50,000, such methods were often adequate. In urbanized areas with larger populations, however, dispatch personnel were finding it progressively more difficult to keep up with the growing number of street locations and the increasing call-processing and record-keeping demands. Consequently, when computer systems of sufficient capability became available at a tolerable price in the early seventies, they were employed to automate some parts of the dispatch operation in these larger facilities (Brenner and Cadoff, 1985).

The introduction of the 9-1-1 calling system in the United States in the late seventies also contributed to the automation of public safety communications. A universal, three-digit telephone number for police, fire, and medical emergencies made public safety agencies more accessible to citizens. This increased accessibility led to increased demand, and to rising expectations of swift, efficient service. Moreover, just as 9-1-1 offered citizens a single number to call for all types of emergencies, it encouraged the consolidation of public safety communications: personnel that had previously been segregated in different departments and housed in separate police, fire, and ambulance dispatch centers were brought together in centralized regional facilities called "public safety answering points," where they now had to process a much higher volume of calls and perform a wider range of work tasks.

Taken together, the increased demand, the public expectation of rapid response, and the creation of more complex and stressful work environments put additional pressure on dispatch operations to introduce automation tools. The use of these tools – what are now referred to as computer-aided dispatch or "CAD" systems – has increased considerably over the past two decades.[1] Today, most dispatch facilities, whether they are large or small, regional or local, use some form of computer-aided dispatch in their work. And there have been significant advances in

CAD technologies in recent years, with each new capability inspiring designers to build still more powerful tools for assisting human performance.[2]

The capacity to build more powerful machines does not in itself guarantee effective performance, however. Unfortunately, we have relatively little under-standing of how CAD applications are utilized by groups of dispatchers in complex, real-world environments, under actual working conditions. We also lack knowledge about whether the various automation tools that have been designed to support dispatch work are truly sensitive to the demands imposed by that environ-ment and to the ordinary work practices dispatchers have evolved to cope with such demands. We run the risk, then, of CAD design and implementation being driven by the ever growing capabilities of computational technology rather than by a detailed analysis of dispatch facilities, of the conditions dispatchers confront and the tool usage problems they encounter. When these problems are acute, personnel can quickly lose confidence in the system.[3]

In this chapter I address these issues by focusing on the design and implementa-tion of CAD technology at a 9-1-1 emergency communications center where I spent some fifteen months as a participant observer and staff member. At this center, Central Lane Communications in Eugene, Oregon, limited but nevertheless bothersome problems developed with the user interface – more specifically, the manner in which it *organized and displayed information* – for an "intelligent decision support" (IDS) application employed in fire and emergency medical dispatching. Although interface design problems have been a regular concern in human factors research on computer applications, such problems – as Woods and Roth (1988) point out – have most often been defined in a fairly restricted, techni-cal manner: windows or no windows, tiled or overlapping windows, command languages versus menus, and so forth. One consequence of this approach is that analysis of the user's tasks with respect to the application becomes focused ex-clusively on performance within the framework of the interface itself, on program manipulations.[4] But interfaces are merely external, machine-based representations of some application world, a medium through which users come to know and act on the world. Plainly, users of an application's interface are engaged in real-world tasks rather than simply program manipulations, and questions about interface design should focus on how well the interface, through the way it displays and provides for the manipulation of information, is sensitive to and supportive of the special features of both the application world (in this case, a world of human beings and their troubles) and the users' accomplishment of real-world tasks in their everyday work environment. Moreover, this work environment is fundamentally, irremediably social in nature, even though it may be saturated with numerous technologies and material artifacts. Thus, from this view, we need to consider not only the features of the material object, the user interface, but the collage of activities involved in making that artifact, with those specific features, into an instrument that is incorporated into the weave of working tasks (Shapiro et al., 1991: 3; see also Whalen, in press).

In addressing these issues, it will be necessary to first describe certain pertinent features of the communications center's organizational environment, focusing on the work tasks of fire dispatchers. This is followed by a review of the systems and tools that have been developed to support this work. The review takes a historical approach, tracing the transition from a manual system to a largely computerized system, including the introduction of an IDS application. We will then be in position to examine the problems that dispatchers experienced with the design or format of the user interface for that application.

9.2 Essential work tasks for fire dispatchers

9-1-1 communications centers, similar to air traffic control facilities, subway line control centers, airline ground operations rooms, and other "centers of coordination," are concerned with the timely provision of services, and preoccupied with the deployment of people and equipment across distances in accord with the emergent requirements of rapid response to what are often time-critical situations (Suchman, in press; see also Suchman, 1993). And, like other centers of coordination, emergency communications facilities make use of a division of labor that temporally orders responsibilities for the performance of this work. At larger centers like Central Lane, the primary work tasks involve the conjoint actions of different persons using a computer-aided dispatch system. Communications specialists functioning as call-takers receive phone calls on both 9-1-1 and non-emergency seven digit lines and, while engaged in interaction with the caller, enter information into a form on their computer screen, assembling a documentary representation of the reported trouble or event.[5] This form is then electronically transmitted to the dispatcher, either police or fire and emergency medical, depending on the type of incident (in Lane County, fire departments are responsible for both fire and medical emergencies).[6] The dispatcher reads the transmitted form and assesses the information, determines when and what organizational response is warranted, and then, via radio, dispatches field units to the scene and coordinates their response.[7]

For fire department dispatchers, the nature of this organizational response will vary by the type of incident for which help is being sought. Whereas police dispatchers have basically only one kind of apparatus, the patrol car, at their disposal, fire dispatchers have many different kinds of apparatus from which to select, each with its own special capabilities and limitations: engines, extension ladder trucks, tankers, battalion chief cars, and paramedic ambulances. Different types of fire or medical incidents require different kinds of apparatus, and department policies dictate the kinds and number of apparatus for each incident type. For example, in all medical incidents that are deemed bona fide emergencies, the policy prescribes an "advanced life support" (ALS) unit in the form of a paramedic ambulance and a "basic life support" (BLS) unit in the form of a fire engine or snorkel/truck. For a house fire, the initial response – referred to as the "first alarm" – is fixed at two engines, a truck, a paramedic unit, and a battalion chief. And if the structure on fire is a high rise or high life building (schools, offices, apartments, and other structures likely to have many people inside, regardless of their height), a third engine and second truck are added to the response. If the incident is an automobile or trash bin fire, however, or involves nothing more than a fire alarm ringing at the location, the initial response is limited to one engine. Finally, should the initial, first-alarm responses to fires prove insufficient with respect to the size and seriousness of the blaze, the specific additional apparatus for a second- (and, if need be, a third-) alarm response is similarly prescribed.

Related to these tasks, fire dispatchers must also make a determination about which individual units to dispatch for each kind of required apparatus – which engine(s) from among all those available, which paramedic unit, and so on. Given the time-critical character of 9-1-1 operations, these judgments must typically be made in a matter of seconds and are based on determining the closest available unit – "available" in the sense of not assigned to another call or activity – to the incident's location. There are a number of complicating factors involved, though. Each fire station under Central Lane's direction is responsible for a specific area of the community, but the distribution of apparatus varies from station to station.[8] Although all stations have one engine, paramedic ambulances and extension ladder trucks are posted at only a few stations. It is not simply a matter, then, of determining the station area in which an incident is located and dispatching the appropriate apparatus from that station. For most types of incidents, apparatus from more than one station will be required.[9]

Moreover, units posted to a station in which an incident is located or to a nearby station may be involved in responding to a prior incident; consequently, they are not available for dispatch to any new incidents. In addition, even when units posted to the pertinent stations are available for a call, they may be out of their home area (and thus their station) at the time of the incident – returning from an earlier call or engaged in a training exercise in a different area, for example – and too far from the location to warrant a dispatch. In order to deal with these complicating factors, dispatchers must closely monitor and continuously track the status (availability) and current location of all units.[10]

9.3 Decision support for dispatching: Run files and notepad

Given the multifarious contingencies facing fire dispatchers and the time-critical features of their work, emergency communications centers have routinely provided their staff members with a variety of support systems to assist them in making

```
┌─────────────────────────────┐
│ 4656  BARGER,   EUG         │
│                             │
│ C1                          │
│                             │
│ M4                          │
│ M9                          │
│ M5                          │
│                             │
│ 7                           │
│ 8                           │
│ T8                          │
│                             │
│ 4                           │
│ 9                           │
│ 2                           │
│ T1                          │
│                             │
│ 1                           │
│ 3                           │
│ 5                           │
└─────────────────────────────┘
```

Figure 9.1.

dispatch decisions and tracking the status of field units. Prior to the development of CAD, Central Lane dispatchers consulted paper-based "run files" that listed all the addresses in the center's response area and the recommended dispatch – the kinds of apparatus and the specific units – for calls to that address. We can examine the use of this fire dispatch decision support system by considering an actual unit recommendation entry from these files (Figure 9.1).

Figure 9.1 shows the run file entry for an address in the city of Eugene, 4656 Barger Street. In this and all other dispatch recommendation listings, each unit is represented by a code consisting of a single number or a letter followed by a number. In both cases, the number indicates the fire station at which that particular unit is posted – its home station; letters are added when the apparatus is a unit other than an engine, such as a paramedic ambulance, truck, or battalion chief. Thus, "8" is the designation for the engine posted at Station 8, and the unit is referred to as Engine 8; "M4" is the designation for the paramedic unit assigned to Station 4, and this unit is known as Medic 4; "T8" stands for the truck posted at Station 8, Truck 8; and "C1" stands for (Battalion) Chief 1.

The listing of units is organized by different "response groups," which are separated from each other by a blank space or a line (it is this separation by space that provides for seeing them as "groups" in the first place). The first group consists of only one unit, the battalion chief; the second consists of paramedic units only; the remaining three groups consist of fire fighting apparatus, which are arranged into first-, second-, and third-alarm responses (Figure 9.2).

Within each of the response groups, units are listed in rank order with respect to dispatch priority or preference. For instance, among the MED or paramedic units,

```
┌─────────────────────────────┐
│  4656  BARGER,   EUG        │
│                             │
│  C1            battalion  chief │
│                             │
│  M4  ⎫                      │
│  M9  ⎬  paramedic   units   │
│  M5  ⎭                      │
│                             │
│  7   ⎫                      │
│  8   ⎬  first   alarm       │
│  T8  ⎭                      │
│                             │
│  4   ⎫                      │
│  9   ⎬  second   alarm      │
│  2   ⎭                      │
│                             │
│  T1  ⎫                      │
│  1   ⎬  third   alarm       │
│  3   ⎭                      │
│  5                          │
└─────────────────────────────┘
```

Figure 9.2.

Medic 4 would be the first choice or "first in" for dispatch to 4656 Barger, Medic 9 the second, and Medic 5 the third or least preferred choice. Recall that these rankings are based on how close each fire station's response area is to the address in question.

Observe that when presenting dispatch recommendations, these file entries do not distinguish between incident types. Instead, after grouping the battalion chief and paramedic units separately, they list the response for the "worst case" possibility – a structure fire at the location – and dispatchers were expected to use that rather broad listing as the basis for making decisions on less serious fire incidents (such as a fire alarm) or medical problems.[11] For instance (keep in mind the rank ordering of units just described), if a medical emergency was reported at 4656 Barger, the recommended dispatch is Medic 4 as the ALS unit and Engine 7 as the BLS unit (as the unit listed first in the first alarm group, Engine 7 is thus the highest ranked among non-MED apparatus). Of course, if a structure fire was indeed reported at 4656 Barger, the units in first alarm group – Engine 7, Engine 8, and Truck 8 – would be the "first in," along with the highest ranked MED unit, Medic 4, and the First Battalion Chief (C1).

These recommendation files do not deal with the issue of unit availability. Dispatchers must determine whether the prescribed "first in" units are in fact available to respond – are not committed to another call (or to a training or drill activity that makes it impossible to respond) and are not too far from their assigned station's area (and thus from the incident location) at the time of the call. They therefore need a system that will allow them to record and track the availability and location of every unit under their authority.

Prior to the use of CAD, Central Lane fire dispatchers employed relatively simple tools, a note pad and pencil, to assist them in this task. Unit movement and status were monitored by radio and any changes were recorded on the note pad. Fairly standard abbreviations for both location and status were used to save time and ensure that the essential information could be gleaned at a glance. Dispatchers, after first determining what apparatus was required and what specific units were recommended or preferred for a call, could review that information to check the availability and current location of all units. If a recommended unit was not available or was out of the pertinent area, a substitution would be made, with dispatchers using the next highest ranked unit for that class of apparatus as the first choice in this regard. For instance, if there was a structure fire at 4656 Barger and Truck 8 was not available, Truck 1 would be substituted. And if neither Engine 7 nor Engine 8 was available for that call, Engine 4 would normally be the first substitute, Engine 9 the second, Engine 2 the third, and so forth. If a different unit from that same apparatus class was *closer* to the incident location, however, the principle of "closest available" would take precedence, regardless of the response ranking of that unit. Thus, if Engine 7 was not available, and Engine 2's current location was for some reason closer to 4656 Barger than Engine 4's, Engine 2 would be dispatched, even though its RES rank in the recommendation listing is below Engine 4's.

We can summarize the import of these observations as follows. The pre-CAD, paper-based dispatch unit recommendation listings, along with the paper-and-pencil tracking of unit status and location, gave dispatchers ready access to information that was crucial to the successful performance of their work tasks; moreover, the organization of the recommendation listing file – the format of this "paper–text user interface," the manner in which information was displayed – served to inscribe textually the most important principles or elements of Central Lane's fire dispatch policies. But this elementary support system only provided dispatchers with basic *evaluation tools* for solving problems and making decisions; as the examples just presented make clear, the system did not actually present dispatchers with *solutions* to those problems (cf. Pew, 1988). Instead, the system depended on dispatchers to use these tools, together with their own reasoning and professional expertise – their understanding of department policy and procedures for responding to different types of incidents, their knowledge of local geography and fire station response areas, their past experience, and the like – to reach the best solution for the problem and circumstances at hand. That is to say, the system's operation rested largely on dispatchers' *practical craft knowledge* (see Collins, 1987; Hutchins, 1983; 1990).

Further, in reaching solutions to such problems, dispatchers are not operating as isolated individuals; rather, they have always acted as members of a local collectivity; their ability to coordinate activities, and to perceive and make sense of information, necessarily relies on a group social organization, a shared (rather than private or personal) body of skills and practices. Recent work in cognitive science and the psychology of work has referred to this organization as a kind of "distributed cognition," a process in which various individuals develop a conjoint, closely interrelated orientation toward a set of tasks and activities (Heath and Luff, 1991; see also Goodwin and Goodwin, 1992). In this sense, "expertise" in the form of craft knowledge and experience is indispensably communal in nature.[12]

9.4 CAD-based support

When Central Lane Communications first converted to CAD, they simply transferred the paper file listing format and organization to the computer. The computer display thus looked much like the paper display, but with a significant addition: rather than being recorded by hand on a note pad, the status and location of each unit listed were entered into the computer system (via the keyboard) by the dispatcher whenever necessary and CAD included this unit status and location information on the dispatch recommendation list display. Moreover, when the "call record form" that had been filled out by a call taker was electronically transmitted to the dispatcher, the CAD system automatically matched up the incident address shown on that form with the appropriate recommendation list for that address, and displayed that list on the dispatcher's computer screen. The computer display (Figure 9.3) also added an explicit identifying code for each response group (BC, MED, 1, 2, and 3).

In the CAD display for 4656 Barger, the identifying codes for response groups are listed under the RES column. The STA column shows a unit's status (entered in abbreviated form) and the LOCATION column provides its current location (also often entered in abbreviated form, with the abbreviation serving as an alias for the site in question). For example, Medic 4 and Engine 8 are shown as having been dispatched, a status that is abbreviated as DSP, to a call at 3435 Echo Hollow Road. Most of the other units are shown to be located and available at their posted or home station, which is indicated by the *absence* of an abbreviation in the STA column. The display also shows that three units are not at their home stations, however: Engine 9 has arrived at Fire Station 5, a status and location abbreviated as ARV and EGF-5, respectively; Engine 4 is shown as en route to their quarters, abbreviated as ENR and QTRS; and Engine 1 has arrived at the department's supply and maintenance shop, abbreviated as S&M.

This CAD-based support system made the dispatcher's job much easier: they did not have to flip through a rack of paper files to find the appropriate address, and they did not have to consult a separately and manually maintained status record and compare it to the file listing. The underlying character of the system was virtually identical to the paper-based one, though. The information was once again organized by the "closest station area" ordering principle, and the entire response framework for the "worst case" scenario, from first through third alarm, was

```
      4656 BARGER, EUG          RESPONSE UNIT STATUS AT 21:53

RES   UNIT  STA  LOCATION
BC    C1                             2    2
MED   M4    DSP  3435 ECHO HOLLOW    2    T1
MED   M9                             3    1      ARV   S&M
MED   M5                             3    3
1     7                              3    5
1     8     DSP  3435 ECHO HOLLOW
1     T8
2     4     ENR  QTRS
2     9     ARV  EGF-5
```

Figure 9.3.

displayed. Note also that the headers for the first choices in each RES category in this scenario – BC, MED, and 1 – were highlighted on the computer screen (represented here by boldface text), further transforming an important part of what could be described as a domain of scrutiny, the boxed CAD screen display, into a zone of special relevance (see Goodwin and Goodwin, 1992).

In addition, as was the case with the paper-based support system, dispatchers were required to draw on their expert knowledge and professional experience when reading and interpreting the CAD display in order to make dispatch determinations. That is to say, CAD did not "make" a decision or attempt to provide a comprehensive solution to dispatch problems; instead, the CAD support system, like the paper file listings and monitoring note pad, provided dispatchers with information for solving those problems. And, through the way CAD arranged that information by response categories and, within those categories, by unit rankings, it presented dispatchers with an instructive "silhouette" of important department policies and procedures that they could then make use of in dealing with many different kinds of situations.

The continued extensive reliance on human expertise under this CAD system can be demonstrated by considering the problems dispatchers would face if they received the following CAD call record or report (Figure 9.4) from a call taker concerning an incident at 4656 Barger and had to make use of the "response unit status" display shown in Figure 9.3 to resolve these problems.

Reviewing just those items on the CAD incident report form that I have shaded for analytic purposes, we can note first that the incident type selected by the call taker (entered in the INC field on the form) is FIRE, ELECTRICAL. The prescribed response for this type of fire is one engine. Competent dispatching requires a great deal more than a simple (and inflexible) execution of department policy with respect to the listed incident type on a call record form, however. For example, dispatchers are expected to use their professional experience and knowledge in assessing whether the incident type selected by a call taker makes sense in light of

```
INC: FIRE, ELECTRICAL      TY: F    FD/CTY: EUG/      ID: EGY093001356
LOC: 4656 BARGER ST      EUG   PR: 1     TY/NM: 1 FAMILY HOUSE
PHO: 345-5565      X:        PH ADR:                              FL:
SRC: 61    XST:    DANEBO AVE     MAP: 62-C6          DIST: 4200
BREATH:    CONSC:   AGE:   SEX:    AGYS: EGF           INI: MLJ
CALLER: RESIDENT         CONT:                             REF:
ADR:                     EUG   DISP:               CSN:
DTL: SOME SMOKE FROM BEDROOM THERMOSTAT
```

Figure 9.4.

the other information that is entered on that form. With an electrical fire in a home, dispatchers would want to know whether there was any indication that more than an electrical device was involved, whether the fire was still burning, and whether the entire structure was then in danger of going up in flames. If there was any evidence that this might be the case, a full first-alarm response would be dispatched.

On the CAD report for 4656 Barger, the text entered in the DTL or "details" field (at the bottom of the form) reads "some smoke from bedroom thermostat." But this account is ambiguous. Does it mean that this is a small and "normal" electrical fire, caused by a short circuit and confined to the thermostat itself, and that the smoke was evident only when the short first occurred? Or does it suggest that the smoke is still visible and the wall around the thermostat is involved or threatened? There is nothing in the computerized support system available to dispatchers – the CAD unit status response display – that offers answers to these vexing questions. Thus, at the very first, with what is perhaps the most important problem faced by dispatchers – determining the nature and seriousness of the reported incident, which will then set the temper of the response – professional judgment and experience play an essential role.[13]

Suppose a dispatcher, after considering the information and consulting with his or her partner, elected to go with a full first alarm, treating the incident as a possible structure fire, not wanting to risk a single-engine response. What specific units should be dispatched? Consider once again the CAD display (Figure 9.5).

I have shaded the RES and UNIT columns of the recommended/prescribed full first-alarm units. Recall, however, that two of the prescribed units – Medic 4 and Engine 8 – are committed to another call (an incident at 3435 Echo Hollow Road). Medic 9, listed as the second choice in the rank ordering of paramedic ambulances, is available at its home station as a replacement for Medic 4, but selecting the best – that is to say, the "closest available" – substitute for Engine 8 presents a more difficult problem. Recapitulating our earlier observations, the highest-ranked engine in the second-alarm response (recall that these units are designated by a "2" header in the RES column) is Engine 4, which is shown as en route to its home

```
         4656 BARGER, EUG          RESPONSE UNIT STATUS AT 21:53

RES    UNIT  STA  LOCATION
BC     C1                            2    2
MED    M4    DSP  3435 ECHO HOLLOW   2    T1
MED    M9                            3    1        ARV  S&M
MED    M5                            3    3
1      7                            3    5
1      8     DSP  3435 ECHO HOLLOW
1      T8
2      4     ENR  QTRS
2      9     ARV  EGF-5
```

Figure 9.5.

station. The display does not indicate in any precise manner Engine 4's current location in the city, however, or where it is coming from, which would then provide some indication of where it might be located relative to Fire Station 4 and to 4656 Barger. The next highest ranked engine, Engine 9, is shown as arrived at Fire Station 5. The lowest ranked engine in the second-alarm group, Engine 2, is indeed available at its home station, but the display also shows that the highest ranked cngine in the third-alarm group, Engine 1, has left its home station and arrived at the department's supply and maintenance facility (S&M).

Which of these four engines is closest to 4656 Barger? The CAD system described earlier does not provide an answer. Rather, to solve this problem, a dispatcher must once again draw on personal knowledge. In this case, this includes knowledge of: (1) recent past activity by Engine 4 – the location from which Engine 4 is returning to its quarters and the amount of time that has elapsed since it left that location; and (2) local geography – the relative distance from 4656 Barger of Fire Station 5, Fire Station 2, the supply and maintenance facility, and, given the prior location of Engine 4 and the time it has been en route to quarters, its probable current location. The use of written notes and memory can help with tracking past activity, as can consultation between dispatchers; in addition, a dispatcher could quickly call Engine 4 on the radio and request its current location.[14] But a detailed, practical understanding of local geography – practical knowledge that would permit someone to recognize whether, for example, the supply and maintenance facility was closer to 4656 Barger than was Fire Station 2 – can only be acquired through experience and study.

9.5 Designing an expert system

After approximately six years of using this CAD unit recommendation system, Central Lane introduced a greater degree of automation into the dispatch decision-making process with a rudimentary intelligent decision support system. There was never any thought given to developing a system that would not only recommend but also implement dispatch decisions concerning such things as the assignment of particular units to an incident, thus taking over control of these matters from the dispatchers. However, the new system's design did attempt to control for or eliminate certain forms of human error by having the machine execute phases of the problem-solving process that had previously been completely managed or resolved by humans:

- Previously, dispatchers had to review the STA (status) entries for all units listed in the CAD unit status response display in order to determine which apparatus was available for a call. The CAD "recommendation" for a particular address was nothing more than a ranked listing of units in terms of their priority, based on the location of their home station, for dispatch to that address, regardless of their current availability. Errors sometimes occurred when dispatchers failed to review adequately or decipher correctly those STA entries. The new system was able to distinguish between available and unavailable units by their STA entries, however, and would recommend only those that were actually available.

- Under the first CAD support system, expert knowledge of local geography was often required for assessing the relative distance of available units from the location of an incident. The new system was designed to reduce this reliance on human expertise and experience and to prevent the inevitable errors in judgment that occurred, such as dispatchers failing to recognize that a particular unit's current location was actually closer to the incident's address than that of another unit. The system would now use algorithms, structured by the predetermined (i.e., programmed into the system) ranking of each fire station's response area with respect to every address in Central Lane's data base, to determine what available unit was the closest to an incident. CAD would then provide specific dispatch recommendations that were predicated on these determinations.

- Where the first CAD system did not distinguish between incident types in suggesting dispatch recommendations, the new system would use the incident code on the call record form to provide incident-sensitive recommendations. This function was intended to help dispatchers avoid errors like failing to follow procedure with regard to exactly what apparatus was required for a particular incident type. The function was also designed to prevent related problems such as dispatchers neglecting to substitute an equivalent type of apparatus for each unavailable unit in a response set.

The new system functioned in the following manner. It first looked at the database's incident code file, which would indicate the "response class" – fire or police and fire together – for the incident type entered in the INC field on the call

```
        4656 BARGER, EUG           RESPONSE UNIT STATUS AT 21:53

RES   UNIT  STA  LOCATION
REC   7
REC   4     ENR  QTRS
REC   T8
REC   CO
REC   M9
      1     ARV  S&M
      9     ARV  EGF-5
```

Figure 9.6.

record form. It then scanned "location type" files (based on county land use data), which indicated the nature of the structure – for example, one family house, duplex, apartment, school – at the reported address. The system next looked at the database's "unit file," and diagnosed the apparatus required for that type of incident at that type of structure. It then determined the current location and status of all units, using information previously entered into CAD by dispatchers, in each of the required apparatus classes. The final step in the algorithm involved scanning the file that ranked, by fire stations, the dispatch priorities for the reported address, with the "first in" or highest priority station for that address ranked number one, the "next in" or second-highest priority station ranked number two, and so on. In the case of 4656 Barger Street, the ordering of stations was 7, 8, 4, 9, 2, 1, 3, and 5. This ranking was then compared with the unit location results from the previous step, and the closest available unit(s) – again, "closest available" is calculated in terms of the fire station response area in which the unit is currently located and the ranking of that station for that address – from each required apparatus class were then recommended to the dispatcher.

The format of the dispatch recommendation screen display, the CAD system's user interface for the decision support component, underwent even more dramatic changes. To illustrate, if a structure fire was reported at 4656 Barger (i.e., if the incident type entered by the call taker was FIRE, STRUCTURE), the recommendation display would look like Figure 9.6. Alternatively, if a medical emergency (e.g., respiratory distress) was reported at the same address, the listing of units in the display would be quite different (Figure 9.7). And if the reported incident was an electrical fire, the display would read as Figure 9.8.

The new interface/display format listed only the recommendations "made" by the system software, based on the "closest available" principle and following the program's algorithms, along with a list of those *available* units that were *not currently located at their home station* (i.e., units that were in quarters and available were not listed). The recommended units have a highlighted **REC** designation

```
      4656 BARGER, EUG              RESPONSE UNIT STATUS AT 21:53

RES   UNIT  STA  LOCATION
REC   M9
REC   7
      1     ARV  S&M
      4     ENR  QTRS
      9     ARV  EGF-5
```

Figure 9.7.

```
      4656 BARGER, EUG              RESPONSE UNIT STATUS AT 21:53

RES   UNIT  STA  LOCATION
REC   7
      1     ARV  S&M
      4     ENR  QTRS
      9     ARV  EGF-5
```

Figure 9.8.

in the RES column. Accordingly, there is no presentation of a broad, "worst-case" framework from which dispatchers then make selections for any and all cases. Instead, and as described earlier, the listing of units is responsive to the specific incident code entered by the call taker on the CAD call record form. That is to say, the display for a structure fire lists, in the form of a recommendation, two engines (7 and 4), a truck (T8), a paramedic ambulance (M9), and a battalion chief or "chief officer," which is the term used in the new system (note that "CO," an abbreviation for chief officer, is used in place of "BC," and no specific chief is prescribed or recommended); the medical emergency display recommends only the prescribed ALS/paramedic and BLS/engine apparatus; and the electrical fire display recommends only the prescribed (for that incident type) single engine. Note also that in making the structure fire dispatch recommendation, the CAD system has resolved the "Which engine should be substituted for Engine 8?" problem discussed earlier. Recall that 8, along with Engine 7, is a "first in" engine for this address, but it has been dispatched to another call and is therefore unavailable; Engine 4 has been selected by the system as the substitute. As we have seen, under the prior system this substitution decision would have been made (and could only have been made) by dispatchers using their knowledge of local geography to determine which of the available engines was closest to 4656 Barger.

One consequence of the new format that was immediately apparent is that if a dispatcher – after reading the details on the call record form, consulting with their partner, and so on – determines that a full first-alarm, structure fire–type response is the better, more prudent dispatch to a call originally entered under a less serious incident code (e.g., electrical or trash bin fire), they could not consult this incident-sensitive display for a ranked listing of the necessary apparatus. To deal with this problem, the new system made that kind of information available on a separate "full first alarm" list, which could be called up on the screen by a keyboard-entered command. Similar lists were available for second- and third-alarm recommendations, as were lists of specific apparatus types (all ranked according to "closest available" criteria) should the dispatch of a single additional engine, truck, ambulance, or other specialized unit to a call become necessary. Related to this, dispatchers could now issue special commands to receive CAD system recommendations for adding particular kinds of apparatus to a dispatch that had already been issued (e.g., adding a truck). In all these cases, then, the new system attempted to compensate for the loss of the comprehensive listing of apparatus that dispatchers, under the old system, would have used to make such selections.

9.6 Problems with the expert system

Despite these efforts to provide information that was comparable with that available under the original CAD system, a number of Central Lane fire dispatchers were uncomfortable with or expressed concerns about – almost always informally, to each other – the new expert system. Moreover, although this expert system was designed to reduce the sophistication of demands on dispatchers, and thus to decrease the likelihood of human error, when errors in failing to dispatch the appropriate unit(s) to an incident continued to occur they were frequently blamed on the system (even though there had not been a dramatic increase in the error rate).[15] "The system," it was often said, had recommended the "wrong" unit(s). "I don't trust it," was a frequently heard refrain. This lack of confidence was further evidenced by the fact that most dispatchers, during the six month period in which both systems were available on-line, either continued to rely exclusively on the old system or routinely compared its recommendations and presentation of information with those of the new before dispatching a call.

Many of these difficulties were undoubtedly rooted in the uncertainty and anxiety that can result from introducing any new automation tool into the workplace, particularly a high-pressured, technologically saturated environment like 9-1-1 communications. And there were a few problems with the expert system's algorithms and database that in some instances produced "incorrect" recommendations, which were then misinterpreted as evidence for the system's basic inadequacy rather than as bugs that could be easily corrected. But there was a common, underlying concern expressed in a number of complaints that pointed to a genuine problem with the new expert system: the manner in which it organized and displayed information on the dispatcher's computer screen when recommending units for a call made it difficult for dispatchers to immediately recognize and correct any errors in or problems with those recommendations.

The basis of this problem appeared to be that the new interface's organization reflected a preference for the automated recommendation system, the "machine expert," over the dispatcher's own reasoning skills and experience as an "expert human practitioner," skills and experience that the earlier system had relied on. As Woods and Roth (1988) have observed for IDS systems in general, this preference – one they describe as a "machine as prosthesis" philosophy – is manifested in the way in which designers all too frequently package and deliver advice (recommendations) to practitioners: they assume advice is synonymous with outputting an answer, with solving the problem for the practitioner. As we have seen, the initial design of Central Lane's unit recommendation screen display showed only the machine expert's choices, with little information about how the machine arrived at that decision; that is to say, the display did not supply much data about the operational "unit selection context" within which that recommendation emerged. This context could be said to include things like the full range of apparatus that could possibly be called on for dispatch on any type of incident to that location, the ranking of those units with respect to dispatch priority, and the system's "understanding" of their current status and location. Without those data, the detection of error could be a rather difficult chore.

It also appeared to be the case that in their complaints, dispatchers implicitly understood that the earlier unit recommendation display, with its comprehensive format, made the operational context readily accessible to practitioners. The most striking evidence for this understanding is the fact that several dispatchers proposed that the old screen display format be retained under the new intelligent decision support system. A few even suggested that the expert system could simply include, in this display, an **REC** marker by those units that were being recommended for the call (given the type of incident that had been reported), thus combining the IDS feature of the new system with the display organization of the old. For a number of technical and resource-availability reasons – it would have required considerable reprogramming, for example – this suggestion was never seriously considered.[16]

The problem of detecting errors when viewing the new unit recommendation display can be illustrated by examining the IDS requirements for entering unit locations, and the operational consequences of those requirements. Recall that dispatchers use abbreviations as aliases for certain locations. These locations are not incident addresses but rather regular fire department destinations such as supply, storage and repair facilities, fire stations, hospitals, and the like. Thus, as I previously noted, S&M is the alias for the fire department's supply and maintenance shop and QTRS is the alias for "quarters" or home station.[17] Under the first CAD system, these particular ways of spelling or recording these and other aliases were a matter of convention more than official policy. That is to say, dispatchers invented these abbreviations over a period of time, as a form of shorthand; indeed, the use of abbreviations for certain locations originated in the days of paper-and-pencil tracking of units.

Because they were simply conventions, there was some small amount of variation in abbreviation spelling and form. For instance, a dispatcher could abbreviate "quarters" as QRTS or QTRS, and "supply and maintenance" as S&M or S-M, as long as other dispatchers could recognize and understand the entries. This variation did not have any consequences for the functioning of the CAD system, because the system did not have an IDS component that provided dispatch recommendations based on *its* reading of the data on unit location. The use of abbreviations as aliases for location entries was primarily to save time and, to a lesser extent, screen display space. Once the IDS component was added to the system, however, data entry procedures, especially for items like aliases, had to be strictly controlled: only those abbreviations recognized by the expert system's software as "genuine" or valid could be used, and the system could not tolerate much, if any, variation. When it came to location aliases, only one abbreviation form (correctly spelled, of course) for each location was permitted. To take one example, QTRS was the only correct alias for "quarters" – the only abbreviation the system could recognize in terms of being able to associate it with a specific location and its address, which in this case is the home station of the unit that is recorded as en route to or secured in that station.

This limitation was greatly complicated by the expert system's treatment of incorrectly recorded location aliases. First, the system did not indicate to the dispatcher that an error had been made. Thus, if a dispatcher typed 4 ENR QRTS instead of 4 ENR QTRS ("Engine 4 en route to quarters"), there was no signal from CAD that this alias entry could not be recognized. Second, and most important, the system regarded units that had an unrecognizable location as unavailable for dispatch. As far as the IDS system was concerned, then, Engine 4 was not en route to its home station and available for dispatch, but rather was at an unknown location *and* was not free to respond to calls. Since the unit recommendation display only listed (1) the recommended units and (2) those available units that were not at their home stations, the display would not show Engine 4 – to use this example once more – as recommended, even if the incident was in its home station's area or its station was ranked as closer to an incident than that of other available units. The expert system would not list Engine 4 in *any* part of the display. This meant that the dispatcher could not detect the incorrect, misspelled QRTS

```
        4656 BARGER, EUG          RESPONSE UNIT STATUS AT 21:53

RES   UNIT  STA  LOCATION
REC   7
REC   T8
REC   1         ARV  S&M
REC   CO
REC   M9
      9         ARV  EGF-5
```

Figure 9.9.

entry by scanning this display – it was not visible. Consequently, if the system now had to make a dispatch recommendation for a structure fire at 4656 Barger, the screen would have looked like Figure 9.9.

Observe that the system would have substituted Engine 1 for Engine 4, because its location, the supply and maintenance facility (S&M), makes it the closest engine to 4656 Barger among all those understood by the system to be available. An experienced dispatcher might recognize in this instance that some type of error had occurred, might recall that Engine 4 had reported being en route to its station and know that if the incident was at 4656 Barger, Engine 4 should therefore have been recommended for dispatch ahead of Engine 1. But dispatchers continuously receive and record a great deal of information, and no matter how experienced or knowledgeable, they cannot be expected to notice every flawed recommendation, especially if they do not have access to the same information the expert system used to generate those recommendations. And it was this problem, the *absence of a shared frame of reference* between the dispatcher and the CAD system, rather than the inability of the system to signal users when they erred in entering data or the system's method of interpreting that erroneous data, that was the principal source of the difficulties. Thus, the technical reason for the flawed or incorrect recommendation isn't really at issue here; incorrect recommendations that were due to bugs in the system's database or algorithms instead of errors in location aliases were equally hard to recognize. If this problem was to be solved, the machine-as-prosthesis logic of the IDS system – its emphasis on providing users with an answer and its concomitant neglect of users' needs for evaluation tools that made better use of their professional expertise – had to be reexamined.

This is precisely what happened at Central Lane in the months following the implementation of the IDS component. Dispatchers' complaints about the system making the "wrong" recommendations and the difficulties they faced in recognizing those errors before units had been dispatched on the call were taken quite seriously. At the time I left Central Lane, a veteran dispatcher who had been very much involved in setting up the new expert system was beginning work on the problem of including additional information on the unit recommendation screen display, and gradually, over the course of several months, more and more data about unit location and status was included in the display. Where the original IDS-produced display listed only the recommended units and those units that were away from their home station but available for calls, the revisions were geared toward adding units that were available at their home stations to the list. This provided dispatchers with greater access to the operational context from which units were selected, somewhat similar to what was obtainable under the old system. The formating of that information also took into account the need for an interface that was less prosthesis and more evaluation tool: the revisions attempted to order units that were available but not recommended according to their dispatch priority rank, which allowed dispatchers more easily to review and compare the lists of "recommended" and "not recommended but available" units so as to identify possible recommendation errors. This identification of error would necessarily be based on their expert knowledge, only now they would have a more extensive and *instructive* display of information to support them in drawing on that expertise. While these revisions, when taken together, never fully realized the comprehensiveness of the old interface, and the ultimate success of those revisions remains at this point unclear, they nevertheless exhibited an orientation to the "system for experts" logic of that prior interface, and represented an attempt to combine elements of that logic with the advantages of the new expert system.

9.7 Expert systems versus systems for experts

Computer system designers and programmers often speak of the "coupling" of human intelligence and expertise with machine power in a single integrated, interactive system that maximizes performance. As Suchman's (1987) pioneering research on human–machine interaction demonstrated, however, the project of building intelligent artifacts confronts some formidable obstacles (see also Button and Sharrock, this volume). It is not primarily a matter of determining how to allocate functions between the machine components and the human elements, as the literature on human factors in expert and automated systems would have us believe.[18] Without denying the relevance of this allocation problem, the most important issue that designers face is how to build systems that take the fundamental *differences* between human practical reasoning and machine operation into account.

The operation of an expert system, in terms of its machine action features, is strictly regulated by the "facts" that are stored in its memory banks and the formal rules that it follows for manipulating that codified information. To use Collins's (1987) terminology, its operation is based on an algorithmic model of knowledge, learning, and communication. The problem is that this model fails miserably as an adequate representation of human knowledge, intelligence, and practice, which is

essentially grounded in commonsense understanding that resists explicit statements and cannot possibly be operationalized.[19] None of this is to say that expert
systems based on algorithmic operations cannot or should not be employed to assist
humans in solving complex problems that require collecting and evaluating a great
deal of information. Plainly, such systems can play an important role in supporting
the performance of complicated tasks, perhaps especially when these tasks are
time-critical in nature. This is certainly the case with the introduction of IDS into
computer-aided dispatch systems. But the key term in this regard is support. A
lesson of the events described in this chapter has been the need to design expert
systems that are actually systems for experts: systems that will support and complement, and not attempt to thoroughly replicate or replace, the communally organized work practices and problem-solving strategies – the professional and practical expertise – of experienced dispatch center personnel.

And this brings us back to the problem of basic differences between human
reasoning and machine operation. System design must recognize the real limitations of machine expertise, and must build an interface that allows the human
practitioner fully to review, assess, and, most important, *understand* the machine's
actions and recommendations, which means being able to comprehend why the
machine made those recommendations or took those actions. Thus, if this coupling
of machine and human intelligence is to succeed, there has to be a mutual intelligibility, a shared frame of reference, between IDS, the expert machine, and
dispatchers, the human experts who are required to interact with it. Another lesson
of the events described in this chapter is the considerable difficulty of establishing
and sustaining this shared frame of reference in and through human–computer
interfaces.

Acknowledgments

This research was supported by a grant from U.S. West Advanced Technologies. My thanks
to Marilyn Whalen and Peter Thomas for many useful comments and suggestions. I would
like to express my deep gratitude to the Eugene, Oregon, Department of Public Safety –
especially the staff of the Central Lane Communications Center – for giving me the
opportunity to work as a communications specialist in their department and permitting
complete access to Central Lane's activities and records. Finally, this chapter could not
have been written without the generous advice and help of Central Lane fire dispatcher Jim
Henry.

Notes

1. E.g., in 1975, only 10 percent of police departments in jurisdictions of more than 100,000
   population employed CAD systems; by the early 1980s over 50 percent of these departments had

installed them, as had several municipalities with smaller populations (Brenner and Cadoff, 1985).

2. In addition to automated calltaking, case number assignment, address verification, status monitoring of units in the field, dispatch recommendations, and information management, CAD tools have been developed to apprise dispatchers about previous incidents of a similar type or at the same location, the presence and type of hazardous materials stored at a site, and alarm records and dispositions. Immediate access to a wealth of additional on-line data is also possible. Further, graphic mapping systems, when linked to automatic vehicle locators, can now provide dispatchers with visual and pictorial (instead of just textual) representations of the status and location of units in the field as well as "best route to incident" recommendations (best-route vehicle routing).

3. As a result, some facilities – the city of Denver's communications center and London's ambulance dispatch operation, to take two relatively recent examples – have had to temporarily abandon their CAD system and return to manual methods.

4. It is worth noting here that while interface design has been an important topic for human factors researchers, it has been a neglected issue in the development of expert systems. As Pew (1988: 931) reminds us, "in the current state of expert system development and dissemination, most development effort is devoted to their internal workings and very little to their user interfaces."

5. An analysis of the embodied courses of practical action and practical reasoning involved in the assembly of this textual record, focusing on the utilization of computer-aided dispatch tools for data entry, can be found in Whalen (in press).

6. Some incidents, such as gunshot wounds and drug overdoses, require a joint fire and police response, and they are routed to both fire and police dispatchers.

7. This division of labor between (1) phone call receipt and information eliciting and (2) radio output and response broadcast is known in the field of public safety communications as horizontal dispatching. In contrast to this tandem team approach, smaller centers most often use a vertical dispatching system, where a single person handles all aspects of a call (see Clawson and Dernocoeur, 1988: 253–254).

8. The size and boundary of each station's area are arranged to equalize the work load among stations as much as possible, so "closest" may not always be judged by actual physical distance.

9. In many larger cities, the distribution of apparatus does not vary significantly from station to station, and fire department dispatchers do not dispatch specific units; rather, they dispatch by station, and the personnel at the fire station determines, based on incident type and availability, what kind of apparatus and which units should respond.

10. For the sake of simplicity, I have described the fire dispatch policies and procedures used for incidents that are located in the two cities, Eugene and Springfield, within Central Lane's response area.

11. Call takers also relied on manual, paper-based methods. Incident information was recorded by hand on cards, which were then time stamped and placed on a conveyer belt that carried them to the dispatcher's work station.

12. In addition, expertise is frequently exhibited in and organized through social interaction at Central Lane: fire dispatchers work in tandem, at work stations that are placed side by side (even if a single dispatcher takes responsibility for particular calls), and rely on vocal exchanges and mutual monitoring of each others' actions to collaboratively manage their work tasks. Quite commonly, then, decision making and problem solving in dispatching calls is accomplished through consultation and discussion between partners.

13. The fact that such problems usually have to be resolved within the span of a minute or so underscores this observation. In this kind of task environment, a dispatcher may not have the time to wait for or seek additional information from the call taker.

14. And if a dispatcher fails to recognize that a unit in the field – one that is not at its home station or another station – is close to the location of an incident, that unit, when it hears the call dispatched over the radio (all units and stations monitor the dispatch frequency), will notify the dispatcher of its current location and offer to respond.

15. I should emphasize here that the overall error rate, under both the old system and the new, was

relatively low, and that there were never any instances during my tenure at Central Lane where lives were lost or even put seriously at risk, or property damaged, because of mistakes by communications center personnel.

16. If the suggestion had been carried out, it would have resulted in a display like the following for a structure fire reported at 4656 Barger:

```
    4656 BARGER, EUG              RESPONSE UNIT STATUS AT 21:53


RES        UNIT STA LOCATION

BC    REC  C1                          2        2

MED        M4   DSP 3435 ECHO HOLLOW   2        T1

MED   REC  M9                          3        1      ARV  S&M

MED        M5                          3        3

1     REC  7    ARV S&M                3        5

1          8    DSP 3435 ECHO HOLLOW

1     REC  T8

2     REC  4    ENR QTRS

2          9    ARV EGF-5
```

17. With respect to incident locations, when dispatchers record (in CAD, via keyboard entry) a unit as dispatched on a particular call, the CAD system lists the incident's address, as it was entered by the call taker in the LOC slot on the call record form, as that unit's location on the unit recommendation screen display (i.e., in the LOCATION column), as well as on all other CAD system lists having to do with unit status.

18. For a useful discussion of this issue by a human factors researcher, see Pew (1988).

19. As Dreyfus (1979: 3) puts it, "Intelligence requires understanding, and understanding requires giving a computer the background of common sense that adult human beings have by virtue of having bodies, interacting skillfully with the material world, and being trained into a culture." (See also Garfinkel, 1967.)

References

Brenner, D. J., and Cadoff, M. A. (1985). *Guide to computer-aided dispatch systems* (Washington, D.C.: National Bureau of Standards, U.S. Department of Commerce).

Clawson, J. J., and Dernocoeur, K. B. (1988). *Principles of emergency medical dispatch* (Englewood Cliffs, N.J.: Prentice-Hall).

Collins, H. M. (1987). Expert systems and the science of knowledge. In W. E. Bijker, T. P. Hughes, and T. J. Pinch (eds.), *The social construction of technological systems: New directions in the sociology and history of technology* (Cambridge, Mass.: MIT Press).

Dreyfus, H. (1979). *What computers can't do: The limits of artificial intelligence*, rev. ed. (New York: Harper and Row).

Garfinkel, H. (1967). *Studies in ethnomethodology*. (Englewood Cliffs, N.J.: Prentice-Hall).

Goodwin, C., and Goodwin, M. H. (1992). Formulating planes: Seeing as a situated activity. In D. Middleton and Y. Engestrom (eds.), *Distributed cognition in the work place* (Beverly Hills, Calif.: Sage).

Heath, C., and Luff, P. (1991). Collaborative activity and technological design: Task Coordination in London underground control rooms. In *Proceedings of the Second European Conference on*

Computer-Supported Cooperative Work, Amsterdam, the Netherlands (Dordrecht: Kluwer), 65–80.

Hutchins, E. (1983). Understanding Micronesian navigation. In D. Gentner and A. Stevens (eds.), *Mental models* (Hillsdale, N.J.: Lawrence Erlbaum).

Hutchins, E. (1990). The technology of team navigation. In J. Gallagher, R. Kraut, and C. Egido (eds.), *Intellectual Teamwork* (Hillsdale, N.J.: Lawrence Erlbaum).

Pew, R. W. (1988). Human factors in expert systems. In M. Helander (ed.), *Handbook of human–computer interaction* (Amsterdam: Elsevier North-Holland), 931–940.

Shapiro, D., Hughes, J., Harper, R., Ackroyd, S., and Soothill, K. (1991). Policing information systems: The social context of success and failure in introducing information systems in the police service. Technical Report EPC-91–117, Rank Xerox, Cambridge EuroPARC.

Suchman, L. (1987). *Plans and situated actions: The problem of human–machine communication.* (Cambridge: Cambridge University Press).

Suchman, L. (1993). Technologies of accountability. In G. Button (ed.), *Technology in working order: Studies of work, interaction and technology* (London: Routledge).

Suchman, L. (in press). Constituting shared workspaces. In Y. Engestrom and D. Middleton (eds.), *Communication and cognition at work* (Cambridge: Cambridge University Press).

Whalen, J. (in press). A technology of order production: Computer-aided dispatch in public safety communications. In G. Psathas and P. ten Have (eds.), *Situated order: Studies in the social organization of talk and embodied activities* (Washington, D.C.: University Press of America).

Woods, D. D., and Roth, E. M. (1988), Cognitive systems engineering. In M. Helander (ed.), *Handbook of human–computer interaction* (Amsterdam: Elsevier North-Holland), 3–34.

10

Conversation analysis and human–computer interaction design

Sarah A. Douglas

10.1 Introduction: From idealism to anarchy: The real world of user interface design

How do we create successful designs for interactive systems? For ten years this rather complex question was answered by a narrow definition of the word "successful" in early and persistent efforts by Card, Moran and Newell (Card, Moran, and Newell, 1983; Newell and Card, 1985; 1986) to create an engineering science of human–computer interaction (HCI) based on a cognitive science of the individual user. In their Tayloresque world "successful" meant reduction of the design to observable and measurable user behavior: achieving minimal speed of routinized performance, achieving minimal speed of learning, elimination of user "errors" which were regarded as wasteful of time, and a completeness of functionality. The ideal designer performed a task analysis involving the specification of the design as a set of user goals accomplished by sequences of user mental or physical actions, such as typing on the keyboard. For an elaborated example of this approach to the design of text editors, see Roberts and Moran (1983).

During the past ten years the HCI community, including both researchers and developers, has failed to accept this approach to design. In particular, the Card-Moran-Newell approach has not been able to deal well with nonroutinized human behaviors of learning, problem solving, and managing trouble. For example, although a cornerstone of the theory depends on the concept of goal-directed behavior, the designer does not actually determine real human intentions but instead "discovers" a Socratic set of ideal and complete goals based on an abstract analysis of what work is to be accomplished – that is, its functionality as a task environment. No attempt is made to analyze the context of work such as what users already know or problems they have with existing products. This makes it devilishly difficult to predict where users will have trouble or make "errors." The entire design effort focuses on the creation of a perfect (i.e., error-free) design rather than a design that can robustly respond to the infinite possibilities of failure.

The design process derived from the Card-Moran-Newell model is typically characterized in the following way. Initial designs are created in a top-down fashion initiated by programmers and then possibly reviewed by an expert in human factors or psychology. The standard design aids are the prior experience of the designer, expert designer heuristics published as user interface guidelines, task analysis tools such as the keystroke model, and simulated user behavior such as the cognitive walk-through. Since the design tools are intended to predict users' behavior, there is no need for contact with real users in real environments of use – in other words, this approach to design is context-free.

Criticism of this context-free methodology has come from both practitioners who have studied the effectiveness of different design tools as well as from researchers with more theoretical interests. A study by Jeffries et al. (1991) compared three methods of evaluating designs without actually involving the human user with a technique called usability testing. The nonempirical methods were human expert evaluation (Nielsen and Molich, 1990), guidelines (Apple Computer, 1987; Mayhew, 1992; Smith and Mosier, 1986), and the cognitive walk-through (Lewis et al., 1990). Usability testing takes a working version of the software and tries it out on a user. Observations as to usability are made by the designers and used to make modifications to the design. The technique seems to encompass any method of direct observation of user performance with the purpose of discovering design flaws. The Jeffries et al. study found that usability testing uncovers the most serious interface failures, is very good at finding recurring and general problems, avoids low-priority problems, and does not produce any false problems. Although initially many readers of the Jeffries et al. study misinterpreted the results, Jeffries and Desurvire in a later article (1992) clarified their results showing that as a design tool, usability testing was preferable to the other three. It is clear that the effectiveness of usability testing lies in the attempt to create some kind of "real" user context for evaluating design.

Continuing the call for adding more context into the development of software, Clayton Lewis, a leader in the HCI research community, elaborates on the failure of the Card-Moran-Newell design approach in his article, "A research agenda for the nineties in human–computer interaction" (Lewis, 1990). He cites three major reasons: the failure to accommodate the context of use, lack of iterative design process, and an inability of this type of theory to modify itself from actual design experience. For Lewis these failures, which he calls *context, process,* and *systems,* should become the major issues for HCI design in the nineties. Due to their importance, a brief review of what Lewis means by context, process, and systems is in order.

Context. Primary criticisms about lack of context have been mainly ethnomethodological arguments (Suchman, 1987) or ethnographic (Whiteside, Bennett and Holtzblatt, 1988). Lewis does not define context in his article other than to characterize Suchman as saying that the "theory is inside out: that the social context in which cognition occurs shapes behavior to such an extent that what is needed is a theory of social interaction modified to account for cognition not the other way around" (Lewis, 1990: 129). In short the Card-Moran-Newell approach fails to take into account *interaction.* Design based solely on an individual psychology of the user ignores the concept of interaction, which requires at a minimum a pair of individuals, be they human–human or human–computer. In some profound sense the Card-Moran-Newell users seem like robots with routine procedures whose only contact with their environment is some sort of triggering event that launches them into an execution of preplanned behavior.

Process. Lewis's second criticism of an engineering science approach involves the process of design itself. He argues that it is more important to worry about how to obtain and act on appropriate feedback on the effectiveness of a design than to worry about the perfection of the initial design. This is called an *open-loop* approach (Gould, 1988).

Systems. The criticism cited by Lewis is the inability of design driven by engineering science to reincorporate the lessons of implementation back into the theory (Carroll and Campbell, 1986; Carroll and Kellogg, 1989). Despite ten years of trying to work through designs based on the Card-Moran-Newell model, new designs are mostly shaped by the systems that have already been built and users' experiences with them. Graphical user interfaces are an example of this.

In some sense, context, process, and systems are very related to each other and point out the complexity or even futility of any science of "applied" human behavior. Providing a context of use to inform the design continuously creates the possibility of improving design through feedback from the cumulative system's experience of both designers and users. This sounds like anarchy to those schooled in the careful task analysis of engineering science, but it emphasizes the design *process* rather than the design *product.* It also requires that the focus of design shift from creating error-free efficient human performance to creating consistency with users' expectations and intentions and a support of users' processes of repair.

In the remainder of this chapter, I will discuss ideas based on conversation analysis that I have been developing over a five-year period that attempt to create a systematic method of design that seriously incorporates context, process, and systems concerns.

10.2 Method: What does talk have to do with it?

In this section I describe this design method in detail. Briefly, a technique called constructive interaction generates context information about the usability of the design by first-time users. The choice of first-time users is made because the trouble they encounter discloses the work required to understand the system's behavior that is masked by the experienced user. Then using conversation analysis as both an analytic as well as a synthetic technique, the developers[1] detect the trouble and decide whether it is a design failure. Further conversation analysis points to repair of the trouble and ultimately offers suggestions for software design changes. Finally, constructive interaction and conversation analysis are placed within an overall design process.

10.2.1 Constructive interaction

Constructive interaction uses two participants who are given problems to solve or tasks to perform. The participants' activities are recorded using both video, audio, and possibly computer-generated records such as keystrokes and pointing actions. It is helpful to compare constructive interaction with "protocol analysis," (Ericsson and Simon, 1984) or "thinking aloud" (Lewis, 1982), another method that has been used extensively in the HCI community. Protocol analysis uses only one participant. This participant is given a set of problems to solve or tasks to perform and encouraged to "think aloud." The participant is recorded in a similar manner to that of constructive interaction. Both constructive interaction and protocol analysis may be repeated with other participants.

The primary goal of protocol analysis is to uncover the underlying mental life of the participant. Protocol analysis is useful in design studies because it provides a method for identifying "problems" users may have with the design, some elaboration as to why, and perhaps ideas for improvement. Unfortunately this method has one major limitation familiar to ethnomethodologists: it fails to recognize language itself as a social process. The presence of the observer and the demand to talk may cause participants to "make up stories." Also, it is highly improbable that reports of a person's own mental processes are scientifically valid. Despite these limitations, protocol analysis provides developers with two critical pieces of information: where the design fails to achieve what developers expect, and some insight into why.

Constructive interaction attempts to elicit verbal information about problems in a more naturally occurring conversation. By using two participants, a situation of collaborative problem solving is created whereby each participant must inform the other in an explicit verbal record about problems, causes, and solutions.

Although the history is somewhat unknown, the first use of constructive interaction as a replacement for protocol analysis to study human problem solving behavior can be attributed to Miyake at the University of California at San Diego who used it to study human repair of a sewing machine. Although her dissertation was not published until 1986, her original research was done from about 1979 to 1982 (J. Grudin, personal communication, November 7, 1993). In the early 1980s both Don Norman's HCI group at San Diego (O'Malley, Draper, and Riley, 1985) and Lucy Suchman at Xerox PARC appear to have been the first to apply it to the analysis of human–computer interaction (Suchman, 1987). In 1989 S. Kennedy of the BNR usability lab published an influential article describing the same technique but calling it "co-discovery learning."

10.2.2 Conversation analysis

Once constructive interaction is completed developers are still left with the problem of systematic analysis of a primarily verbal record. One method is conversa-

Table 10.1. *Suchman's analytic framework. From Suchman (1987).*

THE USERS		THE MACHINE	
I	II	III	IV
Actions not available to the machine	Actions available to the machine	Effects available to the user	Design rationale
E1 E2 E3			

tion analysis (CA). Unlike researchers who have used CA and its "rules" to create design guidelines (cf. Norman and Thomas, 1990) , this use of CA centers entirely on the interpretation of human communication (including so-called nonverbal language) at a very detailed level with a focus on the detection of trouble and analysis of repair.

Suchman (1987) pioneered the use of CA to analyze human–computer interaction. Her primary interest in doing this type of analysis was to compare the behavior of human and machine as an interactive exchange modeled on human–human communication. Suchman was interested in where and why that exchange failed in the broadest sense. She was also interested in the fundamental philosophical issue of whether it is possible to create a software system that could know and explain its own behavior. Although she borrowed heavily from the interactive emphasis of earlier conversational analysts, she radicalized CA by including the computer as one of the "social" participants. In a sense, the program of the machine "stands in" for the human designer-programmer in the interactive exchange. This requires that the programmer attempt to anticipate all possible intentions of the other participant (a hypothetical user) and states of interactive communication. Suchman finds this impossible given the almost infinite number of such states due to the complexity of human behavior.

Consequently Suchman reduced her original videotapes to a simple framework of interaction between a user and the machine. Table 10.1 illustrates the framework for the general process of Suchman's analysis. She created a transcript of the major episodes of trouble, denoted E1, E2, and E3. Included in column I, "Actions not available to the machine," were all verbal and gestural events of users. Column II recorded users' actions at the semantic level of the interface program such as "Selects START button." The third column contained the presentation state of the interface program in either visual or audio messages to users or other physical actions that represented behavior of the machine, such as the sound of initiating a copying process. The final column gave developers' rationale to the effects in column III. Suchman found this a very practical framework since the center columns, II and III, were essentially the "interface," whereas the two outer columns, I and IV, represented the interpretations of users and developers in response to events in II and III.

Suchman found that the coherence of users' actions was largely unavailable to the computer. If the software designer had anticipated a particular sequence of detectable user actions (e.g., a button press) and linked them correctly to users' intent, then the system would respond correctly in spite of the lack of access to other user actions (e.g., gaze). At other times there would be a lack of coherence between user intent and system response.

These failures could be categorized as:

- false alarms, that is, users assumed that things had gone wrong when they hadn't, and
- garden paths, that is, users didn't know that or when things had gone wrong, when in fact they had.

Suchman's analysis was primarily theoretical and basically ended here. However, this use of conversation analysis can be extended to more detailed analysis of design failure. The major insight from the failure of the engineering science approach is the inability to understand a context of use that is primarily interactive and communicative. Suchman's constructive interaction method combined with conversation analysis links user expectations and intentions to actions and in turn to system response. As stated earlier, user expectations and intentions are revealed during breakdowns. Breakdowns are signaled by repetitions and restarts of a sequence of computer-based actions as well as talk about difficulties. However, the record may or may not yield an expressed intent. If it does not, developers as observers of patterns of talk and actions and as members of the cultural community must infer intention.

Although Suchman was interested in complete breakdown – false alarms and garden paths – any breakdown yields valuable information for developers that can potentially be used for redesign. Additionally, the transcript documents users' attempts to repair the breakdown by using the interface as a resource. This suggests appropriate changes to developers: for example, looking for instructions in a help subsystem, trying out a particular interface item whose behavior suggests a repair ("undo" menu item or an icon whose graphics suggest the appropriate function), restructuring the task, or rewording instructions. This synthetic use of conversation analysis has not been exploited in previous HCI research.

The following is a brief synopsis of the method. Since developers are primarily interested in points of breakdown, an entire transcript of the videotapes need not be made. After a brief review of the videotapes, selected areas may need to be transcribed. A transcription is produced of both linguistic and physical actions and may include descriptions of the environment. This transcript may be coded using conventions of CA, which include pauses, breaths, overlaps in talk, stress and pitch changes, gestures including pointing or gaze, and computer input and output events. The transcription conventions found in Luff, Gilbert, and Frohlich (1990) or Suchman (1987) may be used. An issue as to level of detail exists and developers will need to trade off the time and expense of transcription with importance. From my experience the transcript may reveal previously unappreciated issues of users' expectations and intentions.

When I first began to explore the use of CA in the analysis of human–computer interaction design, I found it very difficult to understand exactly what could be used. There did not appear to be a right way to do CA. Ultimately, I found the following concepts of the most value:

- Episode
- Sequentiality (turns, overlapping, etc.)
- Nonverbal communication (gesture, gaze, pointing, etc.)
- Breakdown and repair
- Retrospective intentionality
- Communicative resource

The first three concepts, that of episode, sequentiality, and nonverbal communication, helped me to form a sense of how to create order out of an otherwise almost indecipherable transcript of verbal utterances. These elements can be found in any introduction to CA, such as that by Wooffitt (1990). The concept of using a machine as one of the communication participants (as Suchman does) or even as a form of communicative medium (such as the telephone) may require some additions to the normal analysis. For example, Suchman uses developers' rationale as the intentionality of the computer, and Hopper (1992) when examining turn taking in telephone conversations, extends the Sacks model to encompass issues of syntax and prosody.

The second three themes – breakdown and repair, retrospective intentionality, and communicative resource – helped me to interpret what was really going on in the interactions. Breakdown is critical in that it reveals through retrospective intentionality the structure of human action; and repair, through participants' use of communicative resources, demonstrates other aspects of the structure of interaction. For example, because of the style of user interface most commonly used today, user intentions in interaction are often expressed by the selection of objects and actions. Breakdown occurs when users can't find expected objects or they select the wrong objects ("wrong" in the sense that developers did not intend those objects to be an expression of that particular intention). Breakdown also occurs when users' procedures for accomplishing actions do not match developers' composition of subsequences or termination conditions. Repair is expressed by searching for possible resources of objects and actions available in the designed interface. The usefulness of these concepts will be more apparent in the details of an example offered in the next section.

10.2.3 The overall design process

The information available from the prior analysis of context of use should inform the design from the earliest stages and continuously during development in an iterative model of design. From the programming standpoint the rationale is that the greatest flexibility in design comes earliest when it is much easier to change things on whiteboards than in code. Designs can be implemented in paper story-boards and given to users for a very crude simulation of interaction. Although paper simulations allow earlier feedback on the success of the design, they cannot substitute for the complexity of true interactive computing.

Rapid prototyping (cf. Budde et al., 1984) and high-level programming languages specially designed for user interfaces (cf. Douglas, Doerry, and Novick, 1992) attempt to finesse this problem with automation support designed for flexibility and incompleteness of a design. The difficulty with a rapid prototyping tool is that it may not support all the interface actions desired for the final product, generate efficient code, or generate code in a language that will interface to an application such as a database manager. All prototyping methods require a highly modular implementation strategy for the software. Choosing that modularity may be critical to the success of the prototyping approach.

Based on several years of experience with this new method, I have come to use three pairs of participants at each cycle of design analysis. My reasoning is that it is the minimum number to differentiate universal problems from those which are more unique to individuals. The design team, including users in a participatory design approach, can review the videotapes, selecting problem areas for transcription. After the team discovers all the problem areas and generates design solutions, these design changes are prioritized, trading off severity with complexity of programming. A new prototype is produced and tested again.

10.3 An extended example: Using conversation analysis to design the cardiovascular construction kit

During one extensive software development project beginning in 1987 and extending over a three-year period, I experimented with the use of constructive interaction and conversation analysis in informing design. Previously I had used CA methods to analyze human–human tutoring (Douglas, 1991) in order to determine the feasibility of an AI tutor for teaching Japanese. This experience convinced me of its usefulness on more general software design problems. The next opportunity presented itself with the development of a simulation program called the cardiovascular construction kit (CVCK) to be used in teaching biology laboratories at the university level. In biology labs students often shared computers in a collaborative way, which made constructive interaction very compatible with their actual context of use. The project also required us to develop workbooks for the biology lab exercises that would use the software and were intimately involved with the actual use of the software in a learning environment. This software is now available nationally as a software product in the BIOQUEST biology lab package available from the University of Maryland on CD-ROM and is thus not a "toy" example. This software has also had almost no complaints about the design of the interface or usability.

The design team consisted of myself as the primary developer, two professional programmers, and one biology teacher. Our use of constructive interaction involved bringing two first-year biology students to our HCI laboratory. The two students were of the same gender and had similar age and ethnicity (we discovered that we would get much more cooperative discussion if we paid attention to potential social power asymmetries). For each phase of the design we would typically bring in three pairs of participants. Very early in the design process, prior to software implementation, the participants worked with paper prototypes. Later, while using rapid prototyping tools (Douglas et al., 1992), we worked with software implementations until the final program was completed.

The two participants were left alone in our laboratory and instructed to follow the instructions in the workbook. They were given a buzzer they could use to summon help. Our HCI laboratory was arranged to have three video outputs: one from a camera situated at a high elevation and acute angle behind the pair in such a way that we could see the CRT monitor and where they were pointing, a second camera at a side angle so that we could see the upper half of the participants' bodies with mutual gazes and talking, and a third direct NTSC output from the CRT monitor which was generated by the computer system running the software (see Figure 10.1.) We also recorded from lavaliere mikes on each person to each stereo channel on the second camera output.

After some experimentation we found that the first camera output from the monitor was quite adequate for analysis and thus dropped the third direct NTSC monitor output. We created a final videotape with a picture-in-picture processor with integrated images from the first and second camera. The image of the computer monitor with participants pointing occupied the major portion of the final picture and a reduced version of the long-distance image of the two participants was placed in the upper right-hand corner. This tape was then viewed by the whole team freely discussing possible problems, interpretations, and alternative designs. For events we could not interpret, we produced a written transcript, which we would later individually analyze. This transcript was coded using standard CA techniques for verbal data enhanced with coding for participant pointing and gaze directed toward the computer monitor, participant computer input actions, and any

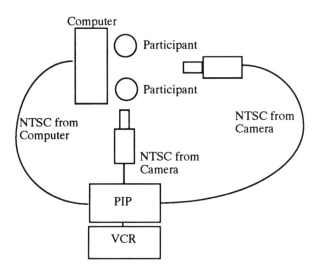

Figure 10.1. Laboratory setup.

significant computer-generated user interface events. After the team had discovered all the problem areas and had generated design solutions, we prioritized the fixes, trading off both severity and the complexity of programming. We then produced a new prototype and repeated the constructive interaction method.

Our experience with the constructive interaction method is a valuable source of information about the use of ethnographics in detailed software design. Four primary aspects stand out. First, we were usually able to detect events where trouble occurred. Second, although we were able to detect such trouble easily, we had difficulty diagnosing the cause. Third, ascribing a cause to the breakdown was often a key to the design solution. Finally, the repairs by the participants often provided us with possible alternative design solutions.

Detecting trouble with the design as revealed by participants' behavior is fairly straightforward since the talk will be laced with expressions easily recognizable to developers: "Oh my! What happened?" "Wait, wait . . . ," and "I don't understand this." What Suchman calls "garden paths" – that is users didn't know that or when things had gone wrong, when in fact they had – were infrequent but more difficult to detect. At a more structural level of analysis we found that we could detect trouble signaled by repetitions and restarts of a sequence of computer-based actions. In fact it was often difficult to pinpoint exactly where the problem started and a great deal of reviewing of the videotape was often necessary.

We found that diagnosing the cause of trouble was often problematic for the developers and dependent upon the ability of the team to recognize users' intent and the failure of the system to respond as expected. At times intent was not verbally expressed and even when expressed, its intelligibility depended greatly

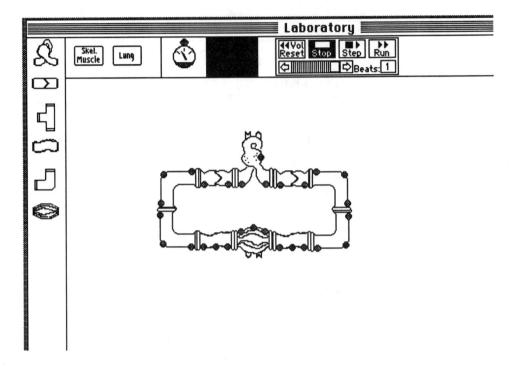

Figure 10.2. CVCK construction for study.

upon the analysts' ability to place themselves in the context of the participants' work as social actors. This requires recreating rich visual and aural images from many sources, not just the already coded transcript (note that we did not code the whole videotape because of cost and time constraints). Group analysis of intent frequently requires argumentation based on empirical evidence. A particular theory had to be convincing to the other members of the team. The evidence that would disclose an underlying intent was often not found in the verbal record, but in a complex interweaving of a history of talk, computer monitor state changes, and user input actions. Participants frequently pointed to areas on the screen and used indexicals for reference resolution, both for the efficiency of communication as well as a lack of lexicon. Again, the full videotape and not a transcript was critical in the analysis. Developers were often able to compare what they expected users' intent to be, that is, the design rationale, with the actual intent. This underlines the domain knowledge necessary to understand what is going on. Showing the videotape to persons not members of the design team and not HCI experts familiar with the domain provided no aid in analysis.

The following is an example from the CVCK development of the richness available from this type of analysis. In this particular episode, after the participants

Table 10.2.

USERS		THE MACHINE	
I Actions not available to the machine	II Actions available to the machine	III Effects available to a user	IV Design rationale

L: OK. OK, what do
  we need
  (L and V read instructions)
V: We need another
  (points to elbow
  icon on palette)			

	L clicks elbow	palette elbow highlights	add component

one . . . we need
two, three more
	L drags elbow
	  from palette
		elbow added to
		  workspace
			place in model
			(selected object
			= elbow)

have read a brief tutorial description of how the software works, they are asked to construct a model system that replicates Figure 10.2. The reader can see that the CVCK interface is a standard tool palette with a central workspace for model construction. A user can select a model component (on the left edge of the palette and from top to bottom) of ventricle, valved pipe, T, straight pipe, elbow, and muscle. A component copy of the icon is dragged into the workspace to the appropriate position. Because components are used in four different rotational positions, a design decision was made to have only one orientation of each component and use a "compass" icon (the cross-shaped double-headed arrows) to create the correct orientation.

The transcript (Table 10.2) begins after the participants have already placed one "elbow," (i.e., right-angled vessel) component in the workspace. (For readability, the transcript has been edited.) The second elbow is successfully added to the workspace and placed into position (Table 10.3). They immediately discover that it is the incorrect orientation and attempt to correct that.

Here, the participants have attempted a direct mapping of their physical actions using the mouse to rotate the object. The first is to move the mouse around in a circle and the second is to actually rotate or twist the mouse by keeping it in one place. Neither works since, in the first place, the hardware recognizes moving the mouse in circles as a circular motion of an object on the screen and not a rotation of that object and, in the second place, the hardware does not recognize twisting the mouse as a meaningful action at all. Thus, these two repair strategies fail (and cannot be used by developers as repairs to the design since they are outside the possibilities of design). They try another approach (Table 10.4).

Table 10.3.

L: No, wait			
How do you //turn this	L moves mouse	elbow moves	change position
thing around	in circles	in circles	
V: //turn it			
L: Oh oh shoot			
V: That's right, just			
move it			
L: No it won't turn			
(twists mouse to		no effects	
turn it)			
V: OK.			

Table 10.4.

L: Oh wait			
V: Put it over here			
L: Oh wait, wait.			
I have an idea.			
Maybe this works,	L clicks on slider	elbow un-highlights	deselect component
	in control panel		(no object selected)
		slider highlights	change simulation
		and moves	rate
this, wait,			
where is that thing?			
here we go	L moves to rotate icon		
	clicks on	highlights rotate icon	rotate component
	right arrow	no effects	(no object selected)

This second strategy is to try to find an action that maps to a control icon that will rotate the elbow. Readers should note how the participants use the interface itself as a resource in their interaction. First the slider in the control panel is used and then L recognizes the "rotate" icon, which is intended by the developers to resemble a compass. The developers intended that a component be selected, then rotated to the desired orientation by selecting one of the four different points of the compass that represents that direction. Note that this is a compound procedure: first select the component, then select the compass point. Unfortunately L deselects the component accidentally by choosing the slider. She then recognizes this and attempts to redo the procedure (Table 10.5).

Table 10.5.

V: OK now, put this one			
	L clicks on elbow	highlights elbow	elbow selected
	L drags it to left	elbow moves	change location
	L points to rotate icon		
	L clicks just outside right arrow	unhighlights elbow (no other effects)	deselect component (no object selected)
L: Darn it!			

Table 10.6.

V: Turn it the opposite way.			
L: It won't turn.			
V: Then bring it back over here. (points to elbow icon in palette)	L clicks on elbow	highlights elbow	elbow selected
	L drags it next to elbow icon in palette	elbow moves	change position
	L clicks on elbow icon in palette	unhighlights elbow component	deselect component
		highlights elbow icon	add component
V: Where where'd that thing go?			

L's failure here is interpreted by the developers as a problem of designing the compass points too small. They are very tiny and this user is unable to "hit the target." A possible design change is to make them larger, but then they will exceed the maximum size of an icon in the interface software. L, however, attempts to follow the advice of her partner and abandon the task (Table 10.6).

This is an unsuccessful attempt to put the elbow component from the workspace

Table 10.7.

L:	There.	L clicks on elbow component	highlights elbow	elbow selected
	Oh!	L points to rotate icon, clicks right arrow	elbow rotates to right	rotate component
	There we go. What'd I do?			

back into the palette and start a completely new problem. It can't be done and L tries one last time to get the rotate icon to work (Table 10.7).

Although L does finally complete the rotation problem, the developers have enough evidence at this point to attempt a new approach to rotation of components.

Once we, as developers, had determined the cause of a particular breakdown, it often suggested design solutions. However, and more crucial to this discussion, the repair efforts by the participants often suggested possible design alternatives. Participants' repairs can be found by examining their detailed talk, and by their other actions in which they use the interface itself as a resource for furthering a repair. The first attempts by L and V to rotate the component, namely by direct physical actions with the mouse, were not possible design alternatives. However, we were impressed by L's three attempts to use an icon to rotate the component and thus remained committed to an icon command on the palette (and did not choose another approach such as a menu-based command). In other words, the design rationale for accomplishing this action closely matched the participants' expectations and intentions. What failed was the actual details of the objects and actions.

We observed three problems with the existing design: a failure to recognize the rotate icon, a failure to select a component before selecting the rotate icon, and a failure to get the cursor inside of a very small target. What we finally decided to do was change the rotate icon to a very simple type of icon button labeled with the word "rotate" that, when pressed, rotates a selected component. This new icon is shown in Figure 10.3. We also decided to add logic for trapping an attempt to use the rotate icon without a selected component. This trap then informs users that a component must be first selected before it is rotated.

We have found that constructive interaction and conversation analysis, as I have described our usage, is an invaluable tool in doing design. Though the method takes time for analysis with the whole design team, it also provides an arena and indeed creative environment for them to work out the design mutually in the presence of real evidence about human behavior.

Figure 10.3. New rotate icon.

10.4 Evaluation: You can lead developers to water, but can you make them drink?

The previous example, I hope, has been compelling in arguing for the usefulness of this method in interface design. It promises to provide, for the first time, a real method of analysis to an otherwise vague area called "usability testing."

The most difficult aspect of the method is that it is primarily qualitative and is best learned through an apprenticeship with experienced analysts. But any design method must prove its value in at least several different ways. First, it must be learnable by those who stand the most to gain from it. Second, it must be practical in that the method is not too costly or too time-consuming. Third, it must be universally valid – that is, developers are able to discover the same problems and derive the same interpretations of cause, although not necessarily the same solutions.

In an attempt to respond to the first two concerns I have taught this general method for several years in my senior/graduate computer science course in user interface design where the students must use it in their final project. Many students have told me that it was the most exciting part of the design process and were very enthusiastic about it. Some of my students are now working for commercial software development companies and have implemented it within their design process. Few of the methods I have taught have had this kind of acceptance.

I still felt unsatisfied with its success, particularly concerning the third issue – universal interpretation. In order to test this out, I took my advanced graduate seminar in HCI and gave them two chapters from Suchman's book: chapter 6, "Case and methods," and chapter 7, "Human–machine communication" (Suchman, 1987). I also had them read Wooffitt's chapter mentioned earlier (Wooffitt, 1990). I then had them review the videotape from the prior design session of CVCK. First, I had them analyze a particular breakdown that I pointed out, and, second, I asked them to find all the remaining breakdowns in one hour of tape. The format of the homework was as follows:

1. In the videotape at approximately 1075, there is an example of interface failure. Please do the following.
   a. Using the framework presented in chapter 7 (cf. p. 122) and the notation of chapter 5 (pp. 96–97), create a transcript of users' breakdown with the system.

   b.   Suchman has stated that "instructions rely upon the recipient's ability to do the implicit work of anchoring descriptions to concrete objects and actions" (p. 101). Discuss where in this example users seem unable to do this.

   c.   We have often discussed the problem of relating intent to behavior. In this episode discuss the programmer's expectations of users' intent and actions, the actual user's intent and actions, and why there is a failure to match here.

   d.   In this episode users are able to repair the trouble they are in. How did they do this? What evidence do you have to support your interpretation *from the videotape?*

   e.   Given your analysis of parts b–d of this problem, how would you redesign the interface?

2.   Find all other episodes in the tape where there is interface design failure and answer parts a–e of question 1 again.

All twelve students in the class independently came to the same identification of breakdowns and almost exactly the same interpretations of causes. They were quite capable of doing the transcriptions although there were minor variations in details, such as a mumbled word. They did complain about the tediousness of transcription, but felt that the transcript was invaluable. The most difficult areas of breakdown for them were the true garden path problems. They had difficulty identifying them and difficulty interpreting them.

10.5 Conclusions

As a result of the informal studies conducted, I have great confidence in the design method proposed here. Only more general utilization will test its ultimate value. In closing, however, I would like to address a few criticisms.

Conversation analysis is an ethnomethodological approach and, by its very nature, takes a radical view of the basis of human action. Part of that view demands that all action is context-based or "situated." But anyone can see that the type of situation created in constructive interaction is not the real situation of use. The participants, while not actors, are recruited. They are given tasks or problems by developers. The environment in which they work has video cameras and other controlled features. Thus, constructive interaction is "situated action," but not exactly the same one that the final software product will encounter. The receding horizon of interaction itself creates a context with its own unique history that will theoretically never be identical to any other. How then, can I assert that this method is valid as a method of creating designs using a context of use?

Ultimately, I am left with the conclusion that design itself is always imperfect. This particular method stands to provide more direct information about context of use since it focuses on actual interaction itself. And, hopefully, I have shown in my informal evaluations that different developers do share a common set of interpretations of action, because they share a common culture with the participants.

There are also those critics that will say that this is not a new method; it is already well received in the HCI community as usability testing. For example, a recent survey (Nielsen, 1993) supports the estimate that 4–6% of corporate and industrial software development budgets are spent on usability engineering. But the most thorough analysis of usability testing defines it in rather vague terms. Nielsen characterizes it as simply any testing that uses "real" users, not specifically addressing the method (Nielsen, 1993: 165). And in the most detailed study to date comparing usability testing with other interface evaluation methods, the authors define it as testing

... in which the interface is studied under real-world or controlled conditions, with evaluators gathering data on problems that arise during its use. These tests can offer excellent opportunities for observing how well the situated interface supports users' work environment. . . . The usability tests were conducted by a human factors professional, for whom product usability testing is a regular part of his job. (Jeffries et al., 1991: 119–120)

These descriptions suggest to me that usability testing is a black art method except for the fact that it brings real users into a laboratory setting. (This distinguishes usability testing from methods such as beta-test site testing.) Using the method I have proposed provides a systematic approach to it that has been sorely lacking.

I have attempted to show in the beginning of this chapter the failure of earlier approaches to human–computer interaction design that were based on engineering science. Engineering science failed to provide information about context of use for the design, an open-loop process where feedback from context is integrated into improvements in the design. Engineering science also fails to recognize that systems design experience rather than abstract scientific principles has created more successful design. I then proposed a method of design usability information collection based on a controlled context of use called constructive interaction. This information is then analyzed using techniques of conversation analysis, which can provide not only a record of breakdown of the interaction but also user-based strategies of repair, which can possibly be incorporated by developers into design improvements. Finally, I discussed an in-depth example of the method's use in a long-term software development project and my success at teaching it to several classes in user interface design. The next step is for wider use and evaluation.

Note

1. I have chosen to substitute the word "developers" for the word "designer" in the remainder of this chapter given the persuasive argument of Grudin (1993): "Using 'the designer' conceals the cumulative and collaborative nature of most system design today."

References

Apple Computer, Inc. (1987). *Human interface guidelines: The Apple Desktop Interface* (Reading, Mass.: Addison-Wesley).

Budde, R., Kuhlenkamp, K., Mathiassen, L., and Zullighoven, H. (eds.). (1984). *Approaches to prototyping* (Berlin: Springer-Verlag).

Card, S. K., Moran, T. P., and Newell, A. (1983). *The psychology of human–computer interaction* (Hillsdale, N.J.: Lawrence Erlbaum).

Carroll, J. M., and Campbell, R. L. (1986). Softening up hard science: Reply to Newell and Card. *Human–Computer Interaction, 2,* 227–249.

Carroll, J. M., and Kellogg, W. A. (1989). Artifact as theory-nexus. In K. Bice and C. Lewis (eds.), *Proceedings of the Conference on Human Factors in Computing Systems: CHI '89* (New York: ACM Press).

Douglas, S. A. (1991). Tutoring as interaction: Detecting and repairing tutoring failures. In P. Goodyear (ed.), *Teaching knowledge and intelligent tutoring* (Norwood, N.J.: Ablex), 123–147.

Douglas, S. A., Doerry, E., and Novick, D. (1992). QUICK: A tool for graphical user-interface construction by non-programmers. *Visual Computer, 8,* 117–133.

Ericsson, K. A., and Simon, H. A. (1984). *Protocol analysis: Verbal reports as data* (Cambridge, Mass,: MIT Press).

Gould, J. D. (1988). How to design usable systems. In M. Helander (ed.), *Handbook of human–computer interaction* (New York: North-Holland), 757–789.

Grudin, J. (1993). Interface: An evolving concept. *Communications of the ACM, 3614,* 110–119.

Hopper, R. (1992). *Telephone conversation* (Bloomington: University of Indiana).

Jeffries, R., and Desurvire, H. (1992). Usability testing vs. heuristic evaluation: Was there a contest? *ACM SIGCHI Bulletin, 24,* 2, 39–41.

Jeffries, R., Miller, J. R., Wharton, C., and Uyeda, K. M. (1991). User interface evaluation in the real world: A comparison of four techniques. *Human Factors in Computing Systems: CHI '91 Proceedings* (New York: ACM Press), 119–124.

Kennedy, S. (1989). Using video in the BNR usability lab. *ACM SIGCHI Bulletin 21,* 2, 92–95.

Lewis, C. (1982). Using the "Thinking-aloud" method in cognitive interface design. Technical Report RC 9265, IBM Thomas J. Watson Research Center, Yorktown Heights, N.Y.

Lewis, C., Polson, P., Wharton, C., and Rieman, J. (1990). Testing a walkthrough methodology for theory-based design of walk-up-and-use interfaces. *Human Factors in Computing Systems: CHI '90 Proceedings,* (New York: ACM Press), 235–242.

Lewis, C. H. (1990). A research agenda for the nineties in human–computer interaction. *Human–Computer Interaction, 5,* 125–143.

Luff, P., Gilbert, N., and Frohlich, D. (eds.). (1990). *Computers and conversation* (London: Academic Press).

Mayhew, D. J. (1992). *Principles and guidelines in software user interface design* (Englewood Cliffs, N.J.: Prentice-Hall).

Miyake, N. (1986). Constructive interaction and the iterative process of understanding. *Cognitive Science, 10,* 151–177.

Newell, A., and Card, S. K. (1985). The prospects for psychological science in human computer interaction. *Human–Computer Interaction, 1,* 209–242.

Newell, A., and Card, S. K. (1986). Straightening out softening up: Response to Carroll and Campbell. *Human–Computer Interaction, 2,* 251–267.

Nielsen, J. (1993). *Usability engineering* (Boston: Academic Press).

Nielsen, J., and Molich, R. (1990). Heuristic evaluation of user interfaces. *Human Factors in Computing Systems: CHI' 90 Proceedings* (New York: ACM Press), 249–256.

Nisbett, R. E., and Wilson, T. D. (1977). Telling more than we can know: Verbal reports on mental processes. *Psychological Review,* 84, 231–259.

Norman, M., and Thomas, P. (1990). The very idea: Informing HCI design from Conversation Analysis. In P. Luff, N. Gilbert, and D. Frohlich (eds.), *Computers and conversation* (London: Academic Press), 51–66.

O'Malley, C., Draper, S., and Riley, M. (1985).Constructive Interaction: A method for studying human–computer–human interaction: *Proceedings of IFIP Conference on Human–Computer Interaction: Interact '84* (Amsterdam: Elsevier), 269–274.

Roberts, T. L., and Moran, T. P. (1983). The evaluation of text editors: Methodology and empirical results. *Communications of the ACM,* 26 (4), 265–283.

Smith, S. L., and Mosier, J. N. (1986). Guidelines for designing user interface software. Technical Report # MTR-10090, MITRE Corp, Boston.

Suchman, L. (1987). *Plans and situated actions: The problem of human–machine communication* (Cambridge: Cambridge University Press).

Whiteside, J., Bennett, J., and Holtzblatt, K. (1988). Usability engineering: Our experience and evolution. In M. Helander (ed.), *Handbook of human–computer interaction* (New York: North-Holland), 791–817.

Wooffitt, R. (1990). On the analysis of interaction: An introduction to Conversation Analysis. In P. Luff, N. Gilbert, and D. Frohlich, (eds.), *Computers and conversation* (London: Academic Press), 7–38.

11

Multimedia tools for social and interactional data collection and analysis

Beverly L. Harrison

11.1 Introduction

In the past, human–computer interface design used psychological methodologies (e.g., Barnard, 1987; Card, Moran, and Newell, 1983; Norman and Draper, 1986; Wickens, 1992) to determine human perceptual, cognitive, and attentional limits, driven by the goal of creating interfaces that better suit the tasks and capabilities of the users. Fields such as learning, memory, cognition, and visual perception have made significant contributions toward achieving this goal. Researchers are now seeking new methods for designing more sophisticated systems that support multiple users performing complex, real-world, collaborative tasks – that is, situated activities (Suchman, 1987). Thus methodologies from sociology and anthropology are being adapted to the needs of human–computer interaction (HCI) research. Examples of relevant methods include social network analysis, time-geography studies, verbal protocol analysis, conversation analysis, ethnographic studies, and ethnomethodology. Several of the chapters in this book explain these methods in more detail (see, e.g., the chapters by Randall and Hughes, Wooffitt and MacDermit, Whalen, and Douglas). Using these methods, researchers attempt to determine which artifacts users require to accomplish their tasks, the context in which these tasks occur, how users collaborate and coordinate tasks, what they communicate about and to whom, and how technological mediation and tools change these work processes. The data resulting from these detailed studies provide designers with a more comprehensive understanding of the human-system interface requirements.

The history of data analysis demonstrates how the conditions under which data are collected influence the methods of data analysis that are developed. Early work in probability and statistics began in astronomy with the problem of variation in readings made by astronomers. In the late nineteenth and early twentieth centuries psychology became a motivating discipline for statistics. For instance, Pearson studied correlation and this statistic formed the basis of studies on personality and general intelligence. This led to factor analysis, which had a central role in debates on the nature of human intelligence (Guilford, 1956; Spearman, 1927). Agriculture also had a significant impact on methods of data analysis. Fisher, for example, developed analysis of variance as a method for assessing whether the differences between plants in different plots of land were statistically significant or not. This led to what are sometimes called split-plot experimental designs and the analysis of variance.

Today, new technologies in human–computer interaction require new foci and methods of data analysis. To capture the rich collection of data resulting from interactions between humans and computers and to facilitate the detailed analysis required, audio and video recordings have become widespread. The resulting data are sequential – that is, they contain a sequence of events that may be encoded in terms of one or more time series. Techniques such as time series analysis, Markov analysis, and lag sequential analysis are being adapted to the needs of video data interpretation (Harrison and Baecker, 1992; Harrison and Owen, 1994; Sanderson, Watanabe, and James, 1991). However, the complexity of the interactions that occur in such data is also leading to an emphasis on exploratory, rather than confirmatory, analyses.

Exploratory data analysis (EDA) (Tukey, 1977) is concerned with developing insights about processes through examining the outputs or data that they generate. This exploration is quite different from the directed data collection of hypothesis-based (confirmatory) analyses. It requires a rich and unrestricted data set that is amenable to a variety of manipulations. EDA allows researchers to formulate hypotheses and visualize relationships among data that might otherwise have been overlooked. This exploratory strategy is ideally suited to studies in HCI where interactions are complex, outcomes are often unpredictable, and hypotheses may be nonintuitive or difficult to generate.

Human–computer interactions produce sequences of events. Exploratory *sequential* data analysis (ESDA) techniques are needed to achieve insight concerning the context of the interactions and the sequential coherence of the resulting events (Sanderson and Fisher, 1994). The data then consist of information about the situational context, temporal dependencies and sequencing, human operator responses and performance, and system responses and states.

Many data collected from a sociological or anthropological perspective are qualitative, such as descriptions of meaningful incidents or events that have been observed. These qualitative data are now being used in HCI to understand work processes, context, and technologically mediated interactions. Naturally, HCI is not the only area that has to deal with quantitative as well as qualitative data. In education, for instance, evaluation through performance testing and behavioral measures may be supplemented by the use of anecdotal records to assess learning outcomes as well as social adjustment (Gronlund, 1985). Regardless of the discipline, there are a number of reasons why use of qualitative analysis may be both desirable and necessary. Frequently, important observational information is inherently categorical in nature and cannot be reasonably reduced to a number scaling. Qualitative data also allow a richness of description that is not otherwise possible. In addition, complex interactions between humans and computers often lead to unexpected patterns of behavior. Open-ended systems of coding are needed to capture the interaction fully. Typically, such open-ended coding is qualitative in nature.

Examples of inherently qualitative information are categories of motivation, descriptions of work processes, and types of errors that are made in using a system. Once collected, qualitative data may languish as an archived set of descriptions or as illustrative reference examples. Alternatively, qualitative data may be analyzed in terms of frequencies, sequencing, patterns, and interrelationships.

In this chapter I discuss the characteristics and challenges unique to collecting, manipulating, and analyzing data sets that contain a large amount of qualitative data. These multimedia, multistream data may include, for example, video records, audio records, observer notes, conversation analysis transcriptions, or gestural analyses. In using time as the common integrating element, the preservation of important sequential dependencies (and hence the contextual dependencies) is ensured. This chapter describes tools and techniques that support the collection, manipulation, and visualization of time-based data and how such tools can simultaneously support both quantitative and qualitative data analysis strategies. Using a case study based on experience in tool design, I describe how one might analyze the rich and complex sequential data from videotapes. The case study illustrates how a variety of time-based data may contribute to understanding diverse problems typical of HCI research. I then describe a number of state-of-the-art data capture and analysis tools that reflect the different approaches taken by tool designers. These systems integrate video technology with a variety of analysis methodologies. They reflect a large design space of tools and techniques for capturing, analyzing, and interpreting different classes of time-based data. Finally, I offer suggestions for those who are building the tools of the future and for those who are working with these tools as a means of exploring the rich sequential data sets resulting from interactional studies.

11.2 The challenges of multimedia time-based data

This section highlights the most significant problems of working with multimedia data. Review of video data has proved invaluable for the detailed analyses required in qualitative analysis or exploratory analysis techniques (e.g., conversation analysis, behavioral analysis of gestures). However, the use of video requires additional "meta" analysis techniques to control the video technology itself. Film makers have made it clear that video is a discursive, not a neutral, recording medium. Intentionally or not, video always represents a perspective or point of view on the actions or events that are recorded. A forced abstraction and filtering on the "data" results from choices in camera angles, field of view, audio sources, focal points, and picture resolution. In video, the simple act of setting up a camera on a tripod may be a discursive act that fundamentally determines important properties of the resulting video.

Abstraction and filtering occur not only in the recording of video but also in its transcription and transformation into a more manageable data set. Capturing key patterns or elements of the video in the resulting data set is largely determined by the properties of the available tools (e.g., ease of use, expressive power, and efficiency). Consider a typical scenario where subjects are "monitored" while videotaping is carried out. The observer is unobtrusively located, viewing the scene either from another room through one-way glass or from a corner within the room. (The observer may also be an active participant, as discussed by Cooper et al. in their chapter in this volume.) In addition to videotaping, the observer may also take personal notes about what is occurring in the scene. The result is a wealth of data. If the observer can rapidly mark some of the important events at this point (with reference to the video recording), it would save a great deal of time in later analysis. In fact, many people attempt to do exactly this using either available analysis tools or, more often, handwritten notes with time references. Given limited resources, events that are not easy to transcribe may be omitted from the resulting data set. Although such data remain archived on the original video, from the perspective of subsequent analysis they may as well not have occurred.

11.2.1 Collecting and translating the data

Ideally, video data are transcribed as they are collected. However, in most realistic situations the flow of information is too great for the human observer to deal with. Observers have to monitor the scene or subjects while noting important events. They must direct visual attention away from the critical data source (the subjects or participants) in order to take notes or locate and select functions in the analysis tool (if they have one). Important events or problems in the study might be missed while the observers focus their attention elsewhere. Observers cannot adequately share attention between all the tasks or events that need to be processed.

In current practice, video records are often viewed repeatedly to capture all the information. The data capture and transcription process are further slowed by the need to rewind and reposition the videotape, and by entry of handwritten notes into word processors or spreadsheets, followed by later editing. The resulting data set consists of multiple data streams, such as transcription of the visual data (e.g., gestural information), transcription of the audio data (e.g., verbal protocols or conversation analysis), observer notes (e.g., information about context, artifact usage), keystroke logs, or other system-generated information. Some of these require careful categorization or classification. Each of these must be entered into the "data analysis tool" (image recognition and speech recognition technologies advances may eventually facilitate this).

Video can provide a rich multimedia source of data, but the coding and annotation of video data require care and effort. Although timing information can be easily and automatically added to video documents, very little of the rich data contained in video can be accessed directly. Researchers are obliged to translate the video data into more tangible and explicit forms that can then be manipulated and analyzed. In carrying out this translation researchers have to make decisions about how they will encode the video data, which types of data they are interested in, and the format the data must take to apply the analysis techniques required. This process has two consequences. First, it imposes the researcher's perspective on the data as it is ultimately transcribed. Often only a subset of the data most salient to the specific research interests and goals is encoded (see, e.g., the case study presented by Douglas). Second, the type, quantity, and quality of the data captured are largely determined by the tools available to encode it. To capture even part of the multiple streams of rich video data is time-consuming and difficult. Not surprisingly, most of the emphasis is on capturing the data to facilitate sorting and searching, and less emphasis is on the exploration or visualization of the data.

11.2.2 Preserving the original detail and context

I have described the data translation that researchers typically undertake to create a workable data file from a video recording. This text-based data file contains information about the original recorded events and timing information, and may contain the observer's personal notes taken during recording. In most cases, at this point the original video and audio record is archived and the researcher works with the transcribed data file. Although this simplifies the quantity and nature of the data set, much of the original context and detail is lost in the analysis. Researchers cannot easily reference the original material to expand their understanding of the transcribed data set. The effect of data transcriptions is to create parallel representations of the underlying events, that is, the original video record and the transcribed summaries thereof. The link between transcribed data and corresponding clips of video is lost and interpretability of the data suffers as a result.

Even with extensive transcription, researchers must (or perhaps should) often refer back to the original videotape. When trying to present or explain the analysis, this original contextual information may be crucial for others to form an accurate impression of the data or its implications. Reference to the original data is also necessary for interjudge reliability when multiple researchers wish to analyze the same portions of video or supplement previously analyzed segments of tape.

The video recording is an integral part of the data set and, as such, should remain linked or connected. Many of the dynamic or temporal properties of the data are lost when the original recordings are no longer referenced. Integrating the media creates data that are vivid and compelling as a presentation mechanism. Transcription and summarization should supplement, rather than replace, the original videotape. Video and its various data representations are then combined into multimedia data streams where the data elements are directly referenced to relevant segments of video or audio.

11.2.3 Exploring and visualizing patterns

In exploratory data analysis the fundamental goal is development of insight. Sadly most of the researchers' efforts (and the tool designers' efforts) are devoted to typing in a representation of the original data. Little time or capability exists to support exploring this qualitative data set to investigate trends and patterns. Of paramount importance is the development of appropriate tools that allow the observer to explore data in a flexible manner that promotes development of insight. Currently, such "exploration" is often confined to the translated text data file, using limited text-based exploration such as simple sorting and keyword searching.

Simple data visualization and exploration encompass sorting the text-based data into various orders that may then be viewed (including examination by the original time sequence). Other forms of visualization include scatterplots, timelines, and other charts or graphs. These visualizations typically emphasize individual occurrences of events. They need to be extended to capture temporal aspects of data and the various interrelationships that exist within data. Recent developments in computer graphics facilitate portraying patterns and trends through animation and the use of color, shape, and size (and dynamic changes within each of these elements).

Data visualization allows observers to capitalize on visual reasoning (Parsaye and Chignell, 1993: chap. 5). Interpretation of visualizations can be assisted through the appropriate use of statistical analyses and summaries. Statistical support generally includes numerical quantities and tests of significance that prevent people from making erroneous conclusions based on visual inspection of possible patterns in graphs and charts. One challenge in exploring and visualizing the information in video data is to coordinate presentations of the basic video, statistical summaries and analyses of coded or transcribed data, and graphical visualizations. User interface design, as well as the packaging of video analysis generally, are both pragmatic issues that are likely to have a large effect on how well video-based observation and analysis will be used in the future.

11.2.4 The pragmatics of using the technology

The development of video or temporal data analysis tools is driven as much by simple pragmatics as by theoretical motivation. Often data are recorded in the field, making portability an important requirement. Fortunately, trends toward portable computing and compact consumer electronics (e.g., video camcorders) favor the development of portable video analysis tools (see Section 3). Many of the video recording and analysis techniques that have been developed for usability analysis in HCI (e.g., Karat, 1990; Nielsen, 1989; 1990) may apply to more general analyses of situated behavior.

Video analysis tends to be most difficult in situations where complex behavior is recorded. In video recordings of group interaction, multiple tapes recording the simultaneous activities of multiple users and screens must be synchronized. Observers must monitor and control multiple views and relate annotations to a specific instance of a particular view. In addition, nonverbal (and nonspeech utterances), as well as verbal behavior must be noted. This type of observation and annotation may require considerable expertise and skill. The same person may need to have domain knowledge about qualitative analysis and HCI, as well as considerable expertise in controlling devices and operating complex technologies. Ideally, the requirements for device control and technological complexity should be minimized so that observers can focus on the data rather than on the processes of obtaining the data. The potential contribution of video-based data is limited only by our ability to design flexible tools that support exploration while preserving context and reducing technological dependencies and complexities.

11.3 The VANNA and Timelines systems: Experiences with temporal data analysis and visualization

For the past four years our laboratory has been developing tools for video annotation and analysis research, building on our earlier experience in data analysis and usability engineering. We conducted extensive reviews of existing automated systems and interviewed the users of these systems. Task analyses were done to study the handwritten notes people used when they had no automated tools. From this background research, we derived a set of design criteria (Harrison and Baecker, 1992) and formulated the design features and functions, which we built into a computer-based system (Harrison, 1991; Harrison and Baecker, 1992; Harrison and Owen, 1994). VANNA (Video ANNotation and Analysis) has been used extensively for the past three years to annotate a variety of temporal data such as video, audio, communication network data, keystroke logs, and verbal transcriptions. It has been used by psychologists, anthropologists, usability experts, engineers, ergonomists, and computer scientists. VANNA was designed to work both as a desktop system and as a portable field system, for real-time note taking and for detailed off-line analyses. User feedback led to numerous iterations and changes in the system functionality and in the controls and display features. Our current system, renamed Timelines, was completed and released at the end of 1993.[1]

To establish context, I first summarize the features in the latest version of our system. I then outline the results of a sample case study, which illustrates the problems and methods employed in analyzing time-based data. This case study (and many others not covered here) contributed greatly to our understanding of the varying needs of researchers (see, e.g., Harrison and Baecker, 1992; Harrison and Owen, 1994). The cases also helped to shape our thinking about the pitfalls and drawbacks in automated systems and about where our research should head in the future.

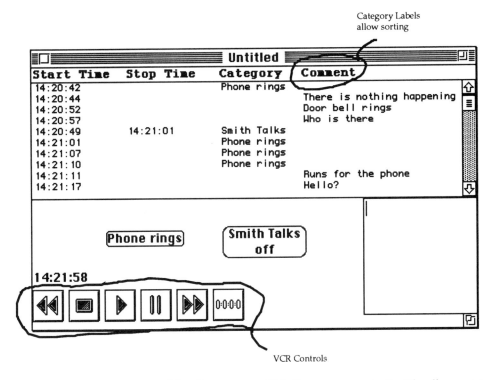

Figure 11.1. The Timelines system. This figure appears in the Timelines user documentation version 1.0.

11.3.1 Description of the VANNA/Timelines system

The VANNA/Timelines system (Harrison, 1991; Harrison and Owen, 1994) integrates various multimedia elements into a single video document (Figure 11.1). The system was originally created to support video data collection and analysis for both software usability testing and behavioral studies in Computer-Supported Cooperative Work (CSCW). In addition to experiments, we also envisaged "note taking" during conferences, seminars, or classes. Interfaces were created using brainstorming sessions, iterative design, and rapid prototyping, resulting in many versions of the system over a short period of time (approximately eight versions in four months). We used direct manipulation interfaces to support a number of key features. Additionally, we designed the system to support a variety of input devices including a touch screen, digital stylus, mouse, and keyboard. The system supports both real-time annotation and the detailed analysis of video data in desktop and portable versions.

Capturing the data

Users define their own labeled index points (event markers) using the "New Event" menu item. Each event marker is assigned a user defined name and optional keystroke equivalency. Users may create event markers based on predetermined items of interest that they anticipate observing or event markers may be created as the video analysis proceeds. A single button press (or keystroke) creates a new data item (event) and automatically links it to the corresponding timed location in the video. These events can reflect ratings of behavioral data such as mood and mood changes, pauses in conversation, overlaps in speech, and the like. This feature is used to capture the instantaneous occurrence of an item of interest. To capture events having durations, an interval is used. Interval markers show not only the user-defined labels but also an indication of their current status (on and running or off). Intervals that are running show the time at which they were started. Intervals that are not currently active show an "off" state. Users create intervals using the "New Interval" menu item and then label each interval. Intervals might be used to indicate the start and end of tasks or conversational turns, for example. Intervals may be set up to be mutually exclusive, where starting one interval automatically stops other related intervals. For example, we might keep track of a person's social remarks or jokes versus task-oriented conversation versus silence where only one type of interval can occur at any one time. A person cannot be silent and joking at exactly the same time. Lastly, textual comments may be entered either alone or in conjunction with an index or interval. These comments can elaborate on existing events or intervals or may be a time-stamped data item themselves. The comment window is variable length, scrollable, and editable. The comment field is typically used to capture observational data or notes about infrequent or unpredictable events, for example, "Subject A seemed very frustrated at this point" or "experimenter had to intervene and restart the computer." Verbal transcriptions or protocols may be thought of as a special case of commenting and are therefore entered in a similar manner.

Manipulating the data

As each event, interval, or comment is entered, it appears highlighted as a new item at the bottom of the data log. This log is shown in the upper half of the Timelines screen. This is a scrolling list of all of the data items formatted into four columns: start time, stop time, category, and comments. Any four column ASCII data file may be loaded into the system and subsequently manipulated.

The data manipulation tools allow users to sort the file, create data subsets, and apply colors to groups of data items. To sort the file, users click on the heading of the column to be used as the sort key. To create multiple views or subsets of the data file, users select items that match specified criteria. The data in these subsets may be hidden from view or colored. Filtering and searching is provided through a number of operations which may be performed on any one of the four columns. These operations are structured as <field name><operator><value specified by the user>. Field name is one of *start time, stop time, category,* or *comment.* Operators for the time fields include *is anything, is greater than, is less than, is equal to,* or *is not equal to.* Operators for the category and comment field include *is anything, is equal to, is not equal to, contains, does not contain,* or *is empty.* The results of each search are highlighted in the data file. Highlighted items may then be hidden from view or a color may be applied. Hidden items are not deleted; they are temporarily removed from the active data set. A menu item allows users to reveal hidden items thereby restoring the data file to its original state.

Visualizing the data

The system supports two forms of data summary or visualization. The first is a quantitative summary of the number of each type of item in the data file. This includes the total number of entries in the file, the number of categories, and the number of colors used. (A category is any or all uniquely labeled events and intervals.) For each individual event and interval (based on the labels) the total number of occurrences is displayed. Intervals additionally have a cumulative and average duration. Summaries are calculated for the currently displayed data set (this excludes items that may have been hidden).

Alternatively, users may produce a graphical visualization that plots the categories (events and intervals) on the y-axis and time along the x-axis (Figure 11.2). For example, these visualizations might be used to compare when different people in a group were speaking or were silent. They could also be used to compare when certain types of errors were made in using a new product. If color was applied to certain data items, this will be reflected in the graphical output. An example of this might be to use color to indicate the severity of a problem that was observed from the video tape. In the visualization, events are shown as short marks, whereas intervals are shown as bars indicating their duration. These aligned timelines allow users to compare visually data for trends and patterns. Items can be reordered along the y-axis to facilitate comparison. For example, one type of subject error noted from the videotape might be observed typically to follow another type of error. Speaking overlaps or pauses in conversation can be immediately noticed by looking at where intervals overlap each other or where there are gaps. Any item in the graph may be selected and the corresponding item in the data file will be shown, should the user wish to see the details about that item. This could include the exact time it occurred at or any comments elaborating on the event. Items in the data file or the visualization may be grouped and automatically played back to review the original raw video data. This allows users to compare items with similar properties back to back in the original video tape.

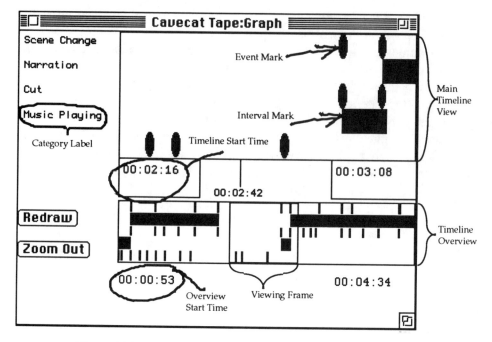

Figure 11.2. Timelines graphical plots. This figure appears in the Timelines user documentation version 1.0.

The portable system

To gain experience in portable video annotation systems we observed users annotating events in real time as the video was recorded. The VANNA portable system integrates computer functionality with video and audio recording. A camcorder is connected to a Macintosh PowerBook™, which automatically collects and stores timing information. We designed the VANNA portable system to support the types of real-time annotations that were characteristic of notes taken *while an experiment or field study was actually in progress*. This meant that the system had to support very fast note-taking mechanisms and would automatically get timing information from the video device *without* affecting the live recording process in any way. From these notes, colleagues can review those sections of the experiment or study of particular interest to them, instead of having to review the entire tape.

11.3.2 Case study: A video conferencing communication study

This case study reflects many of the difficulties and properties typical in detailed unobtrusive observation of people performing real work with their own goals and objectives to meet. In this section I focus on the data collection and manipulation process and the implications for designing video analysis tools. The purpose, experimental design, and discussion of results of the study are reported elsewhere (Harrison, Chignell, and Baecker, 1992a; 1992b).

This study examined, in detail, the characteristic differences in between-site, video-mediated communication versus within-site, face-to-face communication. We were interested in investigating conversational flow, speaking turns, and how video technology influenced the dynamics of interaction. Did the participants experience any particular problems and how did they compensate? Did the objective analysis match participants' perceptions of the conversational dynamics? What were the primary differences between within-site and between-site interactions? A distributed video conference (three sites) was used to collect data for this comparison. Three to five participants were located at each site thereby allowing face-to-face interaction within the site. Participants were discussing a real task and were therefore compelled to work with the other groups across the video links. The task was a review and discussion of a document to which each person had contributed a section. Although we had no control over the task itself (it was a real working meeting), the task had a number of desirable characteristics from the perspective of our study. Participation was highly interactive and highly distributed. Various parties had vested interests in the outcome of the discussion and hence were strongly motivated to represent their views and opinions. For reasons of confidentiality all reports of this study disguise the persons, project, task, and outcome.

The conference was videotaped for later detailed analysis and a questionnaire was filled in by each of the participants upon completion of the conference. We used subjective assessments (questionnaires) to determine attitude differences between video-mediated (between-site) and face-to-face (within-site) communication. Subjects were asked about, for example, visibility of video images, ease of breaking into the conversation, ease of obtaining feedback, ease of providing feedback to others, and how productive they felt. We also used detailed video analysis to collect both qualitative and quantitative data for each of the two "conditions." We counted, for example, speaking turns, failed attempts at gaining floor control, simultaneous speech, and various behaviors used to smooth the interaction when things seemed to go awry (due to technological constraints). One example of our findings showed that video compression resulted in very awkward turn taking because of the delays in transmitting speech between sites. As a result people often started talking simultaneously, then realizing this, both people stop speaking simultaneously, then both would start again. Eventually we saw a variety of "go ahead" gestures or hand-raising "can I speak next" gestures emerge to facilitate speaking turns. Participants were acutely aware of the turn-taking problems but seemed barely aware of the adaptive strategies they adopted. They also tended to overestimate how often these problems occurred, since each single occurrence was so noticeably disruptive. This case study provided us with an interesting blend of qualitative and quantitative data and some compelling anecdotal evidence. In the remainder of this section we will describe the strategies we used to analyze the data and the implications for analysis tool design.

Capturing observational data

The observer-researcher was not an active participant in the meeting but rather sat in a separate room where all of the video signals from all of the sites were displayed and recorded. This allowed for truly unobtrusive observation. All of the meeting participants were informed of this observation and of the video recording before the meeting started. (This is an important ethical point that researchers should enforce when working with video data in particular.)

Data were collected in one of three formats: handwritten notes made by the observer during the meeting, a video and audio recording of the meeting itself, and the questionnaires filled out by the meeting participants. The goal in the research was to investigate the effect of technology mediation on conversational interactions. The observer noted the times (from the VCR counter) and instances of particularly difficult speaking turn switches, problems in floor control, failed turn attempts, side conversations within any site, and interesting gestures used to assist in smoothing conversational dynamics (e.g., raising one's hand to request a turn or waving another person to "go ahead"). The notes were very brief (maximum five words or so) since they were taken as the meeting progressed. They were initially recorded in a personalized "shorthand." The observer went back and elaborated on previously recorded notes to clarify them when possible (during lulls in the meeting). These notes highlighted instances of behavior that related directly to the research interests and hypotheses of the study (either supporting or contradicting). They were free-form and no previously defined categorizations were used.

Video and audio recordings of the entire meeting were made for later detailed analysis using the VANNA system. Multiple passes over the video (in general eight complete passes of the entire meeting, with up to twenty passes over specific segments) were required to capture all of the necessary data. Event markers were used to count instances of simultaneous speech both within a site and across sites, turn interruptions, failed turn attempts, gestures used to smooth or facilitate conversation, gestures or movements used to provide visual feedback, and unusually lengthy or uncomfortable pauses in conversation. These seven event categories were based on the specific research issues under investigation. Comments were used to elaborate on the degree of disruption for simultaneous speech or pauses and to identify the participants involved in each activity marked. For example, for failed turn attempts, comments were used to indicate who was speaking currently and who attempted to break into the conversation. The type of gesture and its purpose were also described by a typed comment (hand waving, hand raising, finger pointing at person X, etc.). Interval markers were used to provide approximate measures of the time spent on task-related work versus social interaction. (One of the interesting effects we found in video communication is that jokes over the video link are very hard to make. The response [laughter] is delayed by the technology so that the association of laughter with the original joke is lost. People end up wondering what someone is laughing at.) Partial transcriptions of the audio were made for those instances where the conversation related directly to the control or facilitation of turn taking. The verbal protocols identified both the content and the speaker (Ericsson and Simon, 1984). The questionnaire data (typically Likert adjective scale ratings) were then compiled and compared with the analysis of the videotape. These data existed in a spreadsheet program, separate from the video analysis data.

Manipulating the data

Although the VANNA system supports four "streams" of data, different types of data and categorizations were used within the streams. The first two streams contain the start and stop times for events or intervals of interest. The third stream of data contained labels for the events and intervals as marked off by the user. This stream contained the seven events and two intervals described previously. Finally the last data stream contained the open-ended comments, which included elaborations or explanations for event items or interval items, observer notes, and verbal protocols. Clearly each of these "types" was a different class of data and served a different purpose. Within the system all data were initially merged into a single data file.

Data were manipulated in one of three ways: by sorting the file according to the time or event/interval labels; by keyword searches on the comments item; or by deleting items (hence creating a subset of the original data file). Sorting by the starting time provided the user with a sense of the sequential coherence of the events and the order in which things occurred and progressed. Sorting by event/interval labels (stream 3 of the data file) allowed users to cluster similar categories and hence get a sense of the frequency of occurrence. For example, we first looked at when instances of difficult turn taking occurred. As the meeting progressed and people developed compensatory behaviors, the frequency of problematic speaker turn exchanges decreased. We then sorted the file by event type, which grouped the turn taking problem events together. This facilitated playback of these items one after the other, since the tool automatically located the items and controlled the video device. We could get a sense of how each turn taking problem resembled or differed from the others.

These transcriptions resulted in a large and very dense file containing many different types of data, making it difficult to read or decipher. Items depicting gestures were mixed in with items about speaking turns and remarks about instances of visual or auditory feedback. By sorting and then deleting select items, separate files were created for the speech-based data (e.g., simultaneous speech, interruptions), the gestural data (e.g., raising a hand for a turn request, waving someone to go ahead), feedback data, and verbal protocol data. This allowed us to work with smaller and more focused data sets. However, although the subfiles provided a better view of particular data sets, the entire file was retained as a baseline to provide context for each data item relative to the others, independent of data type. We could switch between views of the subfiles and views of the entire file.

Finally, keyword searches were used extensively within the comments field to locate specific items of interest. We adopted certain loosely structured and informal rules for categorization through the use of consistently applied keywords. This was used for observer notes and elaborations for events/intervals. The verbal protocol data had more formal structures where each item consisted of <speaker name>: <content of conversation>: <conversation directed to – person's name(s) or all>. Speaker names were entered in bold. Pauses were indicated by ellipses (since the length of the pause was not being measured). Emphatic stress was indicated by italicized words. Who the conversation was directed at was underlined (this information was inferred by the observer). This informal syntax was sufficient for this case study.

Visualizing the data

Even performing simple visual scanning through a text-based data listing, sorted by time, provided a sense of how the meeting progressed and gave a sense of when there were periods of great activity of interest versus little activity. In this research study, great activity meant that many people "battled" for floor control and there were frequent turn changes and failed turn attempts. "Lulls" reflected periods during which one single person held the floor (that person's name was indicated in the comments).

When the data were sorted by event/interval labels, similar items were shown grouped together. This not only facilitated playback itself but allowed the user to investigate the contexts for each group of items to look for further similarities and differences, by referencing the original video records. Several of these data items were specially "marked" and later used in presentations as illustrative and compelling examples of the phenomena of interest. (In fact we later created an event called "good clip" so that we could rapidly indicate the occurrences of particularly good examples that we might later want to present.) This grouping and automated playback facility allowed the user to create a shared understanding with colleagues involved in similar research. Colleagues could review any data file and also get a sense of not only the data but also the original contextual information.

Summary information was obtained for the frequency of occurrence of each event and interval, the cumulative duration, average duration, and a measure of variability of each interval. These summaries, although not "visualizations" per se, provided high-level information about what happened across the entire data file. To obtain a better sense of the data, the observer also broke the data file into pieces, based on time, and then created the summary information. This gave a crude indication of the density of the data in fifteen-minute intervals (the observer selected this granularity). Although crude, the resulting summary data did provide a quantitative measure of the meeting progression from beginning to end and how the communication patterns evolved.

Finally, a graphical visualization was plotted for the data recorded. The events and intervals appeared along the y-axis (dependent variables) and time was plotted along the x-axis. This visualization immediately reflected the patterns in the "density" of the data, that is, where clusters of activity occurred during the meeting versus the lulls. The relative frequency and time of occurrence for the events measured were also visually compared. For example, it was observed that several failed turn attempts in a row often coincided with explicit turn-taking gestures. If there was only one failed turn attempt these gestures were not observed (and by implication were likely not deemed necessary as the turn had either succeeded after one attempt or had been abandoned altogether). Such patterns became apparent using the graphical visualization tool and color coding of data items. These visualizations were also used in a prior study about communication patterns where the audio from four meeting participants was used to generate an automated log of when and who was speaking (Kurtenbach, 1993). These data were similarly plotted over time for each participant. The resulting graph made it immediately obvious when there were speech overlaps, pauses, or conversational bedlam (Sellen, 1992).

11.3.3 Implications for our design

In the early observational studies, handwritten notes were either manually added to the data file or were used to locate the previously noted items on the videotape so that they could then be entered into the system. This lack of initial integration slowed the data collection process considerably. A touch typist could have entered such brief and abbreviated notes on a computer had one been available. Portable versions of the systems were created to support this type of active field observation. Testing on real-time note taking, conducted since this case study, shows that it is possible to capture simple, abbreviated forms of data during observations or experiments.

The analysis of the video data also proved very time-consuming. Much of this resulted from the nature of the studies, but other problems resulted from inadequate tool functionality. For instance, intervals are often mutually exclusive. That is, the occurrence of one type of interval precludes the occurrence of another. In our video communication study, task-oriented behaviors could not occur simultaneously with social interactions. We created a "mutually exclusive" interval capability to address this problem. Turning one interval "on" automatically turns all others in the group "off."

We have found that users require hierarchic category structures, particularly for data from controlled experiments. We are now working on the interface and functions for creating and identifying hierarchic structures.

In our video analysis tools, better mechanisms for entering and manipulating verbal protocol data and conversation analysis data are needed. Thus far, we have had insufficient numbers of users doing research that requires this type of analysis to provide us with feedback and requirements. Although it seems that supporting hierarchic structures would facilitate tagging speech acts with speaker identifiers, we believe that there are many subtle and important aspects in both conversation analysis and verbal protocol analysis that we have not begun to address. This has implications for the number and way in which we have been handling streams of data within our system.

Our initial results indicate that graphical visualizations are powerful exploratory tools, particularly in large data files. The ability to create subsets or alternate views of this data file and redraw the visualizations appears to provide users with substantial flexibility. It has also encouraged our users to think of "video data analysis" in new ways, reinforcing the idea of exploratory data analysis for more general temporal sequential data.

11.3.4 Addressing the challenges: A synopsis of several landmark systems

In this section I illustrate how others have built support tools that facilitate the collection, manipulation, analysis, and exploration of time-based data. I also rely upon earlier discussion about the process by which multimedia data are integrated and analyzed and have used this as a framework. This section discusses common elements and critical ideas incorporated into current tools to support each of the stages in the video data collection and analysis process. Most systems support one phase of process better than other phases. For each of the phases I discuss what appears to have worked in other systems.

Collecting and translating the data

A number of systems have converged on the use of buttonlike objects to mark off labeled index points (e.g., Harrison, 1991; Kennedy, 1989; Losada and Markovitch, 1990; MacKay and Davenport, 1989; Olson and Olson, 1991). This allows the user to mark events of interest, typically with a single button press, mouse click, or keyboard stroke. The user-defined label is saved along with timing information. Once coded, most systems save the data in time-stamped columnlike formats. Several examples of input or coding mechanisms and the resulting data files will be outlined here.

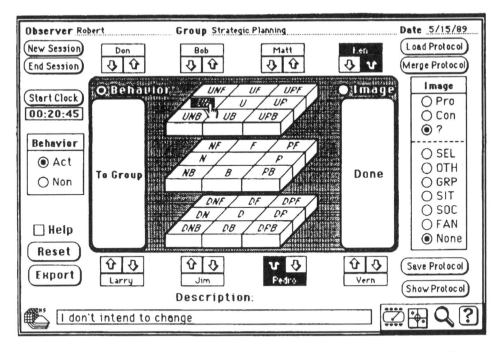

Figure 11.3. GroupAnalyzer coding component. This figure is identified in Losada and Markovitch (1990) as Figure 2.

The GroupAnalyzer (Losada and Markovitch, 1990; Losada, Sanchez, and Noble, 1990) was designed to code and analyze meetings and to provide feedback to the meeting participants about behavioral patterns over time. To accomplish this, it uses the Bales SYMLOG dimensions (Bales, 1983) to describe mood, cooperativeness, and degree of task orientation. Although the application is specialized, once again the buttonlike input mechanisms proved the most useful (Figure 11.3). Each interaction coded requires three buttons: an initiator, a recipient, and a Bales rating of the act. As in the VANNA and Timelines systems, a comment line is available for short textual notes by the researcher. The result of the coding session is a meeting protocol (Figure 11.4).

VideoNoter (a reduced set of functions is available as CVideo) supports five kinds of windows, where each window has a different function (Roschelle and Goldman, 1991; Roschelle, Pea, and Trigg, 1990; Trigg, 1989). In addition to text and graphics windows, user may create customized annotation windows to record initial data. Users may define their own button-oriented "coding templates," used for marking events of interest or categorizing events. Objects within the coding template may be resized and relocated within the window. The worksheet window is used for making textual or simple graphical annotations on a transcription of the

```
1115,Pedro,G,a,F,Gio:people know the
     players
1118,Bob Vern,Pedro,n,PF,Deb:attentive
1125,Don,G,a,F,PAM:writes for gp
1130,Don,G,n,F,Deb:types
1131,Bob,G,a,F,PAM:
1133,Pedro,G,a,DF,Gio:
1139,Bob,G,a,UF,PAM:
1144,Bob,G,a,N,Deb:nobody talks to J. S.
1151,Bob,G,a,F,Deb:
1154,Bob,G,a,UF,Gio:we need to...
1156,Ken,G,a,UN,PAM:interrupts
```

Figure 11.4. Sample meeting protocol. This figure is identified in Losada and Markovitch (1990) as Figure 3.

video (Figure 11.5). This is the primary window for data entry and retrieval of video segments based on marked events. Items are automatically time-stamped, allowing the resulting annotations to be used as indexes to specific frames in the videotape or disk. Users may define their own button-oriented coding template for marking events of interest.

EVA is an interactive video annotation tool that allows both "on-line real-time" coding while an experiment (or observation) is occurring, and "off-line" detailed coding with the stored video record after the video recording is completed (MacKay, 1989; MacKay and Davenport, 1989). To tag events of interest, observers create their own labeled index buttons prior to the start of the session. A generic time-stamp button is used to indicate unanticipated events that the observer wishes to mark. Users may enter notes, verbal transcriptions, keystroke logging for the subjects, and symbolic categories for organizing the recorded data. Later they can go back and add more detail to the analysis. Additionally, observers may make notes in a separate window.

Similar mechanisms are used by the U-test usability tool described by Kennedy (1989). In the U-test system, reminders to the observer may also be programmed in. The tool is preprogrammed, by the experimenter, with a list of tasks that the subjects are to perform. For each task, a detailed list of steps and a set of anticipated possible errors which the subject might make are given. These "error buttons" may be considered specific cases of experimenter-created event indexes. A "timer on" and "timer off" function allows experimenters to set start and stop points for intervals of interest. Experimenters may also enter text comments and observations.

The GALATEA system (Potel and Sayre, 1976; Potel, Sayre, and MacKay, 1980) uses pen-based input as an integral part of the operation of the system. GALATEA is "an interactive animated graphics system for analyzing dynamic phenomena [notably biological cell movement] recorded on a movie film" (Potel et

UN/em-project

Video	Annotations	Challenges	Transcript
			S: Ok this one's too great. Yeah. (1.5)
			G: Initial // speed isn't good enough. Aw (
			S: // Ok ((?)) (.)
			G: //You can't tell.
			S: //Now that looks fine.
			S: that's I think=
			G: =Initial speed is fine?
			S: Just make this one smaller.
			G: Wait you know we could use particle o
·· 00:12:24	⌐G tries to use "initial speed" vocabulary. S ignoring G		speed an::
			S: now // this
			G: // Oh we couldn't convert it to a partic
		Challenge 6	S: Now ok. That's slightly too much. It sl
·· 00:12:36	⌐G has idea of using particle one to test speed. S ignores. G drops idea.		G: .hhh eventually.
			S: Ok (.) so:: (1.0) reset maybe make //
	⌐"It's hard to tell the difference between initial speed and acceleration" G confirms lack of distinction between v and a.		
·· 00:12:48			G: // It's hard to tell the difference betw
			acceleration.
			(4.0)

Figure 11.5. Sample VideoNoter worksheet. This figure is identified in Roschelle et al. (1990) as Figure 1.

Figure 11.6. Frame from a Galatea animation. This figure is identified in Potel et al. (1980) as Figure 12.

al., 1980). Computer graphics or animated images are superimposed on the film (Figure 11.6). Users have the ability to "write directly" on the film with a digitizing stylus when they recognize an item of interest and wish to track it. For example, the user manipulates the pen to follow a moving object, matching the resulting animation in both time and space. Users also have a sketching function for free hand-drawing or handwritten notes.

The SHAPA system (Sanderson, James, and Seidler, 1989) was developed to analyze verbal communications (protocol analysis), originally within the context of flight crew workload studies. SHAPA provides the analyst with information about what was said, the sequence in which it was said, and how often such sequences occurred. It handles single-stream protocol data without time stamps. Each line of transcription in the SHAPA system is numbered. These lines may then be categorized or labeled using a predicate-argument structure defined by the researcher (and described briefly here). A more sophisticated system called Mac-SHAPA (Sanderson et al., 1990; Sanderson et al., 1991) was subsequently developed to aid in video analysis by integrating device control, automatic time stamping, data entry, and data manipulation and analysis. Users may import preexisting data files such as keystroke logs. SHAPA and MacSHAPA use a column-based structure where each column represents a different type of information (as determined by the researcher) arranged by time (Figure 11.7).

The Meeting Plots system (Olson and Olson, 1991; Olson et al., 1992) uses coding templates that consist of user-defined, labeled buttons and free-form text comments. In their research, they were interested in studying design rationale and

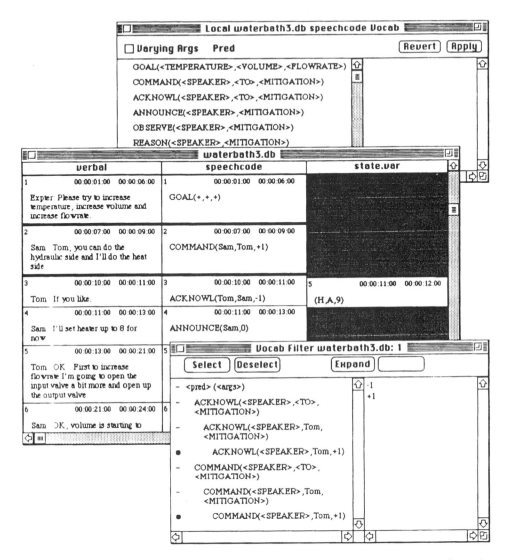

Figure 11.7. MacSHAPA data entry and manipulation screens. This figure is identified in Sanderson (1993) as Figure 5.

decision making. For this reason (as in most systems), the choice of labels reflects their research interests. Items such as issues, alternatives, problems, and goals are used. Their system also allows for verbal transcriptions and free-form comments.

The Observer, Tracker, and Reviewer tools (Hoiem and Sullivan, 1993) were designed for data collection and analysis in usability applications. "Observer" is used for noting observations about an interaction. A coding scheme, created in any text editor, can be loaded and labeled buttons will be automatically created. The

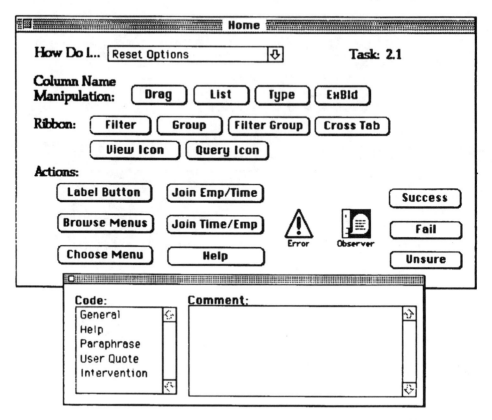

Figure 11.8. Observer system coding screen. This figure is identified in Hoiem and Sullivan (1993) as Figure 1.

labeled buttons indicate the items of interest as they relate to a specific task or usability test. Categories may occur in multiple parallel streams or hierarchical structures. Users may also enter free-form textual comments. The "Tracker" system collects keystroke log data, menu selections, and the like generated by the computer (Figure 11.8).

From a survey of these and other tools, most systems favor buttonlike data entry where the observers predetermine which labels or names their categories require. Virtually all systems also support free-form text-based entry. New category labels and more lengthy text can be created "off-line" when more detailed analyses are carried out. Activities that tend to be coded off-line include user comments or general observations; verbal transcriptions of the conversation; nonverbal information, such as, gesture; personality or mood measures. For rapid data entry a reduced set of functions is typically used. Although independently developed, these systems reflect a surprising similarity in their data collection mechanisms and the resulting data set appearance. One problem many tools have not yet addressed is portability into field sites. Our results over the last year suggest that portable systems are extremely useful and do not require substantial changes from the original software programs, provided that the original software is designed in a flexible way. Finally, while many systems adopt similar approaches in coding, translating, and representing the data, many do not go much further in terms of analytic tools and media integration. In the next two sections I discuss the importance of data manipulation and media integration and describe examples of how several systems have achieved this.

Data manipulation

Although the sequential aspect of video data is preeminent, there is often considerable value in organizing and grouping the key concepts in the data. This can be achieved by simple sorting and searching tools, which allow the users to create data subsets or reorderings. Alternatively, this can be done using cluster analysis methods (Everitt, 1974), in which items or concepts are grouped based on patterns of intercorrelation or similarity. Clustering is often the first step in analysis of the semantic content or meaning of video data. Verbal protocol analysis, conversation analysis, discourse analysis, and content analysis can then be used to summarize the principal features of text using organizing constructs (derived either from a theoretical model or from an empirical method such as cluster analysis). The regrouped data itself may provide interesting insights (as illustrated by the case study described earlier). In addition, these data subsets may be passed on to data analysis and visualization tools for more sophisticated exploration. In this section we briefly present several systems that reflect typical data manipulation mechanisms.

In the VideoNoter system (Roschelle, Pea, and Trigg, 1990), a collections window allows users to group data objects together and create hierarchical organizations. These may be thought of as files and folders, used to organize annotations and link video segments. An object or group of objects within a collection window can be selected to show automatically the corresponding work-sheet entry or to play the corresponding video segment. Searching functions are used to locate words or phrases in the text, or coded events.

The Reviewer tool (Hoiem and Sullivan, 1993) integrates data collected through keystroke logs and the computer system activity with data noted by the observer of the usability test. These time-stamped multistream data files are "merged" and synchronized with the videotape (Figure 11.9).

Virtually all of the systems we have seen allow sorting and keyword searching, and merging of data files. Some allow hierarchically structured events (e.g., Reviewer, MacSHAPA, VideoNoter). From our own research we have determined that there are three basic data manipulation requirements that facilitate the creation of subsets of data for subsequent analysis: sorting, searching (with ability to "hide"

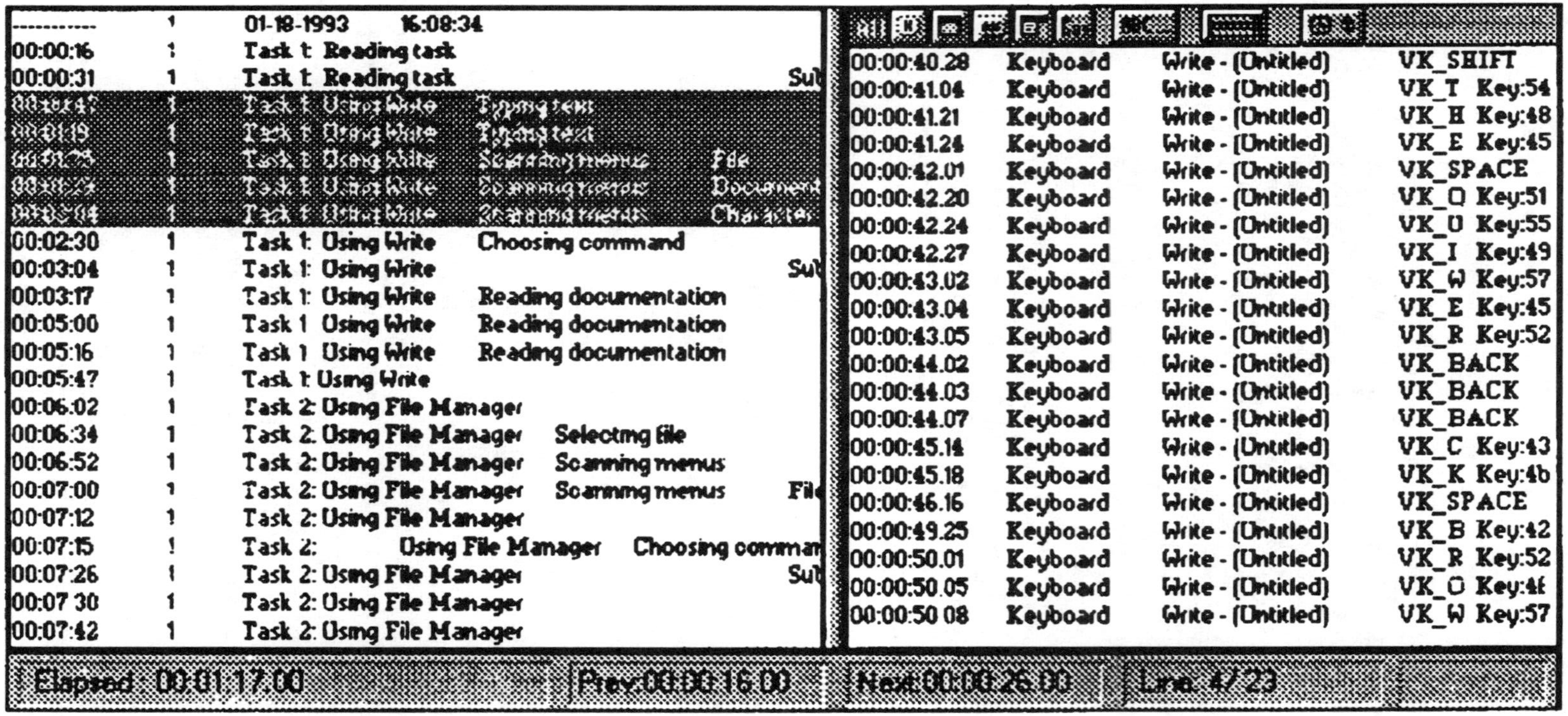

Figure 11.9. Reviewer merged data files. This figure is identified in Hoiem and Sullivan (1993) as Figure 7.

or "reveal" the results of the search), and the use of hierarchical data structures (which can be queried at any level to create subsets). Some systems support better and more sophisticated query capabilities (e.g., MacSHAPA, Timelines, Reviewer). Systems are also starting to use color to differentiate items across subsets (e.g., Timelines).

Media integration: Preserving context and detail

One of the primary problems in creating representative text-based data files from video-recorded events is the preservation of temporal dependencies between events thereby maintaining a sense of context. Viewing data points in a column-based format can be misleading because a gestalt understanding of events is lost. Isolated data items are open to misunderstanding or misinterpretation. Additionally, the original dynamism of the data is not captured using traditional transcriptions and column-based displays. These problems can be addressed in two ways: integration of the original media and better data visualization tools. In this section we discuss media integration, linking the translated data set to the original video recording. When viewing the data elements, a researcher can either explicitly request a playback of the original material or the material could be implicitly played back by virtue of scrolling through elements in the data file. We have found that this integration gives the researcher an important sense that the original video data is not lost and remains an active part of the data set.

As in the VANNA and Timelines systems, the GroupAnalyzer system, the U-Test system, the SHAPA system, and the Meeting Plots system allow the users to play back selected items from the data file automatically, thereby permitting users to observe more detail or context for items of interest. This can be done on a per-item basis by selecting the desired item and then choosing the play option. The images are presented on a separate video monitor.

The VideoNoter system has attempted to smoothly integrate the video device control functionality into the worksheet view. A gray bar indicates the current position of the video device. As the video plays, the bar moves through a dynamically scrolling data file, indicating the items currently being played. The user may select the bar itself and drag it to a new location, moving the video device to the corresponding location. Items may be played back on a separate video monitor by selecting them.

In the EVA system (MacKay and Davenport, 1989) the researcher works at a "visual workstation." Live video from the camera appears in a window on this workstation screen making the integration of the media much smoother and more seamless. The buttons to mark events of interest and the observer notes window are located on the same workstation screen. This allows the researcher to focus on a single source, facilitating the coding process. One interesting capability of this tool during playback is that it allows the text transcriptions to appear as "subtitles," synchronized with the video. One subtitle appears for each participant or for each "event stream," such as an audio transcription. Another facility, not seen in other tools, is the ability to automatically log keystrokes from the subjects and synchronize them with the video.

As should be clear from the description in the previous section, the GALATEA system totally integrates the video image and the tool functionality on a single screen. The data coding and data analysis phases therefore present the video image and corresponding annotations together. (The exception is for statistical or numerical analyses where there is not an obvious coupling of image to output.) Device control is achieved through a graphical control panel on the side of the work space.

The Reviewer system uses mechanisms similar to VideoNoter to achieve media integration. Double clicking on any item (line) in the data file locates that item on the video device and plays it. As the video plays, the corresponding location in the data file is highlighted and this highlight moves in synchronicity with the video.

Whereas most systems support remote control of the video devices, few integrate the resulting video image into a window on the same workstation or permit still frames to be used as index markers between the data file and the video. The use of video windows that are integrated as part of the same tool functionality reinforce the idea of media-based data. Separating the video out onto a separate television monitor has given our subjects a sense of disjoint data sources (along with all of the associated visual time-sharing problems). We are also optimistic about the use of video still frames as context-rich index markers linking the original video data (or audio data) to the associated data elements as transcribed. For example, we are working on "post-its" (one inch by one inch) embedded into the column-based data file. With the emergence of digital video, it is hoped that these capabilities will become more popular and pervasive. Without media integration it becomes difficult to capture the dynamic, temporal sense of the data file. In the next section I describe visualization methods that partially address the problems of capturing these dynamic temporal properties without requiring media integration per se.

Analysis, exploration, and visualization

Once the video has been coded, many different analyses may be applied to the resulting data set. The level of analysis is dependent upon the researchers' objectives, the experimental design, and the goal of the observations. Additionally the structure of the data themselves determines what types of queries can be supported. Interaction patterns, in particular, play a significant role in many analyses. These patterns can be derived using a variety of statistics that show dependencies or relationships or by approximation through visual inspection of carefully formatted output. Both qualitative analyses (e.g., frequency counts, statistical analysis) and qualitative analyses (e.g., timeline visualizations, animations) contribute to the

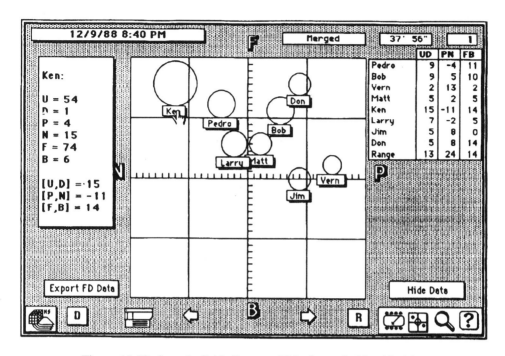

Figure 11.10. Sample field diagram. This figure is identified in Losada and Markovitch (1990) as Figure 4.

researcher's understanding of the data and its implications. In this section we discuss some interesting techniques used by current systems to analyze and visualize the coded data sets.

The GroupAnalyzer system displays include a static field diagram (as shown in Figure 11.10). Simulations of the system have also shown an animated diagram that demonstrates how the group dynamics evolve and change over time. Each circle, representing a participant, expands as the perceived level of dominance increases (and likewise shrinks for decreases in perceived dominance). The participant's circle moves through the various quadrants as the participant becomes more or less friendly and more or less emotionally expressive. To animate the field diagram, observers must record behavioral data at regular intervals. The temporal information automatically logged by the computer is used to coordinate the multiple data streams (one per participant) and the video synchronization. The resulting animation is a series of discrete views played in the order of occurrence (as opposed to more traditional continuous animations).

Time series analysis (spectral analysis) of the data in the GroupAnalyzer system may be displayed as a static network diagram called an interaction diagram. These diagrams display interactive behavioral patterns over time. Each participant is represented by a node, from which directed links extend to connect other nodes. The links signify cross-correlated behaviors. The width of the link is the level of significance. Negative correlations and lag times between interactions are also represented. These network diagrams are popular in a number of systems to represent relationships between data items.

The U-Test system was designed for usability testing applications. As a result the analysis routines and functions are specific to the needs of the researchers in usability. Frequency counts for the number of errors of each type, the number of hints, and the task times are computed. There are no graphical visualization tools per se, since these were not needed for the task at hand.

In the GALATEA system (Potel and Sayre, 1976; Potel et al., 1980), analysis functions include mechanisms to interpolate motion across frames, animations to represent moving skeletal forms, and the ability to draw on one part of the film and copy the graphics to another location. Typical statistical analyses include correlations, linear regressions, Fourier transforms, and simple hypothesis testing. More advanced statistical methods such as time series analyses, multivariate regression, and cluster analysis are available on secondary computers.

The MacSHAPA system (Sanderson, 1993; Sanderson et al., 1990; Sanderson et al., 1991) was built on the experiences gained with the original SHAPA system. In particular it offers a rich set of tools for visualizing patterns and trends in the data either in tabular or graphical formats (Figure 11.11). Unlike most other systems it also incorporates a sophisticated querying capability that allows users to filter and combine the data in interesting and flexible ways.

Meeting Plots (Olson and Olson, 1991; Olson et al., 1992) shows graphical descriptions of the flow of activities in group design meetings over time. Activities serve as indexes to either the original video record or to a transcription of the discussion. In Meeting Plots, the x-axis represents time, while classes of activities that took place during the meeting and artifacts used are shown on the y-axis. Activities may be general (e.g., meeting management, goal setting) or specific (e.g., discussed merits of a specific piece of software). Figure 11.12 shows a graphical representation of a meeting to discuss the redesign of an automated teller machine to reduce waiting queues. It provides a concise overview of the progression of the meeting.

Based on these graphical representations of how the meeting evolved, a network diagram is produced (Figure 11.13). (These are somewhat similar to the diagrams produced by the GroupAnalyzer system described earlier.) Each circular node represents a category of activity in the collaborative process such as meeting management, planning and writing, or summarizing. The size of the circle reflects the total time spent on that particular activity. Black wedges in each circle represent the time spent clarifying that particular topic, whereas the white portion reflects direct discussion of the topic. Arrows between nodes show transitions between

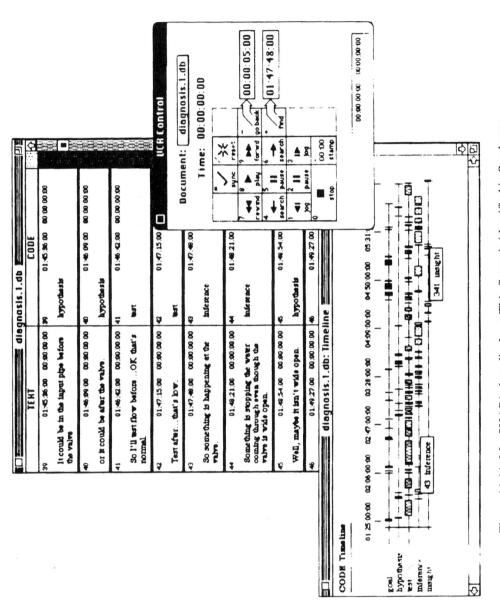

Figure 11.11. MacSHAPA data displays. This figure is identified in Sanderson (1993) as Figure 4.

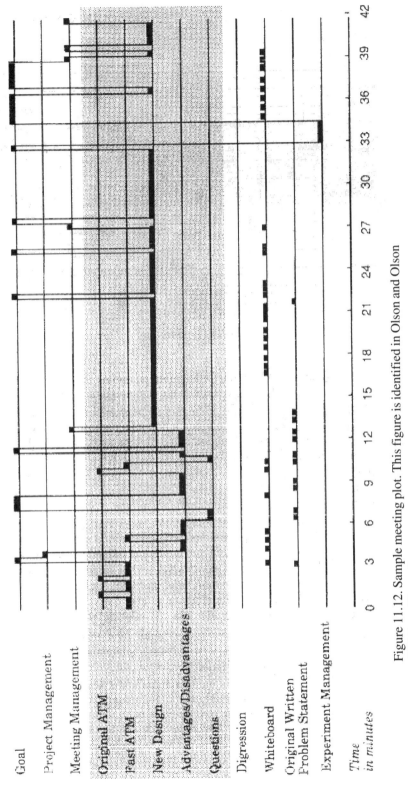

Figure 11.12. Sample meeting plot. This figure is identified in Olson and Olson (1991) as Figure 3.

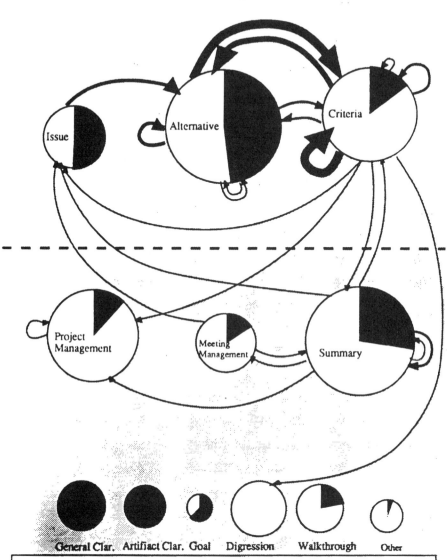

Figure 4: The time spent in various activities and the transitions among them.
The size of the circle represents the total time, with direct presentation in white,
the clarification in black. The width of the arrow represents the frequency of
that transition. Only those transitions above .7% are shown.

Figure 11.13. Sample timing and flow diagram. This figure is identified in
Olson et al. (1992) as Figure 4.

topics, with the width of the arrow indicating the likelihood of going from one node to another (Olson et al., 1992).

The Reviewer system has the relatively simple analysis capabilities typical of usability tools (see, e.g., U-Test). Data can be viewed, filtered, or sorted, and video segments can be reviewed based on the data file. Events of a similar type can be grouped together and played back in sequence for comparison. The majority of the analysis work is carried out by the routines provided in Microsoft Excel. These include frequency counts and basic statistical analyses.

From these descriptions, there are several emerging trends in methods to support exploration and visualization. Timeline representation (with and without color) allows researchers to get a holistic sense of data relationships. Network diagrams also convey similar information about relationship without the emphasis on the time of occurrence, but rather of the strength of the relationship. Finally, several tools for browsing the actual video segments and organizing them into meaningful patterns are being announced.

11.4 Conclusions

In this chapter I have discussed the challenges and opportunities for exploration of time-based qualitative data and, in particular, video data. I have described how these data and the associated transcription and analysis contribute toward a better understanding of human–computer interaction. I presented a case study to illustrate a typical video analysis session and the research questions that might be supported, using our own system as an example tool. Our approach emphasizes the integration of multistream, multimedia, temporal data. I reviewed a number of systems that employ creative approaches to addressing the challenges of exploratory sequential data analysis for a variety of research paradigms and goals. All of these systems support multiple parallel data streams having dynamic properties, where time is the integrating element for these streams. They offer promising suggestions for future work.

Integrated environments are needed that combine the strengths of existing computer-based systems with the insights of traditional exploratory data analysis techniques and statistical techniques. The pragmatics of capturing and summarizing video data are also important, since ease of coding is crucial to data integrity and can impact the type and amount of data that will be entered. In addition to dealing with the coding "bottleneck," future video analysis systems should facilitate the critical tasks of exploration and visualization. While the exploration and visualization facilities reviewed here represent a promising start, there is still a great opportunity to expand on current facilities using digital video, computer graphics, and a variety of methods for charting data and integrating video with the various summarizations that are made of it.

Acknowledgments

I would like to acknowledge Russell Owen's and Ron Baecker's effort in developing the Timelines system. This chapter also benefited from comments and insights from Mark Chignell and discussion with Penny Sanderson concerning exploratory sequential data analysis. Support for our research laboratory has been provided by the Information Technology Research Center of Excellence (ITRC) of Ontario, the National Science and Engineering Research Council (NSERC), the Ontario Telepresence Project, and Apple Computer. Support for the development of the Timelines system was additionally provided by IRIS/PRECARN.

Note

1. Timelines is available by anonymous ftp from our computer network free of charge. To receive instructions on obtaining a copy, please send E-mail to beverly@dgp.utoronto.ca or regular mail to Beverly Harrison, Dept. of Industrial Engineering, University of Toronto, 4 Taddlecreek Road, Toronto, Ontario, Canada, M5S 1A4.

References

Bales, R. F. (1983). SYMLOG: A practical approach to the study of groups. In H. H. Blumberg, A. P. Hare, V. Kent, and M. Davies (eds.), *Small groups and social interaction* (New York: Wiley), 499–523.

Barnard, P. J. (1987). Cognitive resources and the learning of human–computer dialogs. In J. M. Carroll (ed.), *Interfacing thought: Cognitive aspects of human–computer interaction* (Cambridge, Mass.: MIT Press), 112–158.

Card, S. K., Moran, T. P., and Newell, A. (1983). *The psychology of human–computer interaction* (Hillsdale, N.J.: Lawrence Erlbaum).

Ericsson, K. A., and Simon, H. A. (1984). *Protocol analysis: Verbal reports as data* (Cambridge, Mass.: MIT Press).

Everitt, B. S. (1974). *Cluster analysis* (London: Heinemann).

Gronlund, N. E. (1985). *Measurement and evaluation in teaching, 5th Ed.* (New York: Macmillan).

Guilford, J. P. (1956). The structure of intellect. *Psychological Bulletin,* 53, 267–293.

Harrison, B. L. (1991). Video annotation and multimedia interfaces: From theory to practice. In *Proceedings of the Human Factors Society 35th Annual Conference,* San Francisco.

Harrison, B. L., and Baecker, R. M. (1992). Designing video annotation and analysis systems. In *Proceedings of the Graphics Interface '92 Conference,* Vancouver, B.C., May 11–15 (New York: ACM Press), 157–166.

Harrison, B. L., Chignell, M. H., and Baecker, R. M. (1992a). Out of site, still in mind? A case study in video mediated communication. In *Proceedings of the Human Factors Society 36th Annual Conference,* Atlanta, October 12–18, 242–246.

Harrison, B. L., Chignell, M. H., and Baecker, R. M. (1992b). Do perceptions match reality? A comparison of subjective and objective measure in video mediated communication. In *Proceedings of the Human Factors Association of Canada 24th Annual Conference,* Hamilton, Ontario, October 25–28, 21–35.

Harrison, B. L., and Owen, R. (1994). Timelines: A system for temporal data analysis. In *Proceedings of Graphics Interface '94,* Banff, Alberta, Canada, May 16–20.

Hoiem, D. E., and Sullivan, K. D. (1993). Designing and using integrated data collection and analysis tools: Challenges and considerations. *Behavior and Information Technology,* Special Issue on Usability Laboratories, 13 (2).

Karat, C. M. (1990). Cost–benefit analysis of iterative usability testing. In *Proceedings of the IFIP TC 13 Third International Conference on Human–Computer Interaction,* Interact '90, 351–356.

Kennedy, S. (1989). Using video in the BNR usability lab. *ACM SIGCHI Bulletin,* 21 (2), 92–95.

Kurtenbach, G. (1993). The evaluation of an interaction technique based on self-revelation, guidance and rehearsal. Ph.D. dissertation, University of Toronto, Department of Computer Science, April.

Losada, M., and Markovitch, S. (1990). GroupAnalyzer: A system for dynamic analysis of group interaction. In *Proceedings of the 23rd Annual Hawaii International Conference on System Sciences* (IEEE Computer Society), 101–110.

Losada, M., Sanchez, P., and Noble, E. E. (1990). Collaborative technology and group process feedback: Their impact on interactive sequences in meetings. *Proceedings of the Conference on Computer-Supported Cooperative Work (CSCW '90)* (New York: ACM Press), 53–64.

Mackay, W. E. (1989). EVA: An experimental video annotator for symbolic analysis of video data. *ACM SIGCHI Bulletin,* 21 (2), 68–71.

Mackay, W. E., and Davenport, G. (1989). Virtual video editing in interactive multimedia applications. *Communications of the ACM,* 32 (7), 802–810.

Nielsen, J. (1989). Usability engineering at a discount. In G. Salvendy and M. J. Smith (eds.), *Designing and using human–computer interfaces and knowledge based systems* (Amsterdam: Elsevier), 394–401.

Nielsen, J. (1990). Big paybacks from "discount" usability engineering. *IEEE Software,* 7 (3), 107–108.

Nielsen, J. (1991). *Usability engineering* (San Diego, Calif.: Academic Press). [Prereleased information from the author]

Norman, D. A., and Draper, S. W. (1986). *User centered system design: New perspectives on human–computer interaction* (Hillsdale, N.J.: Lawrence Erlbaum).

Olson, G. M., and Olson, J. S. (1991). User-centred design of collaboration technology. *Journal of Organizational Computing,* 1, 61–83.

Olson, J. S., Olson, G. M., Storrosten, M., and Carter, M. (1992). How a group-editor changes the character of a design meeting as well as its outcome. In J. Turner and R. Kraut (eds.), *Proceedings of the Conference on Computer-Supported Cooperative Work (CSCW '92)* (New York: ACM Press), 91–98.

Parsaye, K., and Chignell, M. H. (1993). *Intelligent database tools and applications* (New York: Wiley).

Potel, M. J., and Sayre, R. E. (1976). Interacting with the Galatea Film Analysis System. In *SIGGRAPH '76 Proceedings, ACM Computer Graphics,* 10 (2), 52–59.

Potel, M. J., Sayre, R. E., and MacKay, S. A., (1980). Graphics input tools for interactive motion analysis. *Computer Graphics and Image Processing,* 14, 1–23.

Roschelle, J., and Goldman, S. (1991). VideoNoter: A productivity tool for video data analysis. *Behavior Research Methods, Instruments and Computers,* 23, 219–244.

Roschelle, J., Pea, R., and Trigg, R. (1990). VideoNoter: A tool for exploratory video analysis. IRL Technical Report no. IRL90–0021, March.

Sanderson, P. M. (1993). Designing for simplicity of inference in observational studies of process control: ESDA and MacSHAPA. In *Proceedings of the Fourth European Conference on Cognitive Science Approaches to Process Control (CSAPC '93): Designing for Simplicity.*

Sanderson, P. M., and Fisher, C. (1994). Introduction to the special issue on exploratory sequential data analysis. *HCI Journal,* 6, (4).

Sanderson, P. M., James, J. M., and Seidler, K. S. (1989). SHAPA: An interactive software environment for protocol analysis. *Ergonomics,* 32 (11), 1271–1302.

Sanderson, P. M., James, J., Watanabe, J., and Holden, J. (1990). Human operator behaviour in complex worlds: Rendering sequential records analytically tractable. *Ninth European Annual Conference on Human Decision Making and Manual Control,* Ispra, Italy, September 10–12, 123–132.

Sanderson, P. M., Watanabe, J., and James, J. (1991). Visualization and analysis of complex sequential data using SHAPA (Mac). *Proceedings of the Third European Conference on Cognitive Science Approaches to Process Control,* Cardiff, September 2–6.

Sellen, A. J. (1992). Speech patterns in video-mediated conversations. In *Human Factors in Computing Systems: CHI '92 Proceedings* (New York: ACM), 49–59.

Spearman, C. (1927). *The abilities of man* (London: Macmillan).

Suchman, L.A. (1987). *Plans and situated actions: The problem of human–machine communication* (Cambridge: Cambridge University Press).

Trigg, R. (1989). Computer support for transcribing recorded activity. *ACM SIGCHI Bulletin,* 21 (2).

Tukey, J. W. (1977). *Exploratory data analysis* (Reading, Mass.: Addison-Wesley).

Wickens, C. D. (1992). *Engineering psychology and human performance,* 2nd ed. (Columbus, Ohio: Charles E. Merrill Publishers).

12

Social interaction in the use and design of a workstation: Two contexts of interaction

Deborah Lawrence, Michael E. Atwood, Shelly Dews, and Thea Turner

12.1 Introduction

Interactive system design is most often approached as a problem in human–computer interaction and, correspondingly, is most often studied as one person interacting with a computer. In many instances, however, people interact with a computer in support of their communication with other people. This is the case with telephone operators, travel reservations agents, mail-order service representatives, and others. In these interactions, one person, typically a customer, wants to accomplish some goal with a system but does so by interacting with a human intermediary. The computer operator is, in effect, a "surrogate user." In designing systems for surrogate users, both the human–computer interaction and the human–human interaction must be taken into account. In this chapter, we discuss the use, usability, and human performance demands of such systems.

For the past few years, we have been involved in a project whose goal is to design and field a new workstation for telephone operators. In an attempt to gain an in-depth understanding of the telephone operator's task, we have used CPM-GOMS analyses (Gray, John, and Atwood, 1993), dialogue analysis, and timeline studies. In CPM-GOMS analyses we viewed the human dialogue as part of a complex of timeshared activities by the operator, including keying and visual scanning, in which each contributes to the overall length of a call. Although these analyses were clearly "cognitive" in focus, they nevertheless demonstrated the importance of social interaction in the design and use of interactive computer systems. Dialogue analysis provided a view of the operator's task in which the operator–customer interaction was afforded a sharpened focus. The dialogue analyses, took a more bottom-up approach, in contrast to the model-driven CPM-GOMS analyses, in our attempt to discover the significant variables that contributed to the length of a call. Finally, in timeline studies we looked at the operator's task as one of coordination between two modes of interaction: social interaction and human–computer interaction. These final studies were specifically designed to investigate the extent to which the two forms of interaction were conducted in parallel as opposed to sequentially.

Our work on operator tasks provides an interesting note on the application of what are generally regarded as two incompatible approaches: the "cognitive" and the "social interactional" (e.g., Suchman, 1987; Vera and Simon, 1993). Our several analyses included both approaches. More significantly, even the most "cogni-

tive" approach, CPM-GOMS, clearly demonstrated the importance of social interaction in both design and usability analyses.

Our initial work with operator workstations was in Project Ernestine, where we
compared a workstation that was in use and a proposed workstation by empirical
trial and by the development of CPM-GOMS models. The operators studied in this
project were those you get by dialing "0" and whose basic function is to help
customers complete calls. The CPM-GOMS models used are an extension of those
developed by John (1990) and focus on representing the parallel activities of the
human operator's cognitive, motor, and perceptual processors and the system's
response time. These activities are represented in a project planning formalism
which uses the concept of a critical path. In project planning, the critical path
depicts the sequence of activities that determine the completion time for a project.
In the case of telephone operators, the critical path determines the work time for a
call. By highlighting the critical path through a collection of parallel activities,
these models provide some significant insights.

Initially, we expected our work in Project Ernestine to verify that the proposed
workstation was superior to the one that was then in use. The proposed workstation
was, ergonomically, far superior. It had, for example, a display that used iconlike
symbols, clearly labeled the names of the fields, and was generally sensibly organized. In addition, the keyboard grouped keys by well-defined function, and the
number of keystrokes needed to process a call was, in general, reduced. A trial,
however, revealed that the proposed workstation was 4 percent slower than the
older, less well designed workstation. Practically, this 4 percent difference in
average work time (average call duration) meant millions of dollars per year for a
telephone company. To help us understand this result, we turned to CPM-GOMS
models. They showed how the average work time for a particular call could
increase even when the number of keystrokes was reduced. Since the context
includes multiple forms of interaction with the system as well as social interaction,
savings in one activity does not necessarily result in savings overall. To take an
example from one call, the proposed workstation eliminated a keystroke and
moved another keystroke from the beginning of the call to the end. The net effect
was to place a keystroke on the critical path that was not there before, with the
result of an increase in work time.

The CPM-GOMS models made it possible for us to assess where the operator's
time was spent by showing the proportion of time on the critical path consumed by
a given activity. This information was used to focus our design efforts on those
activities that consume most of the operator's time during the call. The most
striking result of this analysis was that the operator–customer dialogue is the
activity on the critical path that most determines work time. Table 12.1 shows the
percent of work time consumed by waiting for the system (system response time),
keying information into the system (keying), reading information from the screen
(reading), conversing with the customer (talking), and waiting until the called

Table 12.1. *Percentage of time on the critical path consumed by various activities for toll and assistance operators*

Event/Activity	% of Time on the Critical Path	
Listening to customer	43%	
Talking	22%	
Total human dialogue time		**65%**
System response time	16%	
Keying	6%	
Reading	4%	
Total human-computer interaction time		**26%**
Ringing/Coins	5%	
Cognitive	4%	
Total other		**9%**
TOTAL	**100%**	**100%**

number answers or the customer deposits coins (ringing/coins). The percentages shown are the percentage of time that each of these activities is on the critical path in the CPM-GOMS models of the current workstation.

It is illuminating to reflect on the data in Table 12.1 in view of the way that laboratory evaluations and field experiments for workstation design are typically conducted. In typical laboratory experiments, the focus is on designing the computer–human interaction, and the factors of greatest interest are the physical design of keyboards and similar components and the format and content of the displays. As Table 12.1 shows, focus on these factors in designing systems for surrogate users will have relatively small impact on the system in use, although the impact in the laboratory may be statistically significant.

We conjecture that the proposed workstation was designed and evaluated by these traditional means and, while done well by these traditional measures, missed the significance of human–human interactions. Further, we conjecture that the use of traditional design and evaluation methods, which overlook factors of practical significance, is far too common in the design of computer-based systems. An appropriate design philosophy for this type of system would focus on the human–human interaction. This approach requires good understanding of the nature of these interactions, and developing such an understanding is the focus of this chapter.

12.2 The operator as mediator

Our work on the operator-customer dialogue has focused on a different type of telephone operator than those we studied in Project Ernestine. The dialogue studies dealt with directory assistance (DA) operators, the operators who find telephone numbers for customers. DA operators handle approximately eight hundred to a thousand calls per day. For each call, the DA operator takes information offered by the customer, translates it into a database search, reviews the results of the search, elicits more information from the customer if needed, and finally, translates the results of the search for the customer. Table 12.2 illustrates the dialogue and workstation activity in a typical DA call. The required transformations from every-day language to technical language and back are often nontrivial. They rely on the operator's accrued knowledge of the database, workstation, and customer behavior. In addition, the operator's choice of possible transformations is extremely sensitive to the customer, especially to the customer's confidence in the accuracy of the information offered. Because of the critical nature of these transformations, we view the operator as a *mediator between different interaction contexts*. These different contexts might be described as a context of "everyday life" on the one hand, and a context of "technical discourse" on the other. We argue that the coordination of the social and technical contexts is the DA operator's job, and that these contexts in fact determine the structure and content of the operator–customer dialogue.

To obtain an in-depth understanding of the interactions that occur in our surrogate user environment, we used two techniques: dialogue analysis of the verbal exchanges and timeline analysis of the dialogue and operator keystrokes. We have analyzed the content of numerous dialogues in detail; and, for a subset of calls, we have mapped the timing of the speech and pauses onto the timing of the keystrokes. This combination provides a multidimensional view of the DA task that takes into account both how the human dialogue affects the human–computer interaction and how the human–computer interaction affects the human dialogue. Like some ethnographic and ethnomethodological studies described in this volume and elsewhere (e.g., Cooper, Hine, Rachel, and Woolgar, this volume; Douglas, this volume; Nyce and Löwgren, this volume; Randall and Hughes, this volume; and Whalen, this volume), the dialogue and timeline analyses are fine-grained analyses of social and system interaction. Although our methodology is related to ethnology and eth-nomethodology, our orientation is psychological, with our concern primarily on the operator, the human performance demands of the task, and the implications for system design. In spite of our psychological orientation, the results highlight con-textual issues, in particular the differences between "social" and "technical" con-texts and how those differences make performance demands on the operator. Compared with CPM-GOMS analyses, the dialogue/timeline analyses are richer in

Table 12.2. *Outline of dialogue and operator's interaction with the workstation*

Operator-Customer Dialogue	Operator's Human-Computer Interaction
Operator's greeting is played by the workstation (a special case of 'dialog' since the greeting is recorded and automatically played). Operator: *"New York Telephone, Ms Hill."*	Call arrives at workstation.
Customer requests a listing. Customer : *"Hi I need the telephone number of the Syosset Hospital."*	Operator transforms (or begins to transform) the request into database query. Operator types in the LOCALITY field: *S-Y-O*
(Optional) Operator may question the customer about listing details. Operator: *"Do you want General information ma'am?"* Customer: *"Ah, no I need ah for the ah ah I don't know how to say this."* Operator: *"Patient?"* Customer: *"Yes."*	(Optional) Operator completes a database query and/or may perform additional queries if the first is not successful. Operator types in the NAME field: *S -Y-O-S I-N-F-O* [Search key]: *Business*
Pause in dialogue or exchange of polite phrases while the operator types, waits for return of listings, and scans results.	Operator scans results, then selects a listing (or candidates) or determines that no listing is to be found. Operator selects listing: *Patient Information*
(Optional) Operator may announce or discuss results.	Operator releases the call so that the workstation delivers the listing.
Automated response system: *"The number is ...."*	

their analysis of the dialogue content but less detailed in their temporal analysis of events.[1] Because our combination of dialogue and timeline analyses uses a middle ground of detail, it can be applied to a larger sample of instances than CPM-GOMS analyses, which is useful for identifying and validating patterns of behavior. First, the dialogue analysis is described. The timeline analysis is described in detail later.

12.2.1 Dialogue analysis

Our focus with this research has been on how the human–computer interaction affects the human dialogue that it was designed to support and on how the human dialogue affects the human–computer interaction. Our original goals in analyzing the dialogue were to determine inductively the variables that distinguish faster and slower operators and long and short calls. Speed and duration were dimensions of interest, since they have a large economic impact on the telephone companies. More recently, we have used these methods to understand how operators translate the information they receive from the customer into database searches, how they translate the results of these searches to report to the customer, and how these translations affect the structure and content of the dialogue. We have attempted to approach the dialogues inductively by coding a large number of variables and then examining the frequencies and interrelationships among the variables. Admittedly, our approach is not entirely inductive in that the variables we generated were frequently based on hunches that resulted from our initial observations.

We sampled DA calls in four different offices. Taken together, our samples are from three geographical areas and involve three workstations. In each environment, we sampled between five and twenty operators who represented the range of experience levels and average work times for their offices. Each operator was videotaped for an hour as they interacted with customers. At the same time, keystrokes were recorded by software and time stamped. The middle twenty minutes of each videotape, or about forty to sixty calls per operator, were transcribed.

Dialogue coding scheme

We applied two levels of coding to the dialogue. First, basic quantitative coding was applied to all calls. It included the number of words and conversational turns by each speaker, how the call was terminated, its duration, and the number of database searches the operator performed. A second level of coding, which examined the content of the calls in detail, was applied to a smaller set of calls, which were sampled to represent the distribution of typical work times. This coding scheme, which is outlined here, was intended to capture a large number of assorted characteristics of the operator–customer dialogue. Its scope includes both content and phrasing of the speech. For two of the four samples of calls, we also coded how the customer's verbal request mapped onto the characters typed by the operator to search the database for the listing. In all, we coded 180 to 250 variables per call. Following is an outline of the coding scheme; the actual coding made more detailed distinctions than shown in the outline:

- Operator and customer demographics (e.g., gender, accent)
- Operator's greeting (e.g., "New York Telephone"; "What city, please?")

- Customer's request:
    Form of request (e.g., Ability phrasing ["Can you give me . . . ?"], Name only phrasing ["Barnes and Noble on . . ."])
    Content:
        Ancillary phrases (e.g., "Please," "Hello")
        Hedges (e.g., "I think it's on . . .")
        Components (e.g., name, street, town, sublisting information ["billing department"], landmark ["Near Queens Boulevard"])
- Operator's response to the customer's request:
    Acknowledgment (e.g., "Thank you")
    Request for more information (e.g., "Do you know the street?")
    Announcement of results (e.g., "I have a J. Boone on 107th")
- Operator's questions:
    Format:
        YES/NO format (e.g., "Is that in Brooklyn?")
        WH- format (e.g., "What street is it on?")
    Syntax:
        Phrased as question (e.g., "Is that in Manhattan?")
        Phrased as assertion (e.g., "That's in Patchogue?")
        Telegraphic phrasing with the verb omitted (e.g., "In Brooklyn?")
- Operator's presentation of the results
    Successful results (e.g., no verbal presentation; suggestion from listings ["I have a J. Boone on 107th"], stock phrase ["The number is . . ."])
    Unsuccessful results (e.g., "I don't show a Hair Unlimited . . .")
- Customer's response to operator's presentation
- Call summary:
    Number of conversational turns by operator and by customer
    Number of words by operator and by customer
    Duration of each call
    Number of filled pauses by operator and by customer (e.g., "ah" "um")
    Number of polite phrases by operator and by customer (e.g., "Thank you" "I'm sorry")
    Number of searches in each call
    Success or outcome of the call

Translation coding scheme

We also coded how the operator's database queries either transformed or simply echoed the information as stated by the customer. We coded how the operator's query related to each piece of information in the customer's request (e.g., the words in the name, the town). Following is an outline of the translation coding scheme:

- No change: Entered as stated (e.g., customer requests: "ADR"; operator types: A-D-R)
- Standard truncation (e.g., customer requests: "Central Taxi"; operator types: C-E-N-T [space] T-A-X)
- Omit information (e.g., customer requests listing on "Main Street"; operator omits street from search strings)
- Substitute name or part of name (e.g., customer requests: "AHRC"; operator types: A-S-S-O [space] H-E-L-P)

Calls were coded by two independent coders. Spot checks of approximately 7 percent of calls from each sample were coded by both coders independently, and intercoder reliability was over 95 percent in each sample.

12.2.2 The role of mediator

As mediator between the customer and the technology, the DA operator interacts in two contexts, social and technical, and also speaks in two voices, an "everyday life" voice and a "technical" voice. Our understanding of voices draws on Mischler's (1984) notion of voices in medical interviews. Mischler's work contrasts the "voice of the lifeworld" with the "voice of medicine." In his corpus of medical interviews, the doctors speak almost exclusively in only one of these voices – the "voice of medicine." Mischler characterizes this voice as similar to the "scientific" attitude described by Shultz (1962), and the technocratic, or technological consciousness, described by Habermas (1970). In the medical interviews, when the patient speaks in the "voice of the lifeworld," much of what is said is ignored by the doctor. However, unlike Mischler's doctors, telephone operators speak in both of the voices involved in their domain, and in various ways they act as intermediaries between the two contexts. They *act for* the customer as "surrogate users" of the technology, by translating back and forth between the specialized language of the technology and the language of everyday discourse.

To be effective as "surrogate users" operators must be extremely sensitive to both *what* their customers say and to *how* they say it. Operators infer information by attending to the customer's everyday discourse requests and noting subtle signals, such as the customer's degree of uncertainty about the particular components of the information being offered, that may be useful in fulfilling the customer's request. In addition, operators vary their styles depending on how they perceive the customer's style. Often customers themselves seem to assume a technical context of interaction. For example, some customers offer very brief and exact requests without any preliminary verbiage that might serve politeness considerations. With these customers, operators adopt a highly abbreviated style which differs from the style they use with other, less technically oriented customers. However, operators do not just vary their own styles to meet the needs of their customers. They also sometimes introduce technical dialogue into the everyday dialogue with the purpose of advising the customer of the information needed. This introduction of technical information introduces the customer from an everyday life context into the technical context, to a limited extent.

12.2.3 Translation from everyday discourse to database search

Operators must span a wide "gulf of execution," to use Norman's (1986) term, between the customer's request and finding the requested listing in the database. Constructing effective database searches is a problem in many database retrieval contexts (Greene et al., 1990; Reisner, 1981), but operators and other surrogate users have the additional problem of attempting to act on behalf of another person who has no knowledge of how the database is constructed. The everyday life context of interaction and the technical context of interaction differ in a number of ways that help explain the operator's difficulty in coordinating between the two. One important difference is that everyday discourse is less exact than technical discourse, both in the sense of "less accurate" and in the sense of "less completely specified." As the customer's intermediary between everyday discourse and database retrieval, the operator must construct an accurate and well-specified search. Among the problems in doing so is that the search may be based on information that is inaccurate or incomplete. From the customer's point of view, it is not always clear that incomplete or partially incorrect information poses a significant problem for the operator. This is especially true if the customer's model is based on experience with searching for listings in telephone books. For example, a customer might ask for Basset's Book Shop on a given street. The name might be correct, but the street incorrect. Using an incorrect street may pose little problem when looking up a listing in a paper telephone book. One can find the name and then simply observe that it is on a different street than expected. Using a book, even a slightly wrong name may not pose a problem since scanning may allow a person to spot the similar name. However, entering the wrong street or wrong name in a database search may prevent retrieval of the listing (though directory assistance databases vary in the extent to which they allow partial matches in the information the operator types). Thus, operators must decide which parts of the information offered to include, when to substitute information from their own knowledge, and in which fields to enter information.

To locate a listing, operators transform the information offered by the customer into a database query. DA workstations typically have four or five fields for entering retrieval information. These are usually two fields for the name and a field each for the locality (i.e., town or city), street, and building number. Using some combination of the information fields, operators typically construct a query of seven to twelve characters from a customer request of about nine to fifteen words. Usually only the first few characters of a given word are used. But constructing a search string is not simply selecting and truncating key words. Operators must

Table 12.3. *Frequency of transformations of customer requests into database search strings*

Type of transformation	Percent of calls using transformation in the first search[*]
Substitute name or part of name (for *"AHRC,"* enter *A-S-S-O H-E-L-P)*	10%
Omit word in business name (for *"Valley Brook Diner,"* enter *V-A-L B-R-O-O)*	23%
Omit a piece of information (e.g. street, building number, town)	41%
Fields entered as stated (for "K-Mart," enter *KMART)*	20%
Standard truncation (for *"Central Hardware,"* enter *C-E-N-T H-A-R-D)*	85%

[*] Numbers sum to more than 100%, since a search typically involves more than one field.

often rely on their own knowledge and intuitions to specify a search string that is likely to result in a listing that the customer will find acceptable.

Table 12.3 lists the frequency with which operators perform various types of transformations on the basic information offered by the customer. These transformations include substituting a different name or word for all or part of the name offered, omitting a piece of information (such as the street), and performing more minimal transformations (such as simply truncating the words or entering them as stated). For the first search, customers offer on average 2.1 pieces information and operators enter information in about the same number of fields. The most common transformation, standard truncation, is a minimal one; in 85 percent of calls, the first search includes at least one field where the operator simply types the first few letters of a word offered by the customer. However, transformations requiring more expertise, such as omissions and substitutions, occur frequently.

What information should be included?

In transforming an everyday discourse request into a database search, the operator must make judgments about what information to include. Operators omit some component of the information offered by the customer over 40 percent of the time. The frequency with which information is omitted varies with the database and the geographical region. Information is omitted from approximately 70 percent of residence requests but only 40 percent of business or government requests. The street name provided by a customer is frequently incorrect and operators must decide to include it or omit it from the search based on their own geographical knowledge, as well as on their judgment of the customer's geographical knowledge. In fact, it is usually recommended that operators omit the street in their initial search of a business listing, since the street offered is so frequently incorrect. In one sample, street was omitted from the operator's first database search 83 percent of the time. However, in another geographical region, street is more useful. For example, a street name is very informative for Manhattan, where many listings of the same name may be located in a limited geographical area.

Operators must also decide whether the customer's stated request is actually the official name of the requested listing or is simply a name the customer assumes is correct. For example, the operator must decide whether or not to include "PIZ" in a search when the customer requests "Vinnie's pizza restaurant." If the first part of the name is common, including "PIZ," if correct, may be necessary to reduce the number of possible listings. Alternatively, if the first part of the name is relatively rare, including "PIZ" may not be necessary and, if incorrect, may prevent retrieval of the desired listing. Operators are taught some heuristics to use in making this decision, but in most cases they must rely on past experience with customers and with the database.

How is this listed?

Frequently, the name offered by the customer is not the official name of the institution, and it is often up to the operator to generate the listing name. This is especially true for government listings. For example, customers frequently ask for Social Security, which is actually listed under the Department of Social Services. In everyday life the official name may be almost never encountered, and there may rarely be a need to know it. In fact, when speaking to an experienced operator, not knowing the official name rarely causes a problem. The operator simply translates the request into the appropriate search string. But for the operator, knowing how to make such substitutions is critical. Without that knowledge, operators could not find many frequently requested listings such as "the welfare office" or many less frequently requested listings, such as "the Wiltshire movie theater." Operators must be able to substitute information if they are to quickly and accurately fulfill customer requests. The knowledge needed to make such substitutions develops with time and experience, and is probably a factor in the general decrease in work times that occurs as operators gain expertise.

Customers' requests also often include approximate information (see Table 12.4). For example, customers frequently indicate that they are not sure of the exact name, location, or spelling of the listing. They might say that the name is "something like O'Days" or that "it might be in Cambridge," or "it's near Queens Boulevard." Though such information is often useful in an everyday life context, it is much less useful in the operator's technical context because these rough pointers are poorly suited to constructing the exact retrieval strings required for a DA

Table 12.4. *Use of "approximate" information by the customer in initial requests*

Type of Approximate Information	Percent of Requests[*]
"Hedges" in customer's requests, e.g., *"It may be on...."*	7-19%
Location by "landmark" information or "range" information e.g., *"It's in the East 50's"*	2-4%
Description of listing without a name	2-4%
Total (excluding overlaps)	11-23%

*Note: the range of per cent of requests represent the range of averages across the four DA offices sampled.

database search. One way to use this kind of vague information is to do a broad search and then scan through the alternatives. However, workstation design and recommended practices discourage broad searches, since extensive scanning is relatively slow, compared with the time required to type a search string or the system time to return listings. Since the operator's task is designed for speed, many DA workstations limit the amount of scanning by imposing a limit on the number of pages of listings that can be returned. This design practice provides an excellent example of the conflict between the two interaction contexts that operators negotiate. In one context, such approximate information is useful. However, its usefulness is constrained in the other context. The operator's task is to decide how to use the information given the constraints.

Some database retrieval techniques that are used in other contexts to avoid the limitations of searching for an exact match are not applicable to the DA operator's task. One example is latent semantic indexing, which uses samples of text to locate related texts such as papers or news articles (Dumais, 1991). This technique examines the overlap in the words used among sets of related texts, and can be a powerful improvement over keyword indexing. However, it would not be relevant to telephone directory retrievals because it requires natural text of more than a few words. Some of the other techniques for improving the power of database retrievals involve synonym substitution. This approach has been used in directory assistance databases, but its usefulness is limited because of the speed component of the operator's task. When listings containing synonyms of part of the operator's search string are retrieved, the result is typically a relatively large number of listings to scan. As with other ways of broadening a search, synonym retrieval has limited usefulness for an operator because of other constraints.

Given approximate information in the request, operators typically verbally report the exact information before providing the telephone number. This practice serves a dual purpose. First, it provides the customer with the correct information. Second, it serves to remind the customer that exact information is appropriate in the operator's technical context.

O   New York Telephone, what town please?
C   In Melville, I think.
O   Yes.
C   Home Depot.
O   There's a store on 110 in Farmingdale.
C   Yeah, that's it.
O   Thank you.

Which fields should be used?

Peculiarities in a database often make it advisable to use idiosyncratic search strings. In most cases, many possible search strings would return a given listing, and one aspect of the task is to learn to use those search strings that return relatively few listings with relatively short system response times. For example, for the White Plains, N.Y., post office, operators often enter WHIT FISH in the name fields. FISH is a truncation of the street name, but because of the organization of the database, one can retrieve the fewest listings in this case by entering the street in part of the name field. This provides an explicit example of an area in which the human–computer interaction deviates dramatically from the human–human interaction that initiated it. Even if the customer offers the official name, it is to the operator's advantage to ignore the customer's exact request and adhere to the demands of the database.

12.2.4 Introducing the technology context into the dialogue

Mediating between two interaction contexts has discernible effects on the structure and content of DA operator–customer dialogues. Among the effects of mediating between two contexts is that the technical context is often evident in the dialogue in several respects. In many ways, DA dialogues resemble human–computer interactions. These dialogues are highly abbreviated, and the speakers often speak in conventional formulas. In some cases the dialogues end abruptly in a manner that might not be acceptable in other forms of human discourse. These features, abbreviated language, standardized phrases, and abrupt endings, are commonly associated with human–computer interactions and demonstrate how the technical context affects the social context.

DA operator–customer transactions are asymmetrical communications. One party is interacting with a computer that is not visible to the other party. One result is that the surrogate user is partly occupied by their human–computer interaction and therefore less than fully interactive with the other person. In our data, the operator's interspeaker pauses averaged over 750 milliseconds (for both faster and slower operators), almost twice as long as typical pauses in other telephone conversations (Norwine and Murphy, 1938). These relatively long pauses make these dialogues feel less fully interactive than simple one-to-one conversations. A second result is that the customer typically is unaware of the content or structure of the operator's human–computer interaction. Though the operator is actively involved in translating back and forth between everyday discourse and technology, most of this interaction with the technology is invisible to the customer. The technology itself and the search the operator constructs are not witnessed by the customer, and often the operator gives no verbal clues about their interaction with the computer. For example:

> O   New York Telephone. What town please?
> C   In Syosset, ah, Central Hardware, please.
> O   Thank you.
> *[Release to Automated Response System. "The number is . . ."]*

In many cases, the operator introduces, indirectly, some of the technology-related issues onto the dialogue. As mentioned earlier, given approximate or incorrect information in the request, operators typically verbally report the exact information before providing the telephone number. In addition, their frequent questions about the town, street, or spelling of a listing let the customer know the kinds of information needed to find listings. For example, the operator may ask the customer in which database the requested listing is located:

> O   New York Telephone, what town please?
> C   Yes ah, Baldwin, ah, Dan O'Leary?
> O   A residence or a business?

What city please?

Another important means of introducing the technical context into the everyday life context comes with the operator's greeting. The operator's greeting serves to inform the customer about the appropriate context of the transaction. Open-ended greetings, such as "May I help you?" or "New York Telephone, Mr. Lehman" suggest an everyday discourse context in which customers are free to state their requests as they choose. In contrast, "What city, please?" assumes a structured exchange, which more closely resembles a technical interaction than an everyday life interaction. The question alone implies that the customer is going to make a request, demands specific information, and discourages unnecessary verbiage.

We found that the format and content of customers' requests are very different following "What city, please?" than following more open-ended greetings such as "May I help you?" In response to "What city, please?" customers usually use a very terse, implied form of request. They simply state the listing information. For example, they might say, "In Valley Stream, the Seaside Diner." With the more open-ended greetings, explicit requests are more common. For example, a cus-

Table 12.5. *Form and style of customer requests following different operator greetings*

	Operator Greeting			
	"What city please?"	Open-ended greeting, e.g. *"New York Telephone, Tony"*		
Customer's Dialogue	% of Calls			
	Office1	Office2[*]	Office3[*]	Office4
Number words in customer's request	8.7	12.59	15.64	15.8
Use of implied form of request	63%	63%	24%	17%
Use of a greeting by customer (e.g. *"Hello, Operator"*)	2%	4%	6%	18%
Use of *"please* " in customer's request	14%	14%	23%	26%

* Note: Offices 2 and 3 represent the same operators using a different greeting and workstation.

tomer might say, "Can I have the number for the Seaside Diner . . . ?" In addition, customers responding to "What city, please?" are also less likely to include ancillary phrases such as "Hello," "Operator," or "please." The content of customer requests differs mainly in the inclusion of a city name. In response to "What city, please?" customers are more likely to include the city or town in their request. Since some databases are organized around these localities, this information is important. Some DA workstation interfaces also place the cursor in the locality field at the beginning of a call, so getting that information from the customer immediately is important for speed. See Table 12.5 for a summary.

Be brief and to the point

Another way in which these dialogues are influenced by the technical interaction context is that one or both parties are interested in completing the transaction as quickly as possible. Operators work under time constraints, and many customers behaved as if they too were interested in a speedy resolution. In their calls, which were typically short, the dialogue was especially like human–computer interactions. It was brief and factual and included little extra verbiage. Customers in short calls offered more information about the listing than customers in long calls, yet they did so in fewer words. Operators adapted to the style and apparent concerns of the customers and, in short calls, they, like the customers, were especially brief and businesslike. Their conversational turns were shorter and, in asking questions, they usually used telegraphic syntax, omitting the verb (e.g., "In Brooklyn?"). Conversely, in calls with elderly customers and children, most operators slowed down and adopted a less technical, more everyday life mode of interaction.

Hold for the number

To terminate most calls (short and long), operators use an automated voice response system that reads out the number for the customer. In our samples, the customer was nearly always transferred from a human dialogue to a human–machine interaction (actually the automated system was not very interactive, since the customer had no control over it). Operators often buffered the customer from this transition by first indicating in some way that they had found the number. For example, the operator might simply say, "Hold for the number," or offer some description of the exact listing, for example, " Reservations and information." In short calls, operators usually saved time by skipping this transitional step. When the customer seemed to be interested in speed, the operator usually skipped this step and turned the customer over to the automated system without any verbal preparation. Over time, the use of these buffering phrases may decrease as their usefulness declines due to increased customer familiarity with technical interactions. This familiarity will be affected by the customer's DA interactions, other surrogate user interactions, and automated speech recognition interactions.

12.3 The operator as parallel processor

In addition to the dialogue coding, we used timelines of the dialogue and keystrokes to examine how operators coordinate their keying with the dialogue. We wanted to know, for example, how much typing occurs while the customer or operator is speaking, as opposed to during pauses. We were particularly interested in whether different operators might adopt different styles. Do faster and slower operators differ in their rate of speech? Are pauses longer, or more variable, for slower operators?

Eight calls per operator were sampled; calls were selected to represent each individual's typical distribution of work times. The audio portion was digitized, and a timeline of the dialogue was created. The dialogue timeline identified turns, interspeaker pauses, intraspeaker pauses, and overlaps for each speaker. The interspeaker pause preceding a speaker's turn was attributed to that speaker, since that person determined when to begin speaking (i.e., how much space to leave the previous speaker). An example dialogue timeline is shown in Table 12.6. Timestamped keystrokes had been collected by software at the time of the calls. Using the videotape, the beginning time of a call's dialogue timeline was calibrated with the beginning time of the keystrokes as collected by the software. Then, the keystroke timeline was mapped onto the dialogue timeline. In other words, for each keystroke, the dialogue event that occurred at the same time was identified. One example of the mapping of the keystrokes onto the dialogue is given in Table 12.7.

Faster operators conducted their social interaction and technical interaction more in parallel than slower operators. Compared with slower operators, faster

Table 12.6. *Example of dialogue timeline*

Dialogue Event	Begin Time*	End Time	Duration
Pause before Operator's greeting	0.0	.92	.92
Operator Turn 1: Greeting: "*New York Telephone, Ms Sills*"	.92	1.79	.87
Customer Interspeaker pause 2	1.79	1.93	.14
Customer Turn 2: Customer's request, "*Yes in Queen, on Queens Blvd. ah Radio Shack?*"	1.93	4.35	2.42
Operator Interspeaker pause 3	4.35	5.2	.85

* Times are listed in seconds.

Table 12.7. *Mapping of keystrokes to concurrent events in the dialogue*

Keystroke (character typed)	Time* from beginning of call	Concurrent dialogue event
QUEENS [macro key]	4.14	C Turn 2 (customer's request)"*Yes in Queens, on Queens Blvd. ah Radio Shack?*"
R	4.74	O Interspeaker pause 3 (following customer request)
A	4.95	O Interspeaker pause 3 (following customer request)

Table 12.8. *Keying and speech patterns in calls of faster and slower operators*

	Faster Operators	Slower Operators	
% of keying during customer's turns	38.18%	34.24%	$Chi^2_{14}=39.97$, $p<.01$
% of keying during (all) pauses	29.52%	38.4%	$Chi^2_{13}=15.31$, $p<.01$
Mean length of interspeaker pauses (customer and operator pauses combined)	362 msec	454 msec	$t_{488}=2.11$, $p<.05$
Intraspeaker pauses as % of turns	9.94%	12.88%	$Chi^2_1=4.02$, $p<.05$

operators keyed more during the customer's speech, and less during interspeaker and intraspeaker pauses (Table 12.8). Indications from both the timeline mapping and the dialogues themselves suggest that faster operators had a well-paced and smoothly coordinated style. They had fewer interruptions of speech in order to key and fewer interruptions of speech to allow speakers to formulate their next utterance. Their customers responded after briefer pauses, and they also managed to communicate with somewhat briefer utterances. In a sense, faster operators had a "top-down" approach to a call. They seemed to maintain a rhythm in their interaction with the customer, which was not frequently interrupted by "time out" to type or to formulate responses. Slower operators' style was less "top-down." Both the rhythm of their dialogue and their keying as well as what they said to the customer suggest that slower operators operated more in a "respond" mode. Whereas faster operators seemed to establish a direction and proceed toward a smooth execution, slower operators seemed to respond more to the customer's direction. Their calls had more interruptions for typing or formulating. They also keyed less after all conversation was finished, suggesting that they relied more on customer input to direct their human–computer interaction. In fact, slower operators were more likely than faster operators to ask the customer to select among possible listings late in the call (39 percent of calls by slower operators compared with 13 percent of calls by faster operators). Faster operators relied more on what the customer had already said to select a listing.

These results suggest some practical outcomes. The extent to which an operator can interact with the customer and the workstation at the same time is predictive of their speed at the task. Evidence from both CPM-GOMS analyses and the dialogue analyses shows how two specific skills, typing skill and verbal fluency skills, contribute to a person's ability to handle both tasks in parallel. We are currently investigating whether practice drills on some components of the task can develop automatic performance and increase the degree of parallelism. Our next step is to look at verbal fluency skills, their relationship to average call times, and whether they develop with experience.

12.4 Conclusions

Our series of analyses of the directory assistance operators has given us a view of the social interaction in surrogate user tasks and how it affects and is affected by the surrogate user's interaction with the technology. We see the operator's task as mediating between two interaction contexts, one social and one technological. The two contexts are linked to two different forms of discourse – the discourse of everyday life and the discourse of technical interaction. To fulfill a directory assistance request, operators translate back and forth between the two interaction contexts and their related forms of discourse. As a surrogate user, the operator's role is different form that of some other experts, such as physicians, whose own technical voice tends to dominate the interaction. In contrast to some of the other types of experts, operators mediate between everyday and technical discourse without ignoring or excluding the everyday portion.

The types of information suitable in human conversation are often not suitable for the operator's human–computer interactions. It is for this reason that DA database queries require mediation by an expert. In some cases the "gulf of execution" between the customer's request and the requirements of the technology cannot be spanned even by the operator's expertise. In these cases, operators must ask customers to fill the gap and, for example, supply additional information required for a search of the database ("A residence or a business?"). In this way, technical discourse is introduced into the social interaction, interspersed with the discourse of everyday life. In some cases there may be technical solutions used in other contexts (such as library searches, etc.) to help database users to translate everyday discourse requests into successful database queries. For example, synonym substitution may allow more powerful searches. However, for the operator, the usefulness of these technical solutions is limited because of other task demands, in particular the speed requirement. Work practices, especially the emphasis on speed, limit the operator's ability to make use of some of the information customers offer. For example, approximate information ("It's in the 50s") may be usable but may require the operator to perform several searches. In other words, the gulf between everyday discourse and the operator's computer–human interaction is exacerbated by other demands, in particular the speed requirement. The operator's situation is analogous to that of the cashiers in Randall and Hughes's study of a building society (Chapter 8). In both cases, the practitioner balances conflicting sets of demands with speed and throughput on the one hand and "customer satisfaction" on the other.

One way to shorten the semantic distance between everyday discourse and human–computer interaction is to ask customers to change their behavior, and this is frequently the solution in DA dialogues. Sometimes customers volunteer information about which database the operator should search, as a result of operators' questions in previous calls ("It's a residence"). In addition, greetings that are directive and task-oriented (such as "What city, please?") encourage technology-oriented dialogue. In response to these greetings, customers speak relatively tersely, as though they were filling in slots of information. (See Woofitt and MacDermid, this volume, for a discussion of how and why the users of interactive speech systems may or may not adapt their speech to system requirements.)

On a micro level, our analysis of the timing of the dialogue and keystrokes suggests that operators differ in their skill at coordinating their work in the two interaction contexts, and that this difference in skill results in differences in average work times. Operators who are better able to coordinate their interaction with the customer with their interaction with the computer are faster than those who are less able (all coordinate to some extent). Faster operators are better able to conduct the dialogue and workstation activity in parallel.

In other words, telephone operators must not only be skilled at both their social and technical interactions; they must also be skilled at coordinating the two. This requirement distinguishes the tasks of telephone operators and other surrogate users from less time-sensitive database retrieval tasks.

How operators themselves see their job is in keeping with the conception of the operator as a mediator between different types of discourse. When we asked operators to describe what they do, they described their interaction with customers and almost never mentioned the workstation or the activities of typing or scanning listings. Operators seemed to experience their complex coordination of talking and listening with keying and scanning as completely transparent. What operators did describe was the kind of information that customers provided, or failed to provide, and how they, the operators, attempted to deal with that information and the customer.

Note

1. For example, where the dialogue/timeline studies treated a keystroke as a single point in time (specifically, the point when the workstation registered the key contact), the CPM-GOMS analyses also included cognitive preparation time and hand and finger movements to home to the key.

References

Dumais, S. (1991). Improving the retrieval of information from external sources. *Behavior Research Methods, Instruments and Computers*, 23, 229–236.

Gray, W. D., John, B. E., and Atwood, M. E. (1993). Project Ernestine: Validating GOMS analysis for predicting and explaining real-world task performance. *Human Computer Interaction*, 8 , 237–309.

Gray, W. D., John, B. E., Stuart, R., Lawrence, D., and Atwood, M. E. (1990). GOMS meets the phone company: Analytic modeling applied to real-world problems. In D. Diaper, D. Gilmore, G. Cockton, and B. Schackel (eds.), *Human–computer interaction: INTERACT '90*. (Amsterdam: Elsevier North-Holland) 29–34.

Greene, S., Devlin, S., Cannata, P., and Gomez, L. (1990). No IFs, ANDs, or ORs: A study of database querying. *International Journal of Man–Machine Studies*, 32, 303–326.

Habermas, J. (1970). *Toward a rational society* (Boston, Mass.: Beacon Press).

John, B. E. (1990). Extensions of GOMS analyses to expert performance requiring perception of dynamic visual and auditory information. In *Human Factors in Computing Systems: CHI '90 Proceedings* (New York: ACM Press), 107–115.

Mischler, E. G.(1984). *The discourse of medicine: Dialectics of medical interviews* (Norwood, N.J.: Ablex).

Norman, D. A. (1986). Cognitive engineering. In D. A. Norman and S. W. Draper (eds.), *User centered system design* (Hillsdale, N.J.: Lawrence Erlbaum), 31–65.

Norwine, A. C., and Murphy, O. J. (1938). Characteristic time intervals in telephonic conversation. *Bell System Technical Journal*, 17, 281–291.

Reisner, P. (1981). Human factors studies of database query languages: A survey and assessment. *Computing Surveys*, 13, 13–31.

Schultz, A. (1962). *Collected papers, I: The problem of social reality* (The Hague: Martinus Nijhoff).

Suchman, L. (1987). *Plans and situated actions: The problem of human–machine communication* (Cambridge: Cambridge University Press).

Vera, A. H., and Simon, H. A. (1993). Situated action: A symbolic interpretation. *Cognitive Science*, 17, 7–48.

Index

active badge systems, 4, 89–91
  privacy issues, 89, 90, 91, 93–94
activity theory, application to human–computer interaction, 16
adjacency pairs
  request-offer of help, 133
  use in studies of utterance design and turn-taking system, 114, 123n11
advanced life support (ALS), deployment in fire emergencies, 164
Advice System (Frohlich and Luff), 120
air traffic controllers, ethnographic studies, 40, 145
algorithmic operations, expert systems based on, 180
alien culture, computer view as part of, 73
analytical models, for sociality of work, 144
analytic skepticism, in ethnography, 13–14, 23, 33n23
anthropology, 1, 3
  ethnography as research method for, 144
Aristotle, on rhetoric, 96
audio recordings
  of cardiovascular construction kit use, 188
  use in ethnographic studies, 13
  use in human–computer interaction studies, 205
automation, resentment toward, 72

Bales SYMLOG dimensions, use in GroupAnalyzer, 221
basic life support (BLS) unit, deployment in fire emergencies, 164
biologists, collaboration with computer scientists in human genome project, 22
The Bionic Man (TV program), 127
bionic WOZ simulation, 6, 127
  use in studies of flight information service, 129–140
  use in studies of system performance, 6, 127
bottom-up empirical description, in ethnographic studies, 11, 16
brainwashing, organizational communication schemes compared to, 94
breakdown and repair, as concept in conversation analysis, 190–191

brick wall story, of information systems design, 27, 29
building society, cashiers' work with customers in, 148–157
bureaucratic control, description, 71
bureaucratic management thought, 97–98

CAD. *See* computer-aided dispatch (CAD)
Callon, Michel, discourse analysis by, 49
capture model, use to rearrange work activities, 95
cardiovascular construction kit, conversation analysis use in design of, 9, 191–198
Card-Moran-Newell model, for design of interactive systems, 4, 53, 184, 185, 186
cashiers, work with customers, 148–157, 258
cellular telephones, active badges compared to, 90, 91
centers of coordination, response to emergencies by, 163
Central Lane Communications (Eugene, Oregon), computer-aided dispatch use at, 162–179
Chicago School, 144, 158n1
Chinese room argument, 111
cognition, role in ethnography, 14
cognitive map, design for perception use of, 92–93
cognitive psychology
  advances in, 53
  use in human–computer interaction studies, 4, 31, 33n12, 37, 50, 52, 55, 63n2
cognitive representations, of user, 184
cognitivism, 1
collective bargaining strategy, role in computer technology, 71, 72
communication, organizational, 100
communicative breakdowns, 6
communicative resource, as concept in conversation analysis, 190
community, of computer users and scientists, 18–19, 22
computer(s)
  definition and description, 69
  effect on working life, 71
computer-aided dispatch (CAD)
  manual dispatching prior to use of, 167

261

computer-aided dispatch (CAD) (cont.)
    as support system, 161–183
    technology, 8
computerization, as long-term process, 67
computer language, early psychological evaluation, 37
Computers and Conversation (Luff et al.), 129
computer scientists, ethnographic study of, 17–19
computer-supported cooperative work
    (CSCW), 2, 11, 32n9, 123n2, 211
    applications, 41
    concept of formalization in, 80
    description, 7
    in working with customers, 142–160
computer systems
    design and implementation of, 87
    as medium for metaphor design, 88
computer systems design. *See* systems design
conceptions, of user, 99–101. *See also* user
configuration, of user, 22–26
confirmation insertion sequences, use in
    computer-based flight information studies,
    131–135
constructive interaction
    definition and description, 8–9, 187
    use in usability of designs, 186
constructivist, 49, 63n1, 140n4
consumers, involvement in product development, 74–75
context-free design, characteristics, 184–186
contextual design, process of, 38
contextual inquiry
    definition, 38
    into human–computer interaction, 3, 16,
    32n6
control, types, 71
conversation
    naturally occurring, 108
    simulations of, 117–119
    unformalizable character of, 115–116
conversational computers, feasibility of, 139
conversational turn-taking, 108, 114, 121,
    123n5, n10, n11, 190
conversation analysis (CA)
    of human–computer interaction, 5, 6, 11,
    107–125, 129, 204
    human–computer interaction design and,
    184–203
conversation metaphor, for computer systems,
    108
cooperation, as part of computer-supported cooperative work, 143, 158n3
corporate culture, metaphors describing, 87–88

corporatist management thought, 97–98, 99
counterimplementation (CI), managers' tactics
    as, 72
CPM-GOMS, use in studies of telephone operators' tasks, 240, 241–245, 257, 259n1
crisis rhetoric, 48
    second wave and, 57–62
critique of cognitive science, application to
    human–computer interaction, 16
critique of reason, application of technology
    and, 142
CSCW. *See* computer-supported cooperative
    work (CSCW)
customers, computer-supported cooperative
    work studies on, 142–160

data analysis, history, 204
data manipulation, in VANNA/Timelines studies, 217–218
data visualization
    in VANNA/Timelines studies, 213, 218–219
    in video recording studies, 209
dehumanization, in technological society, 67
Descartes, René, on rhetoric, 96
design, for usability, 4
design analysis, conversation analysis use in,
    191
designers
    concept of users, 59, 67, 70
    role in human–computer interaction, 59,
    63n10
    as users, 61
design for perception
    general properties, 92–93
    as manifestation of managerial concept of
    user, 88
design rationale
    Meeting Plots system use to study, 224
    role in system development, 191
    use in cardiovascular construction kit design,
    191
design rationale capture, 81
deskilling, 70
dialogue(s)
    ethnography as, 15, 26–30
    technical versus social, 10
    technology-oriented, 10
dialogue analysis, of directory-assistance operators, 243, 245–247
dialogue coding scheme, for directory-
    assistance operator dialogue, 245–246
directory-assistance operators, dialogue studies
    on, 243

disciplinary rhetoric, of human–computer interaction, 48–66
discourse, of human–computer interaction, 49
discourse analysis, 49–50
dispatch centers
    computer use in, 161–183
    decision support for, 164–168
distributed cognition, in fire dispatchers, 168–169
division of labor, 7
    models, 146–147
double-level languages, effect on system's acceptance by users, 80–81
Durkheim, Émile, on sociologists, 142

ecological research, cognitive psychology as, 33n12
Eliza program, 112
E-mail
    privacy issues, 88
    use by researchers, 17–18, 19, 21, 33n17
Empowering People (CHI '90 conference), 51, 64n4
empowerment
    of designers, 61
    of uscr, 4, 51
    of workers, 98
empowerment and measurement regime, as type of control, 71
engineering, use in usability studies, 38
engineering science approach, to system design, 185–186, 201
episode, as concept in conversation analysis, 190
ESDA. *See* exploratory sequential data analysis (ESDA)
ESPRIT II project, for development of speech-based computerized information service, 128, 140n1
ethnography
    analytic skepticism in, 13–14
    anthropological roots, 33n19, 144
    cognition role in, 14
    definition and description, 12–15, 32n3
    as dialogue, 15, 26–30
    exotic as element of, 12
    field studies, 17–30
    human–computer interaction studies using, 2–3, 8, 9, 11–36, 39–42, 144, 204, 243
    observer's role, 13
    as reportage, 31, 32
    of scientific practice, 17
    technologically driven, 3
    unit of analysis in, 14–15

use in software design, 193
ethnomethodology
    application to human–computer interaction, 11, 16, 107, 109, 200, 204, 243
    definition, 7
EVA, as interactive video annotation tool, 222, 229
evaluation tools, of fire dispatchers, 167
everyday discourse, translation to database search, 248–249
exotic, as element of ethnography, 12
expert evaluation, in usability testing, 185
expert systems
    problems with, 175–179
    versus systems for experts, 161–183
exploratory data analysis (EDA), description and use, 205
exploratory sequential data analysis (ESDA), 9
    use in human–computer interaction studies, 205

face-to-face interaction, in video conferencing communication study, 215
financial processing, in building society office, 151–156
fire dispatchers
    computer-aided support for, 161–183
    work tasks of, 163–164
flight information service, bionic WOZ simulation of, 129–140
Ford Motor Company, 98
formalization
    double-level languages and, 81
    of human work activities, 76
    strong and weak compared, 81, 82
    in systems rationalism, 75, 78–80
formal organization, 146–147
Foucault, Michel, discourse analysis by, 49
foundational analysis
    definition, 39
    of human–computer interaction, 3, 37–47
Freshwater, ethnographic study of information technology in, 27–30
"From human factors to human actors," 58–59
The Functions of the Executive (Barnard), 83

GALATEA, use in analysis of video-image data, 222, 224, 230, 232
genetics, information technology use in, 19
"Going up a Blind Alley" (Button), 108, 110, 113, 119
GroupAnalyzer system, description and use, 221, 229, 231–232
gulf of execution, of directory-assistance operators, 248, 258

HCI. *See also* human–computer interaction (HCI)
HCI discourse, 50, 62
human action, interaction and, 116–117
human–computer interaction (HCI), in telephone operator-customer relations, 240–259
human–computer interaction (HCI)
  cognitive approach, 143
  comparison with human–machine interaction, 56
  constructive interaction applied to, 187
  contextual inquiry, 3
  conversation analysis of, 5, 6, 11, 107–125, 188
  description, 56
  disciplinary rhetoric, 48–66
  discourse, 50
  ethnographic studies, 11–36, 39–42
  evolution, 37
  first-wave, 61–62
  foundational analysis, 3, 37–47
  horror stories based on, 53
  interaction versus interface, 58
  methods used for study, 204
  as obligatory passage point, 49, 52
  progress and, 53–55
  roots, 3
  second wave, 4, 31, 34n24, 57–62
  social and interactional dimensions, 1, 2, 10, 240–259
  unit of analysis, 14–15
human genome project, ethnographic studies on information technology in, 19–22
human–human interactions
  importance in system design, 185, 242–243
  in offices, 158
  in telephone operator–customer conversation, 252
human–machine interaction, problems in, 179
human practical reasoning, built into system design, 179

informal organization, 146–147
information flows, as work outcome, 149
information-processing psychology, 53, 55
Infovox Text to Speech Synthesizer (TTS), use in bionic WOZ simulation, 129, 130
insertion sequences, in conversational interaction, 133–134, 135
institutional forces, effect on concept of user, 95–96
intelligent decision support (IDS), application to fire and emergency medical dispatching, 8, 162, 176, 178, 180

interaction, interface compared to, 58
interactional dimension, of human–computer interfaces, 1–2, 3
interaction analysis, of human–computer interfaces, 11
interaction contexts, importance in system design, 185
interdependencies of work and activities, 146–148
interface
  definition, 32n6, 64n5
  interaction compared to, 58
invisibility, of work-expertise, 76

keyword searches, in VANNA/Timelines studies, 217–218

labor, working division of, 7
language, action and, 43
lifeworld, system compared to, 100
logocentrism, of ethnographic studies, 33n19
London Underground control rooms, computer-supported cooperative work studies on, 145

machine intelligence, traditional models, 41
MacSHAPA system, description and use, 224, 227, 229, 232, 233
management, definition, 83–84
Management (Drucker), 83
managerial conception, of user, 4, 5, 67–69, 83–97
marketing, of new products, 86–87
Marx, Karl, on technological production, 142, 146, 158n2
media integration, 229–230
medical economics, founding of, 64n3
medical emergencies, intelligent decision support applied to, 162
medical informatics, programmer-user misconceptions in, 77–78, 82
medical interviews, dialogue characteristics, 247, 257
Meeting Plots system, description and use, 224, 229, 232
menu-driven screens, utility, 157
metaphors
  for active badge system, 91
  computer systems as medium for, 88
  for conversation, 108
  of corporate culture, 87–88
  for privacy issues, 93–94
  of user community, 93
Miyake, N., use of constructive interaction to study human problem solving, 187

multimedia data, 9
    for social and interactional data collection
        and analysis, 204–239
multistream data, use in human–computer in-
    teraction studies, 206

naturalism, as basic to human–computer inter-
    action studies, 15, 33n11
naturally occurring conversation, 108
neurosurgery, video groupware use in, 41
newspaper industry, UTOPIA as collaborative
    development in, 42
9-1-1 calling system, computer use in, 161–
    183
1984 (Orwell), 89, 93, 94
non-verbal communication, as concept in con-
    versation analysis, 188, 190
normal, natural troubles, produced by work,
    148–152, 157
note pad, in decision support for dispatching,
    164–168

obligatory passage point, human–computer in-
    teraction as, 49, 52, 62
observer, role in ethnography, 13
Observer, Tracker, and Reviewer tools, use for
    data collection and analysis in usability
    applications, 225–226, 227
Office Procedure Specification Language
    (OPSL), use for office-produced docu-
    ments, 149
Olivetti "active badge," 89
ontological gerrymandering, 64n9
operator–customer dialogue, 150, 153–154
organizational communication
    attitudes in, 100
    as type of public relations, 86
other repair, in computer-based flight informa-
    tion studies, 136, 137

Panopticon (Bentham), 89
paperless office, as chimera, 157
participation, of workers, 98
participatory design, basis and use, 42–45, 74,
    80, 82
performing community, 64n7
personal computers (PC), ethnographic studies
    on development and testing, 23–26,
    33n23
practical craft knowledge, of fire dispatchers,
    167
pre-turn tones, in computer-based flight infor-
    mation studies, 131–133
privacy issues

of active badge systems, 89, 90, 91, 93–94
    of E-mail, 88
    of workplace, 94, 95
product development, consumer invovlvement
    in, 74–75
programmers
    misconceptions of users' work by, 77
    physical work environment of, 73
    users compared to, 83
    views of user, 72–74
Project Ernestine, studies of telephone worksta-
    tions in, 241–242
protocol analysis
    constructive interaction compared to, 187
    goal, 187
psychology, role in early human–computer in-
    teraction studies, 37
*The Psychology of Human–Computer Interac-
    tion* (Card et al.), 53–60
public safety answering points, computer use
    in, 161
public safety communications, insertion se-
    quences in calls to, 133–134

quality of work life (QWL), as corporatist tra-
    dition, 98

realist research, cognitive psychology as,
    33n12
reflexivity, 63
    in ethnography, 15
repair in communication, in bionic WOZ simu-
    lation studies, 131, 135–139
repair initiation, in computer-based flight infor-
    mation studies, 137
representation, of user. *See* user
request-offer of help adjacency pair, in
    computer-based flight information studies,
    133
requirements analysis, 11
requirements capture, for end-user system
    design, 32n1
requirements definition, as beginning of design
    work, 75
resistance
    as collective enterprise, 95
    to computer-based technologies, 71, 79–80,
        85, 101
    as symptom of bad design, 85
response groups, listing of emergency dispatch
    units by, 165–166
retrospective intentiality, as concept in conver-
    sation analysis, 190
Reviewer tool, use for integration of multi-
    stream data files, 227, 228, 229, 230, 236

rhetoric, practical aim of, 96
Rhetoric (Aristotle), 96
run files, in decision support for dispatching, 164–168

Scandinavian approach, participatory design as, 42–45, 74, 82
self-repair, in computer-based flight information studies, 136, 137
semantics, of formal structures, 81
sequentiality, as concept in conversation analysis, 190
settings of use, job descriptions based on, 147
SHAPA system, use for analysis of verbal communications, 224, 229
shared frame of reference, between user and system, 8, 178
simple control, description, 71
simulations, of conversation, 117–119
situational context, analysis of, 7–8
Smith, Adam, 146, 159n8
social artifacts, systems as, 5
social concerns, in design science, 107, 123n1
social control
   of user, 6, 7
   wizards and, 126–141
social dimension, of human–computer interfaces, 1, 2, 3
social fields, in organizational informal communication, 81
social interaction, in design and use of workstation, 240–259
sociality, of work, 143–144
social network analysis, of human–computer interaction, 204
social organization
   of computer system development, 101
   of computer use, 67, 77
sociological research, on computer technologies, 11
sociological work, relevance to human–computer interaction studies, 16
sociology
   computer-supported cooperative work and, 142–160
   for human–computer interaction, 2
   of technology, 1
sociology of scientific knowledge (SSK), 11, 12
   laboratory studies on, 31
sociotechnical systems (STS)
   application to computer system design, 85
   work processes as interlinked systems in, 84–85, 93

software design, engineering role in, 38
software packages, deficiencies of, 77
software psychology
   definition, 37
   human–computer interaction from, 37
specialization, in work settings, 159n8
speech, Swedish view of, 43–44
speech-based interfaces, 6
speech systems, computer technology for, 126–127
SSK. *See* sociology of scientific knowledge (SSK)
strong AI position, conversational computers and, 139
structural organization, of calls to flight-information service, 134
Suchman, Lucy, work on human–computer interfaces, 1
SUNDIAL project, for design of speech-based computerized information service, 128
surrogate user, system operator as, 9, 240, 247
surveillance model, of privacy, 93–94
system, lifeworld compared to, 100
system design
   based on sociality of work, 145
   worker involvement in, 74
system-friendly, user-friendly comparison to, 6, 127
systems analysis, as beginning of design work, 75
systems analyst, technical conception of, 97
systems design
   brick wall story, 27, 29
   factors affecting, 7
   role in human–computer interaction studies, 37, 58, 59
   sociotechnical systems methods applied to, 85
   user conceptions in, 67–106
systems rationalism, use in system design, 75

task, 2
Tavistock Institute, sociotechnical system design at, 84
technical conception, of user, 4, 5, 67–69, 72–82, 95–96, 97
technical control, description, 71
technical reason, practical aim of, 96
technologically driven ethnography, 3
technological seduction, cultural, organizational change-making as, 87
technology bargaining, role in participatory design research in Europe, 82
technology-oriented dialogue, 10

telephone, computer basis of, 69
telephone-based flight information service, bionic WOZ simulation of, 129–132
telephone operators
    CPM-GOMS studies of tasks of, 240
    as parallel processors, 255–257
    workstations for, 9
text-editing system, interface deficiency in, 54
thinking aloud, constructive interaction compared to, 187
time-based data, multimedia type use in human–computer interaction studies, 206–210
time-geography studies, of human–computer interaction, 204
Timelines system, description and use, 9, 210–236, 237n1
time-motion studies, notation used in, 75
translation coding scheme, for directory-assistance operator dialogue, 245–246
Turing Test, basis and application of, 110–112
turn-taking arrangements, in conversation, 108, 114, 123n5, n10, n11, 190, 215, 219

underground control rooms, computer-supported cooperative work studies, 145
unions
    role in computer technology, 71, 72
    role in participatory design research in Europe, 82
usability
    criteria for, 9
    definition, 61
    design for, 4
    engineering approach, 38
    laboratory studies, 37–38
    personal-computer testing for, 23–26
usability testing
    characteristics, 185
    constructive interaction and conversation analysis use for, 199, 201
    by video analysis, 209–210
user, 2
    cognitive representations of, 184
    configuration of, 22–26
    definitions and conceptions, 4, 59–60, 68, 97
    empowerment of, 4, 51
    managerial conception, 4, 5, 67–69, 83–96
    operator compared to, 57
    programmers compared to, 83
    representations of, 15, 50–52, 57, 184
    resistance to computer systems, 79
    role in human–computer interaction, 3

social control, 6, 7
technical conception, 4, 5, 67–69, 72–82, 95–96, 97
user-centered design, 4, 49, 52
user cognition, 4
user empowerment, 4
user-friendly
    computer-based speech systems as, 126
    system-friendly comparison to, 6
user interface
    definitions and description, 2, 4
    as site of human–computer interaction knowledge, 48, 52–53, 184
user requirements, 4
user-system interaction, 3
U-test usability tool, description and use, 222, 229, 232, 236
UTOPIA, as cooperative design project, 42
utterance design, in conversational analysis, 113–115

VANNA (Video ANNotation and Analysis), description and use, 9, 210–236
verbal protocol analysis, of human–computer interaction, 204
Vico, Giambattista, on rhetoric, 96
video conferencing communication study, case study, 214–216
video groupware, use in neurosurgery, 41
VideoNoter, use for collection of time-based data, 9, 221–222, 223, 227, 229
video recordings
    of cardiovascular construction kit use, 192–193, 199
    collection and translating data from, 207–208
    data analysis, 219–220
    data capture by, 9, 216–217
    data collection and translation, 220–236
    data manipulation, 217–218
    data visualization, 218–219
    as documents, 9
    preservation of original detail and context of, 208
    use in conversation analysis, 188, 189
    use in ethnographic studies, 13
    use in human–computer interaction studies, 205, 206–207

Weber, Max, 142, 146
Wittgenstein's notion of language games, application to participatory design, 43
The Wizard of Oz (Baum), 127
Wizard of Oz (WOZ) simulations, 127

wizards, social control and, 126–141
women workers, invisible work-expertise of,
    76
work
    interdependencies of, 146–148
    sociality of, 143–144, 145
work-arounds, use by computer users, 79–80
work-expertise, invisibility of, 76–77
working division of labor, 7, 147, 148
working life, computer effects on, 71

workplace, privacy issues, 94, 95
work practices, effect on ethnographic studies,
    18
workstations
    social interaction in design and use of, 240–
    259
    for telephone operators, 9, 240–259

Xerox Corporation, active badge project, 89
Xerox PARC, 1, 41